KT-519-573

International Financial Reporting Standards

A Practical Guide

WITHDRAWN

EDINBURGH NAPIER UNIVERSITY LIBRARY

3 8042 00836 2152

International Financial Reporting Standards

A Practical Guide

Sixth Edition

Hennie van Greuning
Darrel Scott
Simonet Terblanche

THE WORLD BANK
Washington, D.C.

CRL
657.30218 GRE
7day

© 2011 The International Bank for Reconstruction and Development / The World Bank
1818 H Street NW
Washington DC 20433
Telephone: 202-473-1000
Internet: www.worldbank.org

All rights reserved

1 2 3 4 :: 14 13 12 11

The findings, interpretations, and conclusions expressed in this volume are those of the authors and do not necessarily reflect the views of the Executive Directors of The World Bank or the governments they represent.

The World Bank does not guarantee the accuracy of the data included in this work. The boundaries, colors, denominations, and other information shown on any map in this work do not imply any judgement on the part of The World Bank concerning the legal status of any territory or the endorsement or acceptance of such boundaries.

Rights and Permissions
The material in this publication is copyrighted. Copying and/or transmitting portions or all of this work without permission may be a violation of applicable law. The International Bank for Reconstruction and Development / The World Bank encourages dissemination of its work and will normally grant permission to reproduce portions of the work promptly.

For permission to photocopy or reprint any part of this work, please send a request with complete information to the Copyright Clearance Center Inc., 222 Rosewood Drive, Danvers, MA 01923, USA; telephone: 978-750-8400; fax: 978-750-4470; Internet: www.copyright.com.

All other queries on rights and licenses, including subsidiary rights, should be addressed to the Office of the Publisher, The World Bank, 1818 H Street NW, Washington, DC 20433, USA; fax: 202-522-2422; e-mail: pubrights@worldbank.org.

ISBN: 978-0-8213-8428-2
eISBN: 978-0-8213-8555-5
DOI: 10.1596/978-0-8213-8428-2

Library of Congress Cataloging-in-Publication data has been requested.

Contents

PART I   INTRODUCTORY PRINCIPLES

PART II   GROUP STATEMENTS

PART III   STATEMENT OF FINANCIAL POSITION / BALANCE SHEET

Foreword: World Bank Treasury

The publication of this sixth edition follows fairly soon after the previous edition, as the convergence in accounting standards has accelerated, despite some significant challenges. International convergence in accounting standards under the leadership of the International Accounting Standards Board (IASB) and the Financial Accounting Standards Board (FASB) in the United States has now progressed to the point where more than 100 countries currently subscribe to the International Financial Reporting Standards (IFRS).

The rush toward convergence continues to produce a steady stream of revisions to accounting standards by both the IASB and FASB. For accountants, financial analysts, and other specialists, there is already a burgeoning technical literature explaining in detail the background and intended application of these revisions. This book provides a nontechnical yet comprehensive managerial overview of the underlying materials.

The appearance of this sixth edition—already translated into 15 languages in its earlier editions—is therefore timely. In this edition, the World Bank Treasury has partnered with a major bank in a client country to co-author and co-produce the publication. It is a logical step for the Bank to draw on the considerable technical expertise available from such a partner, and it brings an additional practical dimension to this publication by emphasizing strategic and tactical implementation decisions made by financial regulated-statement issuers. The book already forms the basis of a securities accounting workshop offered several times each year to World Bank Treasury clients in central banks and other public sector funds.

Each chapter briefly summarizes and explains a new or revised IFRS, the issue or issues the standard addresses, the key underlying concepts, the appropriate accounting treatment, and the associated requirements for presentation and disclosure. The text also covers financial analysis and interpretation issues and a commentary on implementation decisions to better demonstrate the potential effect of the accounting standards on business decisions. Simple examples in most chapters help further clarify the material. It is our hope that this approach, in addition to providing a handy reference for practitioners, will help relieve some of the tension experienced by nonspecialists when faced with business decisions influenced by the new rules.

Kenneth G. Lay, CFA
Treasurer
The World Bank
Washington, D.C.
December 2010

Foreword: FirstRand Limited

FirstRand Limited is proud to be a co-sponsor of this publication together with the World Bank Treasury. FirstRand is a large, publicly listed financial services group which operates largely in South Africa and on the African continent. Our growth strategy increasingly requires us to develop business opportunities presented by the investment and trade flows resulting from trade corridors that are rapidly emerging between Africa, India, and China. Given that the World Bank is also active in these territories, we believe it is extremely appropriate for us to be associated with such a prestigious development institution, particularly as a key part of the World Bank's mandate is to protect transparency for stakeholders and promote adherence to best practice. These principles are also integral to the way FirstRand aims to communicate with its many stakeholders, who fully support our own strategic intent: to be the African financial services group of choice, creating long-term franchise value and delivering superior and sustainable economic returns to shareholders within acceptable levels of volatility.

In addition to financial sponsorship, the chief financial officer of FirstRand's banking businesses and a team of his staff members actively contributed to the publication by researching and writing on the latest technical IFRS issues. This collaboration is an example of how FirstRand seeks to uplift and empower our highly skilled employees and further demonstrates that our staff members are encouraged to improve their capabilities. Training and education programs at FirstRand are regarded as an essential element of our investment in human capital, and the content of these programs is based on needs identified from industry trends, best practice, and research. Making a publication of this nature accessible to our broader staff, to our clients, and to professionals and students in the areas where we operate not only assists us in fulfilling our commitment to training and education, but also gives members of our own staff an opportunity to contribute to the development of best practice in accounting standards.

Sizwe Nxasana, CA(SA)
CEO
FirstRand Limited
Sandton, South Africa
December 2010

Acknowledgments

The authors are grateful to Ken Lay, vice president and treasurer of the World Bank, who has supported this sixth edition as a means to assist World Bank client countries with a publication to facilitate understanding the International Financial Reporting Standards (IFRS) and to emphasize the importance of financial analysis and interpretation of the information produced through application of these standards.

Our gratitude also extends to the senior management of FirstRand Limited, who devoted staff time and resources to co-produce this publication.

Colleagues in the World Bank Treasury shared their insights into the complexities of applying certain standards to the treasury environment. We benefited greatly from hours of conversation with many colleagues, including Hamish Flett and Richard Williams.

The contributing team from the technical accounting group at FirstRand Limited assisted greatly in researching updates to IFRS. Without the assistance of the team members, this publication could not have succeeded.

Mark Ingebretsen from the World Bank's Office of the Publisher remained patient and helpful throughout the production process. Thank you. Current and former members of the publishing team have provided tremendous support through the various editions of this book: thank you, Santiago Pombo, Stuart Tucker, Jose de Buerba, Mayya Revzina, and Valentina Kalk.

Despite the extent and quality of the inputs that we have received, we are solely responsible for the contents of this publication.

Hennie van Greuning
Darrel Scott
Simonet Terblanche

December 2010

Introduction

This text, based on five earlier editions that have already been translated into 15 languages, is an important contribution to expanding awareness and understanding of International Financial Reporting Standards (IFRS) around the world, with easy-to-read summaries of each standard and examples that illustrate accounting treatments and disclosure requirements.

TARGET AUDIENCE

A conscious decision has been made to focus on the needs of executives and financial analysts in the private and public sectors who might not have a strong accounting background. This publication summarizes each standard, whether it is an IFRS or an International Accounting Standard, so managers and analysts can quickly obtain a broad overview of the key issues. Detailed discussion of certain topics has been excluded to maintain the overall objective of providing a useful tool to managers and financial analysts.

In addition to the short summaries, most chapters contain basic examples that emphasize the practical application of some key concepts in a particular standard. This text provides the tools to enable an executive without a technical accounting background to (1) participate in an informed manner in discussions relating to the appropriateness or application of a particular standard in a given situation, and (2) evaluate the effect that the application of the principles of a given standard will have on the financial results and position of a division or of an entire enterprise.

STRUCTURE OF THIS PUBLICATION

Each chapter follows a common outline to facilitate discussion of each standard:

1. **Objective of Standard** identifies the main objectives and the key issues of the standard.
2. **Scope of the Standard** identifies the specific transactions and events covered by a standard. In certain instances, compliance with a standard is limited to a specified range of enterprises.
3. **Key Concepts** explains the usage and implications of key concepts and definitions.
4. **Accounting Treatment** lists the specific accounting principles, bases, conventions, rules, and practices that should be adopted by an enterprise for compliance with a particular standard. Recognition (initial recording) and measurement (subsequent valuation) are specifically dealt with, where appropriate.

5. **Presentation and Disclosure** describes the manner in which the financial and non-financial items should be presented in the financial statements, as well as aspects that should be disclosed in these financial statements—keeping in mind the needs of various users. Users of financial statements include investors, employees, lenders, suppliers or trade creditors, governments, tax and regulatory authorities, and the public.

6. **Financial Analysis and Interpretation** discusses items of interest to the financial analyst in chapters where such a discussion is deemed appropriate. None of the discussion in these sections should be interpreted as a criticism of IFRS. Where analytical preferences and practices are highlighted, it is to alert the reader to the challenges still remaining along the road to convergence of international accounting practices and unequivocal adoption of IFRS.

7. A **commentary** discusses any debate surrounding a particular standard as well as possible future developments or changes envisaged.

8. **Implementation decisions** related to strategic and tactical policy issues that might arise are discussed in a separate section. No doubt users of this publication will be able to add their own implementation problem points to the bullet points initiated in this new section.

9. **Examples** included at the end of most chapters are intended as further illustration of the concepts contained in the IFRS.

The authors hope that managers in the client private sector will find this format useful in establishing accounting terminology, especially where certain terms are still in the exploratory stage in some countries.

CONTENT INCLUDED

All of the accounting standards issued by the International Accounting Standards Board (IASB) through September 30, 2010, are included in this publication. The IASB texts are the ultimate authority—this publication merely constitutes a summary.

Part I

Introductory Principles

CHAPTER 1

Framework for the Preparation and Presentation of Financial Statements

1.1 OBJECTIVE

An acceptable coherent framework of fundamental accounting principles is essential for preparing financial statements. The major reasons for providing the framework are to

- identify the essential concepts underlying the preparation and presentation of financial statements;
- guide standard setters in developing new accounting standards and reviewing existing standards;
- assist preparers in preparing financial statements and dealing with topics that are not covered by a specific IFRS;
- assist auditors in forming an opinion as to whether a set of financial statements conforms with IFRS; and
- assist users in interpreting the financial information contained in a set of financial statements that comply with IFRS.

The framework sets guidelines and should not be seen as a constitution; nothing in the framework overrides any specific standard. However, because the standard setters are guided by the framework when developing and reviewing specific standards, instances of conflict between the framework and individual standards are not expected to be numerous and are expected to diminish over time.

The framework may be revised over time based on the IASB's experience of working with it.

1.2 SCOPE OF THE FRAMEWORK

The existing framework deals with the

- objectives of financial statements;
- qualitative characteristics of financial statements;
- elements of financial statements;
- recognition of the elements of financial statements;
- measurement of the elements of financial statements; and
- concepts of capital and capital maintenance.

1.3

KEY CONCEPTS

Objective of Financial Statements

1.3.1 The **objective** of financial statements is to provide information about the **financial position** (statement of financial position), **performance** (statement of comprehensive income), and **changes in financial position** (statement of cash flows) of an entity that is useful to a wide range of users in making economic decisions. Users of financial information include present and potential capital providers, employees, lenders, suppliers, customers, and the government.

1.3.2 Financial statements also show the results of **management's stewardship** of the resources entrusted to it. This information, along with other information in the notes to the financial statements, provides users of financial statements with information about the amount, timing, and uncertainty of the entity's future cash flows in order that they can make economic decisions. In order to meet this objective, financial statements contain information about

- assets;
- liabilities;
- equity;
- income and expenses, including gains and losses;
- contributions by and distributions to owners in their capacity as owners; and
- cash flows.

The following table sets out the assumptions underlying the preparation of financial statements, the qualitative characteristics of financial statements, and the constraints of providing financial information.

Fair presentation
The objective of financial statements is to achieve fair presentation.

Materiality
IFRS only applies to material information. An item is material if its omission or misstatement would change the decisions taken by the users of the financial statements.

Underlying assumptions

Accrual basis of accounting Financial statements are prepared based on the **accrual basis of accounting**. Under this basis transactions are recorded when they occur and not as the cash flows take place.	**Going concern** Financial statements are prepared on the assumption that an entity is a **going concern** and will be in operation for the foreseeable future. Hence it is assumed that the entity has neither the intention nor the need to liquidate or materially curtail the scale of its operations.

Qualitative characteristics

Understandability
Information should be readily understandable by users who have a basic knowledge of business, economic activities, and accounting, and who have a willingness to study the information with reasonable diligence.

Relevance
Relevant information influences the economic decisions of users, helping them to evaluate past, present, and future events or to confirm or correct their past evaluations. The relevance of information is affected by its nature and materiality. Information is considered to be material if its omission or misstatement could influence the economic decisions of users taken on the basis of the financial statements.

Reliability
Reliable information is free from material error and bias and can be depended upon by users to represent faithfully that which it either purports to represent or could reasonably be expected to represent. The following factors contribute to reliability:
- faithful representation;
- substance over form;
- neutrality;
- prudence; and
- completeness.

Comparability
Information should be presented in a consistent manner over time and in a consistent manner between entities to enable users to make significant comparisons.

Constraints on financial information

Timeliness Undue delay in reporting could result in loss of relevance but improve reliability. In achieving a balance between relevance and reliability the overriding consideration is how best to satisfy the economic decision-making needs of users.	**Cost versus benefits** Benefits derived from information should exceed the cost of providing it.

1.3.3 Balancing qualitative characteristics. To meet the objectives of financial statements and make them adequate for a particular environment, providers of information must balance the qualitative characteristics in such a way that best meets the objectives of financial statements.

1.3.4 The application of the principal qualitative characteristics and the appropriate accounting standards normally results in financial statements that provide **fair presentation**.

1.4

ACCOUNTING TREATMENT

Elements of Financial Statements

1.4.1 The following elements of financial statements are directly related to the measurement of the financial position:

- **Assets.** Resources controlled by the entity as a result of past events and from which future economic benefits are expected to flow to the entity.
- **Liabilities.** Present obligations of an entity arising from past events, the settlement of which is expected to result in an outflow from the entity of resources embodying economic benefits.
- **Equity.** The residual interest in the assets of an entity after deducting all of its liabilities (may be referred to as shareholders' funds).

1.4.2 The following elements of financial statements are directly related to the measurement of performance:

- **Income.** Increases in economic benefits during the accounting period in the form of inflows or enhancements of assets, or decreases of liabilities that result in an increase in equity (other than those relating to contributions from equity participants). Income comprises both revenue and gains.
- **Expenses.** Decreases in economic benefits during the accounting period in the form of outflows or depletion of assets, or incurrences of liabilities that result in decreases in equity, other than those relating to distributions to equity participants.

Initial Recognition of Elements

1.4.3 Recognition is the process of incorporating in the statement of financial position or statement of comprehensive income an item that meets the definition of an element and satisfies the criteria for recognition. Elements (assets, liabilities, equity, income, and expenses) should only be **recognized** in the financial statements if

- it is **probable** that any future economic benefit associated with the item will flow to or from the entity; and
- the item has a cost or value that can be **measured with reliability**.

Subsequent Measurement of Elements

1.4.4 Measurement is the process of determining the monetary amounts at which the elements of the financial statements are to be recognized and carried in the statement of financial position and statement of comprehensive income. The following bases are used to different degrees and in varying combinations to **measure** elements of financial statements:

- **Historical cost.** Assets are recorded at the amount paid or fair value of consideration given to acquire them at the time of their acquisition. Liabilities are recorded at the amount of proceeds received in exchange for the obligation.
- **Current cost.** Assets are carried at the amount of cash and cash equivalents that would have to be paid if the same or equivalent asset were acquired currently. Liabilities are carried at the undiscounted amount of cash or cash equivalents that would be required to settle the obligation currently.
- **Realizable (settlement) value.** Assets are carried at the amount of cash and cash equivalents that would be obtained by selling the assets in an orderly disposal. Liabilities are carried at their settlement values, that is, the undiscounted amount of cash or cash equivalents expected to be paid to satisfy the liabilities in the normal course of business.

■ **Present value assets** are carried at the present discounted value of the future net cash inflows that the item is expected to generate in the normal course of business. Liabilities are carried at the present discounted value of the future net cash outflows that are expected to be required to settle the liabilities in the normal course of business.

Capital Maintenance Concepts

1.4.5 Capital and capital maintenance include

■ **Financial capital** is synonymous with net assets or equity; it is defined in terms of nominal monetary units. Profit represents the increase in nominal money capital over the period.

■ **Physical capital** is regarded as the operating capability; it is defined in terms of productive capacity. Profit represents the increase in productive capacity over the period.

1.5

PRESENTATION AND DISCLOSURE: TRANSPARENCY AND DATA QUALITY

1.5.1 In forming a safe environment for stakeholders, corporate governance rules should focus on creating a culture of transparency. Transparency refers to making information on existing conditions, decisions, and actions accessible, visible, and understandable to all market participants. Disclosure refers more specifically to the process and methodology of providing the information and of making policy decisions known through timely dissemination and openness. Accountability refers to the need for market participants, including the relevant authorities, to justify their actions and policies and to accept responsibility for both decisions and results.

1.5.2 Transparency is a prerequisite for accountability, especially to borrowers and lenders, issuers and investors, national authorities, and international financial institutions. In part, the case for greater transparency and accountability rests on the need for private sector agents to understand and accept policy decisions that affect their behavior. Greater transparency improves economic decisions taken by other agents in the economy. Transparency also fosters accountability, internal discipline, and better governance, while both transparency and accountability improve the quality of decision making in policy-oriented institutions. Such institutions—as well as other institutions that rely on them to make decisions—should be required to maintain transparency. If actions and decisions are visible and understandable, the costs of monitoring can be lowered. In addition, the general public is better able to monitor public sector institutions, shareholders and employees have a better view of corporate management, creditors monitor borrowers more adequately, and depositors are able to keep an eye on banks. Poor decisions do not go unnoticed or unquestioned.

1.5.3 Transparency and accountability are mutually reinforcing. Transparency enhances accountability by facilitating monitoring, while accountability enhances transparency by providing an incentive for agents to ensure that their actions are disseminated properly and understood. Greater transparency reduces the tendency of markets to place undue emphasis on positive or negative news and thus reduces volatility in financial markets. Taken together, transparency and accountability also impose discipline that improves the quality of decision making in the public sector. This can result in more efficient policies by improving the private sector's understanding of how policy makers may react to events in the future. Transparency forces institutions to face up to the reality of a situation and makes officials more responsible, especially if they know they will have to justify their views, decisions, and actions. For these reasons, timely policy adjustment is encouraged.

1.5.4 The provision of transparent and useful information on market participants and their transactions is an essential part of an orderly and efficient market; it also is a key prerequisite for imposing market discipline. For a risk-based approach to bank management and supervision to be effective, useful information must be provided to each key player: supervisors, current and prospective shareholders and bondholders, depositors and other creditors, correspondent and other banks, counterparties, and the general public. Left alone, markets may not generate sufficient levels of disclosure. Although market forces normally balance the marginal benefits and costs of disclosing additional information, the end result may not be what players really need.

1.5.5 The public disclosure of information is predicated on the existence of quality accounting standards and adequate disclosure methodology. The process normally involves publication of relevant qualitative and quantitative information in annual financial reports, which are often supplemented by biannual or quarterly financial statements and other important information. Because the provision of information can be expensive, disclosure requirements should weigh the usefulness of information for the public against the costs of providing it.

1.5.6 It is also important to time the introduction of information well. Disclosure of negative information to a public that is not sufficiently sophisticated to interpret it could damage an entity (especially if it is a financial institution). In situations where low-quality information is put forth or users are not deemed capable of properly interpreting what is disclosed, public requirements should be phased in carefully and tightened progressively. In the long run, a full-disclosure regime is beneficial, even if some immediate problems are experienced, because the cost to the financial system of not being transparent is ultimately higher than the cost of revealing information.

1.5.7 The financial and capital market liberalization of the past decades brought increasing volatility to financial markets and, consequently, increased the information needed to ensure financial stability. With the advance of financial and capital market liberalization, pressure has increased to improve the usefulness of available financial sector information through the formulation of minimum disclosure requirements. These requirements address the quality and quantity of information that must be provided to market participants and the general public.

1.5.8 Transparency and accountability are not ends in and of themselves; nor are they panaceas to solve all problems. They are designed to improve economic performance and the working of international financial markets by enhancing the quality of decision making and risk management among market participants. In particular, transparency does not change the nature of banking or the risks inherent in financial systems. Although it cannot prevent financial crises, transparency may moderate the responses of market participants to bad news by helping them to anticipate and assess negative information. In this way, transparency helps to mitigate panic and contagion.

1.5.9 A dichotomy exists between transparency and confidentiality. The release of proprietary information may enable competitors to take advantage of a particular situation, a fact that often deters market participants from full disclosure. Similarly, monitoring bodies frequently obtain confidential information from financial institutions, which can have significant market implications. Under such circumstances, financial institutions may be reluctant to provide sensitive information without the guarantee of client confidentiality. However, both unilateral transparency and full disclosure contribute to a regime of transparency. If such a regime were to become the norm, it would ultimately benefit all market participants, even if in the short term it would create discomfort for individual entities.

1.5.10 In the context of public disclosure, financial statements should be easy to interpret. Widely available and affordable financial information supports official and private monitoring of a business's financial performance. It promotes transparency and supports market discipline, two important ingredients of sound corporate governance. Besides being a goal in itself, in that it empowers stakeholders, disclosure could be a means to achieve better governance. The adoption of internationally accepted financial reporting standards is a necessary measure to facilitate transparency and contribute to proper interpretation of financial statements.

1.5.11 In the context of fair presentation, no disclosure is probably better than disclosure of misleading information.

1.6 COMMENTARY

1.6.1 The framework provides robust descriptions and guidance about the concepts underlying current accounting practices. The current framework was published for the first time in July 1989 by the IASB's predecessor body, IASC, and was adopted by the IASB in 2001. Many of the definitions and concepts in the current framework are therefore outdated and are not as useful in the modern business world as they might have been historically. For example, **the current framework does not identify fair value as a possible measurement base.** Although current cost or present value may be close to what we understand fair value to be today, they are not fair value. In the current environment the IASB is moving more and more towards fair value measurement for items recognized in the financial statements, particularly financial instruments. Another example is that equity does not have its own definition, but rather is based on the definition of assets and liabilities. This makes the distinction between equity instruments and financial liabilities in terms of IAS 32 very difficult in complex transactions.

1.6.2 Based on the shortcomings identified above as well as the fact that the framework used to develop IFRS was not aligned to the framework to develop U.S. Generally Accepted Accounting Principles (GAAP), the IASB and the FASB added a project to their agenda in 2004 to update the framework. The project was split into a number of phases with the IASB taking the lead in developing certain phases and the FASB others. The IASB and FASB have agreed to issue each phase as a separate document as they are finalized. When all phases have been finalized they will be consolidated into a single conceptual framework.

1.6.3 The table below sets out the various phases of framework development, which standard setting body is leading the development of the phase, and the progress to date:

Phase	Standard setter responsible	Status
Objectives and qualitative characteristics	IASB	The final chapter is expected to be published in the near future.
Elements and recognition	FASB	Listed on the joint FASB/IASB current technical plan and project updates for 2011.
Measurement	FASB	Listed on the joint FASB/IASB current technical plan and project updates for 2011.
Reporting entity	IASB	Listed on the joint FASB/IASB current technical plan and project updates for 2011.

EXAMPLE: FRAMEWORK FOR THE PREPARATION AND PRESENTATION OF FINANCIAL STATEMENTS

EXAMPLE 1.1

Chemco Inc. produces chemical products and sells them locally. The corporation wishes to extend its market and export some of its products. The financial director realizes that compliance with international environmental requirements is a significant precondition if the company wishes to sell products overseas. Although Chemco already has established a series of environmental policies, common practice expects an environmental audit to be done from time to time, which will cost approximately $120,000. The audit would encompass the following:

- a full review of all environmental policy directives;
- a detailed analysis of compliance with these directives; and
- a report containing in-depth recommendations of those physical and policy changes that would be necessary to meet international requirements.

The financial director of Chemco has suggested that the $120,000 be capitalized as an asset and then written off against the revenues generated from export activities so that the matching of income and expenses will occur.

EXPLANATION

The costs associated with the environmental audit can be capitalized only if they meet the definition and recognition criteria for an asset. The IASB's framework does not allow the recognition of items in the statement of financial position that do not meet the definition or recognition criteria.

To recognize the costs of the audit as an asset, it should meet both the

- definition of an asset; and
- recognition criteria for an asset.

For the costs associated with the environmental audit to comply with the **definition of an asset**, the following should be valid:

i)   The costs must give rise to a resource controlled by Chemco.
ii)   The asset must arise from a past transaction or event, namely the audit.
iii)   The asset must be expected to give rise to a probable future economic benefit that will flow to the corporation, namely the revenue from export sales.

The requirements of (i) and (iii) are not met. Therefore, Chemco cannot capitalize the costs of the audit because of the absence of fixed orders and detailed analyses of expected economic benefits.

To **recognize** the costs as an asset in the statement of financial postion, they must comply with the recognition criteria (see §1.4.3), namely

- The asset should have a cost that can be measured reliably.
- The expected inflow of future economic benefits must be probable.

To properly measure the carrying value of the asset, the corporation must be able to demonstrate that further costs will be incurred that would give rise to future benefits. However, the second requirement poses a problem because of insufficient evidence of the probable inflow of economic benefits and would therefore again disqualify the costs for capitalizing as an asset.

CHAPTER 2

First-Time Adoption of IFRS
(IFRS 1)

2.1

OBJECTIVE

IFRS 1 provides entities with guidance on the process to be followed when adopting IFRS. The purpose of IFRS 1 is to ensure that the entity's first financial statements (including interim financial reports for that specific reporting period) under IFRS contain high-quality information that is transparent and comparable over all periods presented; that provides a suitable starting point for IFRS presentation; and can be generated at a cost that does not exceed the benefits.

2.2

SCOPE OF THE STANDARD

IFRS 1 applies when an entity adopts IFRS for the first time by an explicit and unreserved statement of compliance with IFRS. The standard specifically covers

- comparable (prior period) information that is to be provided;
- identification of the basis of reporting;
- retrospective application of IFRS information; and
- formal identification of the reporting and the transition date.

IFRS requires an entity to comply with each individual standard effective at the reporting date for its first IFRS-compliant financial statements. Subject to certain exceptions and exemptions, IFRS should be applied retrospectively. Therefore, the comparative amounts, including the opening Statement of Financial Position for the comparative period, should be restated from national generally accepted accounting principles (GAAP) to IFRS.

IFRS 1 does not apply to an entity already applying IFRS changes its accounting policies. Changes in accounting policies for entities that already apply IFRS are treated in terms of International Accounting Standard 8 (IAS 8) or in terms of the transitional provisions of a specific standard.

2.3

KEY CONCEPTS

2.3.1 The **reporting date** is the Statement of Financial Position date of the first financial statements that explicitly state that they comply with IFRS (for example, December 31, 2005).

2.3.2 The **transition date** is the beginning of the earliest period for which an entity presents full comparative information under IFRS in its first IFRS financial statements. For an entity to meet the requirements of IAS 1, three statements of financial position should be presented (for example, January 1, 2003, if the reporting date is December 31, 2005).

2.4

ACCOUNTING TREATMENT

Opening Statement of Financial Position (Balance Sheet)

2.4.1 Entities are required to prepare and present an opening IFRS statement of financial position at the date of transition to IFRS. This is the starting point for accounting under IFRS. The opening IFRS Statement of Financial Position should recognize all assets and liabilities whose recognition is required by IFRS, but not recognize items as assets or liabilities whose recognition is not permitted by IFRS. An entity should use the same accounting policies in the opening statement of financial position and throughout all periods presented in its first IFRS financial statements. Those accounting policies should comply with each IFRS that is effective at the end of its first IFRS reporting period subject to certain exemptions and prohibitions provided for. An entity may early adopt an IFRS that is not yet mandatory on transition to IFRS provided that IFRS allows for early adoption.

2.4.2 When preparing the opening Statement of Financial Position an entity should:

- **Recognize** all assets and liabilities whose recognition is required by IFRS. Examples of changes from national GAAP are derivatives, leases, pension liabilities and assets, and deferred tax on revalued assets.
- **Remove** assets and liabilities whose recognition is not permitted by IFRS. Examples of changes from national GAAP are deferred hedging gains and losses, other deferred costs, some internally generated intangible assets, and provisions.
- **Reclassify** items that should be classified differently under IFRS. Examples of changes from national GAAP are financial assets, financial liabilities, leasehold property, compound financial instruments, and acquired intangible assets (reclassified to goodwill). Adjustments required are reclassifications between Statement of Financial Position items.
- Apply IFRS in **measuring** assets and liabilities recognized. Any adjustments resulting from events or transactions that occurred before the date of transition are recorded directly in retained earnings unless another category of equity (for example, share-based payment reserve, or a component of other comprehensive income such as an available for sale reserve) is more appropriate.

Exemptions from Other IFRS

2.4.3 IFRS 1 provides certain exemptions from retrospective application of other IFRS. An entity may elect to apply one or more of these exemptions.

2.4.4 It is not necessary to restate **business combinations** that took place before the transition date. If any are restated, all later combinations must be restated. If information related to prior business combinations is not restated, the same classification (acquisition, reverse acquisition, and uniting of interests) must be retained. Carrying amounts per previous accounting principles (previous GAAP) are treated as deemed costs for IFRS purposes.

However, those IFRS assets and liabilities that are not recognized under national GAAP must be recognized, and those that are not recognized under IFRS must be removed. The necessary adjustments should be made to goodwill for contingent consideration resolved before the transition to IFRS. The impairment tests required for goodwill under IFRS should be performed and any negative goodwill should be credited to retained earnings. Under previous GAAP an entity may not have consolidated a subsidiary that should be consolidated in terms of IFRS. On IFRS adoption, the carrying amount of the subsidiaries' assets and liabilities should be adjusted to comply with IFRS and the deemed goodwill will be the difference between the parent's interest in the net assets and the cost of the subsidiary reflected in the parent's separate financial statements. The exemptions relating to business combinations also apply to associates and joint ventures.

2.4.5 Fair value or revaluation may be used as deemed cost for **property plant and equipment and investment property that is accounted for under the cost model, as well as for intangible assets that may be revalued** in terms of IAS 38. This exemption is not available for any other assets or liabilities.

2.4.6 In respect of **employee benefits** a first time adopter may elect to recognize all cumulative actuarial gains or losses in retained earnings at the date of initial transition even if it uses the corridor approach for later actuarial gains and losses. If an entity intends to apply this exemption it must be applied to all plans.

2.4.7 A first time adopter need not comply with all the requirements for **cumulative translation differences** that existed on the date of transition to IFRS. If this exemption is applied then the cumulative translation differences for all foreign operations are deemed to be zero at the transition date. Any gain or loss from subsequent disposals shall exclude translation differences arising before the date of transition and include all subsequent differences.

2.4.8 A **compound instrument in terms of IAS 32** need not be separated into its equity and liability components if at the date of transition to IFRS the liability component is no longer outstanding.

2.4.9 If a subsidiary adopts IFRS later than its parent the subsidiary may in its own financial statements measure its assets and liabilities based on either the date of transition of its parent or its date of transition. This applies also to associates and joint ventures.

2.4.10 On transition to IFRS a first time adopter may designate a **financial asset** as available for sale. Since September 1, 2006, a first time adopter has been allowed to designate a **financial asset or liability** at fair value through profit or loss provided that the IAS 39 requirements for such designation are met.

2.4.11 A first time adopter is encouraged but not required to apply **IFRS 2** to equity instruments granted before November 7, 2002 or those granted after November 7, 2002 but vested before the transition to IFRS. In these circumstances IFRS 2 may only be applied if the fair value of the equity instruments has been publicly disclosed at the measurement date. Even if IFRS 2 is not applied to equity instruments granted the disclosure required in IFRS 2 is still to be provided. Modifications to schemes to which IFRS 2 was not applied are not accounted for in terms of IFRS 2.

2.4.12 A first time adopter may apply the transitional provisions in IFRS 4 to **insurance contracts**. IFRS 4 restricts the changes in accounting policies for insurance contracts.

2.4.13 IFRIC 1 requires changes in **decommissioning, restoration, and similar liabilities** to be added or deducted from the cost of the asset and the depreciation adjusted prospectively for the remaining useful life of the asset. A first time adopter need not comply with these requirements for changes in liabilities that occurred before the transition date. If this exemption is applied the first time adopter estimates the liability at the transition date and then estimates the amount that would have been included in the cost of the asset on initial recognition, based on present value techniques, and then calculates the accumulated depreciation based on that amount.

2.4.14 A first time adopter may apply the transitional provisions in IFRIC 4. Therefore a first time adopter may determine whether an arrangement existing at the date of transition to IFRS contains a **lease** based on the facts and circumstances at that date.

2.4.15 The transitional provisions in IFRIC 12 may be used by a first time adopter with **service concession arrangements**.

2.4.16 A first time adopter may apply the transitional provisions set out in IAS 23 as revised in 2007 to borrowing costs. The effective date shall be read as being the later of January 1, 2009 and the date of adoption.

2.4.17 In 2009 IFRS 7 was amended to require additional disclosure about fair values. The amendments stated that comparative information was not required the first time that an entity makes these additional disclosures. IFRS 1 was consequently updated to state that when an entity first applies IFRS the same exemption is applicable to the additional fair value disclosures, that is, comparatives are not required when the fair value hierarchy is presented for the first time, even if part of IFRS adoption.

Prohibition of Retrospective Application

2.4.18 IFRS 1 prohibits retrospective application for certain aspects of IFRS.

2.4.19 Derecognition of financial assets and liabilities are applied prospectively from the transition date. Therefore, financial assets and financial liabilities that have been derecognized under national GAAP are not reinstated, unless the information needed to apply IAS 39 was obtained when initially accounting for those transactions. However, all derivatives and other interests retained after derecognition and existing at the transition date must be recognized. All special purposed entities (SPEs) controlled at the transition date must be consolidated; refer to chapter 7 that addresses IAS 27 for more detail on SPEs.

2.4.20 At the date of transition all derivatives must be measured at fair value and all deferred gains or losses under derivatives must be eliminated, that is, deferral reversed and gains or loss recognized in comprehensive income. An entity shall not reflect in its opening statement of financial position a **hedging relationship** that does not meet the hedge accounting criteria in IAS 39. The IAS 39 requirements relating to the discontinuance of hedge accounting should be applied to such hedges. Transactions entered into before the date of transition cannot be retrospectively designated as hedges.

2.4.21 An entity's estimates under IFRS at transition date shall be consistent with the estimates made at the same date under previous GAAP, unless there is objective evidence that those estimates were made in error.

2.4.22 For all transitions to IFRS after January 1, 2005, the first time adopter shall apply **IFRS 5** retrospectively. Prior to this the transitional provisions in IFRS 5 should be applied.

2.4.23 The following requirements in IAS 27 in respect of non-controlling interests should be applied prospectively from the date of transition to IFRS:

- the requirement that total comprehensive income is attributed to non-controlling interests even if this results in a deficit balance;
- the provisions relating to changes in the parent's ownership that do not result in the loss of control; and
- the requirements for accounting for the loss of control over a subsidiary.

2.5	## PRESENTATION AND DISCLOSURE

2.5.1 A statement should be made to the effect that the financial statements are being prepared in terms of IFRS for the first time.

2.5.2 In accordance with IAS 1 the entity's first financial statements should include the current period and two comparative periods for the statement of financial position, the current period and one comparative period for the statement of comprehensive income, and the current and one comparative statement of cash flows. Three years' reconciliations in the statements of changes in equity and related notes follows the underlying statement.

2.5.3 Prior information and historical summaries that cannot be easily converted to IFRS should be dealt with as follows:

- any previous GAAP information should be prominently labeled as not being prepared under IFRS; and
- where the adjustment to the opening balance of retained earnings cannot be reasonably determined, that fact should be stated.

2.5.4 Where IFRS 1 permits a choice of transitional accounting policies, the policy selected should be stated.

2.5.5 The way in which the transition from previous GAAP to IFRS has affected the reported financial position, financial performance, and cash flows should be explained.

2.5.6 With regard to reporting date **reconciliations** from national GAAP (assume December 31, 2005), the following must be disclosed:

- equity reconciliation at the transition date (January 1, 2003) and at the end of the last national GAAP period (December 31, 2004); and
- reconciliation of total comprehensive income for the last national GAAP period (December 31, 2003).

2.5.7 With regard to interim reporting, reconciliations (assume the interim reporting date to be June 30, 2005, and the reporting date to be December 31, 2005), the following must be disclosed:

- equity reconciliation at the transition date (January 1, 2003), at the prior two years comparative date (June 30, 2004 and June 30, 2003), and at the end of the last national GAAP period (December 31, 2004); and
- profit reconciliation for the last national GAAP period (December 31, 2004) and for the prior year comparative date (June 30, 2004).

2.5.8 Impairment losses recognized or reversed for the first time when preparing the opening statement of financial position should be disclosed in terms of IAS 36 in the same way as would be required if the impairment loss or reversal took place in the period beginning with the date of transition to IFRS.

2.5.9 Where fair value is used as a deemed cost, for each line item so measured, the entity shall disclose the aggregate of the fair vales and the aggregate adjustment made to the carrying amounts reported under previous GAAP.

2.6   FINANCIAL ANALYSIS AND INTERPRETATION

The information to be disclosed in terms of IFRS 1 provides users of financial statements with information about how the amounts recognized under the entity's previous GAAP have been changed for the adoption of IFRS. As a result of the fact that comparatives are also restated in the year of adoption, the users will have comparable information.

2.7   COMMENTARY

2.6.1 IFRS 1 achieves its objective by providing exemptions and exceptions that result in relevant and reliable information on adoption of IFRS 1 for which the costs of providing the information do not exceed the benefits derived. IFRS 1 will continually need to evolve to keep up to date with new standards and interpretations issued by the IASB.

2.6.2 The IASB does not have a specific project aimed at revising IFRS 1 for the foreseeable future, but new standards and interpretations are constantly being developed and issued. Therefore, IFRS 1 is often amended and updated through the Annual Improvements Project. Given the extensive scope of the standard, it is necessarily complicated and to some extent inconsistent. The standard requires careful consideration.

2.8   IMPLEMENTATION DECISIONS

The following table sets out some of the strategic and tactical decisions that should be considered when applying IFRS 1.

Strategic decisions	Tactical decisions	Problems to overcome
In some cases the first time adoption of IFRS will be based on a regulatory requirement. However, in other instances management may need to take a strategic decision to as to whether they are going to adopt IFRS and from when they are going to apply it. This decision will be driven by, amongst other things, requirements of stakeholders, in particular equity and debt holders.	IFRS 1 presents a number of exemptions for first time adopters. Management will need to consider which exemptions in IFRS 1 to apply on adoption of IFRS and will need to understand the implications of each exception.	Many of the problems relating to the adoption of IFRS lie in the individual standards and may be overcome by applying the exemptions in IFRS 1. Inconsistent application of exemptions may lead to inconsistent financial statements.
Determining whether the current accounting systems are able to report in terms of IFRS or whether system updates are required.	Whether the current system can be maintained or upgraded or whether an entirely new system should be developed or purchased.	System issues, both related to current and future performance, and historical information.

CHAPTER 3

Presentation of Financial Statements (IAS 1)

3.1 **OBJECTIVE**

The objective of this standard is to prescribe the basis for presentation of general-purpose financial statements in order to ensure that the financial statements are in accordance with IFRS. The key issues are to ensure comparability with the entity's financial statements of previous periods and with the financial statements of other entities. It also enables informed users to rely on a formal, definable structure and facilitates financial analysis.

3.2 **SCOPE OF THE STANDARD**

IAS 1 outlines

- what constitutes a complete set of financial statements;
- the overall requirements for the presentation of financial statements, including guidelines for their structure;
- the distinction between current and noncurrent elements; and
- minimum requirements for the content of financial statements.

An updated IAS 1 was issued in September 2007. Performance reporting and the reporting of comprehensive income are major issues dealt with in the revised standard, and voluntary name changes are suggested for key financial statements. These name changes are mentioned in paragraph 3.4.4 below.

3.3 **KEY CONCEPTS**

3.3.1 Fair presentation. The financial statements should present fairly the financial position, financial performance, and cash flows of the entity. Fair presentation requires the faithful representation of the effects of transactions, other events, and conditions in accordance with the definitions and recognition criteria for assets, liabilities, income, and expenses set out in the framework. The application of IFRS is presumed to result in fair presentation.

3.3.2 Departure from the requirements of an IFRS is allowed only in the extremely rare circumstance in which the application of the IFRS would be so misleading as to conflict with the objectives of financial statements. In such circumstances, the entity should disclose the reasons for and the financial effect of the departure from the IFRS.

3.3.3 **Current assets** are:

- assets expected to be realized or intended for sale or consumption in the entity's normal operating cycle;
- assets held primarily for trading;
- assets expected to be realized within 12 months after the reporting date; and
- cash or cash equivalents, unless the assets are restricted in use for at least 12 months after the reporting period, or are to be used to settle a liability.

3.3.4 **Current liabilities** are:

- liabilities expected to be settled in the entity's normal operating cycle;
- liabilities held primarily for trading;
- liabilities due to be settled within 12 months after the reporting date; and
- liabilities for which the entity does not have an unconditional right to defer settlement for at least 12 months after the reporting period.

3.3.5 **Noncurrent assets and liabilities** are expected to be settled more than 12 months after the reporting date.

3.3.6 The portion of **noncurrent interest-bearing liabilities** to be settled within 12 months after the reporting date can be classified as noncurrent liabilities if:

- the original term is greater than 12 months;
- it is the intention to refinance or reschedule the obligation; or
- the agreement to refinance or reschedule the obligation is completed on or before the reporting date.

3.3.7 **Other comprehensive income** comprises items of income and expenses that are not recognized in profit or loss as permitted or required by other IFRSs. These include:

- changes in revaluation surplus of fixed or intangible assets in terms of IAS 16 and IAS 38 (refer to chapters 10 and 13);
- actuarial gains and losses on defined benefit plans recognized in accordance with IAS 19 (refer to chapter 24);
- gains and losses arising from translating the financial statements of a foreign operation recognized in terms of IAS 21(refer to chapter 21);
- gains and losses on re-measuring available-for-sale financial assets in terms of IAS 39 (refer to chapter 17); and
- the effective portion of gains and losses on hedging instruments in a cash flow hedge in terms of IAS 39 (refer to chapter 17).

3.3.8 Total comprehensive income is the change in equity during a period resulting from transactions, other than those changes resulting from transactions with owners in their capacity as owners—that is, the sum of profit or loss for the period and other comprehensive income.

3.4

ACCOUNTING TREATMENT

3.4.1 Financial statements should provide information about an entity's financial position, performance, and cash flows that is useful to a wide range of users for economic decision making.

3.4.2 Departure from the requirements of an IFRS is allowed only in the extremely rare circumstance in which the application of the IFRS would be so misleading as to conflict with the objectives of financial statements. In such circumstances, the entity should disclose the following:

▦ that management has concluded that the financial statements present fairly the entity's financial position, financial performance, and cash flows;
▦ that it has complied with the applicable IFRSs, except that it has departed from a particular requirement to achieve fair presentation;
▦ the title of the IFRS from which it has departed;
▦ the nature and reasons for the departure; and
▦ the financial effect of the departure, for each period presented.

3.4.3 The **presentation and classification** of items should be consistent from one period to another unless a change would result in a more appropriate presentation, or a change is required by the IFRS.

3.4.4 A **complete set of financial statements** comprises the following:

▦ Statement of Financial Position (formerly Balance Sheet);
▦ Statement of Comprehensive Income (formerly Income Statement);
▦ Statement of changes in equity;
▦ Statement of cash flows;
▦ Notes to the financial statements that contain accounting policies and other explanatory information; and
▦ Statement of financial position for the beginning of the earliest comparative period when an entity applies an accounting policy retrospectively, makes a retrospective restatement of items in its financial statements, or reclassifies items in its financial statements.

Entities are encouraged to furnish other related financial and nonfinancial information in addition to financial statements. This information can include a financial review by management that describes and explains the main features of the entity's financial performance and position, environmental reports, and value-added statements. Reports that are presented outside of the financial statements are outside of the scope of IFRSs.

3.4.5 Fair presentation. The financial statements should present fairly the financial position, financial performance, and cash flows of the entity.

The following aspects should be addressed with regard to **compliance** with the IFRS:

▦ Compliance with the IFRS should be disclosed.
▦ Compliance with **all** requirements of each standard is compulsory.
▦ Disclosure cannot rectify inappropriate accounting treatments.
▦ If the requirements of a new or revised IFRS are adopted before its effective date, this fact should be disclosed.

3.4.6 Financial statements should be presented on a **going-concern basis** unless management intends to liquidate the entity or cease trading, or has no realistic alternative but to do so. If an entity does not present its financial statements on a going-concern basis, it shall disclose the fact, the basis on which it has prepared the financial statements, and the reason why the entity is not considered to be a going concern. Uncertainties related to events and conditions that cast significant doubt on the entity's ability to continue as a going concern should be disclosed.

3.4.7 The **accrual basis** of accounting should be applied when preparing the financial statements, except for cash flow information. Under this basis, items are recognized as assets, liabilities, equity, income, and expenses when they meet the definitions and recognition criteria.

3.4.8 Aggregation of immaterial items of a similar nature and function is allowed. Material items should not be aggregated. Items with a dissimilar nature or function should be presented separately, unless they are immaterial.

3.4.9 Assets and liabilities should not be **offset** unless it is required or allowed by another IFRS (see chapter 33 on IAS 32 and chapter 15 on IAS 12). However, immaterial gains, losses, and related expenses arising from similar transactions and events can be offset.

3.4.10 With regard to comparative information, the following aspects are presented for all amounts reported in the financial statements:

- numerical information for the previous period; and
- relevant narrative and descriptive information.

PRESENTATION AND DISCLOSURE

3.5.1 Financial statements should be clearly identified and distinguished from other types of information in the same published document. Each component of the financial statements should be clearly identified, with the following information prominently displayed:

- name of reporting entity;
- whether the financial statements are of an individual entity (stand-alone) or of a group of entities (consolidated);
- reporting date or period covered;
- presentation currency (refer to chapter 21 on IAS 21); and
- level of precision used in presenting amounts.

Statement of Financial Position (Balance Sheet)

3.5.2 The **Statement of Financial Position** provides information about the financial position of the entity. It should distinguish between major categories and classifications of assets and liabilities.

3.5.3 Current or noncurrent distinction. The Statement of Financial Position should normally distinguish between current and noncurrent assets, and between current and noncurrent liabilities. Assets and liabilities to be recovered or settled within 12 months should be disclosed as current.

3.5.4 Liquidity-based presentation. Where a presentation based on liquidity provides more relevant and reliable information (for example, in the case of a bank or similar financial institution), assets and liabilities should be presented in the order in which they can or might be required to be liquidated.

3.5.5 Irrespective of the method of presentation adopted, an entity should disclose the amount expected to be recovered or settled within and after more than 12 months of the reporting period for each asset and liability line.

3.5.6 **Capital** disclosures encompass the following:

- the entity's objectives, policies, and processes for managing capital;
  - a description of what the entity manages as capital;
  - whether the entity complies with any externally imposed capital adequacy requirements and the nature of those requirements;
  - how it is meeting its objectives for managing capital;

- quantitative data about what the entity regards as capital; and
- consequences of noncompliance with capital requirements, where applicable.

3.5.7 An entity should disclose the following capital information either in the Statement of Financial Position, statement of changes in equity, or in the notes.

- for each class of share capital:
  - number of shares authorized;
  - number of shares issued and fully paid;
  - number of shares issued and not fully paid;
  - par value per share, or that it has no par value;
  - reconciliation of the number of shares at the beginning and end of year;
  - rights, preferences, and restrictions attached to that class, including restrictions on dividends and the repayment of capital;
  - shares in the entity held by the entity itself, subsidiaries, or associates;
  - number of shares reserved for issue under options and sales contracts, including the terms and amounts; and
  - a description of the nature and purpose of each reserve within equity.

3.5.8 Table 3.1 lists the **minimum information** that must be presented on the face of the **Statement of Financial Position:**

TABLE 3.1   Minimum Information for the Statement of Financial Position

Assets	Liabilities and Equity
Property, plant, and equipment	Trade and other payables
Investment property	Provisions
Intangible assets	Financial liabilities
Financial assets	Current tax liabilities
Investments accounted for using the equity method	Deferred tax liabilities
Biological assets	Liabilities included in disposal groups held for sale (see IFRS 5)
Deferred tax assets	**Equity**
Inventories	Issued capital and reserves attributable to owners of the parent
Trade and other receivables	Reserves
Current tax assets	Non-controlling interests
Cash and cash equivalents	
Assets held for sale (see IFRS 5)	
Assets included in disposal groups held for sale	

3.5.9 Other information that must appear on the face of the **Statement of Financial Position or in notes** includes the following:

- nature and purpose of each reserve;
- shareholders for dividend not formally approved for payment; and
- amount of cumulative preference dividend not recognized.

Statement of Comprehensive Income

3.5.10 Information about performance of the entity should be provided in a single Statement of Comprehensive Income or in two statements, a separate income statement followed immediately by a statement displaying components of other comprehensive income. **Minimum information** to be presented on the face of the **Statement of Comprehensive Income** includes the following:

- revenue;
- finance costs;
- share of profits or losses of associates and joint ventures;
- tax expense;
- the total gain or loss on discontinued operations, comprising the post-tax profit or loss of discontinued operations and the post-tax gain or loss recognized on the remeasurement to fair value less costs to sell, or on the disposal of the assets or disposal groups constituting a disposal group;
- profit or loss for the period attributable to non-controlling interest and owners of the parent;
- each component of other comprehensive income classified by nature;
- share of other comprehensive income of associates and joint ventures accounted for using the equity method; and
- total comprehensive income for the period attributable to non-controlling interest and owners of the parent.
- the amount of income tax for each component of other comprehensive income, including reclassification adjustments, either in the Statement of Comprehensive Income or in the notes; an entity may present components of other comprehensive income either:
  - net of related tax effects, or
  - before related tax effects with one amount shown for the aggregate amount of income tax relating to those components.

- Reclassification adjustments (amount reclassified to profit or loss in the current period that were recognized in other comprehensive income in the current or previous period) relating to components of other comprehensive income should be disclosed.

3.5.11 Other information to be presented on the face of the **Statement of Comprehensive Income or in the notes** includes:

- Analysis of expenses based on either their nature or function (see the example at the end of the chapter).
- If expenses are classified by function, disclosure of the following is required:
  - depreciation charges for tangible assets;
  - amortization charges for intangible assets;
  - employee benefits expense; and
  - dividends recognized and the related amount per share.

3.5.12 IFRS no longer allows the presentation of any items of income or expense as extraordinary items.

Statement of Changes in Equity

3.5.13 The **statement of changes in equity** reflects information about the increase or decrease in net assets or wealth.

3.5.14 Minimum information to be presented on the face of the statement of changes in equity includes the following:

- total comprehensive income for the period showing separately the total amounts attributable to owners of the parent and non-controlling interest;
- the effects of retrospective application (for example, for changes in accounting policies) or restatements recognized (for example, correction of errors) in accordance with IAS 8 on each of the components of equity;
- for each component of equity, a reconciliation between the carrying amount at the beginning and the end of the period.

3.5.15 **Other information** to be presented on the face of the statement of **changes in equity or in the notes** includes the following:

- capital transactions with owners and distributions to owners;
- the amounts of dividends recognized as distributions to owners during the period and the related per share information;
- reconciliation of the balance of accumulated profit or loss at beginning and end of the year; and
- reconciliation of the carrying amount of each class of equity capital, share premium, and each reserve at beginning and end of the period

Statement of Cash Flows

3.5.16 For a discussion of the **statement of cash flows**, refer to IAS 7 (chapter 4).

Notes to the Financial Statements

3.5.17 The notes to the financial statements consist of a summary of accounting policies and other explanatory notes. Such information must be provided in a systematic manner and cross-referenced from the face of the financial statements to the notes.

3.5.18 An entity should disclose in the summary of significant accounting policies:

- measurement bases used in preparing financial statements; and
- each accounting policy used, even if it is not covered by the IFRS;

3.5.19 The notes to the financial statements should present information about the basis of preparation of the financial statements and accounting policies, information required by IFRSs but not disclosed elsewhere, and additional information that is not presented elsewhere but is relevant to an understanding of the financial statements.

3.5.20 The notes to the financial statements should include the following information:

- **Judgments made in applying accounting policies**

    Judgments made by management in applying accounting policies that have the most significant effect on the amounts recognized in the financial statements. These include management's judgments in determining:
    - whether financial assets are held-to-maturity investments;
    - when substantially all the significant risks and rewards of ownership of financial assets and lease assets are transferred; and
    - whether the substance of the relationship between the entity and a special purpose entity indicates control.

■ **Estimation Uncertainty**

Key assumptions about the future and other key sources of estimation uncertainty that have a significant risk of causing material adjustment to the carrying amount of assets and liabilities within the next year. The entity should disclose the nature and carrying amount of these assets and liabilities as at the end of the reporting period.

3.5.21 Other disclosures include the following:

■ domicile of the entity;

■ legal form of the entity;

■ country of incorporation;

■ registered office or business address, or both;

■ nature of operations or principal activities, or both;

■ name of the parent and ultimate parent;

■ the amount of dividends proposed or declared before the financial statements were authorized for issue, but not recognized as a distribution to owners during the period, and the related amount per share; and

■ amount of cumulative preference dividend not recognized.

3.6　**FINANCIAL ANALYSIS AND INTERPRETATION**

3.6.1 Financial analysis applies analytical tools to financial statements and other financial data to interpret trends and relationships in a consistent and disciplined manner. In essence, the analyst is in the business of converting data into information, thereby assisting in a diagnostic process that has as its objective the screening and forecasting of information.

3.6.2 The financial analyst who is interested in assessing the value or creditworthiness of an entity is required to estimate its future cash flows, assess the risks associated with those estimates, and determine the proper discount rate that should be applied to those estimates. The objective of the IFRS financial statements is to provide information that is useful to users in making economic decisions. However, IFRS financial statements do not contain all the information that an individual user might need to perform all of the above tasks, because the statements largely portray the effects of past events and do not necessarily provide nonfinancial information. IFRS financial statements do contain data about the past performance of an entity (its income and cash flows) as well as its current financial condition (assets and liabilities) that are useful in assessing future prospects and risks. The financial analyst must be capable of using the financial statements in conjunction with other information to reach valid investment conclusions.

3.6.3 The **notes** to financial statements are an integral part of the IFRS financial reporting process. They provide important detailed disclosures required by IFRS, as well as other information provided voluntarily by management. The notes include information on such topics as the following:

■ specific accounting policies that were used in compiling the financial statements;

■ terms of debt agreements;

■ lease information;

■ financing agreements that are not recognized on the Statement of Financial Position;

■ breakdowns of operations by important segments;

■ contingent assets and liabilities; and

■ detailed pension plan disclosure.

3.6.4 Supplementary schedules can be provided in financial reports to present additional information that can be beneficial to users. These schedules include such information as the five-year performance record of a company, a breakdown of unit sales by product line, a listing of mineral reserves, and so forth.

3.6.5 The management of publicly traded companies in certain jurisdictions, such as the United States, is required to provide a **discussion and analysis** of the company's operations and prospects. This discussion normally includes the following:

- a review of the company's financial condition and its operating results;
- an assessment of the significant effects of currently known trends, events, and uncertainties on the company's liquidity, capital resources, and operating results;
- the capital resources available to the firm and its liquidity;
- extraordinary or unusual events (including discontinued operations) that have a material effect on the company; and
- a review of the performance of the operating segments of the business that have a significant impact on the business or its finances.

The publication of such a report is encouraged, but is currently not required by IFRS.

3.6.6 Ratio analysis is used by analysts and managers to assess company performance and status. Ratios are not meaningful when used on their own, which is why trend analysis (the monitoring of a ratio or group of ratios over time) and comparative analysis (the comparison of a specific ratio for a group of companies in a sector, or for different sectors) is preferred by financial analysts. Another analytical technique of great value is relative analysis, which is achieved through the conversion of all Statement of Financial Position (or Statement of Comprehensive Income) items to a percentage of a given Statement of Financial Position (or Statement of Comprehensive Income) item.

3.6.7 Although financial analysts use a variety of subgroupings to describe their analysis, the following classifications of risk and performance are often used:

- **Liquidity**. An indication of the entity's ability to repay its short-term liabilities, measured by evaluating components of current assets and current liabilities.
- **Solvency**. The risk related to the volatility of income flows, often described as business risk (resulting from the volatility related to operating income, sales, and operating leverage) and financial risk (resulting from the impact of the use of debt on equity returns as measured by debt ratios and cash flow coverage).
- **Operational efficiency**. Determination of the extent to which an entity uses its assets and capital efficiently, as measured by asset and equity turnover.
- **Growth**. The rate at which an entity can grow as determined by its retention of profits and its profitability measured by return on equity (ROE).
- **Profitability**. An indication of how a company's profit margins relate to sales, average capital, and average common equity. Profitability can be further analyzed through the use of the Du Pont analysis.

3.6.8 Some have questioned the usefulness of financial statement analysis in a world where capital markets are said to be efficient. After all, they say, an efficient market is forward looking, whereas the analysis of financial statements is a look at the past. However, the value of financial analysis is that it enables the analyst to gain insights that can assist in making forward-looking projections required by an efficient market. Financial ratios serve the following purposes:

- They provide insights into the microeconomic relationships within a firm that help analysts project earnings and free cash flow (which is necessary to determine entity value and creditworthiness).
- They provide insights into a firm's financial flexibility, which is its ability to obtain the cash required to meet financial obligations or to make asset acquisitions, even if unexpected circumstances should develop. Financial flexibility requires a firm to possess financial strength (a level and trend of financial ratios that meet or exceed industry norms); lines of credit; or assets that can be easily used as a means of obtaining cash, either by selling them outright or by using them as collateral.
- They provide a means of evaluating management's ability. Key performance ratios, such as the ROE, can serve as quantitative measures for ranking management's ability relative to a peer group.

3.6.9 Financial ratio analysis is limited by the following:

- **The use of alternative accounting methods**. Accounting methods play an important role in the interpretation of financial ratios. Ratios are usually based on data taken from financial statements. Such data are generated via accounting procedures that might not be comparable among firms, because firms have latitude in the choice of accounting methods. This lack of consistency across firms makes comparability difficult to analyze and limits the usefulness of ratio analysis. The various accounting alternatives currently found (but not necessarily allowed by IFRS) include the following:
  - first-in-first-out (FIFO) or last-in-first-out (LIFO) inventory valuation methods;
  - cost or equity methods of accounting for unconsolidated associates;
  - straight-line or accelerated-consumption-pattern methods of depreciation; and
  - capitalized or operating lease treatment.

IFRS seeks to make the financial statements of different entities comparable and so overcome the following difficulties:

- **The homogeneity of a firm's operating activities**. Many firms are diversified, with divisions operating in different industries. This makes it difficult to find comparable industry ratios to use for comparison purposes. It is better to examine industry-specific ratios by lines of business.
- **The need to determine whether the results of the ratio analysis are consistent**. One set of ratios might show a problem, and another set might prove that this problem is short term in nature, with strong long-term prospects.
- **The need to use judgment**. The analyst must use judgment when performing ratio analysis. A key issue is whether a ratio for a firm is within a reasonable range for an industry, and the analyst must determine this range. Although financial ratios are used to help assess the growth potential and risk of a business, they cannot be used alone to directly value a company or determine its creditworthiness. The entire operation of the business must be examined, and the external economic and industry setting in which it is operating must be considered when interpreting financial ratios.

3.6.10 Financial ratios mean little by themselves. Their meaning can only be gleaned by using them in the context of other information. In addition to the items mentioned in 3.6.9 above, an analyst should evaluate financial ratios based on the following:

- **Experience**. An analyst with experience obtains a feel for the right ratio relationships.

■ **Company goals.** Actual ratios can be compared with company objectives to determine if the objectives are being attained.

■ **Industry norms (cross-sectional analysis).** A company can be compared with others in its industry by relating its financial ratios to industry norms or a subset of the companies in an industry. When industry norms are used to make judgments, care must be taken, because of the following:

 – Many ratios are industry specific, but not all ratios are important to all industries.

 – Differences in corporate strategies can affect certain financial ratios. (It is a good practice to compare the financial ratios of a company with those of its major competitors. Typically, the analyst should be wary of companies whose financial ratios are too far above or below industry norms.)

■ **Economic conditions.** Financial ratios tend to improve when the economy is strong and to weaken during recessions. Therefore, financial ratios should be examined in light of the phase of the economy's business cycle.

■ **Trend (time-series analysis).** The trend of a ratio, which shows whether it is improving or deteriorating, is as important as its current absolute level.

3.6.11 The more **aggressive the accounting methods**, the lower the quality of earnings; the lower the quality of earnings, the higher the risk assessment; the higher the risk assessment, the lower the value of the company being analyzed (see table 3.2).

3.6.12 Table 3.3 provides an overview of some of the **ratios that can be calculated** using each of the classification areas discussed in 3.6.7.

3.6.13 When performing an analysis for specific purposes, various elements from different ratio classification groupings can be combined, as seen in table 3.4.

TABLE 3.2 Manipulation of Earnings via Accounting Methods that Distort the Principles of IFRS

Financial statement item	Aggressive treatment (bending the intention of IFRS)	"Conservative" treatment
Revenue	Aggressive accruals	Installment sales or cost recovery
Inventory	FIFO-IFRS treatment	LIFO (where allowed—not allowed per IFRS anymore)
Depreciation	Straight line (usual under IFRS) with higher salvage value	Accelerated-consumption-pattern methods (lower salvage value)
Warranties or bad debts	High estimates	Low estimates
Amortization period	Longer or increasing	Shorter or decreasing
Discretionary expenses	Deferred	Incurred
Contingencies	Footnote only	Accrue
Management compensation	Accounting earnings as basis	Economic earnings as basis
Prior period adjustments	Frequent	Infrequent
Change in auditors	Frequent	Infrequent
Costs	Capitalize	Expense

TABLE 3.3 Ratio Categories

1. Liquidity

	Numerator	Denominator
Current	Current assets	Current liabilities
Quick	Cash + marketable securities + receivables	Current liabilities
Cash	Cash + marketable securities	Current liabilities
Receivables turnover	Net annual sales	Average receivables
Average receivables collection period	365	Receivables turnover
Inventory turnover	Cost of goods sold	Average inventory
Average inventory processing period	365	Inventory turnover
Payables turnover	Cost of goods sold	Average trade payables
Payables payment period	365	Payables turnover
Cash conversion cycle	Average receivables collection period + average inventory processing period – payables payment period	N/A

2. Solvency (Business and Financial Risk Analysis)

	Numerator	Denominator
Business risk (coefficient of variation)	Standard deviation of operating income	Income
Business risk (coefficient of variation) – net income	Standard deviation of net income	Mean net income
Sales variability	Standard deviation of sales	Mean sales
Operating leverage	Mean of absolute value of % change in operating expenses	Percentage (%) change in sales
Debt-equity	Total long-term debt	Total equity
Long-term debt ratio	Total long-term debt	Total long-term capital
Total debt ratio	Total debt	Total capital
Interest coverage	EBIT (Earnings before interest and taxes)	Interest expense
Fixed financial cost coverage	EBIT	Interest expense + one-third of lease payments
Fixed charge coverage	EBIT + lease payments	Interest payments + lease payments + preferred dividends / (1 − tax rate)
Cash flow to interest expense	Net income + depreciation expense + increase in deferred taxes	Interest expense
Cash flow coverage of fixed financial cost coverage	Traditional cash flow + interest expense + one-third of lease payments	Interest expense + one-third of lease payments
Cash flow to long-term debt	Net income + depreciation expense + increase in deferred taxes	Book value of long-term debt
Cash flow to total debt	Net income + depreciation expense + increase in deferred taxes	Total debt
Financial risk	Volatility caused by firm's use of debt	N/A

TABLE 3.3 **Ratio Categories** *(continued)*

3. Operational Efficiency (Activity)

	Numerator	**Denominator**
Total asset turnover	Net sales	Average net assets
Fixed asset turnover	Net sales	Average total fixed assets
Equity turnover	Net sales	Average equity

4. Growth

	Numerator	**Denominator**
Sustainable growth rate	Retention rate of earning reinvested (RR) × (ROE)	N/A
RR (retention rate)	Dividends declared	Operating income after taxes
Return on equity (ROE)	Net income − preferred dividends	Average common equity
Payout ratio	Common dividends declared	Net income − preferred dividends

5. Profitability

	Numerator	**Denominator**
Gross profit margin	Gross profit	Net sales
Operating profit margin	Operating profit (EBIT)	Net sales
Net profit margin	Net income	Net sales
Return on total capital	Net income + interest expense	Average total capital
Return on total equity	Net income	Average total equity
Return on common equity	Net income − preferred dividends	Average common equity
Du Pont 1: ROE ROA x Financial Leverage	Net income	Equity
Net profit margin	Net income	Revenue
× Asset turnover	Revenue	Average assets
× Financial leverage	Average assets	Average equity
Du Pont 2: ROE	Net income	Equity
Operating profit margin	Operating profit (EBIT)	Revenue
× Interest burden	Earnings before tax (EBT)	Operating profit (EBIT)
× Tax burden	Net income	Earnings before tax (EBT)
× Asset turnover	Revenue	Average assets
× Financial leverage	Average assets	Average equity

TABLE 3.4   Combining Ratios for Specific Analytical Purposes

Purpose of analysis	Ratio used					
	Liquidity	**Solvency (business and financial risk analysis)**	**Operational efficiency (activity)**	**Growth**	**Profitability**	**External liquidity**
Stock/equity valuation	Debt/equity			Dividend payout rate	Return on equity (ROE)	Market price to book rate value
	Interest coverage			RR (retention rate)	Return on common equity	Market price to cash flow
		Business risk (coefficient of variation of operating earnings)				
		Market price to sales				
		Business risk (coefficient of variation) — net income				
		Sales variability Systematic risk (beta) Sales/earnings growth rates Cash flow growth rate				
Risk measurement	Current ratio	Total debt ratio	Dividend payout		Asset size	Market value of stock outstanding
	Working capital to total assets	Cash flow to total debt				
		Interest coverage				
		Cash flow to total debt				
		Business risk (coefficient of variation of operating earnings/ operating profit margins)				
		Long-term debt ratio	Equity turnover		Net profit margin (ROE)	Market value of stock outstanding
Credit analysis for bond ratings		Total debt ratio	Working capital to sales ratio		Return on assets (ROA)	Par value of bonds

		Ratio used				
Purpose of analysis	**Liquidity**	**Solvency (business and financial risk analysis)**	**Operational efficiency (activity)**	**Growth**	**Profitability**	**External liquidity**
		Cash flow to total debt	Total asset turnover		Operating profit margin	
		Cash flow coverage of fixed financial cost			ROE	
		Cash flow to interest expense				
		Interest coverage				
		Variability of sales/net income and ROA				
Forecasting bankruptcy	Current	Cash flow to total debt	Total asset turnover		ROA	Market value of stock to book value of debt
	Cash	Cash flow to LT debt	Working capital to sales ratio		ROA	
		Total debt ratio			EBIT to total assets	
		Total debt and total assets			Retained earnings to total assets	
Other—not used above	Quick (acid test)	Operating leverage	Fixed asset turnover	Sustainable growth rate	Gross profit margin	Number of securities traded per day
	Receivables turnover	Financial risk (volatility caused by firm's use of debt)			Operating profit margin	Bid/asked spread
	Average receivables collection period	Fixed financial cost coverage			Return on total capital	Percentage of outstanding securities traded per day
	Inventory turnover	Fixed charge coverage			Return on total capital including leases	
	Average inventory processing period				Du Pont 1	
	Payables turnover				Du Pont 2	
	Payables payment period					
	Cash conversion cycle					

3.7   **COMMENTARY**

3.7.1 The IASB and the U.S. FASB are currently collaborating on a project to develop a new, joint standard for financial statement presentation. This is part of the IASB's project to align IFRS with U.S. GAAP. Under IFRSs, the new standard will replace the existing IAS 1 and IAS 7. The boards are conducting the project in three phases:

- Phase A—A complete set of financial statements and requirements for presenting comparative information. This phase has been completed and incorporated in the currently effective version of IAS 1.
- Phase B—Work on more fundamental issues regarding the presentation of information in the financial statements. A discussion paper "Preliminary View on Financial Statement Presentation" was released in October 2008 and the comment period closed in April 2009. In the discussion paper the boards propose a presentation model that requires an entity to present information about its business activities (the way it creates value) and its financing activities (how it finances/funds those activities) separately. The boards are currently considering the comments received.
- Phase C—Presentation and display of interim financial information in U.S. GAAP. The IASB may also reconsider the requirements of IAS 34 Interim Financial Reporting.

3.7.5 As mentioned previously the management of publicly traded companies in certain jurisdictions, such as the United States, is required to provide a discussion and analysis of the company's operations and prospects. The publication of management commentary is currently not a requirement of IFRSs. The IASB released an exposure draft on management commentary in June 2009, with a comment period that closed on March 1, 2010.

3.7.6 The proposals presented in the exposure draft will not result in an IFRS. It will not be a requirement for an entity to comply with the framework for the preparation and presentation of management commentary as a condition for asserting compliance with IFRS.

3.8 **IMPLEMENTATION DECISIONS**

The following table sets out some of the strategic and tactical decisions that should be considered when applying IAS 1.

Strategic decisions	Tactical decisions	Problems to overcome
Determining what information will be presented on the face of the statement of financial position, income statement, and statement of changes in equity, and what information will be presented in the notes to the annual financial statements.	When determining what information will be presented on the face of the various statements and in the notes to the financial statements, management needs to ensure that their presentation is in line with the presentation of other entities within the same industry.	Ensuring that the financial reporting and management reporting systems are adequate to obtain all the information that is required to be presented in terms of IAS 1.
IAS 1 permits presentation on the statement of financial position based on either a current and noncurrent split or on a liquidity basis.	Management should determine what information to present on the face of the statement of financial position, income statement, statement of changes in equity and what information to present in the notes to the annual financial statements. Industry practice and user requirements are useful guidelines. Where the current/noncurrent basis of presentation is selected, management needs to define what is regarded as current and noncurrent based on the entity's normal operating cycle and the guidance provided in IAS 1.	Ensuring that the financial reporting system is adequate to obtain the information required regarding the amounts expected to be recovered or settled within 12 months after the reporting period and more than 12 months after the reporting period.
What information will be presented as forming part of the financial statements and what supplementary information required by certain users will also be presented in the annual report.	Management, in conjunction with the external auditors, should decide what level of assurance will be applied to additional information presented in the annual report.	The annual report should clearly distinguish between information that forms part of the annual financial statements and is subject to sign-off by the auditors. This may necessarily interfere with the flow of commentary.
IAS 1 also provides a choice to present either a single statement of comprehensive income or two statements (an income statement and separate statement of comprehensive income). This decision is primarily dependent on industry practice although entity specific issues may also be relevant	Whether the components of other comprehensive income will be presented net of the related tax effects or gross of the related tax effects, with a single line presented for the tax effects, on the face of the statement of other comprehensive income.	Management reporting systems should be able to provide the following information for each component of comprehensive income: • gains or losses arising in the current year; • reclassification adjustments recognized in profit or loss for the period; and • related income tax effect.
What accounting policies are considered to be significant. Based on this analysis determine which accounting policies will be disclosed in the annual financial statements.	When considering whether a specific accounting policy should be presented, consider whether it would assist users in understanding how transactions, other events, and conditions are reflected in the financial statements. Consideration should also be given to whether the disclosure of certain accounting policies is required by a specific standard.	

EXAMPLE: PRESENTATION OF FINANCIAL STATEMENTS

ABC Group—Statement of Financial Position as at 31 December 20X7

	20X9	20X8
ASSETS		
Noncurrent assets		
Property, plant, and equipment		
Goodwill		
Other intangible assets		
Investments in associates		
Available-for-sale financial assets		
Current assets		
Inventories		
Trade receivables		
Other current assets		
Cash and cash equivalents		
Total assets		
EQUITY AND LIABILITIES		
Equity attributable to owners of the parent		
Share capital		
Retained earnings		
Other components of equity		
Non-controlling interests		
Total equity		
Noncurrent liabilities		
Long-term borrowings		
Deferred tax		
Long-term provisions		
Total noncurrent liabilities		
Current liabilities		
Trade and other payables		
Short-term borrowings		
Current portion of long-term borrowings		
Current tax payable		
Short-term provisions		
Total current liabilities		
Total liabilities		
TOTAL EQUITY AND LIABILITIES		

(continued)

EXAMPLE: PRESENTATION OF FINANCIAL STATEMENTS *(continued)*

ABC Group—Statement of Comprehensive Income for the Year Ended, illustrating the presentation of comprehensive income in one statement and classification of expenses by function

	20X9	20X8
Revenue		
Cost of sales		
Gross profit		
Other income		
Distribution costs		
Administrative expenses		
Other expenses		
Finance costs		
Share of profit of associates		
Profit before tax		
Income tax expense		
Profit for the year from continuing operations		
Loss for the year from discontinued operations		
PROFIT FOR THE YEAR		
Other comprehensive income:		
Exchange differences on translating foreign operations		
Available-for-sale financial assets		
Cash flow hedges		
Gains on property revaluation		
Actuarial gains (losses) on defined benefit pension plans		
Share of other comprehensive income of associates		
Income tax relating to components of other comprehensive income		
Other comprehensive income for the year, net of tax		
TOTAL COMPREHENSIVE INCOME FOR THE YEAR		
Profit attributable to:		
Owners of the parent		
Non-controlling interests		
Total comprehensive income attributable to:		
Owners of the parent		
Non-controlling interests		
Earnings per share		
Basic and diluted earnings		

CHAPTER 4

Statement of Cash Flows
(IAS 7)

4.1　**OBJECTIVE**

In order to assess the viability of any entity, particularly the solvency and liquidity position, the users of financial statements require information about the cash resources of an entity, the ability of the entity to generate cash resources, and the use by an entity of its cash resources.

The purpose of IAS 7 is to provide guidance regarding the manner in which the cash flow information should be presented. The statement of cash flows is also relevant for identifying

- movement in cash balances for the period;
- timing and certainty of cash flows;
- ability of the entity to generate cash resources; and
- prediction of future cash flows (useful for valuation models).

4.2　**SCOPE OF THE STANDARD**

All entities are required to present a statement of cash flows that reports cash flows during the reporting period.

4.3　**KEY CONCEPTS**

4.3.1 An entity should present a **statement of cash flows** that reports cash flows during the reporting period, classified by operating, financing, and investing activities.

4.3.2 Cash flows are inflows and outflows of cash and cash equivalents.

4.3.3 Cash comprises

- cash on hand; and
- demand deposits (net of bank overdrafts repayable on demand).

4.3.4 Cash equivalents are short-term, highly liquid investments (such as short-term debt securities) that are readily convertible to known amounts of cash and that are subject to an insignificant risk of changes in value.

4.3.5 Operating activities are principal revenue-producing activities and other activities that do not include investing or financing activities.

4.3.6 Investing activities are acquisition and disposal of long-term assets and other investments not included as cash-equivalent investments.

4.3.7 Financing activities are activities that change the size and composition of the equity capital and borrowings.

4.4   ACCOUNTING TREATMENT

4.4.1 Cash flows from **operating activities** are reported using either the direct or indirect method:

- The **direct method** discloses major classes of gross cash receipts and gross cash payments (for example, sales, cost of sales, purchases, and employee benefits).
- The **indirect method** adjusts profit and loss for the period for
  - effects of noncash transactions;
  - deferrals or accruals; and
  - investing or financing cash flows.

- Entities are encouraged to use the direct method as it provides additional information that may be useful for estimating future cash flows.

4.4.2 Cash flows from **investing activities** are reported as follows:

- Major classes of **gross cash receipts** and **gross cash payments** are reported separately.
- The aggregate cash flows from acquisitions or disposals of subsidiaries and other business units are classified as investing.

4.4.3 Cash flows from **financing activities** are reported by separately listing major classes of gross cash receipts and **gross cash payments**.

4.4.4 The following cash flows can be reported on a **net** basis:

- cash receipts and payments on behalf of customers; and
- cash receipts and payments for items for which the turnover is quick, the amounts large, and maturities short (for example, purchase and sale of investments by an investment entity).

4.4.5 Interest and dividends paid should be treated consistently as either operating or financing activities. Interest and dividends received are treated as investing inflows. However, in the case of financial institutions, interest paid and dividends received are usually classified as operating cash flows.

4.4.6 Cash flows from taxes on income are normally classified as operating activities (unless they can be specifically identified with financing or investing activities).

4.4.7 A foreign exchange transaction is recorded in the functional currency using the exchange rate at the date of the cash flow.

4.4.8 Foreign operations' cash flows are translated at the exchange rate ruling on the dates of cash flows (an exchange rate that approximates the actual rate can also be used, for example a weighted average rate for the period).

4.4.9 When entities are equity or cost accounted, only actual cash flows from them (for example, dividends received) are shown in the cash flow statement.

4.4.10 Cash flows from joint ventures are proportionately included in the statement of cash flows if the joint venture is proportionally consolidated.

4.5

PRESENTATION AND DISCLOSURE

4.5.1 The following should be disclosed:

- components of cash and cash equivalents in the statement of cash flows and a reconciliation with the equivalent items in the statement of financial position;
- details about noncash investing and financing transactions (for example, conversion of debt to equity); and
- amount of cash and cash equivalents that are not available for use by the group.

4.5.2 The following disclosure is suggested:

- amount of undrawn borrowing facilities available for future operating activities and to settle capital commitments (indicating any restrictions);
- aggregate amount of cash flows from each of the three activities (operating, investing, and financing) related to interest in joint ventures that are proportionally consolidated;
- amount of cash flows arising from each of the three activities regarding each reportable operating segment; and
- distinction between the cash flows that represent an increase in operating capacity and those that represent the maintenance of it.

4.5.3 The following should be shown in aggregate for either the purchase or sale of a subsidiary or business unit:

- total purchase or disposal consideration;
- purchase or disposal consideration paid in cash and equivalents;
- amount of cash and cash equivalents in the entity acquired or disposed; and
- amount of assets and liabilities other than cash and cash equivalents in the entity acquired or disposed.

4.6

FINANCIAL ANALYSIS AND INTERPRETATION

4.6.1 The IFRS statement of cash flows shows the sources of the cash inflows received by an entity during an accounting period, and the purposes for which cash was used. The statement is an integral part of the analysis of a business because it enables the analyst to determine the following:

- the ability of a company to generate cash from its operations;
- the cash consequences of investing and financing decisions;
- the effects of management's decisions about financial policy;
- the sustainability of a firm's cash-generating capability;
- how well operating cash flow correlates with net income;
- the impact of accounting policies on the quality of earnings;
- information about the liquidity and long-term solvency of a firm;
- whether or not the going-concern assumption is reasonable; and
- the ability of a firm to finance its growth from internally generated funds.

4.6.2 Because cash inflows and outflows are objective facts, the data presented in the statement of cash flows represent economic reality. The statement reconciles the increase or decrease in a company's cash and cash equivalents that occurred during the accounting period (an objectively verifiable fact). Nevertheless, this statement must be read while keeping the following in mind:

- There are analysts who believe that accounting rules are developed primarily to promote comparability, rather than to reflect economic reality. Even if this view were to be considered harsh, it is a fact that too much flexibility in accounting can present problems for analysts who are primarily interested in assessing a company's future cash-generating capability from operations.

- As with Statement of Comprehensive Income data, cash flows can be erratic from period to period, reflecting random, cyclical, and seasonal transactions involving cash, as well as sectoral trends. It can be difficult to decipher important long-term trends from less meaningful short-term fluctuations in such data.

4.6.3 Financial analysts can use the IFRS statement of cash flows to help them determine other measures that they wish to use in their analysis—for example, free cash flow, which analysts often use to determine the value of a firm. Defining free cash flow is not an easy task, because many different measures are commonly called free cash flow.

4.6.4 **Discretionary free cash flow** is the cash that is available for discretionary purposes. According to this definition, free cash flow is the cash generated from operating activities, less the capital expenditures required to maintain the current level of operations. Therefore, the analyst must identify that part of the capital expenditure included in investing cash flows that relates to maintaining the current level of operations—a formidable task. Any excess cash flow can be used for discretionary purposes (for example, to pay dividends, reduce debt, improve solvency, or to expand and improve the business). IFRS, therefore, requires disclosure of expenditures as those expenditures that were required to maintain the current level of operations and those that were undertaken to expand or improve the business.

4.6.5 **Free cash flow available to owners** measures the ability of a firm to pay dividends to its owners. In this case, all of the cash used for investing activities (capital expenditures, acquisitions, and long-term investments) is subtracted from the cash generated from operating activities. In effect, this definition states that the firm should be able to pay out as dividends cash from operations that is left over after the firm makes the investments that management deems necessary to maintain and grow current operations.

4.6.6 Generally, the cash generated from operating activities is greater than net income for a well-managed, financially healthy company; if it is not, the analyst should be suspicious of the company's solvency. Growth companies often have negative free cash flows because their rapid growth requires high capital expenditures and other investments. Mature companies often have positive free cash flows, whereas declining firms often have significantly positive free cash flows because their lack of growth means a low level of capital expenditures. High and growing free cash flows, therefore, are not necessarily positive or negative; much depends upon the stage of the industry life cycle in which a company is operating. This is why the free cash flow has to be assessed in conjunction with the firm's income prospects.

4.6.7 Many valuation models use cash flow from operations, thus giving management an incentive to record inflows as operating (normal and recurring), and outflows as related to either investing or financing. Other areas where management discretionary choices could influence the presentation of cash flows follow:

- **Payment of taxes**. Management has a vested interest in reducing current-year payments of taxes by choosing accounting methods on the tax return that are likely to defer tax payments to the future.
- **Discretionary expenses**. Management can manipulate cash flow from operations by timing the payment or incurring certain discretionary expenses such as research and development, repairs and maintenance, and so on. Cash inflows from operations can also be increased by the timing of the receipt of deposits on long-term contracts.
- **Leasing**. The entire cash outflow of an operating lease reduces the cash flow from operations. For a capital lease, the cash payment is allocated between operating and financing, thus increasing cash flow from operations.

| 4.7 | **COMMENTARY** |

4.7.1 IAS 7 is a fairly simple standard and generally easy to implement. Nevertheless, some practical issues have arisen in applying this standard; some of the more important issues include these listed below:

- There is no consensus as to whether or not cash flows should be presented inclusive or exclusive of value added tax (VAT) since the standard does not specifically deal with the treatment of VAT. The IFRIC has recommended that entities should disclose whether the gross cash flows are inclusive or exclusive of VAT.
- It is not clear whether investment in shares or units in money market funds that are redeemable at any time can be classified as cash equivalents. In this regard the IFRIC noted that for an item to meet the definition of cash equivalents, the amount of cash that will be received must be known at the time of the initial investments. The units therefore cannot be considered cash equivalents simply because they can be converted to cash at any time at the market price in an active market.
- There is inconsistent application in the banking industry regarding cash reserves held with the central bank. Certain banks include those cash reserves in cash and cash equivalents as they are considered to be resources available to the banking institution. Other banks exclude these amounts as they do not control access to the funds.
- The indirect method calculates cash flow from operating activities by using information that is already available in the annual financial statements. It does not provide additional information about the actual cash flows. The direct method is therefore recommended and favored by external auditors.
- IAS 7 has been amended and now requires that only an expenditure that results in a recognized asset should be classified as cash flow from investing activities. This amendment became effective for annual periods on January 1, 2010. There are no other future developments expected for IAS 7.

4.8   IMPLEMENTATION DECISIONS

The following table sets out some of the strategic and tactical decisions that should be considered when applying IAS 7.

Strategic decisions	Tactical decisions	Problems to overcome
IAS 7 requires that an entity consider what amounts are cash and cash equivalents and what amounts are managed as the cash resources of the entity. The standard requires, subject to certain restrictions, the entity should make this decision based on its intention.		
Whether to report the cash flows from operating activities using the direct or indirect method.	In making this decision, management should take into account the fact that the standard encourages entities to use the direct method because it provides additional information that may be useful in estimating future cash flows.	Determining whether the accounting system is able to provide cash flow information for the direct or indirect method of presentation.
IAS 7 provides for the classification of interest and dividends received and paid as either investing or operating activities. This decision will be based on the intent of the entity.	It is generally accepted that the dividends received/paid and the interest received/paid will be classified as operating activities for a financial institution. For other types of entities, management should make a decision and apply it on a consistent basis from period to period.	Management should take into account the fact that presenting dividends and interest paid in operating activities allows users to determine the ability of an entity to pay dividends and interest out of operating cash flows; at the same time, some entities may prefer to show dividends and interest paid under financing activities as these are payments to providers of capital.

EXAMPLES: STATEMENT OF CASH FLOWS

EXAMPLE 4.1

During the year ending 20X1, ABC Company completed the following transactions:

1. Purchased a new machine for $13.0 million
2. Paid cash dividends totaling $8.0 million
3. Purchased Treasury stock (own shares) totaling $45.0 million
4. Spent $27.0 million on operating expenses, of which $10.0 million was paid in cash and the remainder put on credit

Which of the following correctly classifies each of the above transaction items in the operating, investing, and financing activities section on the statement of cash flows?

	Transaction 1	Transaction 2	Transaction 3	Transaction 4
a.	Investing inflow	Operating outflow	Financing outflow	All expenses—operating outflow
b.	Financing outflow	Financing outflow	Investing outflow	Cash paid (only)—operating outflow
c.	Investing outflow	Financing outflow	Financing outflow	Cash paid (only)—operating outflow
d.	Financing inflow	Operating outflow	Financing inflow	Cash paid (only)—operating outflow

EXPLANATION

Choice c. is correct. Each transaction had both the proper statement of cash flow activity and the correct cash inflow or outflow direction.

Choice a. is incorrect. This choice incorrectly classifies the cash flow activities for transactions 1, 2, and 4. Choice b. is incorrect. This choice incorrectly classifies the cash flow activities for transactions 1 and 3. Choice d. is incorrect. This choice incorrectly classifies the cash flow activities for transactions 1, 2, and 3. *Note:* Dividends are sometimes classified as an operating cash flow.

EXAMPLE 4.2

Gibson Entities had the following financial data for the year ended December 31, 20X2:

	Millions of $
Capital expenditures	75.0
Dividends declared	1.2
Net income	17.0
Common stock issued	33.0
Increase in accounts receivable	12.0
Depreciation and amortization	3.5
Proceeds from sale of assets	6.0
Gain on sale of assets	0.5

Based on the above, what is the ending cash balance at December 31, 20X2, assuming an opening cash balance of $47.0 million?

a. $13.0 million
b. $17.8 million
c. $19.0 million
d. $43.0 million

Choice c. is correct. The answer is based on the following calculation:

	Millions of $
Operating cash flow	
Net income	17.0
Depreciation and amortization	3.5
Gain on sale of assets	(0.5)
Increase in accounts receivable	(12.0)
Operating cash flow	**8.0**
Investing cash flow	
Capital expenditures	(75.0)
Proceeds from sale of assets	6.0
Investing cash flow	**(69.0)**
Financing cash flow	
Common stock issued	33.0
Financing cash flow	**33.0**
Net change in cash (8 − 69 + 33)	(28.0)
Beginning cash	47.0
Ending cash	**19.0**

Note that the dividends had only been declared, not paid.

EXAMPLE 4.3

The following are the abridged annual financial statements of Linco Inc.

Statement of Comprehensive Income for the Year Ending September 30, 20X4	
	$
Revenue	850,000
Cost of sales	(637,500)
Gross profit	212,500
Administrative expenses	(28,100)
Operating expenses	(73,600)
Profit from operations	110,800
Finance cost	(15,800)
Profit before tax	95,000
Income tax expense	(44,000)
Profit for the period	51,000

Statement of Changes in Equity for the Year Ending September 30, 20X4

	Share capital ($)	Revaluation reserve ($)	Accumulated profit ($)	Total ($)
Balance—beginning of the year	120,000		121,000	241,000
Revaluation of buildings		(20,000)		(20,000)
Profit for the period			51,000	51,000
Dividends paid			(25,000)	(25,000)
Repayment of share capital	(20,000)			(20,000)
Balance—end of the year	100,000	20,000	147,000	267,000

Statement of Financial Position at September 30, 20X4

	20X4 ($)	20X3 ($)
Noncurrent Assets		
Property, plant, and equipment		
Office buildings	250,000	220,000
Machinery	35,000	20,000
Motor vehicles	6,000	4,000
Long-term loans to directors	64,000	60,000
	355,000	304,000
Current Assets		
Inventories	82,000	42,000
Debtors	63,000	43,000
Prepaid expenses	21,000	16,000
Bank	–	6,000
	166,000	107,000
Total Assets	521,000	411,000
Equity and Liabilities		
Capital and Reserves		
Share capital	100,000	120,000
Revaluation reserve	20,000	–
Accumulated profits	147,000	121,000
	267,000	241,000
Noncurrent Liabilities		
Long-term borrowings	99,000	125,000
Current Liabilities		
Creditors	72,000	35,000
Bank	43,000	–
Taxation due	40,000	10,000
	155,000	45,000
Total Equity and Liabilities	521,000	411,000

Additional information

1. The following depreciation charges are included in operating expenses:
   Machinery $25,000
   Motor vehicles $ 2,000
2. Fully depreciated machinery with an original cost price of $15,000 was sold for $5,000 during the year. The profit is included in operating expenses.
3. The financial manager mentions that the accountants allege the company is heading for a possible liquidity crisis. According to him, the company struggled to meet its short-term obligations during the current year.

EXPLANATION

The statement of cash flows would be presented as follows if the **direct method** were used for its preparation:

LINCO INC. Statement of Cash Flows for the Year Ending September 30, 20X4

	$
Cash flows from operating activities	
Cash receipts from customers (**Calculation e**)	830,000
Cash payments to suppliers and employees (**Calculation f**)	(725,200)
Net cash generated by operations	104,800
Interest paid	(15,800)
Taxation paid (**Calculation d**)	(14,000)
Dividends paid	(25,000)
	50,000
Cash flows from investing activities	
Purchases of property, plant and equipment (**Calc. a, b, c**)	(54,000)
Proceeds on sale of machinery	5,000
Loans to directors	(4,000)
	(53,000)
Cash flows from financing activities	
Decrease in long-term loan (125 – 99)	(26,000)
Repayment of share capital	(20,000)
	(46,000)
Net decrease in bank balance for the period	(49,000)
Bank balance at beginning of the year	6,000
Overdraft at end of the year	(43,000)

Commentary

1. The total increase in creditors was used to partially finance the increase in working capital.

2. The rest of the increase in working capital as well as the interest paid, taxation paid, and dividends paid were financed by cash generated from operations.
3. The remaining balance of cash generated by operating activities and the proceeds on the sale of fixed assets were used to finance the purchase of fixed assets.
4. The overdrawn bank account was used for the repayment of share capital and the redemption of the long-term loan.

CALCULATIONS

		$
a.	**Office buildings**	
	Balance at beginning of year	220,000
	Revaluation	20,000
	Purchases (balancing figure)	10,000
	Balance at end of the year	250,000
b.	**Machinery**	
	Balance at beginning of year	20,000
	Depreciation	(25,000)
	Purchases (balancing figure)	40,000
	Balance at end of the year	35,000
c.	**Vehicles**	
	Balance at beginning of year	4,000
	Depreciation	(2,000)
	Purchases (balancing figure)	4,000
	Balance at end of the year	6,000
d.	**Taxation**	
	Amount due at beginning of year	10,000
	Charge in income statement	44,000
	Paid in cash (balancing figure)	(14,000)
	Amount due at end of the year	40,000
e.	**Cash receipts from customers**	
	Sales	850,000
	Increase in debtors (63–43)	(20,000)
		830,000
f.	**Cash payments to suppliers and employees**	
	Cost of sales	637,500
	Administrative expenses	28,100
	Operating expenses	73,600
	Adjusted for noncash flow items:	
	Depreciation	(27,000)
	Profit on sale of machinery	5,000
	Increase in inventories (82–42)	40,000
	Increase in creditors (72–35)	(37,000)
	Increase in prepaid expenses (21–16)	5,000
		725,200

CHAPTER 5

Accounting Policies, Changes in Accounting Estimates, and Errors
(IAS 8)

5.1   OBJECTIVE

IAS 8 provides entities with guidance on the process to be followed when selecting accounting policies to use in preparing financial statements and how the entities should account for a change in the accounting policies. The standard also deals with accounting for changes in estimates and how to account for prior-period error.

5.2   SCOPE OF THE STANDARD

IAS 8 covers situations where the entity

- is selecting and applying accounting policies;
- is accounting for changes in accounting policies;
- has changes in accounting estimates; and
- has corrections of prior-period errors.

5.3   KEY CONCEPTS

5.3.1 Accounting policies are specific principles, bases, conventions, rules, and practices applied by an entity in preparing and presenting financial statements.

5.3.2 Changes in accounting estimates result from new information or new developments and, accordingly, are not corrections of errors or changes in policy. Changes in accounting estimates result in adjustments of an asset's or liability's carrying amount or the amount of the periodic consumption of an asset that results from the assessment of the present status of, and expected future benefits and obligations associated with, assets and liabilities. For example, a change in the method of depreciation results from new information about the use of the related asset and is, therefore, a change in accounting estimate.

5.3.3 Prior-period errors are omissions from and misstatements in the entity's financial statements for one or more prior periods. Errors arise from a failure to use, or a misuse of, reliable information that:

- was available when prior-period financial statements were authorized for issue; and
- could reasonably have been obtained and taken into account in the preparation and presentation of those financial statements.

Such errors include the effects of:

- mathematical mistakes;
- mistakes in applying accounting policies;
- oversights or misinterpretations of facts; or
- fraud.

5.3.4 Omissions or misstatements are **material** if they could, individually or collectively, influence users' economic decisions that are made on the basis of the financial statements.

5.3.5 Impracticable changes are requirements that an entity cannot apply after making every **reasonable effort** to do so. The application of a change in accounting policy or retrospective correction of an error becomes impracticable when:

- effects are not determinable;
- assumptions about management intent in a prior period are required;
- it requires significant estimates of amounts; or
- it is impossible to distinguish between information that provides evidence of circumstances at the prior-period date (and that would have been available at the prior-period date) from other information; in other words, hindsight should not be used.

5.4   ACCOUNTING TREATMENT

5.4.1 When a standard or an interpretation **specifically applies** to a transaction, other event, or condition, the **accounting policy** or policies applied to that item should be **determined (chosen)** by applying the standard or interpretation, considering any implementation guidance issued by the IASB for that standard or interpretation.

5.4.2 In the **absence of specific guidance on accounting policies** (that is, a standard or an interpretation that specifically applies to a transaction, other event, or condition), management should use its judgment in developing and applying an accounting policy that results in relevant and reliable information. In making the judgment, management should consider the applicability of the following factors in the following descending order:

- the requirements and guidance in standards and interpretations dealing with similar and related issues; and
- the definitions, recognition criteria, and measurement concepts for assets, liabilities, income, and expenses in the framework.

To the extent that there is no conflict with the above, in making the judgment, management may also consider the following:

- the most recent pronouncements of other standard-setting bodies that use a similar conceptual framework; or
- other accounting literature and accepted industry practices.

5.4.3 Accounting policies should be **applied consistently** for similar transactions, other events, and conditions (unless a standard or interpretation requires or permits categorization, for which different policies may be appropriate).

5.4.4 A change in accounting policy is allowed only under one of the following conditions:

- the change is required by a standard or interpretation; or
- the change will result in the financial statements providing reliable and more relevant information about the effects of transactions, other events, and conditions.

5.4.5 When a change in accounting policy results from the **application of a new standard** or interpretation, any specific transitional provisions in the standard or interpretation should be followed. If there are no specific transitional provisions, the change in accounting policy should be applied in the same way as a voluntary change.

5.4.6 A **voluntary change in accounting policies** is applied as follows:

- Policies are applied retrospectively and prior periods restated as though the new policy had always applied, unless it is impracticable to do so.
- Opening balances are adjusted at the earliest period presented.
- Policies are applied prospectively if it is impracticable to restate prior periods or to adjust opening balances.

5.4.7 Carrying amounts of assets, liabilities, or equity should be adjusted when **changes in accounting estimates necessitate a change in assets, liabilities, or equity.**

5.4.8 **Changes in accounting estimates** should be included in profit or loss in the period of the change or in the period of change and future periods, if the change affects both.

5.4.9 Financial statements do not comply with IFRS if they contain **prior-period material errors**. In the first set of financial statements authorized for issue after the discovery of a material error, an entity should correct material prior-period errors **retrospectively** by:

- restating the comparative amounts for the prior period(s) presented in which the error occurred; or
- if the error occurred before the earliest prior period presented, restating the opening balances of assets, liabilities, and equity for the earliest prior period presented.

5.5 **PRESENTATION AND DISCLOSURE**

5.5.1 If an entity makes a **voluntary change in accounting policies**, it should disclose:

- the nature of the change;
- the reason or reasons why the new policy provides reliable and more relevant information;
- the adjustment in the current and each prior period presented and the line items affected;
- the adjustment to the basic and diluted earnings per share in current and prior periods;
- the adjustments to periods prior to those presented; and
- if retrospective application is impracticable, the circumstances that led to the existence of that condition and a description of how and from when the change in accounting policy has been applied.

5.5.2 When initial application of a standard or an interpretation has or could have an effect on the current period or any prior period, unless it is **impracticable** to determine the amount of the adjustment, an entity should disclose:

- the title of the standard or interpretation;
- that the change in accounting policy is made in accordance with the standard or interpretation's transitional provisions (when applicable);
- the nature of the change in accounting policy;
- a description of the transitional provisions (when applicable);
- the transitional provisions that might have an effect on future periods (when applicable);

Edinburgh Napier
University Library

■ the adjustment to the basic and diluted earnings per share in current and prior periods; and

■ the amount of the adjustment relating to periods before those presented, to the extent practicable.

5.5.3 In considering an **impending change in accounting policy**, an entity should disclose;

■ the title of the new standard;

■ the nature of the pending implementation of a new standard;

■ the planned application date; and

■ known or reasonably estimable information relevant to assessing the possible impact of new standards.

5.5.4 With reference to a **change in accounting estimates**, an entity should disclose

■ the nature of the change in the estimate; and

■ the amount of the change and its effect on the current and future periods.

If estimating the future effect is impracticable, that fact should be disclosed.

5.5.5 In considering **prior-period errors**, an entity should disclose

■ the nature of the error;

■ the amount of correction in each prior period presented and the line items affected;

■ the correction to the basic and diluted earnings per share;

■ the amount of correction at the beginning of the earliest period presented; and

■ the correction relating to periods prior to those presented.

5.5.6 Financial statements of subsequent periods need not repeat these disclosures.

5.6   FINANCIAL ANALYSIS AND INTERPRETATION

5.6.1 Analysts find it useful to break down reported earnings into recurring and nonrecurring income or losses. Recurring income is similar to permanent or sustainable income, whereas nonrecurring income is considered to be random and unsustainable. Even so-called nonrecurring events tend to recur from time to time. Therefore, analysts often exclude the effects of nonrecurring items when performing a short-term analysis of an entity (such as estimating next year's earnings). They also might include them on some average (per year) basis for longer-term analyses.

5.6.2 The analyst should be aware that, when it comes to reporting nonrecurring income, IFRS does not distinguish between items that are and are not likely to recur. Furthermore, IFRS does not permit any items to be classified as extraordinary items.

5.6.3 However, IFRS does require the disclosure of all material information that is relevant to an understanding of an entity's performance. It is up to the analyst to use this information, together with information from outside sources and management interviews, to determine to what extent reported profit or loss reflects sustainable income and expenses and to what extent it reflects nonrecurring items.

5.6.4 Analysts generally need to identify such items as

- changes in accounting policies;
- changes in estimates;
- unusual or infrequent items; and
- discontinued operations (see chapter 19).

5.7 COMMENTARY

5.7.1 Concluding that retrospective application is impracticable occurs very rarely if ever. An entity would be required to demonstrate that it has exhausted all possible avenues. Sign-off by the audit firm's global technical office will probably be required. Entities should also consider the reputational risk associated with such disclosure.

5.7.2 Determining whether a situation is a change in accounting policy or change in accounting estimate is often not clear and requires judgment and interpretation by management. For example, if the valuation technique of a complex financial instrument is changed, or if the portfolio impairment calculation of a debtor's book is changed, some consider the change to be a change in policy and most others consider it a change in estimate.

5.7.3 Choosing an appropriate accounting policy in the absence of guidance in the standards or interpretations is often a complex process. Inconsistent industry practices exist and/or contradictory guidance is provided by the different standard setting bodies. For example, the accounting treatment of business combinations between entities under *common control* has still not been resolved by the standard setters.

5.8 IMPLEMENTATION DECISIONS

The following table sets out some of the strategic and tactical decisions that should be considered when applying IAS 8.

Strategic decisions	Tactical decisions	Problems to overcome
Establishing accounting policies for transactions both where there is a specific standard or interpretation dealing with the transaction and where there is none.	In determining the accounting policy, management should consider: • the accounting policy alternatives available; • the impact of the alternatives on the financial statements; • how the financial information is managed and how the accounting policy election impacts the presentation; and • industry practice.	Determining whether the current system is compatible with the accounting policy elected.
	If a prior-period error is identified, the disclosure thereof is often very sensitive. Management should consider the best way to present the information.	Determining when the error first occurred and calculating the impact on prior periods to present the current and two comparative periods in the statement of financial position.

EXAMPLES: ACCOUNTING POLICIES, CHANGES IN ACCOUNTING ESTIMATES, AND ERRORS

EXAMPLE 5.1

Which of the following items is not included in profit or loss?

a. The effects of corrections of prior-period errors
b. Income gains or losses from discontinued operations
c. Income gains or losses arising from extraordinary items
d. Adjustments resulting from changes in accounting policies

EXPLANATION

Choice a. is incorrect. An entity should correct material prior-period errors retrospectively in the first set of financial statements authorized for issue after their discovery by

- restating the comparative amounts for the prior period or periods presented in which the error occurred; or
- restating the opening balances of assets, liabilities, and equity for the earliest prior period presented.

Choice b. is correct. Income gains and losses from discontinued operations (net of taxes) are shown on a separate line of profit or loss, called Income (Loss) from Discontinued Operations (see IFRS 5).

Choice c. is incorrect. The items are included in profit or loss but they are not shown as extraordinary items. (Extraordinary items are not separately classified under IAS 1.)

Choice d. is incorrect. Adjustments from changes in accounting policies should be applied retroactively, as though the new policy had always applied. Opening balances are adjusted at the earliest period feasible, when amounts prior to that period cannot be restated.

EXAMPLE 5.2

Unicurio Inc. is a manufacturer of curios that are sold at international airports. The following transactions and events occurred during the year under review:

a. As of the beginning of the year, the remaining useful life of the plant and equipment was reassessed as four years rather than seven years.
b. Bonuses of $12 million, compared with $2.3 million in the previous year, had been paid to employees. The financial manager explained that a new incentive scheme was adopted whereby all employees shared in increased sales.
c. There was a $1.25 million profit on the nationalization of land.
d. During the year, the corporation was responsible for the formation of the ECA Foundation, which donates funds to welfare organizations. This foundation forms part of the corporation's social investment program. The company contributed $7 million to the fund.

How would each transaction and event be treated in profit or loss?

EXPLANATION

Each of the transactions and events mentioned above would be treated as follows **in profit or loss** for the current year:

1. A change in the useful life of plants and equipment is a change in accounting estimate and is applied prospectively. Therefore, the carrying amount of the plant and equipment is written off over four years rather than seven years. All the effects of the change are included in profit or loss. The nature and amount of the change should be disclosed.

2. The item is included in profit or loss. Given its nature and size, it may need to be disclosed separately.

3. The profit is included in profit or loss (that is, it is not an "extraordinary item").

4. The contribution is included in profit or loss. It is disclosed separately if it is material.

Part II

Group Statements

CHAPTER 6

Business Combinations
(IFRS 3)

6.1   **OBJECTIVE**

Business operations often take place within the context of a group structure that involves many interrelated companies and entities. IFRS 3 prescribes the accounting treatment for business combinations on the date that control is established. IFRS 3 prescribes the accounting treatment for business combinations on the date that control is established.

The objective of IFRS 3 is to improve the relevance, reliability, and comparability of the information that a reporting entity provides in its financial statements about a business combination and its effects. To accomplish that, this standard establishes principles and requirements for how the acquirer recognizes and measures the identifiable net assets and goodwill, or its gain from a bargain purchase, acquired in the business combination. The core principle established is that a business should recognize business combination transactions at fair value and disclose information that enables users to evaluate the nature and financial effects of the acquisition.

The IFRS framework for dealing with equity and other securities investments is outlined in table 6.1.

TABLE 6.1   Accounting Treatment of Various Securities Acquisitions

Acquisition of Securities		
Percentage ownership	**Accounting treatment**	**IFRS reference**
Less than 20%	Fair value, amortized cost or cost	IAS 39
Between 20% and 50%	Equity accounting	IAS 28
More than 50%	Consolidation and business combinations	IFRS 3 & IAS 27
Other	Joint ventures	IAS 31

6.2 SCOPE OF THE STANDARD

6.2.1 IFRS 3 applies to all transactions that in substance **meet the definition** of a business combination. It applies to the **initial recognition and measurement** of such combinations and, in a few specific instances, to subsequent measurement.

6.2.2 IFRS 3 sets out:

- the accounting treatment at **date of acquisition**;
- the **purchase method of accounting**;
- fair value as the basis for the initial measurement of the identifiable assets acquired as well as liabilities and contingent liabilities assumed in a business;
- the recognition requirements of liabilities for terminating or reducing the activities of the acquired entity; and
- the accounting issues related to goodwill and intangible assets acquired in a business combination.

6.2.3 IFRS 3 does not apply in the following situations:

- the formation of joint ventures;
- business combinations involving entities or businesses under common control; and
- the acquisition of an asset or group of assets.

6.2.4 In the previous version of the standard, business combinations involving mutual entities and combinations achieved by contract alone (that is, control obtained not by acquiring a portion of the share capital of the subsidiary, but by entering into a contract that establishes control) were specifically excluded from the scope of IFRS 3. In the revised version, detailed in this chapter, both these combination types will result in the application of IFRS 3 accounting.

6.3 KEY CONCEPTS

6.3.1 A **business** is an integrated set of activities and assets *capable* of being conducted and managed to provide a return in the form of dividends, lower costs, or other economic benefits directly to the owners or investors.

6.3.2 A **business combination** is a transaction or other event in which an acquirer obtains control of one or more businesses.

6.3.3 The **acquisition method** views a business combination from the perspective of the combining entity that is identified as the **acquirer**. The **acquirer** is the entity that obtains control over another entity (the acquiree).

6.3.4 **Non-controlling interest** is that portion of a subsidiary attributable to equity interests that are not owned by the parent, either directly or indirectly through subsidiaries. Non-controlling interest is disclosed as equity in the consolidated financial statements.

6.3.5 A **subsidiary** is an entity, including an unincorporated entity such as a partnership, which is controlled by another entity, known as the parent.

6.3.6 **Control** is the power to govern the financial and operating policies of an entity so as to obtain benefits from its activities.

6.3.7 Fair value is the amount for which an asset could be exchanged, or a liability settled, between knowledgeable, willing parties in an arm's-length transaction.

6.3.8 Goodwill is the future economic benefits arising from assets that cannot be individually identified and separately recognized.

6.3.9 Acquisition-related costs are costs incurred to effect a business combination, for example legal, accounting, or valuation fees, any general administration costs, and the costs to register and issue debt or equity instruments. These costs are to be expensed through profit or loss unless the cost to issue debt or equity should be capitalized in terms of IAS 32 and IAS 39.

6.3.10 Reacquired rights are intangible assets that are separately recognized at acquisition date. They relate to any pre-combination right to the use of an asset that was granted by the acquirer to the acquiree, such as a franchise agreement. On acquisition of the acquiree the acquirer effectively "reacquires" this right, and thus a separate intangible asset.

6.3.11 Indemnification assets are assets recognized at acquisition date where the sellers of the acquiree make a contractual guarantee to indemnify the acquirer in respect of the outcome of a specific contingency or uncertainty related to an asset or liability at acquisition. For example, where losses may arise from a particular contingent liability that is included in the net assets, the acquiree guarantees that the liability will not exceed a specific amount. This guarantee is an asset recognized by the acquirer as the same time as recognizing the related contingent liability of the acquiree.

6.3.12 Contingent consideration is an obligation of the acquirer to transfer additional consideration if a specified event occurs or conditions are met. An example would be where the acquirer has the obligation to pay additional consideration if the profits of the acquiree exceed certain levels after acquisition. Contingent arrangements may also give an acquirer the right to the reimbursement of a portion of consideration already paid, which would result in the recognition of a contingent consideration asset.

6.4 ACCOUNTING TREATMENT

6.4.1 The **acquisition method** must be applied by the acquirer for all business combinations entered into. It consists of the following steps:

- identifying a business combination;
- identifying the acquirer;
- determining the acquisition date;
- recognizing and measuring the identifiable net assets of the acquiree; and
- recognizing and measuring goodwill or a gain from a bargain purchase, which includes measuring consideration and non-controlling interest.

Identifying a Business Combination

6.4.2 An entity shall determine whether a transaction or event is a business combination by applying the definitions as above—in other words, there is an acquirer and control is obtained over a business. A business is not necessarily a legal entity. IFRS 3 would also be applicable where a business is purchased out of a legal entity, for example a division.

6.4.3 **Separate transactions** are those that are not a part of the exchange in a business combination, that is, not part of the net assets acquired or the consideration paid. IFRS 3 does not apply to these transactions and they must be separately accounted for per the relevant IFRS. Examples of these types of transactions include the following:

- the effective settlement of preexisting relationships with the acquiree such as a customer/supplier relationship that is automatically settled on acquisition;
- remuneration of the acquiree's former employees for future services to be provided by them; and
- acquisition-related costs (per definition above).

6.4.4 **Common control transactions** are business combinations between entities under the control of the same ultimate holding company both before and after the combination, where control is not transitory. Although these transactions meet the definition of a business combination they are specifically excluded from the scope of IFRS 3 as in substance no control is transferred from a consolidated group perspective. An example of such a transaction is where Entity X acquires 50 percent in Entity Y from its parent Entity Z. Entity Z therefore directly holds 50 percent in Y and indirectly holds the other 50 percent in Y through its 100 percent holding in X. In substance control of Y never passed from Z to X.

Identifying the Acquirer

6.4.5 This standard requires an **acquirer** to be identified for every business combination within its scope. The acquirer is the combining entity that obtains **control** of the other combining entities or businesses.

6.4.6 In the event of **reverse acquisitions**, it may not be clear who the acquirer is for accounting purposes. For example a non-public entity that does not want to register itself on a stock exchange can arrange to be legally acquired by a publicly traded entity. After the transaction, the owners of the non-public entity obtain control over the publicly traded entity for accounting purposes but legally the publicly traded entity is the acquirer. The non-public entity will be the one that must apply IFRS 3 as per the specific guidance on reverse acquisitions provided in the standard.

Determining the Acquisition Date

6.4.7 The **date of acquisition** is the date on which control passes to the acquirer. It is important that this date is established correctly as this is the date on which IFRS 3 must be applied, that is, the date on which all the relevant fair value remeasurements and other calculations must be made.

6.4.8 The date of acquisition is usually the date when the exchange occurs, that is, the date on which the consideration is transferred to the previous owners and the acquirer obtains control over the acquiree's net assets. Control can however be substantially passed either before or after exchange occurs, such as where there are suspensive conditions attached to the business combination agreement. The acquisition date is the date that all the significant conditions have been met. This includes any of the following:

- Where a public offer of shares is made, it is the date when the offer is unconditional.
- Where a private transfer occurs, it is the date the unconditional offer is accepted or all significant conditions of the agreement have been met.
- Where the agreement is subject to the approval of another party, such as a competition commission, the date the authority provides clearance or approval will be the acquisition date.
- Other indicators are the date that the acquirer commences directing the policies of the acquiree or appoints the majority of the board.

Identifiable Net Assets of the Acquiree

6.4.9 At the acquisition date the acquirer must recognize the identifiable assets and liabilities of the acquiree, separately from goodwill. The acquisition-date **recognition criteria** that must all be met are as follows:

- the item must meet the definition of an asset or liability per the Framework;
- the item must be a part of what is exchanged; and
- the item must be identifiable, that is, it must exist at acquisition date.

These recognition criteria may differ from those required per other relevant IFRS for the recognition and measurement of a specific asset or liability (for example IAS 38, Intangible Assets). The requirements of IFRS 3 override other IFRS recognition criteria, but only on *initial recognition through a business combination.*

6.4.10 The acquirer shall **initially measure** the identifiable assets and liabilities at their **acquisition-date fair values**. The fair value must include all uncertainties. Therefore, no separate provisions for impairment should be recognized; rather, the net asset should be recognized. **Subsequent measurement** of the assets and liabilities must be in accordance with the relevant IFRS. Refer to sections 6.4.11, 6.4.12, and 6.4.13 below for exceptions, which must be subsequently measured in terms of IFRS 3.

6.4.11 Contingent liabilities are not recognized as per IAS 37, but instead are recognized if they are a present obligation from a past event with a reliably measurable fair value; that is, ultimate cash outflow does not have to be probable. Probability affects measurement and not recognition. In other words, contingent liabilities are recognized as provisions and not just disclosed in a note to the financial statements

6.4.12 The **exceptions to the general measurement principles** (that is, at fair value) include the following:

- **Reacquired rights:** measured at the fair value per the remaining contractual terms of the original contract, excluding any renewals. A market participant would include renewals in the fair value. The renewals are not however included for IFRS 3 as the contract is no longer being held with a third party and renewals would have to be assumed to be indefinite if they were taken into account.
- **Share-based payment replacements:** any liability or equity item recognized for this replacement must be measured as per IFRS 2.
- **Assets held for sale:** measured at fair value less costs to sell as per IFRS 5.

6.4.13 The **exceptions to both recognition and measurement principles** include income taxes, employee benefits, and indemnification assets. Income taxes and employee benefits are recognized and measured in terms of their relevant IFRSs, that is, IAS 12 and IAS 19 respectively. **Indemnification assets** at acquisition are recognized and measured on the same basis as the indemnified item to which they relate; that is, if the related item is subject to a measurement exception per IFRS 3 then the indemnification asset is also measured on that basis.

6.4.14 Internally generated intangible assets of the acquiree that were not recognized before the combination, as there was no reliable measure of fair value, should be identified separately and recognized as part of the net assets at acquisition date if they meet the requirements of IFRS 3. The only requirement for recognition is that these assets be identifiable, that is, separable or contractually based. They need not meet the definition of IAS 38 (as was required in the previous version of IFRS 3).

6.4.15 If the initial accounting for a business combination is incomplete by the reporting date for the period in which the combination occurs, the acquirer should account for the combination using **provisional amounts**. During the measurement period (12 months from the date of acquisition), the acquirer should retrospectively adjust these provisional amounts to reflect new information obtained about the facts and circumstances that existed at acquisition. **Measurement period adjustments** include all the following situations:

- Provisional accounting was applied in measuring the fair values of the net assets and subsequently more reliable fair values are established that would have been used at acquisition had they been known.
- Assets and liabilities of the acquiree were not recognized at acquisition as they did not meet the recognition criteria and subsequent information obtained reveals that they did in fact meet the criteria.
- Deferred tax assets that arose at acquisition date were not recognized as it did not appear there would be adequate future taxable profits and subsequent information obtained reveals that future taxable profits are probable and this criteria was met at acquisition.
- Adjustments to contingent consideration recognized in combinations before July 1, 2009 for which the contingency is settled in a reporting period after this date.

If any of the above adjustments are required within the measurement period, they shall be made retrospectively to the relevant assets and liabilities with the contra entry *against goodwill*. Subsequent to the measurement period, any required adjustments are not made against goodwill and must be taken through profit or loss.

Measuring Consideration, Non-Controlling Interest, and Goodwill

6.4.16 The **consideration** transferred by the acquirer is the aggregate of the acquisition-date fair values of any assets transferred, liabilities incurred, and equity instruments issued by the acquirer in exchange for control over the acquiree. **Acquisition-related costs** are not included as part of the consideration transferred but are expensed through profit or loss when incurred.

6.4.17 If there is a **contingent consideration arrangement** as part of the acquisition, the fair value of any contingent consideration must be included as part of consideration at acquisition date. At the same time the acquirer must recognize in its own financial statements, a contingent consideration asset, liability, or equity item in terms of the requirements and definitions of IAS 32, IAS 39, and IAS 37. Any subsequent fair value movements in the contingent consideration are not taken against goodwill but recognized as profit or loss, except for an equity item which is not adjusted for fair value changes after initial recognition. On settlement of the contingent consideration, the asset, liability, or equity item is derecognized and the amount paid or received recognized. If the contingency never occurs, and settlement is not required, the item is derecognized in full against profit or loss.

TABLE 6.2 Contingent Consideration: Illustration of Recognition and Measurement

	IAS 39 Liability	**IAS 37 Liability**	**Equity**	**Asset**
Classify	An obligation to settle in cash and it meets the definition of a financial liability per IAS 32.	An obligation to settle in cash and it meets the definition of an IAS 37 provision.	An obligation that will be settled by the issue of the acquirer's own equity.	A right to receive a reimbursement of consideration transferred if a certain event occurs.
Initial recognition and measurement	At fair value per IAS 39, for example, as a payable.	At fair value per IAS 37 as a provision.	At fair value as a reserve in equity.	At fair value per IAS 39, for example, as a receivable.
Fair value movements before settlement	In accordance with IAS 39, that is, through profit or loss.	In accordance with IAS 37, that is, the best estimate of amount payable to third party and movement recognized in profit or loss.	No fair value remeasurements are permitted after initial recognition.	At fair value per IAS 39, that is, either designated through profit or loss or amortized cost. *
Settlement	Derecognize the entire liability and account for the cash paid.	Derecognize the entire liability and account for the cash paid.	Derecognize the other reserve and raise share capital and share premium as necessary.	Derecognize entire asset and account for the cash or other asset received.
Non-occurrence of contingency	Derecognize the entire liability and take the contra entry through profit or loss.	Derecognize the entire liability and take the contra entry through profit or loss.	Derecognize the entire equity reserve item within equity, for example, against retained earnings.	Derecognize the asset and take the contra entry through profit or loss. Any fair value adjustments in other comprehensive income must be recycled to profit or loss in full.

* IFRS 3 requires that contingent consideration assets are subsequently measured at fair value. The recognition and measurement rules override those of IAS 39 and therefore they can be classified as receivables but be carried at fair value instead of amortized cost.

6.4.18 In a business combination achieved in stages (a **step acquisition**), the acquirer obtains control of an entity in which it already held an interest, that is, an IAS 39 investment or an investment in an associate or joint venture. Any change in the nature of an investment such as a change from significant influence to control is considered to be an economic trigger for fair value measurement. The acquirer is deemed to dispose of the previous interest held at fair value at acquisition date. The acquirer must remeasure the previous interest to fair value and recognize a gain or loss in profit or loss for the difference between this fair value and the carrying amount of the investment. The fair value calculated must be included as *part of consideration paid.*

TABLE 6.3 **Illustration of the Effect of Step Acquisitions**

Classification of previously held interest	Gain/loss on deemed disposal
Held for trading	No gain or loss is recognized as the investment was previously carried at fair value.
Designated at fair value through profit or loss	No gain or loss is recognized as the investment was previously carried at fair value.
Available-for-sale investment	No gain or loss is recognized as the investment was previously carried at fair value (remeasured to fair value up to the date immediately before the deemed disposal). The fair value movements previously recognized in reserves should be recycled from other comprehensive income to profit or loss for the period.
Investment in associate or joint venture at cost in stand-alone financial statements	A gain or loss should be recognized for the difference between the fair value and cost on acquisition date.
Investment in associate or joint venture at fair value in stand-alone financial statements	No gain or loss is recognized as the investment was previously carried at fair value.
Investment in associate or joint venture in consolidated financial statements	A gain or loss should be recognized for the difference between the fair value and the equity-accounted carrying amount on acquisition date.

6.4.19 In business combinations where control is obtained but **no consideration is transferred,** such as share buybacks or rights issues or business combinations by contract alone (where no equity is held in acquiree), the consideration used in the calculation of goodwill will be substituted with the acquisition-date fair value of the acquirer's interest in the acquiree determined using a valuation technique.

6.4.20 **Non-controlling interest** is initially measured and recognized as equity of the acquirer at acquisition date. IFRS 3 allows a measurement choice at acquisition date. This measurement choice is not an accounting policy and is available *per business combination.* Non-controlling interest can be measured:

- as its proportionate percentage of the net assets of the acquiree at acquisition date; or
- at fair value. If the acquiree has publicly traded shares the share price per an active market can be used to measure the fair value. If the acquiree does not have publicly traded shares other valuation techniques must be used to determine the fair value.

This initial measurement choice does not affect the subsequent measurement. Subsequently non-controlling interest is always measured as the proportionate percentage of the profit or loss of the subsidiary and its changes in equity, that is, no fair value adjustments are taken into account.

6.4.21 **Goodwill** is calculated at acquisition date. It is calculated as follows:

- consideration transferred by the acquirer (including contingent consideration); plus
- the fair value of the previous interest held in the acquiree; plus
- non-controlling interest at acquisition (amount per measurement choice selected); less
- the fair value of the identifiable net assets of the acquiree.

If this results in a positive amount, it is goodwill. If it results in a negative amount, a gain on bargain purchase has been made.

TABLE 6.4   **Table of Main Differences between Previous IFRS 3 and Revised Standard**

Item	Previous standard	Revised standard	Effect
Accounting method	Purchase method.	Acquisition method—look at when control is acquired.	Could be some transactions that fall in scope that never did before.
Scope	Excluded mutual entities and combinations by contract alone.	No longer excluded.	These types of combinations will be recognized where they never were before.
Acquisition-related costs	Included in consideration and thus goodwill.	Expensed through profit or loss immediately when incurred.	Effect on profit or loss and more/less goodwill.
Step acquisitions	Treat each change in interest separately with its own amount of goodwill. Previous interest held was an equity transaction.	Only when control is obtained is IFRS 3 effective and goodwill is recognized. The previous interest is deemed disposed at fair value, which results in gain/loss in profit or loss and this fair value is included in consideration.	Different goodwill and an effect on profit or loss where there was none before.
Recognition and measurement of net assets	Must be probable, reliable measure and identifiable.	Must meet definition per framework and be identifiable.	May have some assets and liabilities recognized that would not have been before. Effect on goodwill.
Reacquired rights and indemnification assets	No specific guidance.	Specific guidance on recognition and measurement.	Effect on net assets and goodwill. Could have an effect on later periods.
Contingent consideration	All changes and settlement after acquisition date were adjustments against goodwill.	Now recognize item in acquirer's financial statements and all changes through profit or loss.	Potential large effect on profit or loss and items that acquirer must recognize.
Goodwill	Only ever the percentage held by the parent and adjusted subsequently in certain events.	Goodwill measurement choice. No adjustments to goodwill.	New calculation will result in more/less goodwill than would have been recognized.
Non-controlling interest	Only ever percentage of net assets method.	Per transaction choice between percentage of net assets and fair value.	Larger/smaller non-controlling interest balance. Full goodwill if fair value is used.

6.4.22 Goodwill is recognized as a noncurrent asset of the acquirer and should be tested for impairment annually. Goodwill is not amortized.

6.4.23 A **gain on bargain purchase** is recognized in profit or loss (not as negative goodwill). However, before any gain is recognized, the acquirer should reassess the consideration measured and the fair values attributed to the acquiree's net assets to ensure that the measurements correctly reflect all the available information at acquisition date. Such a gain is usually the result of a combination in a forced sale.

6.5   **PRESENTATION AND DISCLOSURE**

6.5.1 The acquirer should disclose information that enables users of its financial statements to evaluate the nature and financial effect of business combinations that were concluded during the period and before the financial statements are authorized for issue (in aggregate where the individual effects are immaterial). The information that should be disclosed includes the following:

- name and description of the acquiree;
- acquisition date;
- the percentage of voting equity instruments acquired;
- the primary reasons for the business combination and how control was obtained;
- acquisition-date fair value of consideration transferred and the fair values of each major class of consideration, such as cash, other assets, liabilities incurred, and equity interests (including the number of equity instruments issued or issuable and the basis for determining that fair value);
- amounts recognized at the acquisition date for each class of the acquiree's assets and liabilities acquired;
- amount of any gain on bargain purchase recognized in profit or loss, the line item in the Statement of Comprehensive Income in which the amount is included, and a description of the reasons why the transaction resulted in a gain;
- a qualitative description of the factors that make up goodwill;
- the amount of the acquiree's revenue and profit or loss since the acquisition date included in the consolidated statement of comprehensive income for the period;
- the revenue and profit and loss of the combined entity for the current period as though the acquisition date for all business combinations concluded during the period had been the beginning of that annual period;
- for any contingent consideration arrangements and indemnification assets recognized, the amount recognized at acquisition, a description of the arrangement, the basis for the amount and an estimate of the undiscounted range of outcomes expected;
- for acquired receivables, the fair value, gross contractual amount receivable, and the best estimate of the contractual cash flows not expected to be collectible at acquisition date;
- for each contingent liability of the acquiree recognized, a brief description of the obligation and expected timing of outflows, an indication of uncertainties, and the amount of any expected reimbursements (if fair value could not be reliably measured the reason why must be disclosed);
- the total amount of goodwill expected to be deductible for tax purposes;
- for separate transactions, such as preexisting relationships and acquisition-related costs, a description of each transaction, how the acquirer accounted for each transaction, the amounts recognized and the line item in which this amount was included, and if the transaction is the effective settlement of a preexisting relationship, the method used to determine the settlement amount;
- for acquisition-related costs, the amount included in expenses and capitalized in terms of IAS 32 must be separately disclosed;
- for each business combination where less than 100 percent interest is held, the non-controlling interest recognized at acquisition and the measurement basis selected to measure the non-controlling interest; if fair value was selected as the valuation technique, disclose the key model inputs used to determine that value; and
- in a step acquisition, the acquisition date fair value of the previous interest held and the gain or loss recognized as a result of remeasurement as well as the line item in which this gain or loss has been recognized.

6.5.2 Information to enable users to evaluate the effects of adjustments that relate to prior business combinations should be disclosed. This includes the following:

▪ if initial accounting is incomplete, the reasons why, the items of net asset and consideration to which provisional accounting was applied and the amount of any measurement period adjustments recognized;

▪ for each period until settlement, any changes in the contingent consideration amount, range of undiscounted outcomes (including reasons for the change) and the valuation techniques and key model inputs to measure contingent consideration; and

▪ the amount and an explanation of any gain or loss recognized in the current period relating to the net assets recognized in a previous period and that is relevant to understanding the consolidated financial statements.

6.5.3 All information necessary to evaluate changes in the carrying amount of goodwill during the period must be disclosed. This must be provided in a reconciliation of the opening and closing carrying amount and must show specific separate reconciling items such as additions, impairment losses, and so forth as specified in IFRS 3 paragraph B67(d).

Business Combinations Concluded after the Reporting Date

To the extent practicable, the disclosures mentioned above should be furnished for all business combinations concluded after the reporting date but before the date of issue. If it is impracticable to disclose any of this information, this fact should be disclosed.

6.6   FINANCIAL ANALYSIS AND INTERPRETATION

6.6.1 When one entity seeks to obtain control over the net assets of another, there are a number of ways that this control can be achieved from a legal perspective: merger, consolidation, tender offer, and so forth. Business combinations occur in one of two ways:

▪ In an **acquisition of net assets:** some (or all) of the assets and liabilities of one entity are directly acquired by another; or

▪ With an **equity (stock) acquisition:** one entity (the parent) acquires control of more than 50 percent of the voting rights of another entity (the subsidiary). Both entities can continue as separate legal entities, producing their own independent set of financial statements, or they can be merged in some way.

Under IFRS 3, the same accounting principles apply to both ways of carrying out the combination.

6.6.2 Under the acquisition method, the assets and liabilities of the acquired entity are combined into the financial statements of the acquiring entity at their fair values on the acquisition date. Because the acquirer's assets and liabilities, measured at their historical costs, are combined with the acquiree's assets and liabilities, measured at their fair market value on the acquisition date, the acquirer's pre- and post-combination Statements of Financial Position might not be easily compared.

6.6.3 The fair value of long-term debt acquired in a business combination is the present value of the principal and interest payments over the remaining life of the debt, which is discounted using current market interest rates. Therefore, the fair value of the acquiree's debt that was issued at interest rates below current rates will be lower than the amount recognized on the acquiree's Statement of Financial Position. Conversely, the fair value of the acquiree's debt will be higher than the amount recognized on the acquiree's Statement of Financial Position if the interest rate on the debt is higher than current interest rates.

6.6.4 In applying the acquisition method, the Statement of Comprehensive Income and the statement of cash flows will include the operating performance of the acquiree from the date of the acquisition going forward. Operating results prior to the acquisition are not restated and remain the same as historically reported by the acquirer. Consequently, the financial statements of the acquirer will not be comparable before and after the combination, but will reflect the reality of the combination.

6.6.5 Despite the sound principles incorporated in IFRS 3, many analysts believe that the determination of fair values involves considerable management discretion. Values for intangible assets such as computer software might not be easily validated when analyzing purchase acquisitions.

6.6.6 Management judgment can be particularly apparent in the allocation of excess consideration. If, for example, the remaining excess consideration is allocated to goodwill, there will be no impact on the firm's net income, because goodwill is not amortized (but is tested for impairment). If the excess were to be allocated to fixed assets, depreciation would rise, thus reducing net income and producing incorrect financial statements.

6.6.7 Under the acquisition method, the acquirer's gross margin usually decreases in the year of the combination (assuming the combination does not occur near the end of the year) because the write-up of the acquiree's inventory will almost immediately increase the cost of goods sold. However, in the year following the combination, the gross margin might increase, reflecting the fact that the cost of goods sold decreases after the higher-cost inventory has been sold. Under some unique circumstances, for instance, when an entity purchases another for less than book value, the effect on the ratios can be the reverse of what is commonly found. Therefore, **there are no absolutes in using ratios, and analysts need to assess the calculated ratios carefully to determine the real effect.**

6.6.8 This points to an important analytical problem. Earnings, earnings per share, the growth rate of these variables, rates of return on equity, profit margins, debt-to-equity ratios, and other important financial ratios have no objective meaning. There is no rule of thumb that the ratios will always appear better under the acquisition method or any other method that might be allowed in non-IASB jurisdictions. The financial ratios must be interpreted in light of the accounting principle that is employed to construct the financial statements, as well as the substance of the business combination.

6.6.9 One technique an analyst can use in reviewing a company is to examine cash flow. Cash flow, being an objective measure (in contrast to accounting measures such as earnings, which are subjectively related to the accounting methods used to determine them), is less affected by the accounting methods used. Therefore, it is often instructive to compare companies, and to examine the performance of the same company over time, in terms of cash flow.

6.6.10 Over the years, **goodwill** has become one of the most controversial topics in accounting. Goodwill cannot be measured directly. Its value is generally determined through appraisals, which are based on appraiser assumptions. As such, the value of goodwill is subjectively determined.

6.6.11 The subject of recognizing goodwill in financial statements has found both proponents and opponents among professionals. The proponents of goodwill recognition assert that goodwill is the "present value of excess returns that a company is able to earn." This group claims that determining the present value of these excess returns is analogous to determining the present value of future cash flows associated with other assets and projects.

Opponents of goodwill recognition claim that the prices paid for acquisitions often turn out to be based on unrealistic expectations, thereby leading to future write-offs of goodwill.

6.6.12 Both arguments have merit. Many companies are able to earn excess returns on their investments. As such, the prices of the common shares of these companies should sell at a premium to the book value of their tangible assets. Consequently, investors who buy the common shares of such companies are paying for the intangible assets (reputation, brand name, and so forth).

6.6.13 There are companies that earn low returns on investment despite the anticipated excess returns indicated by the presence of a goodwill balance. The common share prices of these companies tend to fall below book value because their assets are overvalued. Therefore, it should be clear that simply paying a price in excess of the fair market value of the acquired firm's net assets does not guarantee that the acquiring company will continue earning excess returns.

6.6.14 In short, analysts should distinguish between accounting goodwill and economic goodwill. Economic goodwill is based on the economic performance of the entity, whereas accounting goodwill is based on accounting standards. Economic goodwill is what should concern analysts and investors. So, when analyzing a company's financial statements, it is imperative that the analysts remove goodwill from the statement of financial position. Any excess returns that the company earns will be reflected in the price of its common shares.

6.6.15 Under IFRS 3, goodwill should be capitalized and tested for impairment annually. Goodwill is not amortized. Impairment of goodwill is a noncash expense. However, the impairment of goodwill does affect reported net income. When goodwill is charged against income in the current period, current reported income decreases, but future reported income should increase when the asset is written off or no longer impaired. This also leads to reduced net assets and reduced shareholders' equity on the one hand, but improved return on assets, asset turnover ratios, return on equity, and equity turnover ratios on the other hand.

6.6.16 Even when the marketplace reacts indifferently to these impairment write-offs, it is an analyst's responsibility to carefully review a company's goodwill to determine whether or not it has been impaired.

6.6.17 Goodwill can significantly affect the comparability of financial statements between companies using different accounting methods. As a result, an analyst should remove any distortion that goodwill, its recognition, and impairment might create by adjusting the company's financial statements. Adjustments should be made by:

- computing financial ratios using Statement of Financial Position data that exclude goodwill;
- reviewing operating trends using data that exclude the impairment to goodwill charges; and
- evaluating future business acquisitions by taking into account consideration paid relative to the net assets and earnings prospects of the acquiree.

6.7   **COMMENTARY**

6.7.1 From a practical perspective the revised IFRS 3 presents several challenges, mainly resulting from the fact that the standard is not always explicit and does not provide guidance for all the various possibilities that arise and therefore is open to a large amount of interpretation. This interpretation could be very different from one entity to the next, making for diversity in practice and decreased comparability. Some of the areas where the greatest risk of divergence in practice arise include the following:

- the treatment of common control transactions;
- the accounting treatment of contingent consideration and indemnification assets;
- the recognition and measurement criteria for the net assets of the acquiree, in particular for assets such as indemnification assets and reacquired rights;
- the measurement choice for non-controlling interest and the resultant effect on goodwill;
- the calculation of goodwill or a gain on bargain purchase; and
- the application of fair value accounting for step acquisitions.

6.7.2 Common control transactions are specifically excluded from the scope of IFRS 3. This presents a practical issue because such transactions occur often, particularly in large entities with complex group structures such as banks where reorganization of group entities occur. There is no guidance available elsewhere in IFRS on how to account for such transactions, which further complicates the situation and leads to diversity. For such transactions the general rule of IAS 8 must be applied, that is, management must select an accounting policy by referring to the IFRS requirements for similar transactions or other standard-setting bodies. The IASB is currently working on a project to provide guidance (see point 6.7.7 below for detail). In current practice some entities consider IFRS 3 to be for "similar transactions" and thus apply the basic principles of IFRS 3 for common control transactions. UK GAAP contains guidance on merger accounting and some entities elect to apply merger accounting for business combinations under common control. In terms of merger accounting the assets and liabilities of the acquiree are recognized at the carrying value and goodwill is recognized directly in equity.

6.7.3 The revised requirements of IFRS 3 result in the recognition of items that will have an effect on subsequent periods, such as contingent consideration. In the previous version of the standard all adjustments to acquisition date accounting were taken against goodwill. This could result in income statement volatility because amounts previously recognized against goodwill are now recognized in the income statement.

6.7.4 The measurement choice available for non-controlling interest is available per combination. This presents a practical issue as the choice selected will be a matter of judgment and rests largely on intention. One entity may enter a similar transaction to another but different elections will result in different results. The main difference between the two choices is that the fair value choice results in full goodwill (100 percent) being recognized. Goodwill cannot be changed after initial accounting. This could be considered a useful indicator of what measurement choice best suits the intention of the entity. If the entity intends to eventually hold 100 percent or close to 100 percent of the interest in the acquiree it would seem logical that they would want to hold 100 percent goodwill and that the fair value option would be best suited.

6.7.5 With the large volume of additional disclosure requirements, much more information than was previously required will need to be obtained. Obtaining this information could be difficult, time consuming, and costly.

6.7.6 As part of constant improvements to the standards, the IASB issued "Improvements to IFRSs" in 2010 that include the following:

- **Non-controlling interest:** the initial measurement choice only applies to the instruments of the acquiree that entitle an entity to share in the net assets (for example ordinary shares). Other items of equity are measured in terms of the relevant IFRS (for example share-based payment reserves per IFRS 2).

- **Replacement of share-based payment awards of the acquiree:** the standard will be amended to make the treatment of such replacements clear as follows:
  - The value of any replacements of awards (voluntary or not) that *expire at the acquisition date* are taken in total to the post-combination expenses.
  - The value of any replacements of awards that *do not expire at acquisition* must be split between consideration and post-combination expenses, depending on whether the related services are received before or after the acquisition.
  - Where awards are *not to be replaced at all and are vested at acquisition,* the amount should be included in non-controlling interest at fair value.
  - Where awards are *not to be replaced and they have not yet vested at acquisition,* the amount included in non-controlling interest should be portioned for services rendered before acquisition and the rest will be taken to post-combination expenses.

- **Contingent consideration:** only adjustments in contingent consideration for combinations before July 1, 2009 can be taken against goodwill. All contingent consideration from combinations entered into from July 1, 2009 should be adjustments through profit or loss per IAS 32, 39, or 37.

6.7.7 In 2007 the IASB embarked on a project to provide specific guidance as to the treatment of common control transactions as no such guidance currently exists. The aim of this project is to define what common control is and to consider the accounting treatment of such transactions in separate and consolidated financial statements. At present the project has been suspended and currently there are no further developments.

6.8	IMPLEMENTATION DECISIONS

The following table sets out some of the strategic and tactical decisions that should be considered when applying IFRS 3.

Strategic decisions	Tactical decisions	Problems to overcome
IFRS 3 scopes out business combinations within a group, referred to as common control transactions. Where these occur within an organization, it will be necessary to establish an accounting policy for the treatment for these transactions. Consideration will need to be given to the distribution of affected subsidiary financial statements, industry and jurisdiction practice, and practical implementation.		The substance of these transactions may be difficult to determine. Relevant agreement terms should always be clear on the substance per management's intention.
Establish an accounting policy for the treatment of common control transactions.		
.	For each business combination, whether non-controlling interest is measured at fair value or the percentage of ownership and the resultant impact on goodwill.	

EXAMPLES: BUSINESS COMBINATIONS

EXAMPLE 6.1

H Ltd. acquired a 70 percent interest in the equity shares of F Ltd. for $750,000 on January 1, 20X1. The abridged statements of financial position of both companies at the date of acquisition were as follows:

	H Ltd. $'000	F Ltd. $'000
Identifiable assets	8,200	2,000
Investment in F Ltd.	750	–
	8,950	2,000
Equity	6,000	1,200
Identifiable liabilities	2,950	800
	8,950	2,000

The fair value of the identifiable assets of F Ltd. amounts to $2,800,000, and the fair value of its liabilities is $800,000. The non-controlling interest will be measured as a percentage of net assets of the acquiree. Demonstrate the results of the acquisition.

EXPLANATION

	H Ltd. $'000
Consideration	750
Plus: Non-controlling interest (2,000*30%)	600
	1,350
Less: Net identifiable assets of F Ltd.	(2,000)
Gain on bargain purchase	650

The abridged consolidated statement of financial position at the date of acquisition will appear as follows:

	$'000
Assets	11,000[a]
Shareholders' equity	6,650[b]
Non-controlling interest	600
Liabilities	3,750[c]
	11,000

a = 8,200 + 2,800
b = 6,000 + 650 (gain included in profit or loss)
c = 2,950 + 800

EXAMPLE 6.2

Big Company is buying Small Company for $100,000 plus the assumption of all of Small's liabilities. Indicate what cash balance and goodwill amount would be shown on the consolidated statement of financial position.

Assume that Big Company is planning to fund the acquisition using $10,000 in cash and new borrowings of $90,000 (long-term debt).

At Acquisition Statements of Financial Position

	$ Big	$ Small	$ Small (fair value)
Cash	20,000	3,000	3,000
Inventory	40,000	10,000	15,000
Accounts receivable	20,000	8,000	8,000
Current assets	80,000	21,000	26,000
Property, plant, and equipment	120,000	50,000	60,000
Goodwill	—	—	—
Total assets	200,000	71,000	86,000
Accounts payable	22,000	10,000	10,000
Accrued liabilities	3,000	1,000	1,000
Current liabilities	25,000	11,000	11,000
Long-term debt	25,000	10,000	10,000
Common stock	10,000	1,000	
Share capital	40,000	9,000	
Retained earnings	100,000	40,000	65,000
Total equity	150,000	50,000	65,000
Total equity & liabilities	200,000	71,000	86,000
Common stock			
Par value	10	2	
Market value	80	8	

(continued)

Assume that Big Company is planning to fund the acquisition using $10,000 in cash and new borrowings of $90,000 (long-term debt).

Post-acquisition Statements of Financial Position (Purchase Method)

	$ Big	$ Small	$ Small (fair value)
Cash	10,000	3,000	3,000
Inventory	40,000	10,000	15,000
Accounts receivable	20,000	8,000	8,000
Current assets	70,000	21,000	26,000
Investment in subsidiary	100,000		
Property, plant, and equipment	120,000	50,000	60,000
Goodwill	–	–	–
Total assets	290,000	71,000	86,000
Accounts payable	22,000	10,000	10,000
Accrued liabilities	3,000	1,000	1,000
Current liabilities	25,000	11,000	11,000
Long-term debt	115,000	10,000	10,000
Common stock	10,000	1,000	
Share capital	40,000	9,000	
Retained earnings	100,000	40,000	65,000
Total equity	150,000	50,000	65,000
Total equity & liabilities	290,000	71,000	86,000
Common stock			
Par value	10	2	
Market value	80	8	

EXAMPLE 6.2.A

Using the acquisition method, Big Company's post-acquisition consolidated Statement of Financial Position will reflect a cash balance of:

a. $13,000   b. $20,000   c. $23,000   d. $33,000

EXPLANATION

Choice a. is correct. In an acquisition method business combination, add the cash balances of the two companies together and deduct any cash paid out as part of the combination. Here the two companies have $20,000 + $3,000 = $23,000 less $10,000 paid as part of the acquisition, leaving a balance of $13,000.

EXAMPLE 6.2.B

Using the information provided, complete the consolidated Statement of Financial Position.

EXPLANATION

Completed Postacquisition Statement of Financial Position (Purchase Method)

	$ Big	$ Small	$ Small (fair value)	$ Adjustments	$ Consolidated
Cash	10,000	3,000	3,000		13,000
Inventory	40,000	10,000	15,000		55,000
Accounts receivable	20,000	8,000	8,000		28,000
Current assets	80,000	21,000	26,000		96,000
Investment in subsidiary	100,000			−100,000	
Property, plant, and equipment	120,000	50,000	60,000		180,000
Goodwill	—	—	—	35,000 (b)	35,000
Total assets	290,000	71,000	86,000	25,000	311,000
Accounts payable	22,000	10,000	10,000		32,000
Accrued liabilities	3,000	1,000	1,000		4,000
Current liabilities	25,000	11,000	11,000		36,000
Long-term debt	115,000	10,000	10,000		125,000
Common stock	10,000	1,000			10,000
Paid-in capital	40,000	9,000			40,000
Retained earnings	100,000	40,000	65,000	(65,000) (c)	100,000
Total equity	150,000	50,000			150,000
Total	290,000	71,000	86,000	25,000	311,000
Common stock					
Par value	10	2			
Market value	80	8			

Note: The goodwill is the difference between the fair value of the consideration transferred by Big Company, including debt assumed, and the fair market value of the identifiable net assets of Small Company. In this case, the fair market value of Small's net assets is $86,000. The consideration paid is $121,000 = $10,000 (cash) + $90,000 (debt issued) + $21,000 (liabilities assumed, including Small's accounts payable, accrued liabilities, and long-term debt). The net difference between the $121,000 consideration and the fair market value of the net assets of $86,000 is the goodwill of $35,000.

EXAMPLE 6.3

Parent Company acquires 60 percent interest in Subsidiary Company for $110,000. The market value of the net assets of Subsidiary Company on acquisition date is $100,000. Parent Company estimates that the full 100 percent interest in Subsidiary Company would have cost $160,000. Indicate what the goodwill recognized will be at acquisition date when non-controlling interest is measured:

(a) as a percentage of the net assets of Subsidiary Company; or
(b) at fair value (the full goodwill method).

EXPLANATION

IFRS 3 allows a choice in the initial measurement of non-controlling interest at acquisition date; that is, non-controlling interest can be initially measured as a representative percentage of the net assets of the subsidiary or at fair value at that date. This choice is available for each business combination and is not an accounting policy choice.

The chosen method will have a direct impact on the amount of goodwill recognized at acquisition date. If the fair value option is selected, the full goodwill method is applied where 100 percent of the goodwill is recognized in the consolidated financial statements of Parent Company, that is, the goodwill balance will consist of both the parent's portion and that belonging to non-controlling interest. This will result in a larger goodwill balance but also a larger non-controlling interest balance. Goodwill cannot be adjusted after the initial acquisition date except for measurement period adjustments and impairment.

(a) Non-controlling interest initially measured at the proportionate share of acquisition date net asset value of Subsidiary Company.

Non-controlling interest is calculated as 40 percent of the net asset value of Subsidiary Company (40% × $100,000 = $40,000). Parent Company will calculate the goodwill as the net asset value of Subsidiary Company less the non-controlling interests' share of net assets (40 percent) less consideration, that is, goodwill will only be based on 60 percent of net asset value of Subsidiary Company.

At acquisition	100%	60%	40%
Net asset value	$100,000	$60,000	$40,000
Cost		($110,000)	
Goodwill		$50,000	

(b) Non-controlling interest initially measured at fair value at acquisition date (full goodwill method).

Non-controlling interest is measured at fair value of $50,000. Parent Company will calculate the goodwill as the net asset value of Subsidiary Company less the non-controlling interest at fair value less consideration transferred, that is, goodwill will be based on 100 percent of net asset value of Subsidiary Company.

At acquisition	100%	60%	40%
Net asset value	$100,000	$60,000	$40,000
Cost	($160,000)	($110,000)	($50,000)
Goodwill	$60,000	$50,000	$10,000
Non-controlling interest			$50,000

CHAPTER 7

Consolidated and Separate Financial Statements (IAS 27)

7.1   OBJECTIVE

Users of the financial statements of a parent entity need information about the financial position, results of operations, and changes in financial position of the group as a whole. The main objective of IAS 27 is to define when an entity is a parent and to ensure that parent entities provide consolidated financial statements incorporating all subsidiaries, jointly controlled entities, and associates.

IAS 27 was amended during 2008. The amendments are effective prospectively for annual periods beginning on or after July 1, 2009.

7.2   SCOPE OF THE STANDARD

This standard should be applied in:

- the preparation and presentation of consolidated financial statements for a group of entities under the control of a parent; and
- accounting for investments in subsidiaries, associates, and joint ventures in the separate financial statements of the parent.

The standard does not address the initial accounting on acquisition of a subsidiary. This is addressed in IFRS 3 (see chapter 6).

7.3   KEY CONCEPTS

7.3.1 **Consolidated financial statements** are the financial statements of a group presented as the financial statements of a single economic entity.

7.3.2 **Control** is the power to govern the financial and operating policies of an entity to obtain benefits from the entity's activities. Control is generally evidenced by one of the following:

- **Ownership:** The parent entity owns (directly or indirectly through subsidiaries) more than 50 percent of the voting power of another entity. Control is presumed to exist in such circumstances unless the contrary can be demonstrated.
- **Voting rights:** The parent entity has power over more than 50 percent of the voting rights of another entity by virtue of an agreement with other investors.

- **Policies:** The parent entity has the power to govern the financial and operating policies of the other entity under a statute or agreement.
- **Board of directors:** The parent entity has the power to appoint or remove the majority of the members of the board of directors.
- **Voting rights of directors:** The parent entity has the power to cast the majority of votes at meetings of the board of directors.

7.3.3 A **special purpose entity** (or "SPE") is an entity created to accomplish a narrow and well-defined objective. An SPE may take the form of an unincorporated entity. SPEs are consolidated when the substance of the relationship between an SPE and another entity indicates that the SPE is controlled by that entity. The following circumstances indicate that an entity substantially controls an SPE:

- **Activities**: The activities of the SPE are substantially conducted on behalf of the entity according to its specific business needs so that the entity obtains all the benefits from the operations.
- **Decisions and autopilot:** The entity has the decision-making power to obtain the majority of the benefits from the SPE or has delegated these powers by setting up an autopilot mechanism.
- **Risks and rewards**: The entity has rights to the majority of the benefits of the SPE and is also exposed to the risks incidental to the activities of the SPE.
- **Residual or ownership risk**: In substance the entity retains the majority of the residual or ownership risks related to the SPE or its assets in order to obtain the majority of the benefits from these assets.

7.3.4 A **group** is a parent and all of the parent's subsidiaries.

7.3.5 A **parent** is an entity that has one or more subsidiaries.

7.3.6 Non-controlling interest (previously called minority interest) is the equity in a subsidiary not attributable directly or indirectly to the parent.

7.3.7 Separate financial statements are those presented by a parent, an investor in an associate, or a venturer in a jointly controlled entity, in which the investments are accounted for on the basis of the **direct equity interest** rather than on the basis of the reported results and net assets of the investees.

7.3.8 A **subsidiary** is an entity, including an unincorporated entity such as a partnership, that is controlled by another entity (the parent).

7.4   ACCOUNTING TREATMENT

7.4.1 A parent should present consolidated financial statements as if the group were a single entity.

Consolidated financial statements should include:

- the parent and all its foreign and domestic subsidiaries (including those that have dissimilar activities);
- special purpose entities if the substance of the relationship indicates control (see SIC 12);
- subsidiaries that are classified as held for sale, although the subsidiary is classified as a disposal group held for sale and presented as such (refer to IFRS 5 in chapter 18); and

■ subsidiaries held by venture capital entities, mutual funds, unit trusts, and similar entities (the scope exemption that allows the recognition of associates or joint ventures at fair value is not applicable if the entity is a subsidiary).

7.4.2 Consolidated financial statements combine the financial statements of the parent and its subsidiaries on a line-by-line basis by adding together like items of assets, liabilities, equity, income, and expenses. The basic consolidation procedures include the following:

■ The carrying amount of the parent's investment and its portion of equity of each subsidiary are eliminated in accordance with the procedures of IFRS 3.

■ Non-controlling interests in the net assets of consolidated subsidiaries are identified and presented separately as part of equity. Any losses made by the subsidiary are allocated between the parent and non-controlling interest in proportion to their interests held even if this results in the non-controlling interest having a deficit balance (that is, a debit balance on an equity item).

■ Non-controlling interests in the profit or loss of subsidiaries for the period are identified but are not deducted from profit for the period.

■ Intra-group balances, transactions, and income and expenses are eliminated in full, for example profit or losses from the intra-group sale of assets or inventory, or dividends declared and paid by the subsidiary.

■ Consolidated profits are adjusted for dividends on any cumulative preference shares of the subsidiary, whether or not dividends have been declared. The parent computes its share of profit or losses after these have been adjusted for these dividends.

7.4.3 Consolidated financial statements should be prepared using uniform accounting policies for like transactions and events.

7.4.4 The reporting date of the parent and its subsidiaries should be the same. When the reporting dates of the parent and subsidiaries differ, the subsidiary prepares an additional set of financial statements at the parent's reporting date, unless impracticable. If information on a different reporting date is used, adjustments are made for significant transactions or events that occur between those dates. The difference should be no more than three months.

7.4.5 Changes in the parent's ownership in a subsidiary can result in either:

■ a loss of control of the subsidiary; or
■ control being retained.

Where **control is retained,** the transaction between the parent and the non-controlling interest is considered to be a transaction between the owners of the subsidiary in their capacity as owners. Such changes in interest are accounted for as **equity transactions** and therefore do not have any effect on profit or loss. Any difference that arises between the amount by which the non-controlling interest is adjusted and the fair value of any consideration paid or received should be recognized directly in equity and attributed to the parent, for example recognized through retained earnings. The same principle applies where the parent previously held 100 percent interest in the subsidiary. The amount of non-controlling interest recognized should be initially measured as a percentage of the net asset value of the subsidiary or at fair value with no effect on profit or loss.

7.4.6 Changes that result in the **parent losing control** of the subsidiary could result from the disposal of the entire interest held or only a portion of the interest held. In both cases the parent should do the following:

■ derecognize the entire goodwill balance as at disposal date;
■ derecognize the entire non-controlling interest carrying amount at disposal date;

- derecognize all the assets and liabilities of the subsidiary at their carrying amounts at disposal date;
- recognize the fair value of any proceeds received;
- recognize any **retained investment** in the former subsidiary at fair value at disposal date;
- reclassify to profit or loss or transfer directly to retained earnings any amounts recognized by the subsidiary in other comprehensive income as if the parent has directly disposed of the item; and
- recognize any resulting gain or loss from the above steps in profit or loss; that is, the proceeds received plus the fair value of any retained interest less the net asset value of the subsidiary, goodwill, and non-controlling interest at disposal date.

TABLE 7.1   Accounting Treatment of Changes in Ownership Interest

Change in interest	Effect	Accounting treatment
Financial asset becomes an associate or joint venture	Change in nature of investment. Deemed disposal of previous investment at fair value with gain or loss recognized in profit or loss. The gain or loss is the difference between the carrying amount and fair value of the IAS 39 investment.	IAS 39 is applied until the date that significant influence or joint control is obtained. Gain or loss is recognized in profit or loss.
Control is obtained, i.e., financial asset or associate or joint venture becomes a subsidiary	Change in nature of investment. Deemed disposal of previous investment at fair value with gain or loss recognized in profit or loss. The gain or loss is the difference between the carrying amount and fair value of the financial asset, associate, or joint venture.	IFRS 3 and IAS 27 is applied from the date control is obtained.
Additional interest in an investment with no change in the nature of the investment	No deemed disposal of previous investment. In the case of a subsidiary, the transaction is between equity holders with no effect on profit or loss. In the case of an associate and joint venture, the transaction is treated as an increased investment	Increase the carrying amount of the investment. In the case of a subsidiary, decrease the non-controlling interest and increase parent equity. Recognize any gain or loss in equity per point 7.4.5 above.
Disposal of interest in subsidiary—no loss in control	Equity transaction.	Increase non-controlling interest and decrease parent equity. Gain or loss on disposal recognized in equity per point 7.4.5 above.
Disposal of a subsidiary where control is lost; i.e., a subsidiary becomes an associate, joint venture, or financial asset	Deemed disposal and derecognition of entire investment and recognition of a new investment at fair value. Gain or loss on disposal and recognition of new investment.	Derecognize goodwill, non-controlling interest, and net assets of subsidiary. Recognize fair value of proceeds received. Recognize retained investment at fair value. Recognize any resulting difference as a gain or loss in profit or loss.
Associate or joint venture becomes a financial asset	Deemed disposal and derecognition of entire investment and recognition of a new investment at fair value. Gain or loss on disposal and recognition of new investment.	Equity accounting or proportionate consolidation ceases. Derecognize carrying amount of entire investment in associate or joint venture. Recognize IAS 39 investment and any proceeds received at fair value. Recognize any resulting gain or loss in profit or loss.
Disposal of a financial asset	No change in the nature of the investment.	Apply requirements of IAS 39.

TABLE 7.2   Main Differences between Previous IAS 27 and the Revised IAS 27 (effective July 1, 2009)

Item	Previous standard	Revised standard	Effect
Loss of control over a subsidiary	No specific requirements.	Deemed disposal of entire investment at fair value and acquisition of new investment at fair value.	Gain or loss may be bigger or smaller due to effect of recognizing deemed disposal at fair value.
Change in interest with no loss of control in a subsidiary	No specific guidance but general practice to recognize transactions through profit or loss.	Equity transactions between owners recognized directly in equity. This is applicable for any change in interest where control is not lost, including where the parent initially holds 100% interest in the subsidiary.	No effect on profit or loss.
Losses of subsidiaries	Non-controlling interests only participate in losses until zero carrying value, unless the non-controlling interests guaranteed certain losses.	Losses are carried in proportion to interests held, even if this results in a deficit carrying value of the non-controlling interest.	Can have negative non-controlling interest balance in equity. Less losses recognized by parent but previous excess losses carried cannot be reversed.

7.4.7 A parent need **not present consolidated financial statements** if:

▪ the parent is a wholly owned subsidiary or if its owners, including non-controlling interests, have been informed and do not object;

▪ the parent's debt or equity instruments are not traded in a public market;

▪ the parent did not file, or is not in the process of filing, financial statements with a securities commission or other regulatory body for purposes of issuing instruments in the public market; and

▪ the ultimate parent publishes IFRS-compliant consolidated financial statements that are available for public use.

7.4.8 Investments in subsidiaries, associates, and joint ventures should be accounted for in a parent entity's **separate financial statements** either:

▪ at cost; or

▪ as financial assets in accordance with IAS 39.

The parent should recognize any dividends from these investments in profit or loss of its separate financial statements when the right to receive the dividend is established.

7.5   PRESENTATION AND DISCLOSURE

7.5.1 Consolidated financial statements should include the following disclosures:

▪ the nature of the relationship when the parent does not own (directly or indirectly) more than 50 percent of the voting power;

▪ the reason why the ownership of more than 50 percent of the voting power (directly or indirectly) of an investee does not constitute control.

▪ the reporting date of the subsidiary if this is different to that of the parent and the reason for the difference;

- the nature and extent of any significant restrictions on the ability of the subsidiary to transfer funds, such as cash dividends, or to repay loans or advances;
- a schedule showing the effects of any changes in the parent's ownership interest in a subsidiary that did not result in the loss of control; and
- if control is lost, the gain or loss recognized, the line item in which this amount is included, and the portion of this amount that is attributable to the fair value of the investment retained in the former subsidiary.

7.5.2 If the parent does not present consolidated financial statements, the parent's separate financial statements should include:

- the fact that the exemption from publishing consolidated financial statements has been exercised;
- the name and country of incorporation of the ultimate parent that publishes consolidated financial statements that comply with IFRS; and
- a list of significant subsidiaries, associates, and joint ventures, including the names, countries of incorporation, proportions of interest, and voting rights.

7.5.3 In the parent's separate financial statements, the following should be stated:

- a list of subsidiaries, associates, and joint ventures (as per point 7.5.2);
- the method used to account for investments in subsidiaries, associates, and joint ventures (either cost or IAS 39); and
- the fact that the statements are separate and the reasons why they were prepared if not required by law.

7.5.4 Non-controlling interest should be presented separately within equity in the consolidated Statement of Financial Position. The balance should consist of the initial amount recognized per IFRS 3 and the non-controlling interest's share of changes in equity of the subsidiary since acquisition date.

7.6

FINANCIAL ANALYSIS AND INTERPRETATION (See also chapter 6, section 6.6)

7.6.1 IAS 27 requires that the financial statements of a parent company and the financial statements of the subsidiaries that it controls be consolidated. Control of a subsidiary is presumed when the parent company owns more than 50 percent of the voting rights of a subsidiary, unless control demonstratively does not exist in spite of the parent's ownership of a majority of the voting rights of the subsidiary.

7.6.2 The process of consolidation begins with the Statement of Financial Position and Statement of Comprehensive Income of the parent and the subsidiary constructed as separate entities. The parent's financial statements recognize the subsidiary as an asset (called an investment in subsidiary) and recognize any dividends received from the subsidiary as income from subsidiaries.

7.6.3 When the financial statements of the parent and subsidiary are combined, the consolidated financial statements fully reflect the financial results and financial position of the parent and subsidiary. Consolidation does, however, pose problems:

- Combined financial statements of entities in totally different businesses limit analysis of operations and trends of both the parent and the subsidiary; a problem overcome somewhat by segment information.
- Regulatory or debt restrictions might not be easily discernible on the consolidated financial statements.

7.7 **COMMENTARY**

7.7.1 The application of the requirements of IAS 27 and SIC 12 in identifying transactions that result in control being obtained is a matter of substance over form, which requires a degree of judgment, especially in the case of a special-purpose vehicle. Specific entities to closely consider are securitization or conduit vehicles, insurance cells, employee benefit trusts, and specialized funding vehicles.

7.7.2 Group structures can become complicated and difficult to understand. Complicated structures can have a ripple effect on the accounting for numerous transactions, specifically intergroup transactions and balances. Consolidation procedures, specifically in large entities with complex structures, can be difficult to execute in practice and could be time consuming and costly.

7.7.3 Different countries may have differences in legislation related to group statements, for example company law, taxation law, regulatory reporting, and securities regulations. Consolidation and control may be defined differently as opposed to IFRS and could result in conflicting accounting practice not only between entities in different countries but also by one entity that is required to apply several forms of regulations.

7.7.4 The IASB and FASB embarked on a consolidations project to address the basis and process of consolidation and to provide more guidance around the concept of "control." The end of the project is expected to be an amendment to or replacement of IAS 27 and SIC 12. In December 2008 the IASB issued an exposure draft of proposed amendments to IAS 27.

7.7.5 The main proposals in this exposure draft include:

- A new principle-based definition of control that is easier to apply to a wide range of situations and is more difficult to evade by special structuring. The proposed definition of control is "the power to direct the activities of another entity to generate returns." Power over "activities" is broader than that over "operating and financial decisions" and thus broadens the scope.
- Enhanced disclosure requirements to enable investors to assess the extent of the involvements and related risk of the entity in special structures.

7.8 **IMPLEMENTATION DECISIONS**

The following table sets out some of the strategic and tactical decisions that should be considered when applying IAS 27.

Strategic decisions	Tactical decisions	Problems to overcome
Investments in subsidiaries must be identified by applying the definition of control, with specific identification of special purpose entities.	Processes must be in place to identify such transactions. Intention and related accounting effects that could arise must be considered when entering into investment transactions.	Control is based on substance over legal form and all circumstances would need to be carefully considered to identify the true substance of the transaction.
If the entity is exempt from preparing consolidated financial statements, whether it wants to apply the exemption.		
Where separate financial statements are prepared, an accounting policy decision must be made for the recognition and measurement of the investment.		Care must be taken in applying IAS 39 with regards classification. The accounting policy chosen could have various implications on issues such as future impairments that may arise.

EXAMPLES: CONSOLIDATED FINANCIAL STATEMENTS AND ACCOUNTING FOR INVESTMENTS IN SUBSIDIARIES

EXAMPLE 7.1

The following amounts of profit after tax relate to the Alpha group of entities:

	$
Alpha Inc.	150,000
Beta Inc.	40,000
Charlie Inc.	25,000
Delta Inc.	60,000
Echo Inc.	80,000

Alpha Inc. owns 75 percent of the voting power in Beta Inc. and 30 percent of the voting power in Charlie Inc.

Beta Inc. also owns 30 percent of the voting power in Charlie Inc. and 25 percent of the voting power in Echo Inc.

Charlie Inc. owns 40 percent of the voting power in Delta Inc.

What is the status of each entity in the group, and how is the non-controlling interest in the group after-tax profit calculated?

EXPLANATION

Beta Inc. and Charlie Inc. are both subsidiaries of Alpha Inc., which owns, directly or indirectly through a subsidiary, more than 50 percent of the voting power in the entities.

Charlie Inc. and Echo Inc. are deemed to be associates of Beta Inc., whereas Delta Inc. is deemed to be an associate of Charlie Inc. unless it can be demonstrated that significant influence does not exist.

The non-controlling interest in the group after-tax profit is calculated as follows:

	$	$
Profit after tax of Charlie Inc.		
Own	25,000	
Equity accounted		
Delta Inc. (40% × 60,000)	24,000	
	49,000	
Non-controlling interest of 40%		19,600
Profit after tax of Beta Inc.		
Own	40,000	
Equity accounted:		
Charlie Inc. (30% × 49,000)	14,700	
Echo Inc. (25% × 8,000)	20,000	
	74,700	
Non-controlling interest of 25%		18,675
		38,275

EXAMPLE 7.2

A European parent company, with subsidiaries in various countries, follows the accounting policy of FIFO costing for all inventories in the group. It has recently acquired a controlling interest in a foreign subsidiary that uses LIFO because of the tax benefits.

How is this aspect dealt with on consolidation?

EXPLANATION

IAS 27 requires consolidated financial statements to be prepared using uniform accounting policies However, it does not demand that an entity in the group change its method of accounting in its separate financial statements to that method which is adopted for the group.

Therefore, on consolidation appropriate adjustments must be made to the financial statements of the foreign subsidiary to convert the carrying amount of inventories to a FIFO-based amount.

EXAMPLE 7.3

Below are the statements of financial position and income statements of a parent company and an 80 percent owned subsidiary. The table depicts the method and adjustments required to construct the consolidated financial statements.

	Parent only ($)	Subsidiary only ($)	Adjustments ($)	Consolidated ($)
Cash	50	120		170
Receivables				
From Others	320	20		340
From Subsidiary	30		(30)(a)	—
Goodwill			—(b)	—
Inventories	600	100		700
Plant and Equipment	1,000	500		1,500
Investments				
In Others	800	40		840
In Subsidiary	360		(360)(c)	—
Total Assets	3,160	780	(390)	3,550
Accounts Payable				
To Others	250	100		350
To Parent		30	(30)(a)	—
Long-Term Debt	1,350	200		1,550
Non-controlling Interest			90(c)(d)	90(e)
Common Stock	100	40	(40)(c)	100(f)
Share Capital	300	160	(160)(c)	300(f)
Retained Earnings	1,160	250	(250)(c)	1,160(f)
Total Liabilities and Equity	3,160	780	(390)	3,550

Notes to the Statement of Financial Position:
(a) *The intercompany receivables or payables are eliminated against each other so that they do not affect the consolidated group's assets and liabilities.*

(b) There is no goodwill on consolidation as the parent paid consideration equal to its interest in the subsidiary.

Consideration	$360
Add: non-controlling interest	$90(d)
Less: net asset value of subsidiary	($450)
Goodwill from consolidation	$0

(c) The investment in the subsidiary is eliminated at consolidated level against any goodwill, non-controlling interest and the recognition of the net assets of the subsidiary by the parent.

(d) The parent has elected to measure non-controlling interest as the pro rata share of the net asset value of the subsidiary: 20% of $450 = $90. IFRS 3 also allows a measurement choice where this initial amount may be recognized at fair value.

(e) Note that the non-controlling interest is an explicit item only on the consolidated statement of financial position.

(f) Note that the equity of the consolidated group is the same as the equity of the parent, which is the public entity.

	Parent only ($)	Subsidiary only ($)	Adjustments ($)	Consolidated ($)
Sales to Outside Entities	2,800	1,000		3,800
Receipts from Subsidiary	500		(500)(a)	–
Total Revenues	3,300	1,000	(500)	3,800
Costs of Goods Sold	(1,800)	(400)		(2,200)
Other Expenses	(200)	(50)		(250)
Payments to Parent	–	(500)	500(a)	–
Profit before Tax	1,300	50	–	1,350
Tax Expense (30%)	(390)	(15)		(405)
Net Profit	910	35	–	945
Non-controlling Interest				189(b)

Notes to the income statement:

(a) The receipts from or payable by the subsidiary ($500) are eliminated against each other and do not appear on the consolidated income statement.

(b) The non-controlling interest's share of profits after tax is calculated as its proportionate share of interest held in the subsidiary, that is, $945 × 20% = $189 attributable to non-controlling interest.

EXAMPLE 7.4

Investor Inc. holds a 25 percent interest in the issued share capital of Associate Inc. Investor Inc. acquires an additional 30 percent interest in Associate Inc. for $200. The fair value of 100 percent of the issued share capital of Associate Inc. at that date is $700. The equity accounted carrying amount of the investment at this date is $100. The net asset value of Associate Inc. at that date is $400.

EXPLANATION

IAS 27 requires that when an entity acquires an additional interest in another entity that results in the change of nature of the investment (a step up acquisition), the existing interest held is deemed to be disposed of at fair value at that date. A gain or loss on the remeasurement of the existing interest to fair value should be recognized. For IFRS 3, the fair value of the existing interest should be included as part of the consideration for the additional interest.

In this example, Investor Inc. has acquired a controlling interest in an associate, that is, the interest in Associate Inc. has increased from 25 to 55 percent. The investment has therefore changed in nature from an associate (accounted for under the equity method) to a subsidiary (consolidated). The previous interest of 25 percent is therefore deemed to be disposed of at fair value at the date of acquisition of the additional 30 percent. The steps to recognize the transaction at acquisition are detailed below.

Deemed disposal of the existing interest:
Dr Investment in Associate Inc. $75(a)
Cr Fair value gains $75(a)

Determine amounts for IFRS 3 accounting:
Existing interest $175
Add: Cash paid $200
Total consideration $375
Add: non-controlling interest $315(b)
Less: net asset value acquired ($400)
Goodwill $290

(a) *The existing interest is remeasured to fair value; that is, 25 percent of the 100 percent fair value of Associate Inc. = $700 × 25% – $100 equity accounted carrying amount of investment at that date.*

(b) *Non-controlling interest has been initially measured at fair value = $700 × 45% = $315.*

EXAMPLE 7.5

Parent Inc. holds an 80 percent interest in the issued share capital of Subsidiary Inc. Parent Inc. disposes of 50 percent of its interest in Subsidiary Inc. for $300. The fair value of the 30 percent retained interest in the share capital of Subsidiary Inc. at that date is $180. The carrying amount of the net assets of Subsidiary Inc. at this date is $500 including goodwill of $60. The carrying amount of the non-controlling interest (20 percent) at this date is $88.

EXPLANATION

IAS 27 requires that when an entity partially disposes of its interest in another entity and this results in the change of nature of the investment, the retained interest held is deemed to be acquired at fair value at that date.

In this example, Parent Inc. has lost control of a subsidiary, that is, the interest in Subsidiary Inc. has decreased from 80 to 30 percent. The investment has therefore changed in nature from subsidiary (consolidated) to an associate (equity accounted). The retained interest of 30 percent in Subsidiary Inc. is therefore deemed to be acquired at fair value at the date of disposal of the controlling interest. Parent Inc. will account for this partial disposal as follows:

Dr Bank/cash $300(a)
Dr Investment in Subsidiary Inc. $180(b)
Dr Non-controlling interest $88(c)
Cr Net assets $440(c)
Cr Goodwill $60(c)
Cr Gain on disposal of subsidiary $68(d)

(a) *Consideration received for the disposal of 50 percent interest.*

(b) *The fair value of the retained interest of 30 percent in Subsidiary Inc., deemed to be acquired.*

(c) *Subsidiary Inc. is no longer a subsidiary of Parent Inc. and should no longer be consolidated. Its net assets and non-controlling interest should therefore be derecognized from the financial statements of Parent Inc.*

(d) *Any resulting difference from the derecognition of net assets, goodwill, and non-controlling interest and the recognition of the consideration and retained interest, should be accounted for as a gain or loss on the partial disposal of the subsidiary.*

EXAMPLE 7.6

Parent Inc. acquired 60 percent interest in the issued share capital of Subsidiary Inc. for $300 when the non-controlling interest had a fair value of $200. Two years later, Parent Inc. acquires the remaining 40 percent of its interest in Subsidiary Inc. for $300, effectively acquiring a 100 percent holding. During the two years the net asset value of Subsidiary Inc. has increased by $100.

EXPLANATION

IAS 27 requires that when an entity acquires an additional interest or disposes of a portion of its interest in a subsidiary without a change in control over the entity, such transactions are considered to be transactions with non-controlling interest and should be recognized in equity. No gains or losses are recognized in profit or loss.

In this example, Parent Inc. has acquired the remaining 40 percent in Subsidiary Inc., which is already a subsidiary. Therefore there has been no change in the nature of the investment as control is held by Parent Inc. both before and after the transaction. This is therefore a transaction with the non-controlling interest and should be accounted for through equity. Parent Inc. will account for this partial disposal as follows:

Dr Non-controlling interest $240(*a*)
Dr Equity (e.g., retained earnings) $60(*b*)
Cr Bank/cash $300(*c*)

(a) *Derecognize total non-controlling interest as the entity becomes a wholly owned subsidiary. At acquisition date the carrying amount of non-controlling interest = $200 fair value at initial acquisition + R100 increase in net asset value × 40% = $240.*

(b) *The resulting gain or loss on acquisition, that is, the difference between the adjustment to non-controlling interest and the amount paid. This should go through equity and not profit or loss as it is considered to be an equity transaction.*

(c) *The consideration paid for the acquisition of the additional interest in Subsidiary Inc.*

CHAPTER 8

Investments in Associates
(IAS 28)

OBJECTIVE

Associate entities are distinct from subsidiaries in that the influence and ownership of associates by the parent entity is not as extensive as for subsidiaries (IAS 27). The main issue is identifying the amount of influence needed for an entity to be classified as an associate. Conceptually, a parent entity has "significant" influence over an associate entity. In practical terms, this is measured by the degree of ownership. A conjunct issue of IAS 28 is the appropriate accounting treatment for the parent's investment in the associate.

Due to the significant element of influence over associates, the recognition of a share in profits based purely on distributions received would not amount to fair presentation of the true profits earned from associates. The financial impact of investments in associates therefore needs to be disclosed in relative detail, which is achieved through the application of the equity accounting. The objective of this standard is to provide the principles for equity accounting in order to fairly present the true value of these investments and the related true share in profits.

8.2   SCOPE OF THE STANDARD

8.2.1 IAS 28 applies to each investment in an associate. IAS 28 does not apply to joint ventures or entities that are subsidiaries.

8.2.2 Investments held by the following entities are excluded from the scope of IAS 28 if the investments are designated on initial recognition at fair value through profit or loss in accordance with IAS 39:

- venture capital organizations, for example private equity entities;
- mutual funds;
- unit trusts and similar entities; and
- investment-linked insurance funds.

These investments are measured at fair value through profit or loss and the requirements of IAS 39 are applicable and not the requirements of this standard. However, if an investment in an associate is designated at fair value in terms of the scope exclusion, the disclosure requirements of this standard and IFRS 7 should be met.

8.3

KEY CONCEPTS

8.3.1 An **associate** is an entity (including an unincorporated entity such as a partnership) over which the investor has **significant influence**. An associate is neither a subsidiary (possessing control, that is, the ability to govern the financial and operating policies) nor an interest in a joint venture (possessing joint control, that is, contractually agreed sharing of control).

8.3.2 **Significant influence** is the power to participate in the financial and operating policy decisions of the investee, but is not control or joint control over those policies. If an investor holds, directly or indirectly through subsidiaries, **20 percent or more of the voting power** of the investee, it is presumed to have significant influence, unless it can be clearly demonstrated that this is not the case. Significant influence is evidenced by, among other things, the following:

- representation on the board of directors or governing body of the associate;
- participation in policy-making processes (including decisions about dividends or other distributions);
- material transactions between investor and investee;
- interchange of managerial personnel; or
- provision of essential technical information.

8.3.3 Potential voting rights are instruments (warrants, options, convertible instruments, and so forth) that if exercised or converted will give the investor additional voting power. Currently exercisable or convertible potential voting rights should be included in the assessment of whether significant influence exists or not.

8.3.4 The **equity method** of accounting initially recognizes at cost the investor's share of the net assets acquired and thereafter adjusts for the post-acquisition change in the investor's share of net assets of the investee. The profit or loss of the investor includes the investor's share of the profit or loss of the investee. The equity method is applied in the **consolidated financial statements** of the investor.

8.3.5 **Consolidated financial statements** are the financial statements of a group presented as those of a single economic entity.

8.3.6 **Separate financial statements** are those presented by a parent, an investor in an associate, or a venturer in a jointly controlled entity, in which the investments are accounted for on the basis of the **direct equity interest** rather than on the basis of the reported results and net assets of the investees.

8.4

ACCOUNTING TREATMENT

Initial Recognition

8.4.1 An investment in an associate is **initially recognized and measured** at cost on the date significant influence is obtained.

8.4.2 On acquisition of an investment any difference between the cost of the investment and the investor's share of the fair value of the net assets of the associate is goodwill. This is similar to the approach for recognizing subsidiaries per IFRS 3. This goodwill is included in the carrying amount of the investment and is not separately recognized. If the cost of the investment is less than the share of net assets, the excess is included as income in the determination of the share of profit or loss of the associate in the period in which the investment is acquired.

Subsequent Measurement

8.4.3 In the **separate financial statements** of the investor the investment in an associate is subsequently accounted for in accordance with IAS 27 at either **cost or in accordance with IAS 39.** The investor recognizes dividends from an associate in profit or loss when the right to receive the dividend is established. If the investment is designated at fair value through profit or loss in terms of the scope exemption (refer 8.2.2 above) in the stand-alone financial statements, it continues to be recognized at fair value in the consolidated financial statements.

8.4.4 In the **consolidated financial statements** of the investor, the investment in an associate should be accounted for using the equity method except when:

- it is recognized at fair value in terms of the scope exclusion (refer 8.2.2 above);
- the investment is classified as held for sale per IFRS 5;
- the investor is exempted from preparing consolidated financial statements per IAS 27 paragraph 10; or
- when all of the following apply:
  - the investor is a wholly owned subsidiary or partially owned and its owners are informed that the investor will not apply equity accounting and do not object to this;
  - the investor's debt or equity instruments are not traded in a public market;
  - the investor is not in the process of issuing instruments in a public market; and
  - the ultimate or intermediate parent of the investor produces publicly available consolidated financial statements that are IFRS compliant.

8.4.5 Equity accounting should **commence** from the date that the investee meets the definition of an associate.

8.4.6 The equity method is applied as follows:

- **initial measurement** is at the cost of the investment; and
- **subsequent measurement** involves adjusting the carrying for the investor's share of post-acquisition profit or loss, the investor's share of profit or loss included in the Statement of Comprehensive Income, and the share of other changes included in equity. A group's share in an associate is the aggregate of the holdings by the parent and its subsidiaries. The profits or losses and net assets taken into account to apply the equity method are those recognized in the associate's financial statements, including its share of profits or losses of its own associates and joint ventures.

8.4.7 Many procedures for the equity method are similar to consolidation procedures per IAS 27 and the concepts underlying accounting for the acquisition of a subsidiary per IFRS 3 are also adopted in accounting for an investment in an associate. These procedures include:

- eliminating intra-group profits and losses arising from transactions between the investor and the investee;
- identifying the goodwill portion of the purchase price;
- adjusting for depreciation of depreciable assets, based on their fair values;
- adjusting for the effect of cross-holdings; and
- using uniform accounting policies.

8.4.8 Profits or losses resulting from transactions between an associate and the investor are recognized in the investor's financial statements only to the extent of **unrelated investors' interests in the associate.** For example, if the investor holds 25 percent in the associate, only the effect of 75 percent of the transaction is recognized in the investor's financial statements.

8.4.9 The investor computes its share of profits or losses after adjusting for the cumulative preference dividends, whether or not they have been declared. The investor recognizes its share of losses of an associate until the carrying amount of the investment is zero. Further losses are recognized as a liability only to the extent that the investor has incurred a legal or constructive obligation or has made payments on behalf of the associate. If the associate subsequently makes profits, the investor recognizes its share after any unrecognized share of previous losses.

8.4.10 The same principles outlined for consolidating subsidiaries should be followed under equity accounting, namely using the most recent financial statements and using uniform accounting policies for the investor and the investee. If reporting dates differ, adjustments must be made for significant events after the reporting date of the associate. The difference in reporting dates of the entities should be no more than three months.

8.4.11 Any long-term interest that in substance forms part of the investor's net investment in the associate should be included in the equity accounted carrying amount. Such interests are items for which settlement is neither planned nor likely to occur in the foreseeable future.

Discontinuation and Impairment

8.4.12 Equity accounting should be **discontinued** from the date when the investor ceases to have significant influence and accounted for in one of the following ways:

- The investor disposes of the entire investment and recognizes a gain or loss on disposal (that is, proceeds minus the carrying amount of the investment).
- The investor disposes of only part of the investment and retains an interest in the former associate. A gain or loss on disposal is recognized in profit or loss. The gain or loss is the difference between the fair value of the retained investment plus the proceeds minus the carrying amount of the entire investment in associate at disposal date. The remaining investment should be accounted for at fair value in terms of IAS 39, with the fair value on the date that significant influence ceases, being the fair value on initial recognition.
- The investor increases its interest in the associate and obtains control or joint control of the investee. This is seen as a deemed disposal of the investment at fair value. The difference between the carrying amount and the fair value is recognized as a gain or loss in profit or loss. The investment is thereafter accounted for in accordance with IAS 27 or IAS 31. Where control is obtained, the principles of IFRS 3 must be applied.

8.4.13 With regard to impairment of an investment, the investor applies IAS 39 to determine whether there is an indication that the investment is impaired. If the application of IAS 39 indicates that the investment may be impaired, the investor applies IAS 36 to determine the recoverable amount and the resultant impairment loss. Goodwill is included as part of the carrying amount of the investment and is not tested for impairment separately. Instead the entire investment is tested as a single unit. The impairment loss is allocated against the investment as a whole.

TABLE 8.1   Impairment of an Investment in an Associate

Carrying amount of investment	Fair value less costs to sell of investment	Value in use of investment
Original cost to acquire the investment PLUS Any goodwill on the acquisition PLUS Equity accounting share of profits and changes in equity of associate	The price in a binding sale agreement OR The share price where shares are traded on an active market OR Recent similar transactions LESS Directly attributable costs of disposal	Calculated using: – projected estimated expected future cash flows – discount rate Based on management assumptions and judgment of reasonableness—not fixed per market or contract

8.5   PRESENTATION AND DISCLOSURE

8.5.1 The Statement of Financial Position and notes should include the following:

▦ Investment in associates shown as a separate item on the face of the statement and classified as noncurrent assets.

▦ The notes should contain a list and description of significant associates, including name, nature of the business, and the investor's proportion of ownership interest or voting power (if different from the ownership interest).

▦ If the investor does not equity account the investment, disclose the fact, a description of what the effect would have been had the equity method been applied, and summarized financial information of these associates.

▦ If it is not practicable to calculate adjustments when associates use accounting policies other than those adopted by the investor, the fact should be mentioned.

▦ The investor's share of the contingent liabilities and capital commitments of an associate for which the investor is jointly and severally liable should be disclosed.

8.5.2 The Statement of Comprehensive Income and notes should include the following:

▦ The investor's share of the associate's profits or losses for the period and prior-period items. The investor's share of any discontinued operations of such associates should also be separately disclosed.

▦ The investor's share of changes in other comprehensive income of the associate.

8.5.3 Disclose in the **accounting policy notes** the method used to account for associates.

8.5.4 The fair value of investments in associates for which there are published price quotations should be disclosed.

8.5.5 Summarized financial information of associates should be disclosed, including the aggregated amounts of:

- assets;
- liabilities;
- revenues; and
- profit or loss.

8.5.6 The following disclosures should also be made (usually in the notes):

- the reasons for deviating from the significant-influence presumptions;
- the reporting date of the financial statements of an associate, when such financial statements are used in applying the equity method and differ from the reporting date or period of the investor, and the reason for using a different reporting date or different period;
- the nature and extent of any significant restrictions (for example, resulting from borrowing arrangements or regulatory requirements) on the ability of associates to transfer funds to the investor in the form of cash dividends or repayment of loans or advances; and
- the unrecognized share of losses of an associate, both for the period and cumulatively, if an investor has discontinued recognition of its share of losses of an associate.

8.6   FINANCIAL ANALYSIS AND INTERPRETATION

8.6.1 Under the equity method, the investment in an associate is initially recognized at cost, and the carrying amount is increased or decreased to recognize the investor's share of the profit or loss of the associate after the date of acquisition. The investor's share of the profit or loss of the associate is recognized in the investor's profit or loss. Distributions received from an associate reduce the carrying amount of the investment.

8.6.2 Adjustments to the carrying amount might also be necessary for changes in the investor's proportionate interest in the associate arising from changes in the associate's equity that have not been recognized in the associate's profit or loss. Such changes may arise from the revaluation of property, plant, and equipment and from foreign exchange translation differences. The investor's share of those changes is recognized directly in equity of the investor.

8.7   COMMENTARY

8.7.1 In a big group of entities or an investment holding entity that holds various investments in associates it is often difficult to identify and eliminate intercompany transactions.

8.7.2 Determining when an item, for example a loan or a preference share, in substance forms part of the investment in an associate involves judgment. When an item is considered to be part of the investment, recognizing the interest or preference dividends creates some complexities because there are different accounting views. Certain entities recognize the interest or preference dividends as part of the equity accounted earnings. Other entities recognize the interest or preference dividends as part of interest income.

8.7.3 As part of constant improvements to the standards, the IASB issued improvements to IFRSs in August 2009. The amendments require and clarify the following:

- In the separate financial statements, investments in associates should be tested for impairment in accordance with the principles of IAS 39 and not IAS 36.

▪ Different measurement bases can be applied in consolidated financial statements to portions of an investment in an associate when part of the investment is designated at initial recognition as at fair value through profit or loss in accordance with the scope exception. For example: entity X holds 20 percent in associate A and equity accounts for the investment as it is within the scope of IAS 28. Entity Y also holds 20 percent in associate A but it is outside of the scope of IAS 28 as Entity Y is an insurance company and the investment is part of an investment-linked insurance fund. Entity Y therefore accounts for the investment per IAS 39 at fair value through profit or loss. Both entities X and Y are consolidated by entity Z. Collectively the group holds 40 percent in associate A. At group level, the overall investment of 40 percent is not equity accounted per IAS 28. The two portions are recognized in line with the treatment in the underlying subsidiary's financial statements. This would only apply if the sum of the portions does not exceed 50 percent of the shareholding in the investee. If the sum of the portions exceeds 50 percent, the investee should be consolidated in terms of IAS 27. Different measurements would also not apply if the investees are joint ventures.

8.7.4 If an investment in an associate is designated at fair value through profit or loss in terms of the scope exemption in the stand-alone financial statements, it continues to be recognized at fair value in the consolidated financial statements. The current standard is unclear whether the same principle would apply if within the consolidated group there is more than one investment in the same associate. The IASB has clarified the matter; refer to 8.7.3 above.

8.8 IMPLEMENTATION DECISIONS

In order to implement IAS 34 and develop the information management systems that will allow a smooth transition to this standard, management needs to make strategic implementation choices, which will facilitate ongoing tactical choices. The table below sets out some of the strategic and tactical decisions that should be considered when applying IAS 34:

Strategic decisions	Tactical decisions	Problems to overcome
Investments in associates must be identified by applying the definition of significant influence.	Processes must be in place to identify such transactions. Intention and related accounting effects that could arise must be considered when entering into investment transactions.	Significant influence is based on substance over legal form and all circumstances should be carefully considered to identify the true substance of the transaction.
Where separate financial statements are prepared, an accounting policy decision must be made for the measurement of the investment.	A policy decision must be made as to whether such investments will be carried at cost or as per IAS 39. When making the decision all the implications should be considered, for example the profit or loss volatility of the investment is recognized at fair value through profit or loss.	Care must be taken in applying IAS 39 with regards classification. The accounting policy chosen could have various implications with regards issues such as future impairments that may arise, income statement volatility, and so forth.
Where consolidated financial statements are prepared, ensure that the information required for equity accounting is available.	Processes must be in place to ensure that the entity has access to all the financial information for each associate at the relevant reporting date and that the information complies with the investor's accounting policies and are reliable.	Incorrect, inconsistent, or outdated information.

EXAMPLE: ACCOUNTING FOR INVESTMENTS IN ASSOCIATES

EXAMPLE 8.1

Dolo Inc. acquired a 40 percent interest in the ordinary shares of Nutro Inc. on the date of incorporation, January 1, 20X0, for $220,000. This enabled Dolo to exercise significant influence over Nutro. On December 31, 20X3, the shareholders' equity of Nutro was as follows:

Ordinary issued share capital	$550,000
Reserves	180,000
Retained earnings	650,000
Total	$1,380,000

The following abstracts were taken from the financial statements of Nutro for the year ending December 31, 20X4:

Statement of Comprehensive Income

Profit after tax	$228,000
Extraordinary item	(12,000)
Net profit for the period	$216,000

Statement of Changes in Equity

Retained earnings at the beginning of the year	$650,000
Net profit for the period	216,000
Dividends paid	(80,000)
Retained earnings at the end year	$786,000

In November 20X4, Dolo sold inventories to Nutro for the first time. The total sales amounted to $50,000, and Dolo earned a profit of $10,000 on the transaction. None of the inventories had been sold by Nutro by December 31. The income tax rate is 30 percent.

EXPLANATION

The application of the equity method would result in the carrying amount of the investment in Nutro Inc. being reflected as follows:

Original cost	$220,000
Post-acquisition profits accounted for at beginning of the year (40% x [$180,000 + $650,000])	332,000
Carrying amount on January 1, 20X4	$552,000
Attributable portion of net profit for the period (calculation a)	83,600
Dividends received (40% x $80,000)	(32,000)
Total	$603,600
Calculation a: Attributable Portion of Net Profit	
Net profit (40% x $216,000)	$86,400
After-tax effect of unrealized profit [40% x (70% x $10,000)]	(2,800)
All	$83,600

CHAPTER 9

Interests in Joint Ventures
(IAS 31)

9.1   **OBJECTIVE**

Joint ventures occur when there is an arrangement to undertake an activity where control is shared jointly by two or more business entities. This is different from arrangements where a parent has sole control over a subsidiary or a significant influence over an associate. The overall objective of IAS 31 is to provide users with information concerning the investing owners' (venturers') interest in the earnings and the underlying net assets of the joint venture.

9.2   **SCOPE OF THE STANDARD**

9.2.1 IAS 31 applies to all interests in joint ventures and the reporting of the joint venture's assets, liabilities, income, and expenses in the financial statements of the venturers, regardless of the joint ventures' structures or forms. The standard specifically outlines

- the characteristics necessary to be classified as a joint venture, and
- the distinction between jointly controlled operations, assets, and entities and the specific accounting requirements for each.

9.2.2 IAS 31 does not apply to venturers' interests in jointly controlled entities held by:

- venture capital organizations, for example private equity entities,
- mutual funds,
- unit trusts and similar entities, and
- investment-linked insurance funds that upon initial recognition are designated as at fair value through profit or loss or are classified as held for trading and accounted for in accordance with IAS 39. Such investments are measured at fair value with changes in fair value recognized in profit or loss in the period of the change.

9.2.3 A venturer is exempt from applying proportionate consolidation or the equity method if it meets the scope exemption above and:

- the interest is classified as held for sale in accordance with IFRS 5, or
- the investor does not prepare consolidated financial statements in accordance with the exception in IAS 27; or

- all the following conditions apply:
  - the venturer is a wholly owned or partially owned subsidiary and its owners have been informed and do not object to the venturer not applying proportionate consolidation or the equity method;
  - the venturer's debt or equity instruments are not traded in a public market;
  - the venturer is not in the process of issuing instruments that will be traded in a public market; and
  - the ultimate or any intermediate parent of the venturer produces consolidated financial statements available for public use that comply with IFRS.

9.3 KEY CONCEPTS

9.3.1 A **joint venture** is a contractual arrangement whereby two or more parties undertake an economic activity that is subject to joint control.

9.3.2 The following are **characteristics of all joint ventures:**

- Two or more venturers are bound by a contractual arrangement.
- A joint venture establishes joint control; that is, the contractually agreed sharing of control over a joint venture is such that no one party can exercise unilateral control.
- A venturer is a party to a joint venture and has joint control over that joint venture.

9.3.3 The existence of a **contractual arrangement** distinguishes joint ventures from associates. It is usually in writing and deals with such matters as:

- activity, duration, and reporting;
- appointment of a board of directors or equivalent body and voting rights;
- capital contributions by venturers; and
- sharing by the venturers of the output, income, expenses, or results of the joint venture.

9.3.4 IAS 31 identifies three forms of joint ventures: jointly controlled operations, jointly controlled assets, and jointly controlled entities.

9.3.5 **Jointly controlled operations** involve the use of resources of the venturers; they do not establish separate structures. An example is when two or more parties combine resources and efforts to manufacture, market, and jointly sell a product.

9.3.6 **Jointly controlled assets** refers to joint ventures that involve the joint control and ownership of one or more assets acquired for and dedicated to the purpose of the joint venture (for example, factories sharing the same railway line). The establishment of a **separate entity** is unnecessary.

9.3.7 **Jointly controlled entities** are joint ventures that are conducted through a **separate entity** in which each venturer owns an interest. An example is when two entities combine their activities in a particular line of business by transferring assets and liabilities into a jointly owned legal entity.

9.3.8 **Proportionate consolidation** is a method of accounting whereby a venturer's share of each of the assets, liabilities, income, and expenses of a jointly controlled entity is combined line by line with similar items in the venturer's financial statements or reported as separate line items in the venturer's financial statements.

9.3.9 The equity method is a method of accounting whereby an interest in a jointly controlled entity is initially recorded at cost and adjusted thereafter for the post-acquisition change in the venturer's share of net assets of the jointly controlled entity. The profit or loss of the venturer includes the venturer's share of the profit or loss of the jointly controlled entity.

9.3.10 Separate financial statements are those presented by a parent, an investor in an associate, or a venturer in a jointly controlled entity, in which the investments are accounted for on the basis of the direct equity interest rather than on the basis of the reported results and net assets of the investees.

9.4

ACCOUNTING TREATMENT

9.4.1 For interests in **jointly controlled operations**, a venturer should recognize in its separate and consolidated financial statements:

- the assets that it controls;
- the liabilities that it incurs;
- the expenses that it incurs; and
- its share of the income that the joint venture earns.

9.4.2 For the **jointly controlled assets**, a venturer should recognize in its separate and consolidated financial statements:

- its share of the assets;
- any liabilities that it has incurred;
- its share of any liabilities incurred jointly with the other venturers in relation to the joint venture;
- any income it receives from the joint venture;
- its share of any expenses incurred by the joint venture; and
- any expenses that it has incurred individually from its interest in the joint venture.

9.4.3 An entity should account for its interest as a venturer in **jointly controlled entities** using either proportionate consolidation or the equity method.

1. **The equity method.** Refer to chapter 8, which addresses that accounting treatment of investments in associates.
2. **Proportionate consolidation**, whereby the following principles apply:

- One of two formats could be used:
  - combining items line by line, or
  - listing separate line items.
- The interests in the joint ventures are included in the consolidated financial statements of the venturer, even if it has no subsidiaries.
- Proportionate consolidation commences when the venturer acquires joint control.
- Proportionate consolidation ceases when the venturer loses joint control.
- Many procedures for proportionate consolidation are similar to **consolidation procedures**, described in IAS 27.

9.4.4 The following **general accounting considerations** apply:

▪ Transactions between a venturer and a joint venture are treated as follows:
  – The venturer's share of unrealized profits on sales or contribution of assets to a joint venture is eliminated.
  – Full unrealized loss on sale or contribution of assets to a joint venture is eliminated.
  – The venturer's share of profits or losses on sales of assets by a joint venture to the venturer is eliminated.
  – An investor in a joint venture that does not have joint control should report its interest in a joint venture in the consolidated financial statements in terms of IAS 39 or, if it has significant influence, in terms of IAS 28.
  – Operators or managers of a joint venture should account for any fees as revenue in terms of IAS 18.

9.5   **PRESENTATION AND DISCLOSURE**

9.5.1 The following contingent liabilities (IAS 37) should be shown **separately** from others:

▪ liabilities incurred jointly with other venturers;
▪ share of a joint venture's contingent liabilities; and
▪ contingencies for liabilities of other venturers.

9.5.2 Commitments amounts shown separately include the following:

▪ capital commitments incurred jointly with other venturers; and
▪ share of a joint venture's capital commitments.

9.5.3 Present a list of significant joint ventures, including the names of the ventures, a description of the investor's interest in all joint ventures, and the investor's proportion of ownership.

9.5.4 A venturer that uses the line-by-line reporting format or the equity method should disclose aggregate amounts of each of the current assets, long-term assets, current liabilities, long-term liabilities, income, and expenses related to the joint ventures.

9.5.5 A venturer should disclose the method it uses to recognize its interests in jointly controlled entities.

9.5.6 A venturer not issuing consolidated financial statements (because it has no subsidiaries) should nevertheless disclose the above information.

9.6   **FINANCIAL ANALYSIS AND INTERPRETATION**

9.6.1 Entities can form joint ventures in which none of the entities own more than 50 percent of the voting rights in the joint venture. This enables every member of the venturing group to use the equity method of accounting for unconsolidated affiliates to report their share of the activities of the joint ventures. They can also use proportionate consolidation and each venturer need not use the same method if they are not part of the same group. If the venturers are part of the same group, each venture can elect their accounting policy, but from a consolidated perspective all joint ventures should be recognized consistently.

9.6.2 If they use the equity method, joint ventures enable firms to report lower debt-to-equity ratios and higher interest-coverage ratios, although this does not affect the return on equity.

9.7   COMMENTARY

9.7.1 The proportionate consolidation method leads to a conceptual problem on the statement of financial position, because the venture reports assets that it does not control in its statement of financial position. On the other hand, if proportionate consolidation is prohibited, the equity method will be applied for two different types of investments, associates (investor has significant influence) and joint ventures (investor has joint control).

9.7.2 In September 2007, the IASB issued an exposure draft (ED 9) to replace the existing standard. The main focus of ED 9 is as follows:

- Entities should move away from the method of accounting for joint arrangements based on the legal *form* of the arrangements to a method based on the rights and obligations agreed by the parties.
- Remove the choice in IAS 31 by requiring parties to recognize both the individual assets to which they have rights and the liabilities for which they are responsible, even if the joint arrangement operates in a separate legal entity. If the parties only have a right to a share of the outcome of the activities, their net interest in the arrangement would be recognized using the equity method.
- Entities should disclose summarized financial information relating to an entity's interests in joint ventures.

9.7.3 The IASB is currently redeliberating on the issues raised and considering the consequential amendments of the proposals to other standards.

EXAMPLES: INTERESTS IN JOINT VENTURES

EXAMPLE 9.1

Techno Inc. was incorporated after three independent engineering corporations decided to pool their knowledge to implement and market new technology. The three corporations acquired the following interests in the equity capital of Techno on the date of its incorporation:

- Electro Inc.   30 percent
- Mechan Inc.   40 percent
- Civil Inc.   30 percent

The following information was taken from the financial statements of Techno as well as one of the owners, Mechan.

Abridged Statement of Comprehensive Income for the Year Ending June 30, 20X1

	Mechan Inc. ($'000)	Techno Inc. ($'000)
Revenue	3,100	980
Cost of sales	(1,800)	(610)
Gross profit	1,300	370
Other operating income	150	–
Operating costs	(850)	(170)
Profit before tax	600	200
Income tax expense	(250)	(90)
Net profit for the period	350	110

Mechan sold inventories with an invoice value of $600,000 to Techno during the year. Included in Techno's inventories on June 30, 20X1 is an amount of $240,000, which is inventory purchased from Mechan at a profit markup of 20 percent. The income tax rate is 30 percent.

Techno paid an administration fee of $120,000 to Mechan during the year. This amount is included under "Other operating income."

EXPLANATION

To combine the results of Techno Inc. with those of Mechan Inc., the following issues would need to be resolved:

■ Is Techno an associate or joint venture for financial reporting purposes?
■ Which method is appropriate for reporting the results of Techno in the financial statements of Mechan?
■ How are the above transactions between the entities to be recorded and presented for financial reporting purposes in the consolidated Statement of Comprehensive Income?

First issue

The existence of a **contractual agreement**, whereby the parties involved undertake an economic activity subject to joint control, distinguishes a joint venture from an associate. No one of the venturers should be able to exercise unilateral control. However, if no contractual agreement exists, the investment would be regarded as an associate because the investor holds more than 20 percent of the voting power and is therefore presumed to have significant influence over the investee.

Second issue

If Techno is regarded as a joint venture, the proportionate consolidation method or the equity method must be used. However, if Techno is regarded as an associate, the equity method would be used.

Third issue

It is assumed that Techno is a joint venture for purposes of the following illustration.

Consolidated Statement of Comprehensive Income for the Year Ending June 30, 20X1

	$'000
Revenue (Calculation a)	3,252
Cost of sales (Calculation b)	(1,820)
Gross profit	1,432
Other operating income (Calculation c)	102
Operating costs (Calculation d)	(870)
Profit before tax	664
Income tax expense (Calculation e)	(281)
Net profit for the period	383

Remarks

- The proportionate consolidation method is applied by adding 40 percent of the Statement of Comprehensive Income items of Techno to those of Mechan.
- The transactions between the corporations are then dealt with by recording the following consolidation journal entries:

	Dr ($'000)	Cr ($'000)
Sales (40% x 600)	240	
Cost of sales		240 (Eliminating intragroup sales)
Cost of sales (40% x 20/120 x 240)	16	
Inventories		16 (Eliminating unrealized profit in inventory)
Deferred taxation (Statement of Financial Position) (30% x 16)	4.8	
Income tax expense (Statement of Comprehensive Income)		4.8 (Taxation effect on elimination of unrealized profit)

Note: The administration fee is eliminated by reducing other operating income with Mechan's portion of the total fee, namely $48,000, and reducing operating expenses accordingly. The net effect on the consolidated profit is nil.

Calculations	
	$'000
a. **Sales**	
Mechan	3,100
Intragroup sales (40% x 600)	(240)
Techno (40% x 980)	392
	3,252
b. **Cost of sales**	
Mechan	1,800
Intragroup sales	(240)
Unrealized profit (40% x 20/120 x 240)	16
Techno (40% x 610)	244
	1,820
c. **Other operating income**	
Mechan	150
Intragroup fee (40% x 120)	(48)
	102
d. **Operating costs**	
Mechan	850
Techno (40% x 170)	68
Intra-group fee (40% x 120)	(48)
	870
e. **Income tax expense**	
Mechan	250
Unrealized profit (30% x 16 rounded-up)	(5)
Techno (40% x 90)	36
	281

Part III

Statement of Financial Position/ Balance Sheet

CHAPTER 10

Property, Plant, and Equipment
(IAS 16)

10.1

OBJECTIVE

The objective of IAS 16 is to prescribe the accounting treatment for property, plant, and equipment (PPE), including

- timing of the recognition, derecognition, and amortization;
- determination of the carrying amount of the assets under the cost model and the revaluation model;
- depreciation charges and impairment losses to be recognized in profit or loss; and
- disclosure requirements.

10.2

SCOPE OF THE STANDARD

This standard deals with all property, plant, and equipment, including that which is held by a lessee under a finance lease (IAS 17).

This standard does not apply to

- property, plant, and equipment that is classified as held for sale (see IFRS 5, Noncurrent Assets Held for Sale and Discontinued Operations);
- biological assets related to agricultural activity (see IAS 41, Agriculture);
- exploration assets (see IFRS 6 Exploration for and Evaluation of Mineral Assets); or
- mineral rights and mineral reserves, such as oil or natural gas or similar non-regenerative resources.

10.3

KEY CONCEPTS

10.3.1 Property, plant, and equipment are tangible items that are

- held for use in the production or supply of goods or services, for rental to others, or for administrative purposes; and
- expected to be used during more than one period.

10.3.2 Cost is the amount of cash or cash equivalents paid or the fair value of any other consideration given to acquire an asset at the time of its acquisition or construction. Where applicable, another standard may attribute an amount for the cost of an asset, for example IFRS 2 if the property, plant, and equipment is acquired as part of a share-based payment transaction.

10.3.3 **Fair value** is the amount for which an asset could be exchanged between knowledgeable, willing parties in an arm's-length transaction.

10.3.4 **Carrying amount** is the amount at which an asset is recognized after deducting any accumulated depreciation and impairment losses.

10.3.5 **Depreciable amount** is the cost of an asset, or other amount substituted for cost, less its residual value.

10.3.6 **Depreciation** is the systematic allocation of the depreciable amount of an asset over its useful life.

10.3.7 An **impairment loss** is the amount by which the carrying amount of an asset exceeds its recoverable amount. **Recoverable amount** is the higher of an asset's net selling price and its value in use. (See also IAS 36 for guidance on impairment.)

10.3.8 The **residual value** of an asset is the estimated amount that an entity would currently obtain from disposal of the asset, after deducting the estimated costs of disposal (assuming the asset is already of the age and in the condition expected at the end of its useful life). If the intent is to scrap an asset, it will have no residual value.

10.3.9 **Useful life** is the intended period over which an asset is expected to be available for use by an entity, or the number of production or similar units expected to be obtained from the asset by an entity.

10.4

ACCOUNTING TREATMENT

Initial Measurement

10.4.1 An item of property, plant, and equipment should be **recognized** as an asset only if

- it is probable that future economic benefits associated with the item will flow to the entity; and
- the cost of the item can be reliably measured.

10.4.2 Property, plant, and equipment is initially recognized at cost. The standard does not prescribe the unit of account for property, plant, and equipment and judgment is required in applying the recognition criteria to the entity's specific circumstances. It may be appropriate to aggregate insignificant items such as molds and tools and apply the criteria to the aggregated amount.

10.4.3 Safety and environmental assets qualify as property, plant, and equipment if they enable the entity to increase future economic benefits from related assets in excess of what it could derive if they had not been acquired (for example, chemical protection equipment).

10.4.4 Costs incurred in respect of day-to-day servicing are recognized in profit or loss as incurred and are not capitalized to the property, plant, and equipment. Spare parts and servicing equipment are usually carried as inventory and recognized in profit in loss when consumed.

10.4.5 Parts of some items of property, plant, and equipment may require replacement at regular intervals. The cost of such replacement items is included in the carrying amount of the asset when the recognition criteria are met. The parts being replaced are derecognized when the derecognition criteria are met. Major inspection costs can be capitalized and any amounts relating to a previous inspection are derecognized when a new inspection is capitalized.

10.4.6 The **cost** of an item of property, plant, and equipment **includes**

- its **purchase price** and duties paid;
- any costs directly attributable to bringing the asset to the location and condition necessary for it to be capable of operating in its intended manner, for example professional fees, installation and assembly costs, initial delivery and handling, and site preparation;
- the initial estimate of the costs of dismantling and removing the asset and restoring the site (see IAS 37); and
- materials, labor, and other inputs for **self-constructed assets**.

10.4.7 The **cost** of an item of property, plant, and equipment **excludes**

- general and administrative expenses; and
- start-up costs.

10.4.8 The **cost** of an item of property, plant, and equipment **might** include the effects of **government grants** (IAS 20) deducted from cost or set-up as deferred income.

10.4.9 When assets are exchanged and the transaction has commercial substance, items are recorded at the fair value of the asset(s) received, if the fair value can be reliably measured. In other cases, items are recorded at the carrying amount of the asset(s) given up.

10.4.10 The amount expected to be recovered from the future use (or sale) of an asset, including its residual value on disposal, is referred to as the **value in use**. The carrying amount should be compared with the higher of value in use or fair value less costs to sell (that is, the recoverable amount) whenever there is an indication of impairment. If the recoverable amount is lower, the difference is recognized as an expense (IAS 36).

Subsequent Measurement

10.4.11 **Choice of cost or fair value.** Subsequent to initial recognition, an entity should choose either the **cost model** or the **revaluation model** as its accounting policy for items of property, plant, and equipment and should apply that policy to an entire class of property, plant, and equipment.

10.4.12 Under the **cost model,** the **carrying amount** of an item of property, plant, and equipment is its cost less accumulated depreciation and impairment losses. Assets classified as held for sale are shown at the lower of fair value less costs to sell and carrying value.

10.4.13 In terms of the **revaluation model** the **carrying amount** of an item of property, plant, and equipment is its fair value less subsequent accumulated depreciation and impairment losses. The revaluation model can be applied if fair value can be reliably measured with sufficient regularity. Assets classified as held for sale are shown at the lower of fair value less costs to sell and carrying value.

10.4.14 If an item of property, plant, and equipment is revalued, the entire class of property, plant, and equipment to which that asset belongs should be revalued. Furthermore, when the revaluation model is adopted assets should be revalued with sufficient regularity so that the carrying value does not differ materially from the fair value.

Income and Expenses

10.4.15 **Revaluation gains or loss.** Adjustments to the carrying value are treated as follows:

- Increases should be **credited** directly to **other comprehensive income** under the heading "Revaluation surplus." A reversal of an increase previously taken to other comprehensive income can be debited to other comprehensive income.
- Decreases should be recognized (debited) in profit or loss. A reversal of a previous loss for the same asset is reported in profit or loss to the extent that it reverses the previous loss.

10.4.16 **Depreciation** of an asset is recognized as an expense unless it is included in the carrying amount of a self-constructed asset, for example inventory. The following principles apply:

- The depreciable amount is allocated on a systematic basis over the useful life.
- The method reflects the pattern of expected consumption.
- Each part of an item of property, plant, and equipment with a cost that is significant in relation to the total cost of the item should be depreciated separately at appropriate different rates.
- Component parts are treated as separate items if the related assets have different useful lives or provide economic benefits in a different pattern (for example, an aircraft and its engines or land and buildings).

10.4.17 The **depreciation method** applied to an asset should be reviewed at least at each financial year-end. If there has been a significant change in the expected pattern of consumption of the future economic benefits embodied in the asset, the method should be changed to reflect the changed pattern. Such a change should be accounted for as a change in an **accounting estimate** in accordance with IAS 8.

10.4.18 Depreciation starts when the asset is ready for use and ends when the asset is derecognized or classified as held for sale. Depreciation does not cease when the asset becomes idle or retired from use, unless the asset is fully depreciated. It may happen that when depreciation is based on hourly usage, the depreciation charge is zero when the assets are not in use; that is depreciation continues, but the charge is zero.

10.4.19 Impairment of property, plant, and equipment is dealt with in IAS 36. If compensation is receivable from third parties for property, plant, and equipment impaired, for example an insurance recovery, such compensation should be included in profit or loss when it becomes receivable.

10.4.20 The carrying amount of an item of property, plant, and equipment is derecognized on disposal or when no future economic benefits are expected from its use or disposal. The gain or loss should be included in profit or loss when the item is derecognized, except for sale and leaseback transactions, which have specific rules in IAS 17. The gain or loss is the difference between the net proceeds on disposal and the carrying amount.

10.5   ## PRESENTATION AND DISCLOSURE

10.5.1 For **each class** of property, plant, and equipment, the following must be presented:

- the measurement **bases** used for determining the gross carrying amount;
- the depreciation **methods** used;
- the useful lives or the depreciation **rates** used;
- the **gross** carrying amount and the **accumulated** depreciation (together with accumulated impairment losses) at the beginning and end of the period; and

▓ a **reconciliation** of the carrying amount at the beginning and end of the period, showing:

- additions and disposals, including assets classified as held for sale;
- depreciation;
- acquisitions through business combinations;
- increases or decreases resulting from revaluations and impairment losses recognized or reversed directly in other comprehensive income;
- impairment losses recognized in profit or loss;
- impairment losses reversed in profit or loss;
- net exchange differences arising on the translation of the financial statements; and
- other changes.

10.5.2 The financial statements should also disclose:

▓ restrictions on title and assets pledged as security for liabilities;

▓ expenditures recognized in the carrying amount in the course of construction;

▓ contractual commitments for the acquisition of property, plant, and equipment; and

▓ compensation from third parties for impairments included in profit or loss.

10.5.3 The depreciation methods adopted and the estimated **useful lives or depreciation rates** must be disclosed as well as:

▓ current year depreciation, whether recognized in profit or loss or as a part of the cost of other assets, during a period; and

▓ accumulated depreciation at the end of the period.

10.5.4 Disclose the nature and effect of a **change in an accounting estimate** with respect to:

▓ residual values;

▓ the estimated costs of dismantling, removing, or restoring items;

▓ useful lives; and

▓ depreciation methods.

10.5.5 If items of property, plant, and equipment are stated at **revalued amounts**, the following must be disclosed:

▓ effective date of revaluation;

▓ whether an independent valuator was involved;

▓ methods and significant assumptions applied in estimating the fair value;

▓ reference to observable prices in an active market or recent arm's-length transactions;

▓ carrying amount that would have been recognized had the assets been carried under the cost model; and

▓ revaluation surplus.

10.5.6 Users of financial statements can also find the following information relevant to their needs:

▓ carrying amount of temporarily idle property, plant, and equipment;

▓ gross carrying amount of fully depreciated items still in use;

▓ the carrying amount of items retired from active use and held for disposal; and

▓ fair value of property, plant, and equipment when this is materially different from the carrying amount per the cost model in use.

10.6

FINANCIAL ANALYSIS AND INTERPRETATION

10.6.1 The original cost of acquired fixed assets is usually recognized over time by systematically writing down the asset's book value on the Statement of Financial Position and reporting an expense in profit or loss as the benefits arising from the asset are consumed by the entity. The systematic expensing of the original cost of physical assets over time is called **depreciation**. The systematic expensing of the original cost of natural resources over time is called **depletion**. The systematic expensing of the original cost of intangible assets over time is called **amortization**. Essentially, all three of these concepts are the same. The cost of acquiring land is never depleted because land does not get used up over time. However, if the land has a limited useful life, the cost of acquiring it can be depreciated.

10.6.2 Depreciation is a method of expensing the original purchase cost of physical assets over their useful lives. It is neither a means of adjusting the asset to its fair market value nor a means to provide funds for the replacement of the asset being depreciated.

10.6.3 There are several methods of determining **depreciation expense** for property, plant, and equipment on the financial statements. Depreciation methods include the straight-line method, sum-of-the-years' digits, double-declining balance, and units-of-production (service hours). Regardless of the terminology used, the principles that should be applied in IFRS financial statements are:

- the depreciable amount is allocated on a systematic basis over the asset's useful life; and
- the method used must reflect the pattern of expected consumption.

10.6.4 The straight-line depreciation method is the most common method of providing for depreciation. Both sum-of-the-years' digits and the double-declining balance methods are classified as **accelerated depreciation** (or rather, accelerated consumption-pattern methods; they are often used for tax purposes and do not comply with IFRS if they do not reflect the pattern of the expected consumption of the assets).

10.6.5 In some countries, management has more flexibility than is permitted by IFRS when deciding whether to expense or capitalize certain expenditures. Capitalizing could result in the recognition of an asset that does not qualify for recognition under IFRS. Expensing a transaction that would otherwise qualify as an asset under IFRS means avoiding depreciating it over time. This flexibility will impact the Statement of Financial Position, Statement of Comprehensive Income, a number of key financial ratios, and the classification of cash flows in the statement of cash flows. Consequently, the analyst must understand the financial data effects of the capitalization or expensing choices made by management.

10.6.6 Table 10.1 summarizes the effects of expensing versus capitalizing costs on the financial statements and related key ratios.

TABLE 10.1   Effects of Capitalizing vs. Expensing Costs

Variable	Expensing	Capitalizing
Shareholders' Equity	**Lower** because earnings are lower	**Higher** because earnings are higher
Earnings	**Lower** because expenses are higher	**Higher** because expenses are lower
Pretax Cash Generated from Operating Activities	**Lower** because expenses are higher	**Higher** because expenses are lower
Cash Generated from Investing Activities	**None** because no long-term asset is put on the Statement of Financial Position	**Lower** because a long-term asset is acquired (invested in) for cash
Pretax Total Cash Flow	**Same** because amortization is not a cash expense	**Same** because amortization is not a cash expense
Profit Margin	**Lower** because earnings are lower	**Higher** because earnings are higher
Asset Turnover	**Higher** because assets are lower	**Lower** because assets are higher
Current Ratio	**Same** on a pretax basis because only long-term assets are affected	**Same** on a pretax basis because only long-term assets are affected
Debt-to-Equity	**Higher** because shareholders' equity is lower	**Lower** because shareholders' equity is higher
Return on Assets	**Lower** because the earnings are lower percentage-wise than the reduced assets	**Higher** because the earnings are higher percentage-wise than the increased assets
Return on Equity	**Lower** because the earnings are lower percentage-wise than the reduced shareholders' equity	**Higher** because the earnings are higher percentage-wise than the increased shareholders' equity
Stability over Time	**Less stable** earnings and ratios because large expenses may be sporadic	**More stable** earnings and ratios because amortization smooths earnings over time

10.6.7 Management must make three choices when deciding how to depreciate assets:

- the method of depreciation that will be used (straight-line, accelerated consumption, or depletion in early years);
- the useful life of the asset, which is the time period over which the depreciation will occur; and
- the residual value of the asset.

In IFRS financial statements, these choices are determined by the application of the principles in IAS 16.

10.6.8 The easiest way to understand the impact of using **straight-line versus accelerated depreciation** is as follows: An accelerated consumption method will increase the depreciation expense in the early years of an asset's useful life relative to what it would be if the straight-line method were used. This lowers reported income and also causes the book value of the long-term assets reported on the Statement of Financial Position to decline more quickly relative to what would be reported under the straight-line method. As a result, the shareholders' equity will be lower in the early years of an asset's life under accelerated depreciation. Furthermore, the percentage impact falls more heavily on the smaller income value than on the larger asset and shareholders' equity values. Many of the key financial ratios that are based on income, asset values, or equity values will also be affected by the choice of depreciation method.

10.6.9 No matter which depreciation method is chosen, the total accumulated depreciation will be the same over the entire useful life of an asset. Thus, the effects shown in table 10.2 for the early year or years of an asset's life tend to reverse over time. However, these reversals apply to the depreciation effects associated with an **individual asset**. If a company's asset base is growing, the depreciation applicable to the most-recently acquired assets tends to dominate the overall depreciation expense of the entity. The effects described in the table will normally apply over time because the reversal process is overwhelmed by the depreciation charges applied to newer assets. Only if an entity is in decline and its capital expenditures are low will the reversal effects be noticeable in the aggregate.

10.6.10 The determination of the **useful life** of an asset also affects financial statement values and key financial ratios. The intended usage period—not the actual life—should determine the useful life. All other factors being held constant, the shorter the useful life of an asset, the larger its depreciation will be over its depreciable life. This will raise the depreciation expense, lower reported income, reduce asset values, and reduce shareholders' equity relative to what they would be if a longer useful life were chosen.

Reported cash flow will not be affected, because depreciation is not a cash expense. However, key financial ratios that contain income, asset values, and shareholders' equity will be affected. A shorter useful life tends to lower profit margins and return on equity, while at the same time raising asset turnover and debt-to-equity ratios.

10.6.11 Choosing a large **residual value** has the opposite effect of choosing a short useful life. All other factors being constant, a high salvage (residual) value will lower the depreciation expense, raise reported income, and raise the book values of assets and shareholders' equity relative to what they would be if a lower salvage value had been chosen. Cash flow, however, is unaffected because depreciation is a noncash expense. As a result of a high salvage value, an entity's profit margin and return on equity increase, whereas its asset turnover and debt-to-equity ratios decrease.

10.6.12 Although the *objective* of the depreciation charge is not to provide for the replacement of assets, it is important to keep in mind that when the prices of capital goods increase over time, the depreciation accumulated over the life of such assets will fall short of the amount needed to replace them when they wear out.

To understand this concept, consider equipment that costs $10,000, has a five-year useful life, and has no salvage value. If straight-line depreciation is used, this asset will be depreciated at a rate of $2,000 per year for its five-year life. Over the life of the equipment, this depreciation will accumulate to $10,000. If there had been no inflation in the intervening period, the original equipment could then be replaced with a new $10,000 piece of equipment. Historical-cost depreciation makes sense in a zero-inflation environment, because the amount of depreciation expensed matches the cost to replace the asset.

However, suppose the inflation rate over the equipment's depreciable life had been 10 percent per year, instead of zero. When it is time to replace the asset, its replacement will cost $16,105 ($10,000 × 1.105). The accumulated depreciation is $6,105 less than what is required to physically restore the entity to its original asset position. In other words, the real cost of the equipment is higher, and the reported financial statements are distorted.

This analysis illustrates that, during periods of inflation, depreciating physical assets on the basis of historical cost, in accordance with the financial capital maintenance theory of income, tends to understate the true depreciation expense. As such, it overstates the true earnings of an entity from the point of view of the physical capital maintenance (replacement cost) theory of income.

TABLE 10.2 **Impact of Changes on Financial Statements and Ratios**

Variable	Change from straight-line to depreciation based on accelerated consumption pattern in early years	Change from accelerated consumption pattern in early years to straight-line depreciation	Increase (decrease) in asset depreciable life (duration of consumption)	Increase (decrease) in residual value
Earnings	**Lower** due to higher depreciation expense	**Higher** due to **lower** depreciation expense	**Higher (lower)** due to lower (higher) depreciation expense	**Higher (lower)** due to lower (higher) depreciation expense
Net Worth	**Lower** due to higher asset write-down	**Higher** due to lower asset write-down	**Higher (lower)** due to lower (higher) asset write-down	**Higher (lower)** due to lower (higher) asset write-down
Cash Flow	No effect	No effect	No effect	No effect
Profit Margin	**Lower** due to lower earnings	**Higher** due to higher earnings	**Higher (lower)** due to higher (lower) earnings	**Higher (lower)** due to higher (lower) earnings
Current Ratio	None; only affects long-term assets	None; only affects long-term assets	None; only affects long-term assets	None; only affects long-term assets
Asset Turnover	**Higher** due to lower assets	**Lower** due to higher assets	**Lower (higher)** due to higher (lower) assets	**Lower (higher)** due to higher (lower) assets
Debt-to-Equity	**Higher** due to lower net worth	**Lower** due to higher net worth	**Lower (higher)** due to higher (lower) net worth	**Lower (higher)** due to higher (lower) net worth
Return on Assets	**Lower** due to a larger percentage decline in earnings versus asset decline	**Higher** due to a larger percentage rise in earnings versus asset rise	**Higher (lower)** due to a larger (smaller) percentage rise in earnings versus asset rise	**Higher (lower)** due to a larger (smaller) percentage rise in earnings versus asset rise
Return on Equity	**Lower** due to a larger percentage decline in earnings versus equity decline	**Higher** due to a larger percentage rise in earnings versus equity rise	**Higher (lower)** due to a larger (smaller) percentage rise in earnings versus equity rise	**Higher (lower)** due to a larger (smaller) percentage rise in earnings versus equity rise

10.6.13 Table 10.2 provides an overview of the impact of changes in consumption patterns, depreciable asset lives (duration of consumption), and salvage values on financial statements and ratios. Comparisons of a company's financial performance with industry competitors would be similar to the effects of changes in table 10.2's variables if competitors use different depreciation methods, higher (or lower) depreciable asset lives, and relatively higher (or lower) salvage values.

10.7 EVALUATION

10.7.1 There are relatively few difficulties experienced by entities when applying IAS 16. The most significant judgments required relate to determining the most appropriate depreciation method, useful life, particularly whether components should be depreciated differently, and residual value and the impact on the calculation of deferred tax. These judgments should be reviewed annually and any changes are recorded as changes in estimated. For entities with significant factories and plant, the application is time consuming, but not complex.

10.7.2 Determining whether to follow the cost or revaluation model could have a significant impact on the results of the entity. It would also have a significant impact on the cost, time, and effort involved in applying this standard.

10.8   FUTURE DEVELOPMENTS

Currently the IASB does not have an active project nor is it conducting research into the accounting requirements for property, plant, and equipment. Other than minor changes that may arise as the result of the annual improvements process, no significant changes are expected to this standard in the near future.

10.9   IMPLEMENTATION DECISIONS

The following table sets out some of the strategic and tactical decisions that should be considered when applying IAS 16.

Strategic decisions	Tactical decisions	Problems to overcome
Property, plant, and equipment should be categorized into classes, for example, buildings or vehicles, according to the nature of the assets.	Assets with separate components should be separated into their components and the components depreciated separately. The different components should be identified.	The identification of property, plant, and equipment is generally straightforward and does not result in significant complexity.
The accounting policy, either cost model or revaluation model, for the various asset classes should be determined.	If the revaluation model is selected a decision should be taken as to how frequently the revaluation should take place and what methodology should be used.	Because of its nature it may be difficult to determine the fair value of property, plant, and equipment regularly. The fixed asset register and system should be set up to accommodate the revised carrying amount and recalculate depreciation based on the new revalued amount.
A depreciation policy should be determined for each asset class.	The useful lives and the residual value of the property, plant, and equipment should be assessed annually.	The useful lives of assets and their residual values may change significantly over the life of the asset and these changes should be accounted for as changes in estimates. The fixed asset register and system should be set up to accommodate changes and to recalculate depreciation in accordance with the revised information.
Determining the residual value of items, especially in a mining or manufacturing environment where property, plant, and equipment makes up a significant portion of the balance sheet.	Methodology for determining the value as if the asset was already at the age and condition as expected at the end of its useful life.	

EXAMPLES: PROPERTY, PLANT, AND EQUIPMENT

EXAMPLE 10.1

An entity begins the year with assets of $8,500, consisting of $500 in cash and $8,000 in plant and equipment. These assets are financed through current liabilities of $200 and $2,000 of 7 percent long-term debt, and $6,300 of common stock. During the year, the entity has sales of $10,000 and incurs $7,000 of operating expenses (excluding depreciation), $1,000 of construction costs for new plant and equipment, and $140 of interest expense. The entity depreciates its plant and equipment over 10 years (no residual [salvage] value). Ignoring the effect of income taxes, develop **pro forma** Statements of Comprehensive Income and Statements of Financial Position for the company's operations for the year if it expenses the $1,000 of construction costs and if it capitalizes these costs.

The effect of the expense-or-capitalize-cost decision on the company's shareholders' equity, pretax income, pretax operating and investing cash flows, and key financial ratios should be analyzed.

It is assumed that construction costs will be depreciated over four years and that the resulting asset will be ready for use on the first day of Year 1.

The results of the expense-or-capitalize-cost decision should be summarized.

EXPLANATION

	Expense construction costs		Capitalize construction costs		
	Year 0 ($)	Year 1 ($)	Year 0 ($)	Year 1 ($)	
Sales		10,000		10,000	
Operating expenses		7,000		7,000	
Construction costs		1,000		–	
Depreciation expense		800		800	(8000–0/10)
Amortization expense		–		250	(1000/4)
Interest expense		140		140	
Pretax Income		1,060		1,810	
Cash	500	2,360	500	2,360	
Plant and equipment	8,000	7,200	8,000	7,200	($8,000–$800)
Construction costs	–	–	–	750	($1,000–$250)
Total Assets	8,500	9,560	8,500	10,310	
Current Liabilities	200	200	200	200	
Long-term debt	2,000	2,000	2,000	2,000	
Common stock	6,300	6,300	6,300	6,300	
Retained earnings	–	1,060	–	1,810	
Total Liabilities and Capital	8,500	9,560	8,500	10,310	
Shareholders' equity		7,360		8,110	
Pretax earnings		1,060		1,810	
Operating cash flow (pretax + depreciation and amortization)		1,860		2,860	
Investing cash flow		–		(1,000) (construction cost)	
Net Cash Flow		1,860		1,860	
Pretax Profit Margin		10.6%		18.1%	
Asset Turnover (Sales/ Average Assets)		1.11x		1.06x	
Current Ratio		11.8x		11.8x	
Long-Term Debt-to-Equity		27.2%		24.7x	
Pretax ROE (Income/ Average Equity)		15.5%		25.1%	

EXAMPLE 10.2

On January 1, 20X1, Zakharetz Inc. acquired production equipment in the amount of $250,000. The following further costs were incurred:

	$
Delivery	18,000
Installation	24,500
General administration costs of an indirect nature	3,000

The installation and setting-up period took three months, and an additional $21,000 was spent on costs directly related to bringing the asset to its working condition. The equipment was ready for use on April 1, 20X1.

Monthly managerial reports indicated that for the first five months, the production quantities from this equipment resulted in an initial operating loss of $15,000 because of small quantities produced. The months thereafter showed much more positive results.

The equipment has an estimated useful life of 14 years and a residual value of $18,000. Estimated dismantling costs are $12,500.

What is the cost of the asset and what are the annual charges in the Statement of Comprehensive Income related to the consumption of the economic benefits embodied in the assets?

EXPLANATION

Historical cost of equipment

	$
Invoice price	250,000
Delivery	18,000
Installation	24,500
Other costs directly related to bringing the asset to its working condition	21,000
Initial estimate of dismantling costs	12,500
	326,000

Annual charges related to equipment

	$
Historical cost	326,000
Estimated residual value	(18,000)
Depreciable amount	308,000

The annual charge to the Statement of Comprehensive Income is $22,000 ($308,000 ÷ 14 years). However, note that in the year ending December 31, 20X1, the charge will be $16,500 (9/12 × $22,000), because the equipment was ready for use on April 1, 20X1, after the installation and setting-up period.

EXAMPLE 10.3

Delta Printers Inc. acquired its buildings and printing machinery on January 1, 20X1, for the amount of $2 million and recorded it at the historical acquisition cost. During 20X3, the directors made a decision to account for the machinery at fair value in the future, to provide for the maintenance of capital of the business in total.

Will measurement at fair value achieve the objective of capital maintenance? How is fair value determined? What are the deferred tax implications?

EXPLANATION

Maintenance of capital

The suggested method of accounting treatment will not be completely successful for the maintenance of capital due to the following:

- No provision is made for maintaining the current cost of inventory, work-in-process, and other nonmonetary assets.
- No provision is made for the cost of holding monetary assets.
- No provision is made for backlog depreciation.

Fair value

The fair value of plant and equipment items is usually their market value determined by appraisal. When there is no proof of market value, due to the specialized nature of plant and equipment and because these items are rarely sold (except as part of a going concern), then the items are to be valued at net replacement cost.

Deferred tax implication of revaluation

Deferred taxation is provided for on the revaluation amount for the following reasons:

- The revalued carrying amount is recovered through use, and taxable economic benefits are obtained against which no depreciation deductions for tax purposes are allowed. Therefore, the taxation payable on these economic benefits should be provided.
- Deferred taxation, as a result of revaluation, is charged directly against the revaluation surplus (other comprehensive income).

CHAPTER 11

Investment Property
(IAS 40)

OBJECTIVE

Entities may own property for use in their business or as an investment. In understanding the amount, timing, and nature of future cash flows, users of financial statements would want information about properties held for use separately from properties held for investment purposes. The objective of IAS 40 is therefore to prescribe the accounting treatment and disclosure requirements for investment property. The main issue in accounting for investment properties is to distinguish these properties separately from owner-occupied properties. The standard then gives entities a choice as to whether to measure all of their investment properties at fair value or at cost. Whichever choice is exercised, the standard specifies that the fair value amount of investment property should be disclosed.

11.2

SCOPE OF THE STANDARD

11.2.1 IAS 40 applies to all investment property.

11.2.2 Investment property includes land and buildings or part of a building or both. It excludes

- owner-occupied property (Property, Plant, and Equipment, IAS 16),
- property held for sale in the short term in the ordinary course of business (Inventories, IAS 2),
- property being constructed or developed on behalf of third parties (Construction Contracts, IAS 11),
- property held by a lessee under an operating lease (Leases, IAS 17),
- biological assets (Agriculture, IAS 41), and
- mining rights and mineral resources (Exploration for and Evaluation of Mineral Resources, IFRS 6).

11.3

KEY CONCEPTS

11.3.1 Investment property is property (land and building or part of a building or both) that is held by the owner or by the lessee under a finance lease to earn rentals, or for capital appreciation, or both, rather than for use in the production or supply of goods or services or for administration or for sale in the ordinary course of business.

11.4   **ACCOUNTING TREATMENT**

Recognition

11.4.1 An investment property is recognized as an asset if

- it is **probable** that the future economic benefits attributable to the asset will flow to the entity; and
- the cost of the asset can be **reliably measured**.

11.4.2 A **property interest that is held by a lessee under an operating lease** may be accounted for as an investment property if the property would otherwise meet the definition of an investment property and the fair value model is applied to the leased property interest. This classification is available on a property-by-property basis, but once the election has been made then all other property classified as investment property must be accounted for in terms of the fair value model.

Initial Measurement

11.4.3 On **initial recognition**, investment property is recognized at its cost. Total cost comprises the purchase price and any directly attributable transaction costs (for example, legal services, transfer taxes, and other transaction costs). However, general administrative expenses as well as start-up costs are excluded. Cost is determined the same way as for other property (see IAS 16, chapter 10). For investment property acquired under a finance lease, the asset and liability should be measured at the lower of fair value and the present value of future minimum lease payments.

Subsequent Measurement

11.4.4 An entity might choose to **subsequently** measure all of its investment property, using either of the following:

- **Cost model**. Measures investment property at cost less accumulated depreciation and impairment losses. Under the cost model the requirements of IAS 16 are applied to the measurement of investment property.
- **Fair value model**. Measures investment properties at fair value. Gains and losses from changes in the fair value are recognized in profit or loss as they arise. **Fair value** is defined as the amount at which an asset could be exchanged between knowledgeable, willing parties in an arm's-length transaction.

11.4.5 The following principles are applied to determine the **fair value** for investment property:

- The fair value of an investment property shall reflect market conditions at the end of the reporting period.
- The fair value of investment property reflects rental income from current leases and reasonable, supportable assumptions that represent what knowledgeable, willing parties would assume about rental income from future leases in light of current conditions.
- The best evidence of fair value is given by current prices in an active market for similar property in the same location and condition and subject to similar lease and other contracts. An entity must identify differences in the nature, condition, and location of the properties and amend the valuation where necessary.
- In the absence of current prices in an active market an entity may look to an active market for properties of a similar nature, recent prices of similar properties in a less active market, or discounted cash flow projections based on reliable estimates of future cash flows.

- There is a rebuttable presumption that an entity can reliably determine the fair value of an investment property. However, in exceptional circumstances it may happen that it is clear when the investment property is first acquired or classified as such that the entity will not be able to determine its fair value on a continuing basis. In such circumstances the property is measured using the benchmark treatment in IAS 16 until its disposal date. The entity measures all of its other investment property for which fair value is determinable at fair value.

11.4.6 Transfers to or from investment property should be made when there is a change in use. Special provisions apply for determining the carrying value at the date of such transfers.

11.4.7 An investment property should be derecognized on disposal or when the investment property is permanently withdrawn from use and no future economic benefits are expected from its disposal. Gains or losses arising from the retirement or disposal of an investment property shall be recognized in profit or loss, unless another standard provides for different treatment. For example, IAS 17 has specific rules for the recognition of gains or losses arising from sale and leaseback transactions.

11.5 PRESENTATION AND DISCLOSURE

11.5.1 Accounting policies should specify the following:

- whether the entity applies the fair value or cost model to investment properties;
- if the fair value model is applied then under what circumstances property interests under operating leases are classified as investment property; and
- the criteria used to distinguish investment property from owner-occupied property.

11.5.2 The following disclosures relating to **significant estimates and assumptions** should be provided:

- methods and significant assumptions applied in determining **fair value;**
- the extent to which the fair value has been determined by an external, independent valuer;
- measurement bases, depreciation methods, and rates for investment property valued according to the **cost model;**
- the existence and amounts of restrictions on the investment property; and
- material contractual obligations to purchase, construct, or develop investment property or for repairs or enhancement to the property.

11.5.3 The **Statement of Comprehensive Income and notes** should include the following:

- rental income from investment property;
- direct operating expenses arising from an investment property that generated rental income; and
- direct operating expenses from an investment property that did not generate rental income.

11.5.4 The **Statement of Financial Position and notes** should include the following:

- When an entity applies the **fair value model:**
  - A detailed reconciliation of movements in the carrying amount during the period should be provided.

- In exceptional cases when an investment property cannot be measured at fair value (because of a lack of fair value), the reconciliation above should be separately disclosed from other investment property shown at fair value. In addition, a description of the property should be provided as well as an explanation of why fair value cannot be determined and the range of possible estimates within which fair value is likely to lie.

- When an entity applies the **cost model:**
  - All the disclosure requirements of IAS 16 should be furnished.
  - The fair value of investment property is disclosed by way of a note.

Decision Tree

Figure 11.1 summarizes the classification, recognition, and measurement issues of an investment property. The diagram is adapted from a decision tree in IAS 40.

FIGURE 11.1   Decision Tree

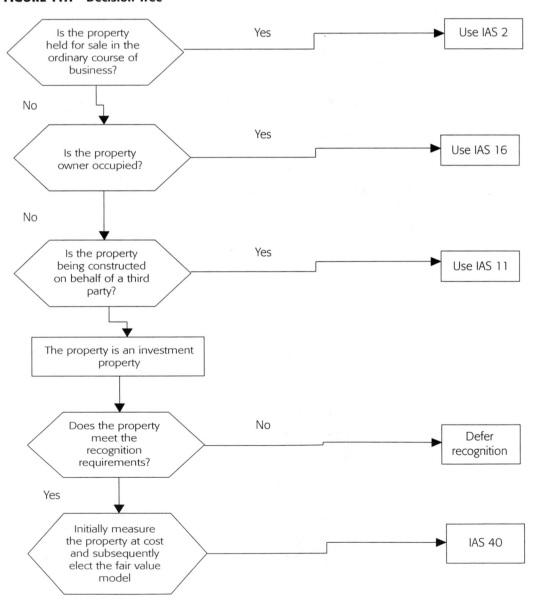

| 11.6 | **FINANCIAL ANALYSIS AND INTERPRETATION** |

Investment properties generate cash flows differently from properties used to house the entity's operating activities. By presenting investment properties separately from owner-occupied properties, users of the financial statements are able to distinguish between these two types of properties and obtain an understanding of the amount, timing, and nature of expected future cash flows.

| 11.7 | **COMMENTARY** |

11.7.1 While the application of the standard is relatively straightforward, there are some complications around the accounting for deferred tax on investment properties. The general principles relating to deferred tax are that deferred tax is provided at the rate that is expected to apply when the carrying amount of the asset is recovered. The tax laws and rates that are substantively enacted at the balance sheet date are used as an indicator of the laws and rates that will apply on realization of the asset. Per the definition of investment properties, the realization of the asset will happen either through rental income or sale. Therefore, the tax laws applicable to either rental income or capital sale will be applied on the realization of the asset. In many jurisdictions the tax rates applicable to capital sales differ from the tax rates applicable to rental income. In this case there is uncertainty about which rate should be used to determine the deferred tax applicable to the investment property. Some believe that a blended rate should be used that incorporates both rentals and the eventual sale of the property; others believe that only the rate applicable to the sale should be used. Yet others believe that the rate applicable to the rental income is appropriate.

11.7.2 There is a proposal in the IASB 2009 Annual Improvements project to remove the requirement to account for investment properties held for sale as inventory and instead account for such properties as noncurrent assets held for sale in terms of IFRS 5. There are no other significant future developments being proposed or considered for IAS 40. It is expected that the deferred tax complications described above will be considered by the IASB as part of their project on income taxes rather than as a project dealing with investment properties.

| 11.8 | **IMPLEMENTATION DECISIONS** |

The following table sets out some of the strategic and tactical decisions that should be considered when applying IAS 40.

Strategic decisions	Tactical decisions	Problems to overcome
The accounting policy, either cost model or revaluation model, should be decided on.	The methodologies to be used to determine fair value should be decided on.	It is generally difficult to determine the fair value of properties.
From time to time management may make a strategic decision that results in a change in the classification of investment property.	Changes in the classification of investment properties should be accounted for as transfers to or from investment property. Once the change has been decided on, the most appropriate classification should be confirmed.	These changes are expected to be infrequent and not result in significant problems in accounting for investment properties.

EXAMPLE: INVESTMENT PROPERTY

EXAMPLE 11.1

Matchbox Inc. manufactures toys for boys. The following information relates to fixed property owned by the company:

	$'000
Land—Plot 181 Hatfield	800
Buildings thereon (acquired June 30, 20X0)	2,100
Improvements to the building to extend rented floor capacity	400
Repairs and maintenance to investment property for the year	50
Rentals received for the year	160

Approximately 6 percent of the property's floor space is used as the administrative head office of the company. The property can be sold only as a complete unit. The remainder of the building is leased out under operating leases. The company provides lessees with security services.

The company values investment property using the fair value model. On December 31, 20X0, the Statement of Financial Position date, Mr. Proper (an independent valuer) valued the property at $3.6 million.

EXPLANATION

To account for the property in the financial statements of Matchbox Inc. at December 31, 20X0, the property should first be classified as either investment property or owner-occupied property. It is classified as an **investment property** and is accounted for in terms of the fair value model in IAS 40. As the portions of the property cannot be sold separately the entire property must be assessed under IAS 40. The motivation for classifying the whole property as investment property is that the portion occupied by the company for administrative purposes (6 percent) is insignificant and the security services rendered to the lessees are also insignificant. Furthermore, the majority of the floor space is used to generate rental income.

The accounting treatment and disclosure of the property in the financial statements of Matchbox Inc. are as follows:

Statement of Financial Position at December 31, 20X0

	Note	$'000
Noncurrent Assets		
Property, plant, and equipment		Xxx
Investment property (Calculation a)	4	3,600

Accounting policies

Investment property is property held to earn rentals. Investment property is measured at fair value with all changes in fair value recognized in profit or loss. The fair value is determined at the reporting date by an independent valuator based on market evidence of the most recent prices achieved in arm's-length transactions of similar properties in the same area.

Notes to the Financial Statements

Investment Property

	$'000
Opening balance	–
Additions	2,900
Improvements from subsequent expenditure	400
Net gain in fair value adjustments	300
Closing balance at fair value	3,600

Calculation a

Carrying Amount of Investment Property

	$'000
Land	800
Building	2,100
Improvements to building	400
	3,300
Fair value	(3,600)
Income	(300)
Increase in value shown in Statement of Comprehensive Income	300

CHAPTER 12

Agriculture (IAS 41)

12.1   **OBJECTIVE**

IAS 41 prescribes the accounting treatment, financial statement presentation, and disclosures related to biological assets and agricultural produce at the point of harvest insofar as they relate to agricultural activity.

Agricultural activity is a specialized industry, and therefore its accounting treatment is not covered by other standards. IAS 41 prescribes a fair value model for the accounting of agricultural produce, with the objective of recognizing changes in the fair value of biological assets over their lifetime rather than on sale or realization.

The accounting treatment of related government grants is also prescribed in IAS 41 (see also chapter 28, IAS 20).

12.2   **SCOPE OF THE STANDARD**

This standard should be applied to the following when they relate to agricultural activity:

- biological assets;
- agricultural produce at the point of harvest; and
- government grants.

This standard does **not** apply to:

- land related to agricultural activity (see chapter 10, IAS 16, Property, Plant, and Equipment; or chapter 11, IAS 40, Investment Property); or
- intangible assets related to agricultural activity (see chapter 13, IAS 38 Intangible Assets).

IAS 41 does not deal with processing agricultural produce after harvest; for example, it does not deal with processing grapes into wine or wool into yarn. Such processing is accounted for as inventory in accordance with IAS 2, Inventory (refer to chapter 16).

12.3 KEY CONCEPTS

12.3.1 Agricultural activity is the management by an entity of the biological transformation and harvest of biological assets for sale, or for conversion into agricultural produce or into additional biological assets. The key criterion for determining whether an activity represents agricultural activity is the active management of biological transformation. For example, fish farming would be considered agricultural activity, as the biological transformation is actively managed. Harvesting from unmanaged sources, such as fishing in the ocean, is not agricultural activity.

12.3.2 Agricultural produce is the harvested product of the entity's biological assets.

12.3.3 A **biological asset** is a living animal or plant.

12.3.4 Harvest is the detachment of produce from a biological asset or the cessation of a biological asset's life processes.

These concepts can be explained by the following table, reproduced from IAS 41:

Biological assets	Agricultural produce	Products that are the result of processing after harvesting
Sheep	Wool	Yarn, carpet
Trees in a plantation forest	Felled trees	Log, lumber
Plants	Cotton	Thread, clothing
	Harvested cane	Sugar
Dairy cattle	Milk	Cheese
Pigs	Carcass	Sausages, cured hams
Bushes	Leaf	Tea, cured tobacco
Vines	Grapes	Wine
Fruit trees	Picked fruit	Processed fruit

12.3.5 Fair value is the amount for which an asset could be exchanged between knowledgeable, willing parties in an arm's length transaction.

12.3.6 An **active market** is a market where all the following conditions exist:

- The items traded within the market are homogeneous.
- Willing buyers and sellers can normally be found at any time.
- Prices are available to the public.

12.4 **ACCOUNTING TREATMENT**

Recognition

12.4.1 An entity should **recognize** a biological asset or agricultural produce when, and only when

- the entity controls the asset as a result of past events;
- it is probable that future economic benefits associated with the asset will flow to the entity; and
- the fair value or cost of the asset can be measured reliably.

Measurement

12.4.2 A biological asset should be **measured on initial recognition** and at each subsequent reporting date at its fair value less estimated point-of-sale costs. However, if on initial recognition it is determined that fair value cannot be measured reliably, a biological asset should be measured at cost less accumulated depreciation and any accumulated impairment losses. Once the fair value of such an asset becomes reliably measurable, it should be measured at fair value less estimated point-of-sale costs.

12.4.3 Agricultural produce **harvested** from an entity's biological assets should be measured at its fair value less estimated point-of-sale costs at the point of harvest. Such measurement is the cost at that date when applying IAS 2 or any other applicable IFRS.

12.4.4 If an **active market** exists for a biological asset or harvested produce, the quoted price in that market is the appropriate basis for determining the fair value of that asset. The fair value of an asset is based on its current location and condition and reflects the market price less transport and other costs necessary to get an asset to the market. Entities often enter into contracts to sell biological asset or agricultural produce at a future date. The fair value of biological assets or agricultural produce is not adjusted because of the existence of a contract.

12.4.5 If an active market does not exist, an entity uses one or more of the following in determining fair value:

- the most recent market transaction price;
- market prices for similar assets; or
- sector benchmarks such as the value of an orchard expressed per export tray, bushel, or hectare, and the value of cattle expressed per kilogram of meat.

12.4.6 In some circumstances, reliable market-based prices may not be available for a biological asset in its current condition. In these circumstances an entity should determine the fair value with reference to the present value of net expected cash flows from the asset discounted at a current market-determined rate. IAS 41 provides guidance on the determination of the expected cash flows and discount rate.

12.4.7 A **gain or loss** on the **initial recognition** of a biological asset or agricultural produce at **fair value** (less estimated point-of-sale costs) and from a **change in fair value** (less estimated point-of-sale costs) of a biological asset should be included in net profit or loss for the period in which the gain or loss arises.

12.4.8 An unconditional **government grant** related to a biological asset measured at its fair value (less estimated point-of-sale costs) should be recognized as income only when the grant becomes receivable. If the government grant related to a biological asset measured at its fair value (less estimated point-of-sale costs) is conditional, an entity should recognize the grant in profit or loss when the conditions attaching to the grant are met. Government grants related to a biological asset measured at cost less accumulated depreciation and any accumulated impairment losses are accounted for in terms of IAS 20.

12.5 PRESENTATION AND DISCLOSURE

12.5.1 An entity should present the **carrying amount** of its biological assets **separately** on the face of its Statement of Financial Position.

12.5.2 An entity should disclose the **aggregate gain or loss** arising during the current period on initial recognition of biological assets and agricultural produce and from the change in fair value less estimated point-of-sale costs of biological assets.

12.5.3 An entity should provide a **description** of each group of biological assets.

12.5.4 An entity should **describe**

- the nature of its activities involving each group of biological assets; and
- nonfinancial measures or estimates of the physical quantities of:
  - each group of biological assets at the end of the period; and
  - output of agricultural produce during the period.

12.5.5 An entity should **disclose**

- the methods and significant assumptions applied in determining the fair value of each group of agricultural produce and biological assets;
- fair value less estimated point-of-sale costs of agricultural produce harvested during the period, determined at the point of harvest;
- the existence and carrying amounts of biological assets whose title is restricted, and the carrying amounts of biological assets pledged as security for liabilities; and
- the amount of commitments for the development or acquisition of biological assets and the financial risk-management strategies related to its agricultural activity.

12.5.6 An entity should **disclose** the following related to government grants received:

- the nature and extent of government grants recognized in the financial statements;
- unfulfilled conditions and other contingencies attaching to government grants; and
- significant decreases expected in the level of government grants.

12.5.7 An entity should present a **reconciliation** of changes in the carrying amount of biological assets between the beginning and the end of the current period, including:

- decreases due to sales;
- decreases due to harvest;
- increases resulting from business combinations;
- net exchange differences arising on the translation of financial statements of a foreign entity; and
- other changes.

12.5.8 The standard requires additional disclosures for biological assets measured at cost less accumulated depreciation and any accumulated impairment losses.

12.6   FINANCIAL ANALYSIS AND INTERPRETATION

12.6.1 As with any fair value standard, users should pay particular attention to the disclosure of key assumptions used to determine fair value and the consistency of those assumptions from year to year.

12.6.2 In particular, the discount rate estimation and estimation techniques used to determine volumes of agricultural assets are likely to have a significant impact on the fair value numbers.

12.7   COMMENTARY

12.7.1 IAS 41 requires that agricultural activities are initially measured at fair value, which is different from the historical cost model widely applied to the initial measurement of other assets in terms of IFRSs. The fair value model was adopted by the IASB as they believed that it provides more relevant information relating to the future economic benefits expected from biological assets.

12.7.2 The main factor that distinguishes agricultural activities from other activities is the active management of biological transformation. Management facilitates biological transformation by enhancing, or at least stabilizing, conditions necessary for the process to take place—for example, nutrient levels, moisture, temperature, fertility, and light.

12.7.3 Biological assets are measured at fair value and there is a rebuttable presumption that fair value can be reliably measured. The presumption can be rebutted only on initial recognition, for biological assets for which market-determined prices or values are not available and for which other alternative fair value estimates (such as present value of discounted cash flows) are determined to be clearly unreliable. Where the fair value of the biological asset cannot be reliably determined the biological asset should be measured at cost less accumulated depreciation and any accumulated impairment losses.

12.7.4 If the fair value of biological assets cannot be determined directly from quoted market prices or with reference to market prices, the fair value should be calculated as the present value of net expected cash flows. Determining the future cash flows and discount rate requires the entity to make estimates and judgments. These estimates and judgments need to be disclosed.

12.7.5 IAS 41 is only applied to biological assets and agricultural produce up to the point of harvest. From this point IAS 2 or another applicable IFRS will be applied. Ageing or maturation processes that occur after harvest are specifically excluded from the scope.

12.7.6 Currently the guidance on measuring fair value is dispersed across the various IFRSs and is not always consistent. The IASB is currently busy with a project on fair value measurement and will issue a standard that will establish a single source of guidance for all fair value measurements. The standard will clarify the definition of fair value and related guidance and will enhance the disclosures about fair value measurements.

12.7.7 The IASB issued an Exposure Draft of the proposed Fair Value Standard in 2009 and will most likely issue a final standard in 2010. The guidance relating to the determination of fair value currently contained in IAS 41 will be replaced by the new standard on fair value measurement.

12.8   **IMPLEMENTATION DECISIONS**

The following table sets out some of the strategic and tactical decisions that should be considered when applying IAS 41.

Strategic decisions	Tactical decisions	Problems to overcome
Determining whether the fair value of biological assets can be measured reliably.	A process should be implemented to decide how the fair value of each major class of biological asset will be determined. For each major class of biological assets, fair value should be determined: • based on market quoted prices; • with reference to market determined prices; • at the present value of future expected net cash flows from the asset; or • at cost (if market determined prices cannot be determined reliably).	Determining the fair value of biological assets in the following instances: • there are no quoted market prices in an active market for the specific agricultural products; • there are no market-determined prices for the assets in their present condition; • the fair value of biological assets cannot be reliably determined; and • where the fair value is determined using discounted cash flows, management should determine the appropriate market-related discount rate.
Determining when the point of harvest is for biological assets.	Distinguishing between produce, biological assets, and products that are a result of processing after harvest. For each major class of biological asset, an entity should document which processes are related to post-harvest processing and biological transformation.	

EXAMPLES: AGRICULTURE

EXAMPLE 12.1: XYZ DAIRY LTD. FINANCIAL STATEMENTS

Statement of Financial Position

XYZ Dairy Ltd. Statement of Financial Position	Notes	December 31, 20X1	December 31, 20X0
ASSETS			
Noncurrent Assets			
Dairy livestock—immature		52,060	47,730
Dairy livestock—mature		372,990	411,840
Subtotal Biological Assets	3	425,050	459,570
Property, plant, and equipment		1,462,650	1,409,800
Total Noncurrent Assets		1,887,700	1,869,370
Current Assets			
Inventories		82,950	70,650
Trade and other receivables		88,000	65,000
Cash		10,000	10,000
Total Current Assets		180,950	145,650
TOTAL ASSETS		2,068,650	2,015,020
EQUITY AND LIABILITIES			
Equity			
Issued capital		1,000,000	1,000,000
Accumulated profits		902,828	865,000
Total Equity		1,902,828	1,865,000
Current Liabilities			
Trade and other payables		165,822	150,020
Total Current Liabilities		165,822	150,020
TOTAL EQUITY AND LIABILITIES		2,068,650	2,015,020

An enterprise is encouraged but not required to provide a quantified description of each group of biological assets, distinguishing between consumable and bearer biological assets or between mature and immature biological assets, as appropriate. An enterprise discloses the basis for making any such distinctions.

(continued)

EXAMPLE 12.1, continued

Statement of Comprehensive Income

XYZ Dairy Ltd. Statement of Comprehensive Income	Notes	Year Ended December 31, 20X1
Fair value of milk produced		518,240
Gains arising from changes in fair value less estimated point-of-sale costs of dairy livestock	3	39,930
Total Income		**558,170**
Inventories used		(137,523)
Staff costs		(127,283)
Depreciation expense		(15,250)
Other operating expenses		(197,092)
		(477,148)
Profit from Operations		**81,022**
Income tax expense		(43,194)
Net Profit for the Period		37,828

Statement of Changes in Equity

XYZ Dairy Ltd. Statement of Changes in Equity	Year Ended December 31, 20X1		
	Share Capital	**Accumulated Profits**	**Total**
Balance at January 1, 20X1	1,000,000	865,000	1,865,000
Net profit for the period		37,828	37,828
Balance at December 31, 20X1	1,000,000	902,828	1,902,828

Statement of Cash Flows

XYZ Dairy Ltd. Cash Flow Statement	Notes	Year Ended December 31, 20X1
Cash Flows from Operating Activities		
Cash receipts from sales of milk		498,027
Cash receipts from sales of livestock		97,913
Cash paid for supplies and to employees		(460,831)
Cash paid for purchases of livestock		(23,815)
		111,294
Income taxes paid		(43,194)
Net Cash from Operating Activities		68,100
Cash Flows from Investing Activities		
Purchase of property, plant, and equipment		(68,100)
Net Cash Used in Investing Activities		**(68,100)**
Net Increase in Cash		0
Cash at Beginning of Period		10,000
Cash at End of Period		10,000

Notes to the Financial Statements

Note 1. Operations and Principal Activities

XYZ Dairy Ltd. ("the Company") is engaged in milk production for supply to various customers. At December 31, 20X1, the Company held 419 cows able to produce milk (mature assets) and 137 heifers being raised to produce milk in the future (immature assets). The Company produced 157,584 kg of milk with a fair value less estimated point-of-sale costs of 518,240 (determined at the time of milking) in the year ended December 31,20X1.

Note 2. Accounting Policies

Livestock and milk.

Livestock are measured at their fair value less estimated point-of-sale costs. The fair value of livestock is determined based on market prices of livestock of similar age, breed, and genetic merit. Milk is initially measured at its fair value less estimated point-of-sale costs at the time of milking. The fair value of milk is determined based on market prices in the local area.

Note 3. Biological Assets

Reconciliation of Carrying Amounts of Dairy Livestock	20X1
Carrying Amount at January 1, 20X1	459,570
Increases due to purchases	26,250
Gain arising from changes in fair value less estimated point-of-sale costs attributable to physical changes	15,350
Gain arising from changes in fair value less estimated point-of-sale costs attributable to price changes	24,580
Decreases due to sales	(100,700)
Carrying Amount at December 31, 20X1	425,050

Note 4. Financial Risk-Management Strategies

The Company is exposed to financial risks arising from changes in milk prices. The Company does not anticipate that milk prices will decline significantly in the foreseeable future and, therefore, has not entered into derivatives or other contracts to manage the risk of a decline in milk prices. The Company reviews its outlook for milk prices regularly in considering the need for active financial risk management.

Source: International Accounting Standards Board, IAS 41: Agriculture, pp. 2361–365. Used with permission.

EXAMPLE 12.2: PHYSICAL CHANGE AND PRICE CHANGE

Background

The following example illustrates how to separate physical change and price change. Separating the change in fair value less estimated point-of-sale costs between the portion attributable to physical changes and the portion attributable to price changes is encouraged but not required by this standard.

Example

A herd of 10 two-year-old animals was held at January 1, 20X1. One animal 2.5 years of age was purchased on July 1, 20X1, for $108, and one animal was born on July 1, 20X1. No animals were sold or disposed of during the period. Per-unit fair values less estimated point-of-sale costs were as follows:

Animal Details	$	$
2-year-old animal at January 1, 20X1	100	
Newborn animal at July 1, 20X1	70	
2.5-year-old animal at July 1, 20X1	108	
Newborn animal at December 31, 20X1	72	
0.5-year-old animal at December 31, 20X1	80	
2-year-old animal at December 31, 20X1	105	
2.5-year-old animal at December 31, 20X1	111	
3-year-old animal at December 31, 20X1	120	
Fair value less estimated point-of-sale costs of herd on January 1, 20X1 (10 × 100)		1,000
Purchase on July 1, 20X1 (1 × 108)	108	
Increase in fair value less estimated point-of-sale costs due to price change:		
10 × (105 − 100)	50	
1 × (111 − 108)	3	
1 × (72 − 70)	2	55
Increase in fair value less estimated point-of-sale costs due to physical change:		
10 × (120 − 105)	150	
1 × (120 − 111)	9	
1 × (80 − 72)		8
1 × 70	70	237
Fair value less estimated point-of-sale costs of herd on December 31, 20X1		
11 × 120	1,320	
1 × 80	80	1,400

Source: International Accounting Standards Board, IAS 41: Agriculture, p. 2301. Used with permission.

EXAMPLE 12.3

In year 20X0, a farmer plants an apple orchard that costs him $250,000. At the end of year 20X1, the following facts regarding the orchard are available:

Disease. There has been widespread disease in the apple tree population. As a result there is no active market for the orchard, but the situation is expected to clear in six months. After the six months, it should also be clear which types of trees are susceptible to infection and which ones are not. Until that time, nobody is willing to risk an infected orchard.

Precedent. The last sale by the farmer of an orchard was six months ago at a price of $150,000. He is not sure which way the market has gone since then.

Local values. The farmers in the region have an average value of $195,000 for their orchards of a similar size.

National values. The farmer recently read in a local agricultural magazine that the average price of an apple tree orchard is $225,000.

What is the correct valuation of the apple tree orchard?

EXPLANATION

The valuation would be the fair value less estimated point-of-sales costs. Fair value is determined as follows:

- Use active market prices—there are none, due to the disease.
- Use other relevant information, such as
  - The most recent market transaction $150,000
  - Market prices for similar assets $195,000
  - Sector benchmarks $225,000

If the fair value **cannot** be determined, then the valuation would be determined at cost, less accumulated depreciation and accumulated impairment losses: $250,000.

However, there are other reliable sources available for the determination of fair value. Such sources should be used. The mean value of all the available indicators above would be used (in the range of $150,000 to $225,000).

In addition, the farmer would consider the reasons for the differences between the various sources of other information, prior to arriving at the most reliable estimate of fair value.

In the absence of recent prices, sector benchmarks, and other information, the farmer should calculate the fair value as comprising the cost price, less impairments, less depreciation—resulting in a valuation of $250,000.

Source: Deloitte Touche Tohmatsu.

CHAPTER 13

Intangible Assets (IAS 38)

| 13.1 | **OBJECTIVE** |

An intangible asset is one that has no physical form, although it exists from contractual and legal rights and has an economic value. The objective of IAS 38 is to allow entities to identify and recognize separately the value of intangible assets on the Statement of Financial Position, providing certain conditions are satisfied. IAS 38 enables users to more accurately assess the value as well as the makeup of assets of the entity.

| 13.2 | **SCOPE OF THE STANDARD** |

IAS 38 applies to all intangible assets that are not specifically dealt with in another standard. Examples include brand names, computer software, licenses, franchises, intangibles under development, and goodwill. Examples of assets dealt with by other standards include Financial Instruments, addressed in IAS 32, and the Exploration for and Evaluation of Mineral Resources, addressed in IFRS 6.

IAS 38 prescribes the accounting treatment of intangible assets, including

- the definition of an intangible asset;
- recognition as an asset;
- determination of the carrying amount;
- determination and treatment of impairment losses; and
- disclosure requirements.

| 13.3 | **KEY CONCEPTS** |

13.3.1 An intangible asset is an identifiable nonmonetary asset

- without physical substance;
- that is separable—in other words, that is capable of being separated from the entity and sold, transferred, licensed, rented, or exchanged, either individually or together with a related contract, asset, or liability; or
- that arises from contractual or other legal rights, regardless of whether those rights are transferable or separable from the entity or other rights and obligations.

13.3.2 **Development** is the application of research findings or other knowledge to a plan or design for the production of new or substantially improved materials, devices, products, processes, systems, or services before the start of commercial production or use.

13.3.3 **Research** is original and planned investigation undertaken with prospect of gaining new scientific or technical knowledge and understanding.

13.4   ACCOUNTING TREATMENT

Recognition

13.4.1 An intangible asset is **recognized** as an asset (in terms of the framework) if

- it meets the definition of an intangible asset;
- it is **probable** that the future economic benefits attributable to the asset will flow to the entity; and
- the cost of the asset can be **measured reliably**.

13.4.2 Internally generated goodwill may not be recognized. Other internally generated intangible assets that may not be recognized include brands, mastheads, customer lists, and similar items that are not acquired through a business combination.

13.4.3 **Development expenditure** is recognized as an intangible asset if *all* of the following can be demonstrated:

- the technical feasibility of completing the intangible asset so that it will be available for use or sale (the "eureka" moment where one can state with certainty that a product will result from the efforts);
- the availability of adequate technical, financial, and other resources to complete the development of the intangible asset and to use or sell it;
- the intention to complete the intangible asset and use or sell it;
- the ability to use or sell the intangible asset;
- the demonstration of how the intangible asset will generate probable future economic benefits; and
- the ability to measure the expenditure.

13.4.4 **Development expenditure** previously recognized as an expense cannot be subsequently capitalized as an asset.

13.4.5 **Research expenditure** is recognized as an expense when incurred.

13.4.6 Expenses related to the following categories are *not* recognized as intangible assets and are **expensed**:

- internally generated brands (externally purchased brand names might qualify for capitalization if independently valued)
- mastheads, publishing titles, customer lists, and so on;
- start-up costs;
- training costs;
- advertising and promotion;
- relocation and reorganization expenses;
- redundancy and other termination costs; and
- expenses after the asset is capable of operating for its intended purpose.

TABLE 13.1 Items Included in Cost at Initial Recognition

Initial measurement	Cost	
	Included	**Excluded**
Separate acquisition	▪ cash paid ▪ import duties and nonrefundable taxes less rebates ▪ costs of employee benefits (as defined in IAS 19) ▪ directly related professional fees ▪ costs of testing whether the asset is functioning properly	▪ costs of introducing a new product or service ▪ costs of conducting business in a new location or with a new class of customer ▪ administration and other general overhead costs ▪ operating losses ▪ costs incurred while asset is capable of operating as intended but has not been brought into use
Developed intangible asset	▪ costs of materials and services used ▪ costs of employee benefits (as defined in IAS 19) ▪ fees to register a legal right ▪ amortization of patents and licenses that are used	▪ selling, administrative, and other general overhead expenditure unless this expenditure can be directly attributed to preparing the asset for use ▪ identified inefficiencies and initial operating losses incurred before the asset achieves planned performance ▪ expenditure on training staff to operate the asset
Exchange of asset	Fair value on date of exchange transaction	
Through a business combination	Fair value on acquisition date	

Initial Measurement

13.4.6 On initial recognition, an intangible asset is measured at cost, whether it is acquired externally or developed internally.

13.4.7 For any internal project to create an intangible asset, the research phase and development phase should be distinguished from one another. **Research expenditure** is treated as an expense. **Development expenditure** qualifying for recognition is measured at **cost**.

Subsequent Measurement

13.4.8 Subsequent to initial recognition, an entity should choose either the **cost model** or the **revaluation model** as its accounting policy for intangible assets and should apply that policy to an entire class of intangible assets:

- **Cost model.** The **carrying amount** of an intangible asset is its cost less accumulated amortization.
- **Revaluation model.** The **carrying amount** of an intangible asset is its fair value less subsequent accumulated amortization and impairment losses.

Assets classified as held for sale are shown at the lower of fair value less costs to sell and carrying amount.

TABLE 13.2 Examples of Research and Development Activities

Research phase	Development phase
In the research phase of an internal project, an entity cannot demonstrate that an intangible asset exists that will generate probable future economic benefits.	In the development phase of an internal project, an entity can identify an intangible asset and demonstrate that the asset will generate probable future economic benefits.
The following are examples of research activities: ▨ activities aimed at obtaining new knowledge; ▨ the search for, evaluation and final selection of, applications of research findings or other knowledge; ▨ the search for alternatives for materials, devices, products, processes, systems, or services; and ▨ the formulation, design, evaluation, and final selection of possible alternatives for new or improved materials, devices, products, processes, systems, or services.	The following are examples of development activities: ▨ the design, construction, and testing of pre-production or pre-use prototypes and models; ▨ the design of tools, jigs, moulds, and dies involving new technology; ▨ the design, construction, and operation of a pilot plant that is not of a scale economically feasible for commercial production; ▨ the design, construction, and testing of a chosen alternative for new or improved materials, devices, products, processes, systems, or services.

13.4.9 An entity should assess whether the **useful life** of an intangible asset is **finite** or **infinite**. If finite, the entity should determine the length of its life or the number of production or similar units constituting its useful life. Amortization and impairment principles apply as follows:

▨ An intangible asset with a **finite** useful life is amortized on a systematic basis over the best estimate of its useful life. The amount amortized is the cost of the asset less its residual value. An impairment test should be performed if an impairment indicator is identified.

▨ An intangible asset with an **infinite** useful life should be tested for impairment annually, but not amortized.

An entity should review the useful life and the residual value on an annual basis.

13.4.10 **Revaluation gains or loss.** Adjustments to the carrying value are treated as follows:

▨ Increases should be **credited** directly to **other comprehensive income** under the heading of revaluation surplus. A reversal of a previous loss for the same asset is reported in profit or loss.

▨ Decreases should be recognized (debited) in profit or loss. A reversal of a profit previously taken to other comprehensive income can be debited to other comprehensive income.

13.4.11 To assess whether an **intangible asset** might be **impaired**, an entity should apply IAS 36, Impairment of Assets. Also, that standard requires an entity to estimate, at least annually, the recoverable amount of an intangible asset that is not yet available for use.

13.4.12 In the case of a business combination, expenditure on an intangible item that does not meet both the definition and recognition criteria for an intangible asset should form part of the amount attributed to goodwill.

13.4.13 An intangible asset should be derecognized on disposal or when no future economic benefits are expected from its use or disposal. The gain or loss that arises from the derecognition should be included in profit or loss.

13.5　PRESENTATION AND DISCLOSURE

13.5.1 Each class of intangible assets should distinguish between **internally generated** and **other** intangibles.

13.5.2 Accounting policies should specify

- measurement bases;
- amortization methods; and
- useful lives or amortization rates (this could also be disclosed elsewhere in the financial statements as it is an accounting estimate).

13.5.3 The **Statement of Comprehensive Income and notes** should disclose

- the amortization charge for each class of asset, indicating the line item in which it is included; and
- the total amount of research and development costs recognized as an expense.

13.5.4 The **Statement of Financial Position and notes** should disclose the following:

- gross carrying amount (book value) less accumulated depreciation for each class of asset at the beginning and the end of the period;
- detailed itemized reconciliation of movements in the carrying amount during the period;
- if an intangible asset is amortized over more than 20 years, evidence that rebuts the presumption that the useful life will not exceed 20 years;
- carrying amount of intangibles pledged as security;
- carrying amount of intangibles whose title is restricted;
- capital commitments for the acquisition of intangibles;
- a description, the carrying amount, and remaining amortization period of any intangible that is material to the financial statements of the entity as a whole;
- for intangible assets acquired by way of a government grant and initially recognized at fair value:
  - the fair value initially recognized for these assets;
  - their carrying amount; and
  - whether they are measured at the benchmark or allowed alternative treatment.

13.5.5 Additional disclosures required for revalued amounts are as follows:

- effective date of the revaluation;
- carrying amount of *each* class of intangibles had it been carried in the financial statements on the historical cost basis;
- amount as well as a detailed reconciliation of the balance of the revaluation surplus; and
- any restrictions on the distribution of the revaluation surplus.

13.6　FINANCIAL ANALYSIS AND INTERPRETATION

13.6.1 This accounting standard determines that the intangible assets reported on a statement of financial position are only those intangibles that have been purchased or manufactured (in limited instances). However, companies have intangible assets that are not recorded on their statements of financial position; these intangible assets include management skill, valuable trademarks and name recognition, a good reputation, proprietary products, and so forth. Such assets are valuable and would fetch their worth if a company were to be sold.

13.6.2 Analysts should try to assess the value of such assets based on a company's ability to earn economic profits or rents from them, even though it is difficult to do so.

13.6.3 Financial analysts have traditionally viewed the values assigned to intangible assets with suspicion. Consequently, in adjusting financial statements, they often exclude the book value assigned to intangibles (reducing net equity by an equal amount and increasing pretax income by the amortization expense associated with the intangibles).

13.6.4 This arbitrary assignment of zero value to intangibles might also be inadvisable. The analyst should decide if there is any extra earning power attributable to goodwill or any other intangible asset. If there is, it is a valuable asset.

13.6.5 An issue to be considered when comparing the returns on equity or assets of various companies is the degree of recognized intangible assets. An entity that has acquired many of its intangible assets in mergers and acquisitions will typically have a significantly higher amount of such assets in its Statement of Financial Position (and hence lower returns on equity and assets) than an equivalent entity that has developed most of its intangible assets internally.

13.7   EVALUATION

13.7.1 In practice there are differing views regarding when the research phase stops and when the development phase starts. There are also different views regarding which costs may be recognized as an intangible asset.

13.8   FUTURE DEVELOPMENTS

13.8.1 The IASB issued an exposure draft on rate regulated activities in July 2009. The proposed standard will apply where a regulator places a restriction on an entity's ability to set the prices to be charged for its services or products. The proposal is in line with U.S. SFAS 71, Accounting for the Effects of Certain Types of Regulation.

13.8.2 The exposure draft proposes that where an entity has the right or obligation to increase or decrease rates in future periods as a result of the actual or expected actions of the regulator, the entity must recognize the following:

- a regulatory asset for its right to recover specific previously incurred costs and to earn a specified return; or
- a regulatory liability for its obligation to refund previously collected amounts and to pay a specified return.

13.9   IMPLEMENTATION DECISIONS

The following table sets out some of the strategic and tactical decisions that should be considered when applying IAS 38.

Strategic decisions	Tactical decisions	Problems to overcome
Identifying the research and development phase of an internally generated intangible asset.	Management should put measures in place to separate the research phase and the development phase. If the research and the development phase cannot be separated, the whole cost should be expensed.	The treatment of variances during the research and development phase.
The accounting policy, being either the cost model or revaluation model should be determined.	If management wants to elect the revaluation model, an active market must exist where fair values can be obtained regularly. If the revaluation model is selected, a decision should be taken as to how frequently the revaluation should take place.	The existence of an active market for intangible assets is uncommon.
An amortization policy should be determined.	The useful lives and the residual value of the intangible should be assessed annually. The residual value of an intangible asset with a finite useful life should be assumed to be zero unless a third party has committed to purchase the intangible or there is an active market for the asset.	Determining whether an intangible asset has a finite or indefinite useful life could be difficult.

EXAMPLE: INTANGIBLE ASSETS

EXAMPLE 13.1

Alpha Inc., a motor vehicle manufacturer, has a research division that worked on the following projects during the year:

- **Project 1:** The design of a steering mechanism that does not operate like a conventional steering wheel, but reacts to the impulses from a driver's fingers

- **Project 2:** The design of a welding apparatus that is controlled electronically rather than mechanically

The following is a summary of the expenses of the particular department:

	General $'000	Project 1 $'000	Project 2 $'000
Material and services	128	935	620
Labor			
Direct labor	–	620	320
Department head salary	400	–	–
Administrative personnel	725	–	–
Overhead			
Direct	–	340	410
Indirect	270	110	60

The department head spent 15 percent of his time on Project 1 and 10 percent of his time on Project 2.

EXPLANATION

The capitalization of development costs for the year would be as follows:

	$'000
Project 1. The activity is classified as research, and all costs are recognized as expenses	—
Project 2. (620 + 320 + 10% x 400 + 410 + 60)	1,450
	1,450

CHAPTER 14

Leases (IAS 17)

14.1	**OBJECTIVE**

Lease accounting is mainly concerned with the appropriate criteria for the recognition, as well as the measurement, of the leased asset and liability from the perspectives of both a lessor and lessee. Associated with this objective is the distinction between a finance lease (which is recognized as an asset by the lessee and is depreciated) and an operating lease (which is expensed by the lessee as the charges occur). Substance over legal form is imperative in lease accounting as the legal form of lease transactions does not always coincide with its substance and resulting accounting treatment.

14.2	**SCOPE OF THE STANDARD**

14.2.1 This standard should be applied in accounting for **all leases** other than:

- leases to explore for or use minerals, oil, natural gas, and similar non-regenerative resources; and
- licensing agreements for such items as motion picture films, video recordings, plays, manuscripts, patents, and copyrights.

However, this standard should also *not* be applied as the basis of measurement for:

- property held by lessees that is accounted for as investment property (see IAS 40);
- investment property provided by lessors under operating leases (see IAS 40);
- biological assets held by lessees under finance leases (see IAS 41); or
- biological assets provided by lessors under operating leases (see IAS 41).

14.2.2 The standard prescribes, for **lessees** and **lessors**, the appropriate accounting policies and disclosure that should be applied to various types of lease transactions. It specifies the criteria for distinguishing between finance leases and operating leases, the recognition and measurement of the resulting assets and liabilities, as well as disclosures.

14.3	**KEY CONCEPTS**

14.3.1 A **lease** is an agreement whereby the **lessor** conveys to the **lessee**, in return for a payment or series of payments, the **right to use** an asset for an agreed period of time.

14.3.2 **Finance leases** transfer substantially all the risks and rewards incidental to ownership of an asset, whether title is or is not eventually transferred.

14.3.3 The characteristics of **finance leases can** include the following:

- The lease transfers ownership of the asset to the lessee at the expiration of the lease.
- The lessee has an option to purchase the asset at less than fair value and at inception it is reasonably certain that the option will be exercised.
- The lease term is for a major part of the economic life of the asset.
- At inception, the present value of the minimum lease payments approximates substantially all of the fair value of the leased asset.
- The leased asset is of a specialized nature and suitable only for use by the lessee.
- The lessee can cancel the lease and on cancellation will bear cancellation losses.
- The gains or losses on the fluctuation of the fair value of the residual value accrue to the lessee, such as a rent rebate at the end of the lease that is equal to most of the sales proceeds.
- The lessee has the option to continue the lease for a secondary period at substantially lower than market rent.

14.3.4 **Operating leases** are leases other than finance leases.

14.3.5 **Minimum lease payments** are the payments over the lease term that the lessee is required to make to the lessor. Certain contingent rental and other items are excluded. However, if the lessee has an option to purchase the asset at a price that is expected to be sufficiently less than fair value at the date the option becomes exercisable, the minimum lease payments comprise the minimum payments payable over the lease term to the expected date of exercise of this purchase option plus the payment required to exercise it.

14.3.6 **Guaranteed residual value** is that part of the residual value of a leased asset that is guaranteed by the lessee or a third party. The third party must be related to the lessee, unrelated to the lessor, and financially capable of paying the guarantee. It is a guarantee for the maximum amount that could become payable and is excluded from the minimum lease payments.

14.3.7 **Unguaranteed residual value** is that portion of the residual value of the leased asset, the realization of which is not guaranteed or is guaranteed by a party related to the lessor.

14.3.8 **The inception date of the lease** is the date on which a lease is classified as operating or finance and the relevant amounts determined (such as the present value of the minimum lease payments). It is the earliest of the lease agreement date and the date the parties commit to the principal provisions of the lease.

14.3.9 **The commencement date of the lease** is the date from which the lessee is entitled to use the related asset. This is the date that the lease is originally recognized in the financial statements of both parties.

14.4   **ACCOUNTING TREATMENT**

Identification of Lease Transactions

14.4.1 In identifying lease transactions to which this lease accounting should be applied, substance over legal form is imperative as there may be transactions that are leases in their legal form but not in substance and vice versa. The following interpretations address these situations:

- **SIC 27:** Applicable where transactions are leases in legal form but not in substance. These legal leases fall outside of the scope of IAS 17. When transactions take the legal form of a lease (for example they state the words "lease" on the contract), the transactions should be evaluated to ascertain if they are in fact leases in substance. This is determined by applying the definition of a lease per IAS 17—that is, an agreement that conveys the right of use of an asset in exchange for payments.
- **IFRIC 14:** Applicable where transactions are leases in substance and not in legal form. These legal leases fall within the scope of IAS 17. Conditions that indicate such transactions include where the contract's fulfillment depends on the use of a specific asset and where the arrangement conveys right of use of an asset. Other costs related to the transaction should be separated from the lease costs and should be separately accounted for (that is, not under IAS 17).

Classification of Leases

14.4.2 The **classification** of leases as operating or finance is done at the **inception** of the lease. The substance rather than the legal form of the lease contract is indicative of the classification. The classification is based on the extent to which risks and rewards incidental to ownership of a leased asset lie with the lessor or the lessee. If **substantially all** of the risks and rewards are transferred to the lessee it is a finance lease. This is usually indicated by certain conditions or clauses within the contract as described under point 14.3.3 above.

- **Risks** include potential losses from idle capacity, technological obsolescence, and variations in return because of changing economic conditions.
- **Rewards** include the expectation of profitable operation over the asset's economic life and of gain from appreciation in value or the realization of a residual value.

14.4.3 Leases of land are normally considered to be operating leases as land has an indefinite useful life and the lessee does not receive all the risks and rewards of ownership (unless title specifically transfers to the lessee at the end of the lease). Where there is a lease of land and buildings the lease must be **considered separately** for the portion related to land and the portion related to the buildings and classified accordingly. This may result in classification of the two portions as different types of leases.

14.4.4 In terms of IAS 40 it is possible for a lessee to classify a **property interest held under an operating lease** as an investment property. In this situation, the property interest is accounted for as if it were a **finance lease**. The interest will continue to be accounted for as a finance lease even if the property is no longer classified as investment property.

TABLE 14.1 Classification of a Lease—Summary

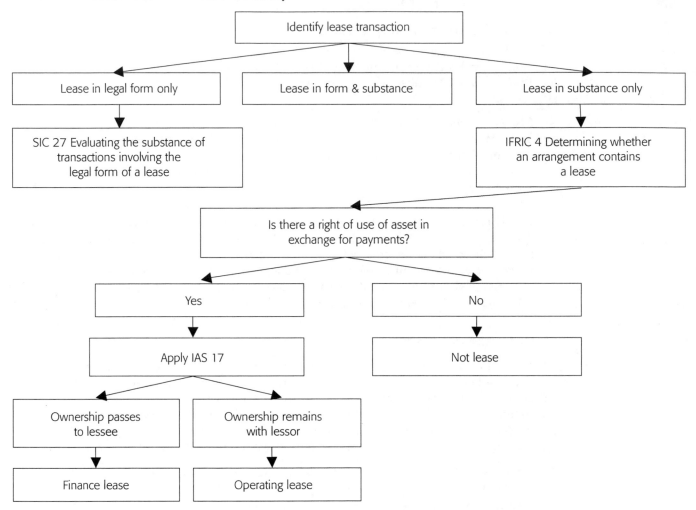

Accounting by Lessees

14.4.5 Under a **finance lease** the accounting treatment is as follows:

▨ At commencement date, the asset and a corresponding liability for future lease payments are recognized at the same amount, which is the lower of the fair value of the leased asset or the present value of the minimum lease payments at that date.

▨ Initial direct costs in connection with lease activities are capitalized to the asset.

▨ Lease payments consist of the finance charge and the reduction of the outstanding liability.

▨ The finance charge is to be a constant periodic rate of interest on the remaining balance of the liability for each period. It must be allocated to profit or loss for each period.

▨ Depreciation and impairment of the leased asset is recognized in terms of IAS 16, IAS 38, and IAS 36. The asset must be depreciated over the shorter of its useful life or the lease term.

14.4.6 Operating lease payments (excluding costs for services such as insurance) are recognized as an expense in the Statement of Comprehensive Income on a straight-line basis over the period of the lease, or a systematic basis that is representative of the time pattern of the user's benefit, even if the payments are not on that basis. The difference between the straight-line expense recognized and the actual rentals paid for a year is recognized as an operating lease asset or liability at reporting date in the statement of financial position.

14.4.7 **Operating lease incentives** provided by the lessor (such as reimbursements, interest free or rent free periods) are added or subtracted from the lease payments for the period and recognized on a straight-line basis over the period of lease.

Accounting by Lessors

14.4.8 Under a **finance lease** the lease is originally recognized on commencement date. The lessor derecognizes the related asset from its statement of financial position and recognizes a receivable for the minimum lease payments. In substance the lessor has sold the asset to the lessee and provided financing for this transaction.

14.4.9 The accounting treatment is as follows:

- The finance lease receivable is initially recognized and measured at the net investment in the lease, that is, the present value of the minimum lease payments that will be received.
- Finance income is recognized in the income statement based on a pattern reflecting a constant periodic rate of return on the net investment.
- Initial direct costs are deducted from the finance lease receivable (except for manufacturer or dealer lessors).

14.4.10 **Manufacturer or dealer lessors** recognize a selling profit or loss in the same manner as for outright sales (that is, as part of revenue) in the period in which the lease commences. If artificially low interest rates are quoted on the lease, the selling profit to be recognized is limited to the profit that would arise if a market-related interest rate was charged. Costs incurred in negotiating and arranging the lease are recognized as expenses (cost of sales) when the related revenue is recognized.

14.4.11 In an **operating lease**, the lessor continues to exercise ownership of the related asset and the asset is recognized per IAS 16 or IAS 38 in the Statement of Financial Position of the lessor. The accounting treatment is as follows:

- Depreciation on the asset is recognized in terms of IAS 16 and IAS 38.
- Lease income is recognized in the Statement of Comprehensive Income on a straight-line basis over the lease term, unless another systematic basis is more representative.
- Initial direct costs are either recognized immediately as an expense or allocated against rent income over the lease term on the same basis as the rental.
- The difference between the straight-line expense recognized and the actual rentals paid for a year is recognized as an operating lease asset or liability at reporting date in the Statement of Financial Position.

Sale and Leaseback Transactions

14.4.12 A **sale and leaseback** is a transaction where one entity sells an asset to another entity (often a bank) and leases back the same asset. If it results in a **finance lease** ownership never really passes and remains with the seller/lessee. If it results in an **operating lease** ownership passes to the buyer/lessor.

14.4.13 If the leaseback is a **finance lease**, it is inappropriate to recognize the profit as income immediately. Any excess of sales proceeds over the carrying amount of the related asset should be deferred (an unearned income liability is recognized) and amortized to profit and loss over the lease term. The transaction is a means whereby the lessor **provides finance** to the lessee and the lessor retains risks and rewards of ownership.

TABLE 14.2 Treatment of Sale and Leaseback Operating Leases

	Carrying amount of asset = its fair value	Carrying amount of asset < its fair value	Carrying amount of asset > its fair value
1. Selling price = fair value	No profit/loss.	Recognize profit in profit/loss immediately.	Recognize loss in profit/loss immediately.
2. Selling price < fair value			
* loss compensated by rentals	Defer loss and amortize over lease period.	Defer loss and amortizes over lease period.	Carrying amount of asset should be written down to fair value.
* loss not compensated by rentals	Recognize loss in profit/loss immediately.	Recognize loss in profit/loss immediately.	Carrying amount of asset should be written down to fair value.
3. Selling price > fair value	Defer profit and amortize over lease period.	Defer profit and amortize over lease period.	Defer profit and amortizes over lease period (profit = fair value – selling price). If a loss, the carrying amount of the asset should be written down to fair value.

14.4.14 If the leaseback is classified as an **operating lease**, there is a sale and thus if the transaction is concluded **at fair value**, sales profit and loss is recognized immediately. Transactions **below or above fair value** are recorded as follows:

- If the **fair value is less than the carrying amount** of the asset, a loss equal to the difference is recognized immediately.
- If the **sale price is above fair value**, the excess over fair value should be deferred and amortized over the lease term.
- If the **sale price is below fair value**, any profit or loss is recognized immediately unless a loss is compensated for by future lease payments at below market price; in this case, the loss should be deferred and amortized in proportion to the lease payments.

14.5 PRESENTATION AND DISCLOSURE

14.5.1 Lessees—Finance Leases:

- the net carrying amount at reporting date for *each* class of asset;
- a reconciliation between the total future minimum lease payments and the present values of the lease liabilities in **three periodic bands**, namely:
  - not later than one year;
  - later than one year but not later than five years; and
  - later than five years;
- all related disclosures under IAS 16, IAS 36, IAS 38, and IAS 40 as relevant to the leased asset;
- general description of material leasing arrangements, such as the basis for contingent rent, the existence and terms of renewal, purchase options and escalation clauses, and restrictions imposed for further leasing;
- distinction between current and noncurrent lease liabilities;
- the total future minimum sublease payments expected to be received under non-cancellable subleases at reporting date;
- contingent rents recognized in expenses for the period; and

- the relevant requirements of IFRS 7, for example liquidity analysis, impairment, and credit risk.

Lessees—Operating Leases:

- general description of significant leasing arrangements (same information as for finance leases above);
- lease and sublease payments recognized as an expense in the current period, separating minimum lease payments, contingent rents, and sublease payments;
- future minimum noncancellable lease payments in the **three periodic bands** as described for finance leases; and
- the total future minimum sublease payments expected to be received under noncancellable subleases at reporting date.

14.5.2 Lessors—Finance Leases:

- a reconciliation of the total gross investment in the lease and the present value of minimum lease payments receivable at reporting date, in the **three periodic bands** as described under point 14.5.1 above;
- unearned finance income;
- the accumulated allowance for uncollectible minimum lease payments receivable;
- contingent rents recognized in income in the period;
- general description of material leasing arrangements; and
- unguaranteed residual values accruing to the lessor.

Lessors—Operating Leases:

- all related disclosures under IAS 16, IAS 36, IAS 38, and IAS 40 as relevant to the leased asset;
- general description of leasing arrangements;
- total future minimum lease payments under noncancellable operating leases in the **three periodic bands** as described under point 14.5.1; and
- total contingent rents recognized in income for the period.

14.5.3 For **sale and leaseback transactions**, the same disclosure requirements as for lessees and lessors above apply. Some items might be separately disclosable in terms of IAS 1.

14.6   **FINANCIAL ANALYSIS AND INTERPRETATION**

14.6.1 The effects of accounting for a lease in the financial statements of the lessee as an operating lease versus a finance lease can be summarized as follows:

- **Operating lease** accounting reports the lease payments as rental expense in the Statement of Comprehensive Income.
- The Statement of Financial Position is impacted only indirectly when the rental expense flows through to retained earnings via net income.
- The rental expense is reported as an **operating cash outflow** (as a part of the entity's net income) on the statement of cash flows.
- The total reported expense over the lease term should normally be the same for a **finance lease** as the total reported expense over the lease term would be under the **operating lease** method. However, costs are higher in the early years under the finance lease method, which causes the earnings trend to rise over the lease term.

- The **finance lease** method places both an asset and a net amount of debt on the Statement of Financial Position, whereas no such asset or debt items are reported under the **operating lease** method.

- Under **finance lease** accounting, the total lease payment is divided into an interest component and the repayment of principal. A depreciation component also arises when the principal (capital portion) is depreciated in terms of IAS 16. Under the **operating lease** method, the payment is simply a rental expense.

- Under the **operating lease** method, lease payments are reported as **operating cash outflows** (interest can be classified as a financing cash flow as well), whereas under the **finance lease** method, the cash outflow is normally allocated between operating and financing activities.

- The interest portion of the **finance lease** payment is normally reported as an **operating cash outflow**, whereas the repayment of the lease obligation portion is treated as a **financing cash outflow**. However, the net effect on total cash is the same in both methods.

- That portion of the lease obligation that is paid or eliminated within one year or one operating cycle, whichever is longer, is classified as a current liability. The remainder is classified as a long-term liability.

14.6.2 Why do companies lease assets and under what conditions will they favor operating or finance leases? Several possible answers can be given to this question, but it must be considered within the context of a specific situation; in other words, circumstances could arise that would invalidate the assumptions on which answers are based.

- Companies with low marginal tax rates or low taxable capacity generally find leasing to be advantageous, because they do not need or cannot obtain the tax advantages (depreciation) that go with the ownership of assets. In this case, either type of lease is appropriate. Companies with high tax rates prefer finance leases, because expenses are normally higher in early periods.

- Operating leases are advantageous when management compensation depends on return on assets or invested capital.

- An operating lease is advantageous when an entity wants to keep debt off of its Statement of Financial Position. This can help them if they have indenture covenants requiring low debt-to-equity ratios or high interest-coverage ratios.

- Finance leases are favored if an entity wants to show a high cash flow from operations.

- Finance leases have advantages when there is a comparative advantage to reselling property.

Table 14.3 summarizes the different effects of operating and finance leases on lessees' accounting, and table 14.4 summarizes the effects on lessors.

TABLE 14.3   Effect of Operating and Finance Leases on Lessee Financial Statements and Key Financial Ratios

Item or ratio	Operating lease	Finance lease
Statement of Financial Position	No effects because no assets or liabilities are created under the operating lease method.	A leased asset (equipment) and a lease obligation are created when the lease is recorded. Over the life of the lease, both are written off, but the asset is usually written down faster, creating a net liability during the life of the lease.
Statement of Comprehensive Income	The lease payment is recorded as an expense. These payments are often constant over the life of the lease.	Both interest expense and depreciation expense are created. In the early years of the lease, they combine to produce a higher expense than is reported under the operating method. However, over the life of the lease, the interest expense declines, causing the total expense trend to decline. This produces a positive trend in earnings. In the later years, earnings are higher under the finance lease method than under the operating lease method. Over the entire term of the lease, the total lease expenses are the same under both methods.
Statement of Cash Flows	The entire cash outflow paid on the lease is recorded as an operating cash outflow.	The cash outflow from the lease payments is allocated partly to an operating or financing cash outflow (interest expense) and partly to a financing cash outflow (repayment of the lease obligation principal). The depreciation of the leased asset is not a cash expense and, therefore, is not a cash flow item.
Profit Margin	Higher in the early years because the rental expense is normally less than the total expense reported under the finance lease method. However, in later years, it will be lower than under the finance lease method.	Lower in the early years because the total reported expense under the finance lease method is normally higher than the lease payment. However, the profit margin will trend upward over time, so in the later years it will exceed that of the operating lease method.
Asset Turnover	Higher because there are no leased assets recorded under the operating lease method.	Lower because of the leased asset (equipment) that is created under the finance lease method. The ratio rises over time as the asset is depreciated.
Current Ratio	Higher because no short-term debt is added to the Statement of Financial Position by the operating lease method.	Lower because the current portion of the lease obligation created under the finance lease method is a current liability. The current ratio falls farther over time as the current portion of the lease obligation rises.
Debt-to-Equity Ratio	Lower because the operating lease method creates no debt.	Higher because the finance lease method creates a lease obligation liability (which is higher than the leased asset in the early years). However, the debt-to equity ratio decreases over time as the lease obligation decreases.
Return on Assets	Higher in the early years because profits are higher and assets are lower.	Lower in the early years because earnings are lower and assets are higher. However, the return on asset ratio rises over time because the earnings trend is positive and the assets decline as they are depreciated.
Return on Equity	Higher in the early years because earnings are higher.	Lower in the early years because earnings are lower. However, the return on equity rises over time because of a positive earnings trend.
Interest Coverage	Higher because no interest expense occurs under the operating lease method.	Lower because interest expense is created by the finance lease method. However, the interest-coverage ratio rises over time because the interest expense declines over time.

TABLE 14.4   Effects of Leasing Methods Used by Lessors on Financial Statements and Ratios

Item or ratio	Operating lease	Sales-type financial lease	Direct-financing lease
Size of Assets	Lowest, because no investment write-up occurs. Low asset values tend to raise asset turnover ratios.	Highest, largely because of the sale of the leased asset. High asset value tends to lower asset turnover.	Middle, because there is an investment write-up, but no sale of the leased asset.
Size of Shareholders' Equity	Lowest, because no asset write-up occurs. Low shareholders' equity tends to raise returns on equity and debt or equity ratios.	Highest, largely because of the gain on the sale of the leased asset. High shareholders' equity tends to lower returns on equity and debt or equity ratios.	Middle, because the investment write-up adds to equity, but there is no sale of the leased asset.
Size of Income in Year Lease Is Initiated (Year 0)	No effect on income when lease is initiated.	Highest, because of the gain on the sale of the leased asset. High income tends to raise profit margins and returns on assets and equity.	No effect on income when lease is initiated.
Size of Income during Life of Lease (Years 1–3)	Middle, based on terms of the lease and method of depreciation. Income tends to be constant over time if lease receipts are fixed and straight-line depreciation is used.	Lowest, because of the relatively low prevailing interest rate. Interest income tends to decline over time. Low income tends to lower profit margins and returns on assets and equity.	Highest, because of the high effective return on the lease. Interest income tends to decline over time. High income tends to raise profit margins and returns on assets and equity.
Operating Cash Flow at Time Lease Is Initiated (Year 0)	No effect, because no cash flow occurs when lease is initiated.	Highest, because of the gain on the sale of the leased asset.	No effect, because no cash flow occurs when lease is signed.
Operating Cash Flow over Term of the Lease (Years 1–3)	Highest, because of the terms of the lease and the method of depreciation.	Lowest, because interest income is low.	Middle, because interest income is high due to high effective return on the lease.

14.7   **COMMENTARY**

14.7.1 As part of the second annual improvements project, separate consideration and classification of land and buildings in a lease will no longer be applicable for years beginning on or after January 1, 2010. The lease as a whole should be considered using the normal classification rules for finance and operating leases and the total lease must then be classified as either lease type based on the substance of the overall transaction.

14.7.2 In 2003 the IASB and FASB ("the Boards") embarked on a project to improve lease accounting by making it more consistent with the conceptual framework and definitions of assets and liabilities. The aim of the project is to amend or replace IAS 17. In March 2009 the Boards released their preliminary views in a discussion paper. During August 2010, the Boards released an exposure draft setting out their proposed accounting model for leases. The discussion paper only addressed the accounting treatment for lessees, while the exposure draft addresses both the accounting for lessees and lessors. The **most significant proposals** in the exposure draft include the following:

- There will be a **single accounting model** for all leases. That is, there will no longer be a split between the accounting treatment of finance and operating leases. All leases will result in the recognition of an asset (for the rights related to the lease) and a liability (for the obligation related to the lease).

- *The following are the main proposals relating to the accounting model to be applied by lessees:*
  - Rights arise in a lease transaction where there is a **right to use an asset**. This meets the definition of an asset in the framework and will result in an **asset being recognized for this right**.
  - The **obligation to pay rentals** and return the asset at the end of a lease term (where relevant) meets the definition of a liability in the framework and will result in the **recognition of a liability for this obligation**.
  - The **right-of-use asset** will be recognized and presented as a separate class of property, plant, and equipment. The asset will initially be measured at the present value of the lease payments plus any initial direct cost incurred. Subsequently the asset will either be amortized over the shorter of the lease term or its economic life or carried at its revalued amount.
  - The **obligation to pay rentals** will be recognized as a financial liability and will initially be measured at the present value of the lease payments. Subsequently the liability will be on an amortized cost basis.

- The exposure draft provides the following guidance relating to measurement:
  - Discount rate—this would be the lessee's incremental borrowing rate or the rate charged by the lessor if it can be readily determined.
  - Lease term—the lease term should be based on the longest possible lease term that is more likely than not to occur.
  - Contingent rentals, residual value guarantees, and term option penalties—these should be estimated and included in the lease payments based on a probability weighted average for a reasonable number of outcomes.

- *The following are the main proposals relating to the accounting model to be applied by lessors:*
  - When the lease transfers significant risks or benefits of the underlying asset to the lessee, the lessor would apply the **derecognition** approach.
  - When the lessor retains exposure to significant risks or benefits of the underlying asset, the lessor would apply the **performance obligation** approach.
  - The derecognition approach requires the lessor to derecognize a part of the underlying asset from its statement of financial position and recognize a right to receive lease payments. Under this approach, the lessor could record a gain upon commencement of the lease.
  - The performance obligation approach requires the lessor to continue recognizing the underlying asset on its statement of financial position. The lessor would recognize a right to receive lease payments and a liability to permit the lessee to use the underlying asset. Under this approach, the lessor records income over the expected life of the lease.
  - The lessor would initially recognize a right to receive lease payments and the liability to receive payments at the present value of the lease payments. Subsequently the right to receive lease payments is measured at amortized cost, using the effective interest rate method. The liability is amortized on the basis of use of the underlying asset, or on a straight-line basis if the pattern of use cannot be reliably determined.

- The guidance applicable to the measurement for the lessor is similar to that of the-lessee, with the exception of the following:
  - The discount rate would be the rate that the lessor charges the lessee.
  - Contingent rentals and amounts receivable under residual value guarantees would be included only if the lessor can measure them reliably.

EXAMPLES: LEASES

EXAMPLE 14.1

A manufacturing machine that costs $330,000 is acquired by a finance lease agreement under the following terms:

- The effective date is January 1, 20X2.
- The lease term is three years.
- Installments of $72,500 are payable half-yearly in arrears.
- The effective rate of interest is 23.5468 percent per year.
- A deposit of $30,000 is immediately payable at inception of the lease.

EXPLANATION

The amortization table for this transaction would be as follows:

	Installment $	Interest $	Capital $	Balance $
Cash Price	330,000			
Deposit	30,000	–	30,000	300,000
Installment 1	72,500	35,320	37,180	262,820
Installment 2	72,500	30,943	41,557	221,263
Subtotal	175,000	66,263	108,737	
Installment 3	72,500	26,050	46,450	174,813
Installment 4	72,500	20,581	51,919	122,894
Installment 5	72,500	14,469	58,031	64,863
Installment 6	72,500	7,637	64,863	–
TOTAL	465,000	135,000	330,000	

The finance lease would be recognized and presented in the financial statements as follows:

Books of the Lessee

An asset of $330,000 will be recorded and a corresponding liability will be raised on January 1, 20X2.

If it is assumed that the machine is depreciated on a straight-line basis over six years, the following expenses would be recognized in the **Statement of Comprehensive Income** for the first year:

Depreciation (330,000/6)	$55,000
Finance lease charges (35,320 + 30,943)	$66,263

The **Statement of Financial Position** at December 31, 20X2, would reflect the following balances:

Machine (330,000 – 55,000)	$275,000 (Asset)
Long-term finance lease liability	$221,263 (Liability)

Books of the Lessor

The gross amount of $465,000 due by the lessee would be recorded as a debtor at inception of the contract, that is, the deposit of $30,000 plus six installments of $72,500 each. The unearned finance income of $135,000 is recorded as a deferred income (credit balance). The net amount presented would then be $330,000 ($465,000 – $135,000).

The deposit and the first two installments are credited to the debtor account, which will then reflect a debit balance of $290,000 at December 31, 20X2.

A total of $66,263 ($35,320 + $30,943) of the unearned finance income has been earned in the first year, which brings the balance of this account to $68,737 at December 31, 20X2.

The **Statement of Comprehensive Income** for the year ending December 31, 20X2, will reflect finance income earned in the first year in the amount of $66,263.

The **Statement of Financial Position** at December 31, 20X2, will reflect the net investment as a long-term receivable at $221,263 ($290,000 – $68,737), which agrees with the liability in the books of the lessor at that stage.

EXAMPLE 14.2

Using the following information, what is the entry to record the assets being leased at the time of signing the lease (inception date)?

Asset 1: Lease payment of $15,000 per year for 8 years, $20,000 fair market value purchase option at the end of Year 8 (guaranteed by the lessee to be the minimum value of the equipment), estimated economic life is 10 years, fair market value of the leased asset is $105,000, and the interest rate implied in the lease is 10 percent.

Asset 2: Lease payment of $15,000 per year for 8 years, $35,000 fair market value purchase option at the end of Year 8 (guaranteed by the lessee to be the minimum value of the equipment), estimated economic life is 12 years, fair market value of the leased asset is $105,000, and the interest rate implied in the lease is 10 percent. The company's incremental borrowing rate is 11 percent.

Options:

a. No entry
b. $89,354 increase in assets and liabilities
c. $192,703 increase in assets and liabilities
d. None of the above

EXPLANATION

Issue 1: Determine whether the leases are finance or operating.

Issue 2: Determine the accounting entries needed.

Asset 1

The lease term is for a major part of the asset's life, 80 percent (8 out of 10 years). No further work is needed with respect to the criteria, because only one criterion (or a combination of criteria) has to be met to result in the lease being recorded as a finance lease (see IAS 17, paragraph 10). The amount to record is the present value of the 8 years of $15,000 lease payments, plus the present value of the $20,000 purchase option. The discount rate to use is 10 percent, which is the lower of the incremental borrowing rate and the lease's implicit rate. The present value is $89,354. This amount will be recorded as an asset and as a liability on the Statement of Financial Position.

Choice b. is correct. The entry required is to record an asset and liability in the amount of $89,354.

Asset 2

The lease term is less than a major part of the asset's life, defined as 67 percent (8 out of 12 years). There is no indication of a bargain purchase option, and the property does not go the lessee at the end of the lease (unless the lessee opts to pay $35,000). The present value of the lease payments, including the purchase option, is $96,351. The present value of the minimum lease payments does not approximate the fair market value of $105,000. Asset 2 does not meet any of the finance lease conditions and is accounted for using the operating lease method.

Choice d. is correct. No entries are required under the operating lease method when the lease is entered into.

EXAMPLE 14.3

Which of the following assets would have a higher cash flow from operations in the first year of the lease? (Assume straight-line depreciation, if applicable.)

Asset 1: Lease payment of $15,000 per year for 8 years, $20,000 fair market value purchase option at the end of Year 8 (guaranteed by the lessee to be the minimum value of the equipment), estimated economic life is 10 years, fair market value of the leased asset is $105,000, and the interest rate implied in the lease is 10 percent.

Asset 2: Lease payment of $15,000 per year for 8 years, $35,000 fair market value purchase option at the end of Year 8 (guaranteed by the lessee to be the minimum value of the equipment), estimated economic life is 12 years, fair market value of the leased asset is $105,000, and the interest rate implied in the lease is 10 percent. The company's incremental borrowing rate is 11 percent.

Options

a. Asset 1.
b. Asset 2.
c. Both assets would have the same total cash flow from operations.
d. Insufficient information given.

EXPLANATION

Asset 1

The lease term is for a major part of the asset's life, 80 percent (8 out of 10 years). No further work is needed with respect to the criteria, because only one criterion (or a combination of criteria has to be met to result in the lease being recorded as a finance lease (see IAS 17, paragraph 10). The amount to record is present value of the 8 years of $15,000 lease payments, plus the present value of the $20,000 purchase option. The discount rate to use is 10 percent, which is the lower of the incremental borrowing rate and the lease's implicit rate. The present value is $89,354. This amount will be recorded as an asset and as a liability on the Statement of Financial Position. The cash flows in the first year will consist of the $15,000 payment, which is allocated between operating cash flow (an outflow for the interest portion of the payment) and financing cash flow (an outflow for the principal portion of the payment):

Total payment	=	$15,000
Interest portion = 10 percent x $89,354	=	$8,935
Principal portion	=	$6,065

Asset 2

The lease term at 67 percent (8 out of 12 years) is less than a major part of the asset's life. There is no indication of a bargain purchase option, and the property does not go to the lessee at the end of the lease (unless the lessee opts to pay $35,000). The present value of the lease payments is $96,351. Therefore, the present value of the minimum lease payments does not approximate the fair market value of $105,000. Asset 2 does not meet any of the finance lease conditions and is accounted for using the operating lease method. The annual lease payment of $15,000 is an operating cash outflow.

Choice a. is correct. There is the issue of whether the leases are finance or operating. Once this issue is resolved, then the amount and classification of the cash flows can be determined. As the explanation above shows, the total cash flows are the same—a negative $15,000. Asset 1, being a finance lease, results in a portion of this outflow being considered a financing cash flow. Thus it shows a lower operating cash outflow, meaning a higher cash flow from operations.

Choice b. is incorrect. Assuming the leases are of similar size, the finance lease will reflect a higher operating cash flow than the operating lease. This is true for every year of the lease term, because a portion of the lease payment is shifted under a finance lease to being a financing cash outflow.

Choice c. is incorrect. The only way for each to have the same operating cash flows in this scenario would be if both were treated as operating leases. But Asset 1 is required to be accounted for as a finance lease.

Choice d. is incorrect. Sufficient information has been provided.

EXAMPLE 14.4

The "capitalization" of a finance lease by a lessee will increase which of the following:

a. Debt-to-equity ratio
b. Rate of return on assets
c. Current ratio
d. Asset turnover

EXPLANATION

Choice a. is correct. Because the capitalization of a finance lease by a lessee increases the debt obligation and lowers net income (equity), the entity will be more leveraged as the debt-to-equity ratio will increase.

Choice b. is incorrect. Given that net income declines and total assets increase under a finance lease, the rate of return on assets would decrease.

Choice c. is incorrect. Because the current obligation of the finance lease increases current liabilities while current assets are unaffected, the current ratio declines.

Choice d. is incorrect. Finance leases increase a company's asset base, which lowers the asset turnover ratio.

EXAMPLE 14.5

All of the following are true statements regarding the impact of a lease on the statement of cash flows regardless of whether the finance lease or operating lease method is used—**except** for:

a. The total cash flow impact for the life of the lease is the same under both methods.

b. The interest portion of the payment under a finance lease will affect operating activities, whereas the principal reduction portion of the finance lease payment will affect financing activities.

c. Over time, a cash payment under the finance lease method will cause operating cash flow to decline, whereas financing cash flows will tend to increase.

d. Cash payments made under an operating lease will affect operating activities only.

EXPLANATION

Choice c. is false. When finance leases are used, operating cash flow will **increase** over time as the level of interest expense declines and more of the payment is allocated to principal repayment, which will result in a **decline** in financing cash flows over time.

Choice a. is true. Total cash flows over the life of the lease are the same under the operating and finance lease methods.

Choice b. is true. A finance lease payment affects operating cash flows and financing cash flows.

Choice d. is true. The operating lease payment is made up of the rent expense, which affects operating cash flow only.

EXAMPLE 14.6

On January 1, 20X1, ABC Company, lessee, enters into an operating lease for new equipment valued at $1.5 million. Terms of the lease agreement include five annual lease payments of $125,000 to be made by ABC Company to the leasing company.

During the first year of the lease, ABC Company will record which of the following?

a. Initially, an increase (debit) of leased equipment of $625,000 and an increase (credit) in equipment payables of $625,000. At year-end, a decrease (debit) in equipment payable of $125,000 and a decrease (credit) to cash of $125,000.

b. An increase (debit) in rent expense of $125,000 and a decrease (credit) in cash of $125,000.

c. No entry is recorded on the financial statements.

d. An increase (debit) in leased equipment of $125,000 and a decrease (credit) in cash of $125,000; no Statement of Comprehensive Income entry.

EXPLANATION

Choice b. is correct. Because the above transaction is an operating lease, only rent expense is recorded on the Statement of Comprehensive Income, with a corresponding reduction to cash on the Statement of Financial Position to reflect the payment.

Choice a. is incorrect. Operating leases do not include the present value of the asset on the Statement of Financial Position.

Choice c. is incorrect. Rent expense is recorded on the Statement of Comprehensive Income for operating leases.

Choice d. is incorrect. The leased asset is not recorded on the Statement of Financial Position for operating leases.

CHAPTER 15

Income Taxes (IAS 12)

OBJECTIVE

The key objectives of IAS 12 are to prescribe the accounting treatment for income taxes and the reconciliation of the legal tax liability (actual tax payable per tax regulations) with the tax liability and expense for accounting disclosure purposes. Other issues addressed include:

- the distinction between permanent and timing differences;
- the future recovery or settlement of the carrying amount of deferred tax assets or liabilities in the Statement of Financial Position; and
- recognizing and dealing with losses for income tax purposes.

SCOPE OF THE STANDARD

This standard must be applied to accounting for **all income taxes**, including domestic, foreign, and withholding taxes, as well as the income tax consequences of dividend payments.

KEY CONCEPTS

15.3.1 Accounting profit is net profit or loss for a period before deducting tax expense.

15.3.2 Taxable profit (or tax loss) is the profit (or loss) for a period, determined in accordance with the rules established by the taxation authorities, based on which income taxes are payable (or recoverable).

15.3.3 Tax expense (or tax income) is the aggregate amount included in the determination of net profit or loss for the period in respect of current tax and deferred tax.

15.3.4 Current tax is the amount of income taxes payable (or recoverable) on the taxable profit (or tax loss) for a period, in accordance with the rules established by the tax authorities.

15.3.5 Deferred tax liabilities are the amounts of income taxes payable in future periods for taxable temporary differences.

15.3.6 Deferred tax assets are the amounts of income taxes recoverable in future periods for:

- deductible temporary differences;
- the carry-forward of unused tax losses; and
- the carry-forward of unused tax credits.

15.3.7 **Temporary differences** are differences between the carrying amount of an asset or liability in the Statement of Financial Position and its tax base. Temporary differences may be either:

- **taxable temporary differences**, which are temporary differences that will result in taxable amounts in determining taxable profit (or tax loss) of future periods when the carrying amount of the asset or liability is recovered or settled; or
- **deductible temporary differences**, which are temporary differences that will result in amounts that are deductible in determining taxable profit (or tax loss) of future periods when the carrying amount of the asset or liability is recovered or settled.

In consolidated financial statements, temporary differences are determined by comparing the carrying amounts of the consolidated assets and liabilities to their tax bases as determined by reference to either the consolidated tax return, or where no such return is prepared, the individual tax returns of the consolidated entities.

15.3.8 The **tax base** of an asset or liability is the amount attributed to that asset or liability for tax purposes.

- The tax base of an asset is the amount **deductible for tax purposes** against any taxable economic benefits that will flow to the entity as it recovers the carrying amount of the asset through use or sale.
- The tax base of a liability is an amount **taxable for tax purposes** in respect of the liability in future periods.

15.4   ## ACCOUNTING TREATMENT

Current Taxation Assets and Liabilities

15.4.1 **Current tax** should be recognized when taxable profits are earned in the period to which it relates in the following manner:

- A current tax expense or income item should be recognized in the income statement.
- A current tax liability should be recognized to the extent that amounts owing are unpaid to tax authorities.
- A current tax asset should be recognized for any amounts paid in excess of the amounts due for the relevant period. In jurisdictions where this is relevant, the benefit of a tax loss carried back to recover tax paid with respect to a prior period should be recognized as an asset.

15.4.2 Current tax liabilities and assets are measured at the amount expected to be paid to or recovered from the taxation authorities using the tax rates and laws that have been **enacted or substantively enacted** (announced by the government) at the reporting date. For current tax this is the rate that is relevant to the financial reporting period regardless of the date on which it is announced. A change in tax rate is a change in estimate per IAS 8 (see chapter 5).

Deferred Taxation Assets and Liabilities

15.4.3 A **deferred tax liability** is recognized for **all taxable temporary differences**, except when those differences arise from:

- the initial recognition of goodwill; or
- the initial recognition of an asset or liability in a transaction that is not a business combination, and at the time of the transaction affects neither accounting nor taxable profit or loss.

15.4.4 A **deferred tax asset** is recognized for all deductible temporary differences to the extent that it is probable that they are recoverable from future taxable profits. A recent loss is considered evidence that a deferred tax asset should not be recognized. A deferred tax asset is not recognized when it arises from the initial recognition of an asset or liability in a transaction that is not a business combination and at the time of the transaction affects neither accounting nor taxable profit or loss.

15.4.5 Deferred tax balances are **measured** using the following:

■ tax rates and tax laws that have been substantively enacted at the reporting date;

■ tax rates that reflect how the asset will be recovered or liability will be settled (through use, disposal, or settlement); and

■ the tax rate enacted or substantively enacted that is expected to apply to the period when the asset is realized or the liability settled.

15.4.6 Deferred tax assets and liabilities are not discounted. The carrying amount of any recognized and previously unrecognized deferred tax assets should be reviewed at each reporting date. The carrying amount should be reduced where it is no longer probable that sufficient taxable profit will be available; conversely, an asset should be recognized where future profits have become probable.

15.4.7 Temporary differences that arise when the carrying amounts of investments in subsidiaries, branches, associates, or joint ventures are different from their tax bases will result in the recognition of a deferred tax liability or asset, except when both the following occur:

■ The parent, investor, or venturer can control the timing of the reversal of temporary differences (for example, it controls the dividend policy of the investee entity).

■ It is probable that the temporary difference will not reverse (in the case of a liability) or will reverse (in the case of an asset) in the foreseeable future. If a deferred tax asset is recognized there must be taxable profit against which the temporary difference can be utilized.

TABLE 15.1 Calculating Deferred Taxation

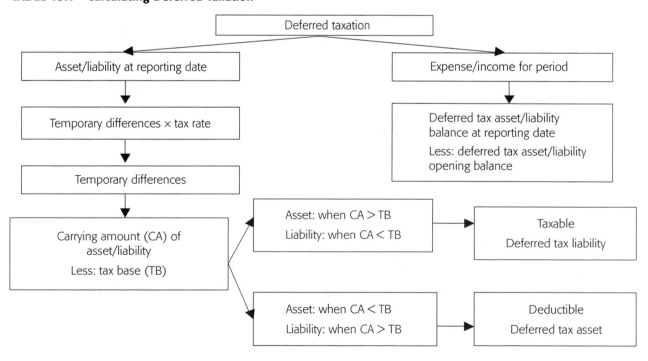

TABLE 15.2   **Examples of Temporary Differences That Arise and Their Deferred Tax Treatment**

Item	Carrying amount	Tax base	Temporary difference	Deferred tax
General principle for assets and liabilities				
Any asset/liability on initial recognition	Cost/fair value at **initial recognition**	Nil	Cost/fair value at initial recognition	Nil—exempt
Any asset/liability on subsequent reporting date	Per IFRS	Equal to carrying amount	Nil	None
Rules applicable to specific assets and liabilities				
Depreciable asset	Cost less accumulated depreciation	Cost less tax allowances	Taxable: CA > TB Deductible: CA < TB	Liability Asset
Land	Cost	Cost	Nil	None—exempt
Assets carried at fair value, e.g., investment property	Fair value at reporting date	Cost	Taxable: CA > TB Deductible: CA < TB	Liability Asset
Goodwill	IFRS 3 amount less impairment	Nil	IFRS 3 amount less impairment	None—exempt
Internally generated intangible assets	Development costs less accumulated depreciation	Cost less tax allowances (if any)	Taxable: CA > TB Deductible: CA < TB	Liability Asset
Research costs on intangible assets	Nil (expensed)	Tax allowance (if any)	Deductible	Asset
Prepayments	Amounts prepaid at reporting date	Nil (future expense)	Taxable	Liability
Provisions	Provision at reporting date	Tax allowance (if any) or nil (only taxed when actually paid)	Deductible	Asset
Operating lease	Operating lease asset/ liability (straight line)	Actual amounts paid/ received (no straight lining)	Taxable/ Deductible	Liability/ Asset
Deferred income, e.g., interest receivable	Amount deferred at reporting date	Nil (not actually received yet)	Deductible	Asset
IFRS 3 business combinations at acquisition date	Fair values of assets and liabilities of acquiree at acquisition date	Carrying amount or cost before acquisition	Taxable	Liability (affects amount of goodwill recognized)
Sale of tangible assets	Accounting profit/ (loss)	Recoupments or scrapping allowances for tax (if any)	Taxable/ Deductible	Liability/ Asset at capital gains rate
Compound financial instrument	Liability component balance at reporting date	Full balance of instrument (liability + equity)	Taxable	Liability

Item	Carrying amount	Tax base	Temporary difference	Deferred tax
Assessed losses carried forward and unused tax credits	Amount unused at current reporting date	Nil	Deductible	Asset (provided future taxable profit)
Retirement benefit liability	Carrying amount at reporting date	Nil (deductible as actually paid)	Deductible	Asset
Investments in subsidiaries, branches, associates, and joint ventures	Carrying amount at reporting date	Usually cost	Taxable/ Deductible	Liability/ Asset (limited)

Current and Deferred Tax Expenses or Income

15.4.8 Current and deferred taxation **expense or income** must be recognized in the same manner in which the underlying item is recognized, that is:

- If the tax relates to an item that affects profit or loss (such as a depreciable asset) then the related taxation is recognized in profit or loss except if the tax arises from a business combination.
- If the tax relates to an item that affects other comprehensive income (such as an available-for-sale asset) or directly in equity (such as the equity component of a compound financial instrument), then the related taxation is recognized in other comprehensive income or equity.

15.4.9 The income tax consequences of **dividends** are recognized when a liability to pay the dividend is recognized.

15.5 PRESENTATION AND DISCLOSURE

15.5.1 Taxation balances should be presented as follows:

- The balances are shown separately from other assets and liabilities in the Statement of Financial Position.
- Deferred tax balances are distinguished from current tax balances.
- Deferred tax balances are noncurrent.
- Taxation expense (income) should be shown for ordinary activities on the face of the Statement of Comprehensive Income.
- Current tax balances can be **offset** when:
  - there is a legal enforceable right to offset; and
  - there is an intention to settle on a net basis.
- Deferred tax balances can be **offset** when:
  - there is a legal enforceable right to offset; and
  - deferred tax assets and liabilities relate to the same tax authority on either:
    - the same taxable entity; or
    - different taxable entities that intend to settle on a net basis.
- The tax expense or income related to profit or loss from **ordinary activities** shall be presented in the statement of comprehensive income.

15.5.2 **Accounting policy disclosure**: the method used for deferred tax should be disclosed.

15.5.3 **The Statement of Comprehensive Income and notes** should contain:

- major components of tax expense (income), shown separately, including:
  - current tax expense (income);
  - deferred tax expense (income) related to the origination and reversal of temporary differences and changes in tax rate;
  - any adjustments recognized in the current period for tax of prior periods;
  - tax benefits arising from previously unrecognized tax losses, credits, or temporary differences of a prior period that is used to reduce the current or deferred tax expense as relevant;
  - deferred tax arising from the write-down (or reversal of a previous write-down) of a deferred tax asset; and
  - deferred amount relating to changes in accounting policies and fundamental errors treated in accordance with IAS 8–allowed alternative;

- reconciliation between tax amount and accounting profit or loss in monetary terms, or a numerical reconciliation of the applicable tax rate;
- the amount of income tax relating to each component of other comprehensive income;
- in respect of discontinued operations:
  - the amount of tax expense related to the gain or loss on discontinuance; and
  - the amount of tax expense related to the profit or loss from ordinary activities of discontinued operation for the period;

- explanation of changes in applicable tax rates compared to previous period(s); and
- for each type of temporary difference, and in respect of each type of unused tax loss and credit, the amounts of the deferred tax recognized in the Statement of Comprehensive Income.

15.5.4 **The Statement of Financial Position and notes** should include:

- aggregate amount of **current** and **deferred** tax charged or credited directly to equity;
- amount (and expiration date) of deductible temporary differences, unused tax losses, and unused tax credits for which no deferred tax asset is recognized;
- aggregate amount of temporary differences associated with investments in subsidiaries, branches, associates, and joint ventures for which deferred tax liabilities have not been recognized;
- for each type of temporary difference, and in respect of each type of unused tax loss and credit, the amount of the deferred tax assets and liabilities;
- amount of a deferred tax asset and nature of the evidence supporting its recognition, when:
  - the utilization of the deferred tax asset is dependent on future taxable profits; or
  - the enterprise has suffered a loss in either the current or preceding period;

- amount of income tax consequences of dividends to shareholders that were proposed or declared before the reporting date, but are not recognized as a liability in the financial statements; and
- the nature of the potential income tax consequences that would result from the payment of dividends to the enterprises' shareholders, that is, the important features of the income tax systems and the factors that will affect the amount of the potential tax consequences of dividends.

15.6   **FINANCIAL ANALYSIS AND INTERPRETATION**

15.6.1 The first step in understanding how income taxes are accounted for in IFRS financial statements is to realize that **taxable profit** and **accounting profit** have very different meanings. Taxable profit is computed using procedures that comply with the relevant tax regulations of a country and is the basis upon which income taxes are paid. Accounting profit is computed using accounting policies that comply with IFRS.

15.6.2 When determining taxable profit, an entity might be allowed or required by the tax regulations to use measurement methods that are different from those that comply with IFRS. The resulting differences might increase or decrease profits. For example, an entity might be allowed to use accelerated depreciation to compute taxable profit and so reduce its tax liability, while at the same time it might be required to use straight-line depreciation in the determination of IFRS accounting profit.

15.6.3 The second step is to understand the difference between current taxes, deferred tax assets and liabilities, and income tax expense. **Current taxes** represent the income tax owed to the government in accordance with tax regulations. **Deferred taxes** represent the future tax consequences of the recovery of assets and settlement of liabilities resulting from the difference between taxable profit and accounting profit. **Income tax expense** is an expense reported in the Statement of Comprehensive Income, and it includes both the current and deferred tax expense. This means that the income tax paid or payable to the government in an accounting period usually differs significantly from the income tax expense that is recognized in the Statement of Comprehensive Income.

15.6.4 Analysts sometimes question whether deferred taxes are a liability or equity. An entity's deferred tax liability meets the definition of a liability. However, deferred tax liabilities are not current legal liabilities, because they do not represent taxes that are currently owed or payable to the government. Taxes that are owed to the government but have not been paid are called current tax liabilities. They are classified as current liabilities on the Statement of Financial Position, whereas deferred tax liabilities are classified as noncurrent liabilities.

15.6.5 If an entity is growing, new deferred tax liabilities may be created on an ongoing basis (depending on the source of potential timing differences). Thus, the deferred tax liability balance will probably never decrease. Furthermore, changes in the tax laws or a company's operations could result in deferred taxes never being paid. For these reasons, many analysts treat deferred tax liabilities as if they are part of a company's **equity capital**.

15.6.6 Technically, treating deferred tax liabilities as if they were part of a company's equity capital should be done only if the analyst is convinced that the deferred tax liabilities will increase or remain stable in the foreseeable future. This will be the case when a company is expected to acquire new (or more expensive) assets on a regular basis so that the aggregate timing differences will increase (or remain stable) over time. Under such circumstances, which are normal for most entities, deferred tax liabilities could be viewed as being zero-interest loans from the government that will, in the aggregate, always increase without ever being repaid. The rationale for treating perpetually stable or growing deferred tax liabilities as equity for analytical purposes is that a perpetual loan that requires no interest or principal payments takes on the characteristics of permanent equity capital.

15.6.7 If an entity's deferred tax liabilities are expected to decline over time, however, they should be treated as liabilities for analytical purposes. One consideration is that the liabilities should be discounted for the time value of money; the taxes are not paid until future periods.

An analyst should also consider the reasons that have caused deferred taxes to arise and how likely these causes are to reverse.

15.6.8 In some cases, analysts ignore the deferred tax liabilities for analytical purposes when it is difficult to determine whether they will take on the characteristics of a true liability or equity capital over time. Ultimately, the analyst has to decide whether deferred tax liabilities should be characterized as liabilities, equity, or neither based on the situation's unique circumstances.

15.6.9 Entities must include income tax information in their footnotes, which analysts should use to:

- understand why the entity's effective income tax rate is different from the statutory tax rate;
- forecast future effective income tax rates, thereby improving earnings forecasts;
- determine the actual income taxes paid by an entity and compare them with the reported income tax expense to better assess operating cash flow; and
- estimate the taxable income reported to the government and compare it with the reported pretax income reported in the financial statements.

15.7   **COMMENTARY**

15.7.1 The industry and country in which an entity operates will have a large practical effect on the recognition and measurement of deferred tax, which could complicate comparisons between entities even within the same industry. Practical differences may arise as a result of the following conditions:

- The tax regulations of different countries and jurisdictions may be vastly different for a specific type of asset or liability, which would result in very different tax bases and deferred tax consequences between entities. Often special tax breaks are made available to certain industries to encourage growth and investment.
- The intentions that an entity has for a certain asset (for use or for disposal) may determine the rate at which an entity recognizes deferred tax (either the normal or the capital gains tax rate). Different entities, even within the same industry, may view one asset type differently, which could result in different deferred tax being recognized for similar asset types.

15.7.2 The recognition of a deferred tax asset is largely based on judgment as to the future probability of profits. Though some guidance is provided on how this may be assessed, the likelihood of difference in practice between entities is high. Tax planning opportunities also play a large role in making such assessments. Entities will not always have similar tax planning opportunities available. This will also be affected by the relevant tax legislation (such as ring fencing of losses) with which the entity must comply, as well as the entity's group structure.

15.7.3 Indirect tax is tax on items other than income, for example value-added tax and stamp duties. Each tax jurisdiction will have its own indirect taxes (for example value-added tax). The inclusion of these amounts in an entity's financial statements could have a negative impact on the performance and financial position and provide an inaccurate picture of the entity to analysts and investors. Care must be taken to separately disclose and deduct these amounts before calculating direct tax.

15.7.4 As part of its overall convergence project with the FASB, the IASB embarked on a project to eliminate the differences in accounting treatment of taxes between IFRS and U.S. GAAP. In March 2009 the IASB issued an exposure draft that would replace IAS 12. The proposals retain the basic approach to accounting for income tax as in IAS 12—that is, the temporary difference approach. The IASB does, however, propose to **remove most of the exceptions currently available** in IAS 12.

15.7.5 The most significant proposed changes in the exposure draft include the following:

- The expected recovery of the asset is assumed to be sale. There will no longer be judgment allowed as to whether the asset is recovered through use or through sale.
- The exemption for recognizing deferred tax on the initial recognition of assets and liabilities has been removed for most assets and liabilities.
- The exception for the recognition of deferred tax on investments in associates, joint ventures, and branches has been changed to apply only to foreign branches and joint ventures. It will no longer apply to associates at all.
- Deferred tax assets must be recognized in full and an allowance account raised to reduce the carrying amount to the realizable amount (based on probable future profits being available).

15.7.6 The comments received on the exposure draft were largely negative, because most respondents felt that rather than improving the standard, the exposure draft introduced complex new rules. In response, the IASB is reviewing how to proceed with this project and is considering splitting it into short-term and long-term objectives. A group of IASB members is currently investigating priority issues for a short-term project.

15.8   IMPLEMENTATION DECISIONS

Strategic Decisions

15.8.1 IAS 12 prescribes a judgmental test before recognition of deferred tax assets is allowed. The judgmental test is based on the probability of future taxable profits being earned and/or the availability of tax planning opportunities. An entity will have to assess these probabilities, taking account of market conditions, jurisdictional conditions, and the reason the deferred tax asset initially arose. This may involve consideration of business plans.

EXAMPLES: INCOME TAXES

EXAMPLE 15.1

Difir Inc. owns the following property, plant, and equipment at December 31, 20X4:

	Cost $'000	Accumulated depreciation $'000	Carrying amount $'000	Tax base $'000
Machinery	900	180	720	450
Land	500	–	500	–
Buildings	1,500	300	1,200	–

In addition:

- Machinery is depreciated on the straight-line basis over 5 years. It was acquired on January 1, 20X4.
- Land is not depreciated.
- Buildings are depreciated on the straight-line basis over 25 years.
- Depreciation of land and office buildings is not deductible for tax purposes. For machinery, tax depreciation is granted over a period of 3 years in the ratio of 50/30/20 (percent) of cost, consecutively.
- The accounting profit before tax amounted to $300,000 for the 20X5 financial year and $400,000 for 20X6. These figures include nontaxable revenue of $80,000 in 20X5 and $100,000 in 20X6.
- Difir had a tax loss on December 31, 20X4, of $250,000. The tax rate for 20X4 was 35 percent, and for 20X5 and 20X6 it was 30 percent.

EXPLANATION

The movements on the deferred tax balance for 20X5 and 20X6 will be reflected as follows in the accounting records of the enterprise:

Deferred tax liability	$'000 Dr/(Cr)
January 1, 20X5, balance	
Machinery (Calculation a: 270 × 35%)	(94.5)
Tax loss carried forward (250 × 35%)	87.5
	(7.0)
Rate change (7 × 5/35)	1.0
Temporary differences: – Machinery (Calculation a)	(27.0)
–Loss utilized (Calculation b: 190 × 30%)	(57.0)
December 31, 20X5, balance	(90.0)
Temporary difference: – Machinery (Calculation a)	–
December 31, 20X6, loss utilized (Calculation b: 60 × 30%)	(18.0)
December 31, 20X6, balance	(108.0)

Calculations

a. Machinery	Carrying amount $'000	Tax base $'000	Temporary difference $'000	Deferred tax $'000
January 1, 20X4, purchase	900	900		
Depreciation	(180)	(450)	270	94.5
December 31, 20X4	720	450	270	94.5
Rate change (5/35 × 94.5)				(13.5)
Depreciation	(180)	(270)	90	27.0
December 31, 20X5	540	180	360	108.0
Depreciation	(180)	(180)	–	–
December 31, 20X6	360	–	360	108.0

b. Income tax expense	20X6 $'000	20X5 $'000
Accounting profit before tax	400	300
Tax effect of items not deductible/taxable for tax purposes:		
Nontaxable revenue	(100)	(80)
Depreciation on buildings (1,500/25)	60	60
	360	280
Temporary differences	–	(90)
Depreciation: accounting	180	180
Depreciation: tax	(180)	(270)
Taxable profit	360	190
Assessed loss brought forward	(60)	(250)
Taxable profit/(tax loss)	300	(60)
Tax loss carried forward	–	(60)
Tax payable/(benefit) @ 30%	90	(18)

EXAMPLE 15.2

Lipreaders Company has net taxable temporary differences of $90 million, resulting in a deferred tax liability of $30.6 million. An increase in the tax rate would have the following impact on deferred taxes and net income:

Deferred taxes	Net income
a. Increase	No effect
b. Increase	Decrease
c. No effect	No effect
d. No effect	Decrease

EXPLANATION

Choice b. is correct. Deferred tax is a liability that results when tax expense on the Statement of Comprehensive Income exceeds taxes payable. The amount of deferred tax liability will rise if tax rates are expected to rise. In effect, more taxes will be paid in the future as the timing differences reverse. This increase in the deferred tax liability will flow through the Statement of Comprehensive Income by raising income tax expense. Thus, net income will decrease.

Choice a. is incorrect. When deferred taxes increase, net income will be lower.

Choice c. is incorrect. The above scenario affects both deferred taxes and net income.

Choice d. is incorrect. Although net income would decrease, deferred taxes would increase because tax rates in the future will be higher.

EXAMPLE 15.3

There are varying accounting rules throughout the world that govern how the income tax expense is reported on the Statement of Comprehensive Income. IFRS requires the use of the **liability method**. To illustrate the essential accounting problem posed when different accounting methods are used to develop financial information for tax and financial reporting purposes, consider the Engine Works Corporation. In the year just ended, Engine Works generated earnings from operations before depreciation and income taxes of $6,000. In addition, the company earned $100 of tax-free municipal bond interest income. Engine Works only assets subject to depreciation are two machines, one that was purchased at the beginning of last year for $5,000, and one that was purchased at the beginning of this year for $10,000. Both machines are being depreciated over five-year periods. The company uses an accelerated-consumption method to compute depreciation for income tax purposes (worth $5,200 this year) and the straight-line method to calculate depreciation for financial reporting (book) purposes.

EXPLANATION

1. Based on this information, Engine Works' income tax filing and Statement of Comprehensive Income for the **current** year would be as follows:

Income Tax Filing ($)		Statement of Comprehensive Income ($)	
Income from operations before depreciation and income taxes	6,000	Income from operations before depreciation and income taxes	6,000
Tax-free interest income	—[a]	Tax-free interest income	100
Depreciation—tax allowance	5,200	Depreciation	3,000[b]
Taxable income	800	Pretax income	3,100
Income taxes payable (35%)	280	Income tax expense	?

a. Tax-free interest income is excluded from taxable income.
b. $1/5 \times \$5,000 + 1/5 \times \$10,000 = \$3,000$.

2. Based on the income tax filing, the income tax that is owed to the government is $280. The question is what income tax expense should be reported in Engine Works' Statement of Comprehensive Income? There are two reasons why accounting profit and taxable profit can be different: **temporary** and **permanent differences** (not a term specifically used in IFRS 12).

3. **Temporary differences** are those differences between accounting profit and taxable profit for an accounting period that arise whenever the measurement of assets and liabilities for income tax purposes differs from the measurement of assets and liabilities for IFRS purposes. For example, if an entity uses straight-line depreciation of its assets for IFRS purposes and accelerated depreciation for income tax purposes, the IFRS carrying amount of the assets will differ from the tax carrying amount of those assets. For income tax purposes, tax depreciation will be greater than IFRS depreciation in the early years and lower than IFRS depreciation in the later years.

4. **Permanent differences** are those differences between IFRS accounting profit and taxable profit that arise when income is not taxed or expenses are not tax deductible. For example, tax-free interest income is not included in taxable income, even though it is part of IFRS accounting profit.

5. Permanent differences affect the current accounting period's **effective income tax rate** (the ratio of the reported income tax expense to pretax income), but do not have any impact on future income taxes. Temporary differences, on the other hand, affect the income taxes that

FIGURE 15.3 **Income Difference before Taxes—Engine Works**

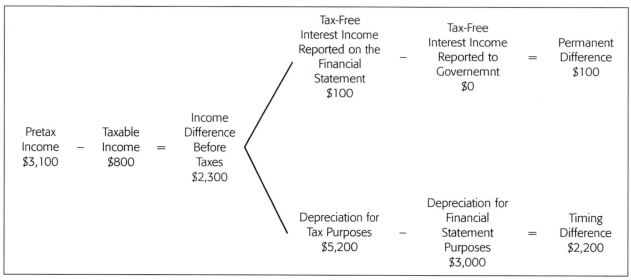

will be paid in future years because they represent a deferral of taxable income from the current to subsequent accounting periods (or an acceleration of taxable income from the future into the current accounting period).

6. The $2,300 difference between pretax income and taxable income is attributable in part to the $100 of tax-free interest income that will never be taxed, but is included in the Statement of Comprehensive Income. This is a **permanent difference** because this income is permanently excluded from taxation; the amount of tax on it that has to be paid now or in the future is zero.

7. The $2,200 difference between the $5,200 accelerated consumption depreciation and the $3,000 straight-line depreciation is a **timing (temporary) difference** because the taxes that are saved in the current year are only deferred to the future when the timing differences **reverse**. Over the life of the equipment, the total depreciation expense will be the same for income tax and book purposes. The $2,200 is a reflection of the difference in the amount of the total cost of the equipment that is **allocated** to this period by the two methods of accounting for depreciation. The Statement of Comprehensive Income has a lower depreciation cost than the tax filing, which results in higher reported income. These differences will reverse over time when the straight-line depreciation rises above the double-declining balance depreciation.

CHAPTER 16

Inventories (IAS 2)

16.1	**OBJECTIVE**

Inventory comprises the goods held for sale and the cost associated with the production thereof. It is often the heart of entities and defines their business and industry. IAS 2's objective is to prescribe the accounting treatment of inventories, including the calculation of the cost of inventory, the type of inventory method adopted, the allocation of cost to assets and expenses, and valuation aspects associated with any write-downs to net realizable value.

16.2	**SCOPE OF THE STANDARD**

This standard deals with all inventories of assets that are:

- held for sale in the ordinary course of business;
- in the process of production for sale;
- in the form of materials or supplies to be consumed in the production process; and
- used in the rendering of services.

In the case of a service provider, inventories include the costs of the service for which the related revenue has not yet been recognized (for example, the work in progress of auditors, architects, and lawyers).

IAS 2 does not apply to the measurement of inventories held by producers of agricultural and forest products, agricultural produce after harvest, or minerals and mineral products to the extent that they are measured at net realizable value in accordance with well-established practices in those industries. Living plants, animals, and harvested agricultural produce derived from those plants and animals are also excluded (see IAS 41, chapter 12).

Although IAS 2 excludes construction contracts (IAS 11) and financial instruments (IAS 39), the principles in IAS 2 are still applied when deciding how to implement certain features of the excluded standards (see example 16.5).

IAS 2 does not apply to commodity broker-traders who acquire inventories principally for the purpose of selling in the near future and generating a profit from fluctuations in the price or to earn a broker-trader's margin. Broker-traders typically measure commodities at fair value less cost to sell, with changes in fair value recognized in profit or loss in the period of change. It is not clear whether the intention of the standard is that commodity broker-traders have the option to apply fair value or IAS 2 or whether the fair value measurement is compulsory. The interpretation developed in practice, based in the wording in the standard, is that broker-traders have the option to choose fair value or IAS 2.

16.3	**KEY CONCEPTS**

16.3.1 Inventories should be **measured** at the lower of cost and net realizable value.

16.3.2 **Cost of inventories comprises** all the costs of purchase, costs of conversion, and other costs incurred in bringing the inventories to their **present location and condition**.

16.3.3 **The net realizable value (NRV)** is the estimated selling price less the estimated costs of completion and costs necessary to make the sale.

16.3.4 **When** inventories are sold, the carrying amount of those inventories should be recognized as an expense in the period in which the related revenue is recognized (see chapter 23).

16.3.5 **The amount of any write-down** of inventories to NRV and all losses of inventories should be recognized as an expense in the period of the write-down or loss.

16.4	**ACCOUNTING TREATMENT**

Measurement Techniques

16.4.1 The cost of inventories that are not ordinarily interchangeable and those produced and segregated for specific projects are assigned by **specific identification** of their individual costs.

16.4.2 The cost of inventories, other than those dealt with in paragraph 16.4.1, should be assigned by using either of the following **cost formulas**:

- weighted average cost; or
- first in, first out (FIFO).

16.4.3 The following **techniques** can be used to measure the cost of inventories if the results approximate cost:

- **Standard cost:**
  - Normal levels of materials, labor, and actual capacity should be taken into account.
  - The standard cost should be reviewed regularly to ensure that it approximates actual costs.
- **Retail method:**
  - Sales value should be reduced by gross margin to calculate cost.
  - Average percentage should be used for each homogeneous group of items.
  - Marked-down prices should be taken into consideration.

Cost and NRV

16.4.4 Cost of inventories consists of:

- purchase costs, such as the purchase price, import charges, non-recoverable taxes, and other directly attributable transport and handling costs;

- costs of conversion;
  - direct labor; and
  - production overheads, including variable overheads and fixed overheads allocated at normal production capacity; and
- other costs, such as design and borrowing costs.

16.4.5 **Cost** of inventories excludes:

- abnormal amounts of wasted materials, labor, and overheads;
- storage costs, unless they are necessary prior to a further production process;
- administrative overheads; and
- selling costs.

16.4.6 **NRV** is the estimated selling price less the estimated costs of completion and costs necessary to make the sale. These estimates are based on the most reliable evidence at the time the estimates are made. The purpose for which the inventory is held should be taken into account at the time of the estimate. Inventories are usually written down to NRV based on the following principles:

- Items are treated on an item-by-item basis.
- Similar items are normally grouped together.
- Each service is treated as a separate item.

16.5   PRESENTATION AND DISCLOSURE

The financial statements should disclose the following:

- accounting policies adopted in measuring inventories, including the cost formulas used;
- total carrying amount of inventories and amount per category;
- the amount of inventories recognized as an expense during the period, that is, cost of sales;
- amount of inventories carried at fair value less costs to sell;
- amount of any write-downs and reversals of any write-downs;
- circumstances or events that led to the reversal of a write-down; and
- inventories pledged as security for liabilities.

16.6   FINANCIAL ANALYSIS AND INTERPRETATION

16.6.1 The **accounting method** used to value inventories should be selected based on the order in which products are sold, relative to when they are put into inventory. Therefore, whenever possible, the costs of inventories are assigned by specific identification of their individual costs. In many cases, however, it is necessary to use a cost formula—for example, first-in, first-out (FIFO)—that represents fairly the inventory flows. IAS 2 does not allow the use of last-in, first-out (LIFO) because it does not faithfully represent inventory flows. The IASB has noted that the use of LIFO is often tax driven and concluded that tax considerations do not provide a conceptual basis for selecting an accounting treatment. The IASB does not permit the use of an inferior accounting treatment purely because of tax considerations.

16.6.2 Analysts and managers often use **ratio analysis** to assess company performance and condition.

TABLE 16.1 Impact of Inventory Valuation on Financial Analysis

Valuation element or manipulation	Effect on company
Beginning inventory overstated by $5,000	Profit will be understated by $5,000
Ending inventory understated by $2,000	Profit will be understated by $2,000
Inventory accounting method effect on cash flows	Taxes will be affected by the choice of accounting method
Early recognition of revenue on a sale	Understatement of inventory Overstatement of receivables Overstatement of profit

TABLE 16.2 The Impact of LIFO vs. FIFO on Financial Statement Variables

Financial statement variable	LIFO	FIFO
Cost of goods sold (COGS)	Higher—more recent prices are used	Lower
Income	Lower—COGS is higher	Higher
Cash flow	Higher—taxes are lower	Lower
Working capital	Lower—current assets are lower	Higher

The valuation of inventories can influence performance and cash flow through the events or manipulations in the presentation of data shown in table 16.1.

16.6.3 Although LIFO is no longer allowed in IFRS financial statements, some jurisdictions continue to allow the use of LIFO. When comparing entities in the same industry, inventories should be adjusted to FIFO to ensure comparability. (In a similar manner, analysts should adjust the statements of non-IFRS entities prior to comparing them with IFRS entities.)

16.6.4 FIFO inventory balances constitute a closer reflection of economic value because FIFO inventory is valued at the most recent purchase prices. Table 16.2 summarizes the effects of using FIFO and LIFO on some of the elements in financial statements.

16.7   COMMENTARY

16.7.1 The calculation of the cost of inventory involves complex cost allocation and cost tracking systems and can vary significantly between entities. IAS 2 addresses these cost accounting principles only at a very high level and the costing of inventory is therefore effected more by cost accounting methodologies in general use, as opposed to strict theoretical prescriptions.

16.7.2 Inconsistency exists in the treatment of rebates and discounts that can be deducted from the cost of inventories. The IFRIC notes that IAS 2 requires only rebates and discounts received as a reduction in the purchase price to be deducted from the cost of the inventories (for example, cash discounts and volume rebates). Rebates that specifically refund the selling expenses should not be deducted from the costs of inventories.

TABLE 16.3 Equivalent FIFO and LIFO Financial Statements and the Key Financial Ratios They Produce

FIFO ($)	LIFO ($)	FIFO ($)
Cash	34	70
Accounts receivable	100	100
Inventories	200	110
Plant and equipment	300	300
Total Assets	634	580
Short-term debt	40	40
Long-term debt	200	200
Common stock	50	50
Paid-in capital	100	100
Retained earnings	244	190
Total Liabilities and Capital	634	580
Sales	600	600
Cost of goods sold	410	430
Interest expense	15	15
Pretax Income	175	155
Income tax expense	70	62
Net Income	105	93
Net profit margin	17.5%	15.5%
Current ratio	8.4x	7.0x
Inventory turnover	2.1x	3.9x
Long-term debt or equity	50.8%	58.8%
Return on assets	16.6%	16.0%
Return on equity	26.6%	27.4%

16.8　**IMPLEMENTATION DECISIONS**

Strategic Decisions

16.8.1 IAS 2 provides a number of alternative methods for calculating the cost of inventory. An entity will need to establish the most appropriate cost formula to allocate the cost of inventory, taking account of industry practice and the nature of the entity's processes.

Tactical Decisions

16.8.2 The cost formula elected as the accounting policy impacts the carrying value of the inventory recognized, the cost of sales number and the profit margin. In making the decision, management should consider how they would like to see the costs come through the financial statements.

16.8.3 Management should consider implementing a process to ensure that inventory is valued at the lower of cost or NRV.

EXAMPLES: INVENTORIES

EXAMPLE 16.1

Slingshot Corporation purchased inventory on January 1, 20X1, for $600,000. On December 31, 20X1, the inventory had an NRV of $550,000. During 20X2, Slingshot sold the inventory for $620,000. Based on the above, which of the following statements is true?

a. The December 31, 20X1, Statement of Financial Position reported the inventory at $600,000.

b. The December 31, 20X1, Statement of Financial Position reported the inventory at $620,000.

c. When the inventory was sold in 20X2, Slingshot reported a $20,000 gain on its income statement.

d. For the year ending December 31, 20X1, Slingshot recognized a $50,000 loss on its Statement of Comprehensive Income.

EXPLANATION

Choice d. is correct. Because IFRS requires the lower of cost or NRV reporting on inventory, the company must recognize a $50,000 loss ($550,000 – $600,000) on the Statement of Comprehensive Income for 20X1. When the inventory is sold in 20X2, a profit of $70,000 ($620,000 – $550,000) is recognized on the Statement of Comprehensive Income.

Choice a. is incorrect. The inventory must be written down to market value at year-end 20X1.

Choice b. is incorrect. The fact that the inventory was sold for $620,000 in 20X2 has no impact on the inventory balance at December 31, 20X1.

Choice c. is incorrect. The sale of the inventory at $620,000 must recognize the inventory market value of $550,000, resulting in a gain of $70,000.

EXAMPLE 16.2

The financial statements of Parra Imports for 20X0 and 20X1 had the following errors:

	20X0	**20X1**
Ending inventory	$4,000 overstated	$8,000 understated
Rent expense	$2,400 understated	$1,300 overstated

By what amount will the 20X0 and 20X1 pretax profits be overstated or understated if these errors are not corrected?

EXPLANATION

20X0. Because the ending inventory is overstated for 20X0, the COGS will be understated, resulting in pretax profits being overstated by $4,000. In addition, because rent expense is understated by $2,400, pretax profits will be overstated by an additional $2,400, for a total overstatement of $6,400.

20X1. The beginning inventory was overstated by $4,000 for 20X1, so COGS will be overstated by $4,000, resulting in a profit understatement of $4,000. Because ending inventory is also understated by $8,000, the impact of this error will be an additional COGS overstatement of $8,000 and additional profit understatement of $8,000. The overstatement of $1,300 for the rent will result in an additional understatement of profit, for a total pretax profit understatement of $13,300 (see below).

20X1

	Correct ($)	Wrong ($)	Misstatement ($)
Beginning inventory	6,000	10,000	4,000
Purchases	20,000	20,000	0
Total	26,000	30,000	4,000
Ending inventory	−18,000	−10,000	8,000
COGS	8,000	20,000	12,000
Sales	30,000	30,000	0
Rent			1,300
Profit	22,000	10,000	13,300

EXAMPLE 16.3

The following information applies to the Grady Company for the current year:

Purchases of merchandise for resale	$300,000
Merchandise returned to vendor	3,000
Interest on notes payable to vendors	6,000
Freight-in on merchandise	7,500

Grady's inventory costs for the year would be

a. $297,000   b. $300,000   c. $304,500   d. $316,500

EXPLANATION

Choice c. is correct. The answer was derived from the following calculation:

Purchase	$300,000
+ Freight-in	7,500
− Returns	(3,000)
	$304,500

Choice a. is incorrect. Freight-in must also be included as part of the inventory costs.

Choice b. is incorrect. In addition to purchases of merchandise, the merchandise returned to the vendor and the freight-in must be included in the inventory calculation.

Choice d. is incorrect. Interest costs on financing are not part of inventory cost (exceptions are in IAS 23).

EXAMPLE 16.4

An entity has a current ratio greater than 1.0. If the entity's ending inventory is understated by $3,000 and beginning inventory is overstated by $5,000, the entity's net income and the current ratio would be

Net Income	Current Ratio
a. Understated by $2,000	Lower
b. Overstated by $2,000	Lower
c. Understated by $8,000	Lower
d. Overstated $8,000	Higher

EXPLANATION

Choice c. is correct. The answer was derived from the following calculations:

$$\Delta \text{ COGS} = \Delta \text{ Beginning Inventory} + \Delta \text{ Purchases} - \Delta \text{ Ending Inventory}$$
$$= \$5,000 + P - (- \$3,000)$$

Assuming Δ P = 0

$$\Delta \text{ COGS} = \$5,000 + \$3,000 = \$8,000$$

If COGS is overstated by $8,000, then net income is understated by $8,000 (assuming taxes are zero). If the ending inventory is understated, then the current ratio is also lower because inventory is part of current assets.

EXAMPLE 16.5 (READ TOGETHER WITH IAS 39)

A portfolio manager purchases and sells the following securities over a four-day period. On day 5, the manager sells five securities at $4 each. Although IFRS does not allow LIFO as a cost formula, determine

i) the cost price of the securities, using the FIFO, LIFO, and weighted average cost (WAC) formulae; and

ii) the profit that will be disclosed under each of the three alternatives.

EXPLANATION

Determining the "Buy" Cost Related to the Sell

Day	Buy Par	Sell Par	FIFO	LIFO	WAC
1	10 at $1		5 at $1		
2	15 at $2				
3	20 at $3			5 at $3	
4		5 at $4			
Average	45 at $2.22				5 at $2.22
(a) Cost price Selling price			5 (20)	15 (20)	11 (20)
(b) Profit			(15)	(5)	(9)

EXAMPLE 16.6

Arco Inc. is a manufacturing company in the food industry. The following matters relate to the company's inventories:

A. In recent years the company utilized a standard costing system as an aid to management. The standard cost variances had been insignificant to date and were written off directly in the published annual financial statements. However, the following two problems were experienced during the year ending March 31, 20X3:

- Variances were far greater as a result of a sharp increase in material and labor costs as well as a decrease in production.
- A large number of the units produced were unsold at year-end. This was partially attributable to the products of the company being considered overpriced.

    The management of the company intends, as in the past, to write off these variances directly as term costs, and to also write off a portion of the cost of surplus unsold inventories.

B. Chocolate raw material inventories on hand at the end of the year represent eight months of usage. Inventory levels normally represent only two months' usage. The current replacement value of the inventories is less than the initial cost.

EXPLANATION

A. Both writing off the variances in labor and material as term costs and writing off a portion of the unsold inventories are unacceptable for the following reasons:

- The write-offs of the large variances result in the standard values not approximating cost according to IAS 2.
- Standard costs should be reviewed regularly and revised in light of the current conditions. The labor and material variances should be allocated to the standard cost of inventories. The production overhead variance resulting from idle capacity should be recognized as an expense in the current period.
- The term "overpriced" is arbitrary, and any write-down of inventory should be done only if the NRV of the inventory is lower than its cost.

B. The abnormal portion of raw material on hand (representing six months of production) might need to be written down to NRV. The other raw materials (representing two months of production) should be written down to NRV only if the estimated cost of the finished products will be more than the NRV.

CHAPTER 17

Financial Instruments: Recognition and Measurement (IAS 39)

IAS 32 and 39 and IFRS 7 were issued as separate standards. However, in practice they are applied as a unit because they deal with the same accounting and financial risk issues. IAS 39 deals with the recognition and measurement issues of financial instruments. IAS 32 (chapter 33) deals with presentation issues, and IFRS 7 deals with disclosure issues (see chapter 34). IAS 39 will be superseded by IFRS 9 after 2012. IFRS 9 is discussed in chapter 18.

17.1 OBJECTIVE

IAS 39 establishes principles for recognizing and measuring financial instruments in the financial statements. IAS 39 significantly increases the use of fair value in accounting for financial instruments, particularly on the asset side of the Statement of Financial Position. The standard is complex and often difficult to apply in practice, in part because it contains many provisions to avoid the manipulation of results (for example, derecognition rules and hedge accounting). The standard is also complex from an analysis perspective, in that it allows a number of alternatives for the recognition and measurement of financial instruments.

17.2 SCOPE OF THE STANDARD

The standard distinguishes between four classes of financial assets: held at fair value through profit and loss (for example, trading and other elected securities); available for sale; held to maturity; and loans and receivables. In addition, IAS 39 identifies two classes of financial liabilities: those held at fair value, and those shown at amortized cost. The standard outlines the accounting approach in each case. It also categorizes and sets out the accounting treatment for three types of hedging: (i) fair value, (ii) cash flow, and (iii) net investment in a foreign operation.

IAS 39 should be applied to all financial instruments (refer table 17.1), with the exception of the following:

- subsidiaries, associates, and joint ventures (IAS 27, IAS 28, and IAS 31);
- rights and obligations under leases, other than derecognition of lease receivables and payables and the impairment of lease receivables (IAS 17);
- employee benefit plan assets and liabilities (IAS 19);
- rights and obligations under insurance contracts (IFRS 4);
- equity instruments issued by the reporting entity;

- financial guarantee contracts related to the failure by a debtor to make payments when due, if the issuer has specifically stated at inception that such contracts are considered to be insurance contracts (IFRS 4);
- contracts to enter into a business combination at a future date (IFRS 3);
- share-based payment transaction (IFRS 2); and
- loan commitments, unless they are designated at fair value, net settled, or provide a below-market interest rate (IAS 37).

The standard has a general scope exception for contracts entered and held for the purpose of receipt or delivery of a nonfinancial item, in line with the entity's purchase, sale, or usage requirements. An example of this exemption would be when a manufacturer that uses steel in its manufacturing process forward-purchases steel in order to fix a price and ensure availability of future supplies. The manufacturer will use the steel in its manufacturing process and therefore it forms part of its usage requirements. The forward contract therefore falls outside the scope of IAS 39 and the manufacturer is not required to recognize a derivative at fair value.

However, any contract to buy or sell a nonfinancial item that can be settled net falls within the scope of the standard.

17.3   **KEY CONCEPTS**

Financial Instruments

17.3.1 **Financial instruments** are contracts that give rise to both:

- a financial asset of one entity; and
- a financial liability of another entity.

17.3.2 A **derivative** is a financial instrument or other contract for which:

- the value changes in response to changes in an underlying interest rate, exchange rate, commodity price, security price, credit rating, and so on;
- little or no initial investment is required; and
- settlement takes place at a future date.

17.3.3 An **embedded derivative** is a component of a hybrid instrument that includes a nonderivative host contract—with the effect that some of the cash flows of the combined instrument vary in a way similar to a stand-alone derivative. A derivative that is attached to a financial instrument but is contractually transferable independently of that instrument, or has a different counterparty from that instrument, is not an embedded derivative, but a separate financial instrument.

Valuation and Market Practice

17.3.4 **Fair value** is the amount at which an asset could be exchanged, or a liability settled, between knowledgeable, willing parties in an arm's-length transaction.

17.3.5 **Mark-to-market (MTM—fair value adjustments to financial assets and liabilities)** is the process whereby the value of financial assets measured at fair value (for example, those held for trading and that are available for sale) and fair value liabilities are adjusted to reflect current fair value. Such adjustments are often made on a daily basis.

17.3.6 **Amortized cost** is the amount at which the financial asset or financial liability is measured at initial recognition

- minus any principal repayments;
- plus or minus the cumulative amortization of the premiums or discounts on the instrument, and fees and costs that are an integral part of the effective interest rate; and
- minus any reduction for impairment or lack of collectability.

The amortization calculation should use the effective interest rate (not the nominal rate of interest).

17.3.7 The **effective interest rate** is the rate that discounts the expected future cash flows on the assets to zero. The effective interest is not necessarily equal to the coupon received. For example, if an instrument is issued at a discount the effective interest rate will take that discount into account, while the coupon received would be based on the contractual interest. The effective interest rate will be different from the contractual or coupon rate if the instrument is issued or redeemable at a premium or discount or there are fees or income that must be included in the effective interest rate.

17.3.8 **Trade or settlement date accounting** arises when an entity chooses to recognize the purchase of an instrument in its financial statements on either (a) the date when the commitment arises from the transaction (trade date), or (b) the date that the liability is settled (settlement date). Most treasury accountants prefer trade date accounting, because that is when the risks and rewards of ownership transfer—and when marking to market commences in any case (regardless of whether the asset has already been recognized in the statement of financial position).

17.3.9 **Total return** is the actual return achieved on financial assets and the amount used to assess the performance of a portfolio; it includes income and expenses recorded in the profit and loss account (for example, interest earned, realized gains and losses) and **unrealized** gains and losses recorded in profit and loss or other comprehensive income (for example, fair value adjustments to available-for-sale securities).

Hedging

17.3.10 A **fair value hedge** hedges the exposure to changes in fair value of a recognized asset or liability or an unrecognized firm commitment (for example, changes in the fair value of fixed-rate bonds as a result of changes in market interest rates).

17.3.11 A **cash flow hedge** hedges the exposure of cash flows related to a recognized asset or liability (for example, future interest payments on a variable-rate bond), or to a highly probable forecast transaction (for example, an anticipated purchase or sale of inventories).

17.3.12 The **hedge of a net investment in a foreign operation** hedges the exposure related to changes in foreign exchange rates on an investment in a foreign operation.

17.4   **ACCOUNTING TREATMENT**

Recognition and Classification

17.4.1 All financial assets and financial liabilities (including derivatives) should be **recognized when** the entity becomes a party to the contractual provisions of an instrument.

17.4.2 For the purchase or sale of **financial assets** where market convention determines a fixed period between trade and settlement dates, either the trade or settlement date can be used for recognition. As stated above, IAS 39 allows the use of either date, but trade date accounting is preferred by most treasury accountants.

17.4.3 Management should establish policies for the classification of portfolios into various asset and liability classes (see table 17.1).

TABLE 17.1   Financial Asset and Liability Categories

Category	Measurement	Financial assets categories	Financial liabilities categories	Comments
1	Fair value through profit and loss	Trading securities	Trading liabilities	Mandatory classification if short sales or issued debt with intention to repurchase shortly or recent short-term profit taking
		Derivatives	Derivatives	Unless designated as qualifying hedging instruments
		Other elected assets	Other elected liabilities	Fair value option (elected)—accounting inconsistencies reduced or where part of a documented group risk management strategy, or if contain embedded derivatives
2	Amortized cost	Held-to-maturity securities	n.a.	Quoted or unquoted debt instruments where intention and ability to hold till maturity.
3	Amortized cost	Loans and receivables	n.a.	Debt instruments not quoted in an active market
4	Fair value through other comprehensive income	Available-for-sale securities	n.a.	Designated as such or default classification

Initial Measurement

17.4.4 Financial assets and financial liabilities are **recognized initially at their fair value**, which, unless evidence exists to the contrary, is the consideration given or received (that is, the transaction price). Transaction costs are included for all instruments not recognized at fair value through profit or loss. Certain hedging gains or losses are also included.

17.4.5 Interest is *not* normally **accrued** between trade and settlement dates, but mark-to-market adjustments are made regardless of whether the entity uses **trade date** or **settlement date** accounting.

Subsequent Measurement

17.4.6 **Unrealized gains or losses** on remeasurement to fair value of financial assets and financial liabilities are **included in net profit or loss for the period**. However there are **two exceptions to this rule:**

- Unrealized gains or losses on an available-for-sale financial asset must be recognized in other comprehensive income until it is sold or impaired, at which time the cumulative amount is transferred to net profit or loss for the period. (See also chapter 21 and example 17.1 at the end of this chapter.)
- When financial assets and financial liabilities (carried at amortized cost) are being hedged, special hedging rules apply.

17.4.7 **Impairment losses** are included in net profit or loss for the period irrespective of the category of financial assets. An entity should **assess**, at each reporting date, whether financial assets should be impaired.

- When impairment losses occur for **available-for-sale financial assets** (where fair value remeasurements are recognized in other comprehensive income), an amount should be transferred from other comprehensive income to net profit or loss for the period to the extent that the decline is below the original cost. Impairment losses on equity instruments may never be reversed through profit or loss. Impairment losses on debt instruments are reversed through profit or loss.
- A **financial asset** or a group of financial assets (for example, **loans and receivables**) measured at amortized cost is impaired if there is objective evidence (which includes observable data) as a result of one or more events that have already occurred after the initial recognition of the asset.
- When performing a collective assessment of impairment, assets must be grouped according to similar credit risk characteristics, indicative of the debtors' ability to pay all amounts due according to the contractual terms.
- Loss events must have an impact that can be reliably estimated on future cash flows.
- Losses expected as a result of future events, no matter how likely, are not recognized. (This conditionality appears to create a conflict with bank supervisory approaches that require a general percentage provision for loan losses, based on empirical evidence that such losses have actually occurred somewhere in the portfolio.)

17.4.8 **Subsequent measurement** of financial securities is summarized in table 17.2.

FIGURE 17.1 Decision Tree for Impairment of Available-for-Sale Financial Assets

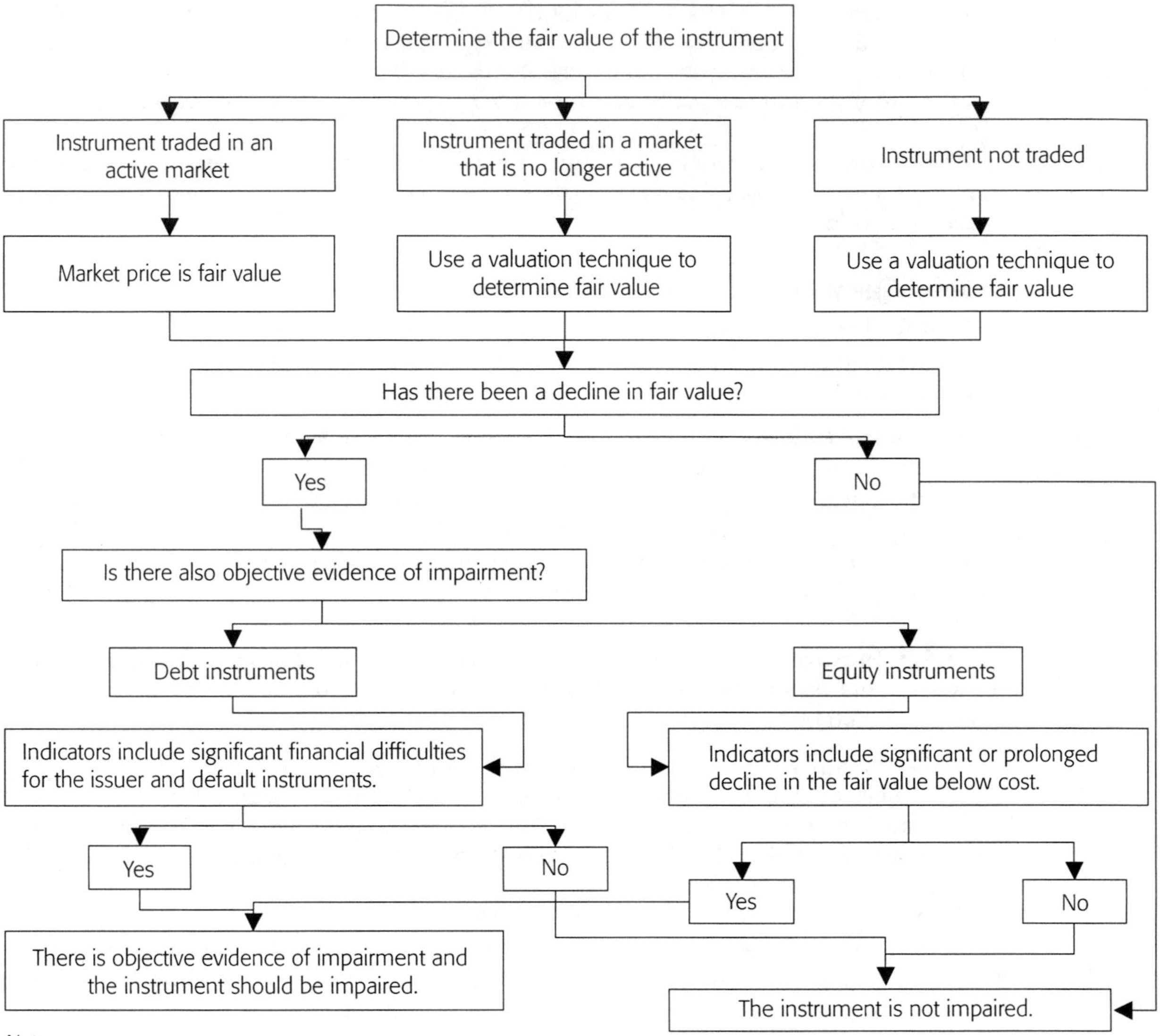

Note:

Objective evidence includes:

- significant financial difficulty of the issuer or obligor;
- a breach of contract, such as a default or delinquency in interest or principal payments; and
- granting the borrower a concession that the lender would not otherwise consider.

An impairment loss could be **reversed** in future periods, but the reversal may not exceed the amortized cost for those assets that are not remeasured at fair value (for example, held-to-maturity assets).

TABLE 17.2 Financial Impact of Various Portfolio Classification Choices under IAS 39

Classification	Element	Statement of Financial Position	Income statement	Other comprehensive income	Impairment
Fair value through profit or loss					
- held for trading	Assets and liabilities	Fair value	Fair value movements		
- designated at fair value	Assets and liabilities	Fair value	Fair value movements		
Available-for-sale	Assets	Fair value	Debt—interest at effective interest rate and foreign currency translation differences Equity—dividends Debt and equity— recycle from other comprehensive income on derecogntion	Debt and equity—fair value movements until instrument is derecognized Equity—foreign currency translation differences	Debt—recognized in profit or loss if default or financial difficulty and may be reversed Equity—recognized in profit or loss if significant or prolonged decline in fair value below cost and may not be reversed
Loans and receivables	Assets	Amortized cost	Interest at the effective interest rate		Recognized in profit or loss if objective evidence of impairment
Held to maturity	Assets	Amortized cost	Interest at the effective interest rate		Recognized in profit or loss if objective evidence of impairment
Amortized cost liabilities	Liabilities	Amortized cost	Interest at the effective interest rate		

Embedded Derivatives

17.4.9 An embedded derivative should be separated from its host and separately accounted for as a derivative if:

- the economic risks and characteristics of the host contract and embedded derivative are not closely related;
- the embedded derivative was a separate contract it would have met the definition of a derivative; and
- the combined instrument is not measured at fair value through profit or loss.

Derecognition

17.4.10 A **financial asset**, or portion thereof, is **derecognized** when the entity is no longer exposed to the substantial risks and rewards of ownership of the financial asset. If the extent of the entity's exposure to the risks and rewards of the asset is unclear, then the entity's ability to control the asset is considered (see figure 17.2).

FIGURE 17.2   Derecognition of Financial Assets

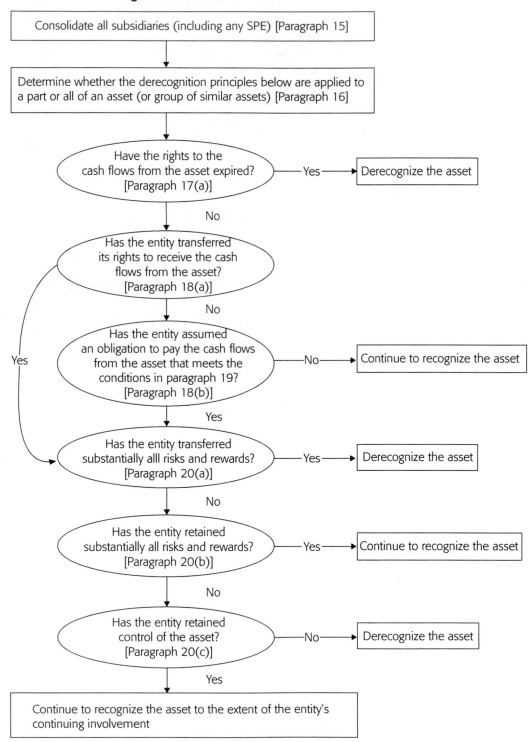

Arrangements under which an entity retains the contractual rights to receive the cash flows of a financial asset, but assumes a contractual obligation to pay the cash flows to one or more recipients (paragraph 18(b))

Source: IAS 39 Financial Instruments: Recognition and Measurement.

17.4.11 When a financial asset is derecognized, the difference between the proceeds and the carrying amount is included in the profit or loss for the period. Any prior cumulative revaluation surplus or shortfall that had been recognized directly in other comprehensive income is also included in the profit or loss for the period. When a part of a financial asset is derecognized, the carrying amount is allocated proportionally to the part sold using fair value at date of sale, and the resulting gain or loss is included in the profit or loss for the period.

17.4.12 A **financial liability is derecognized** when it is extinguished, that is, when the obligation is discharged, cancelled, or expires.

Reclassification

17.4.13 Assets designated as **fair value** through profit or loss may not be reclassified.

17.4.14 Assets classified as held for trading and recognized at fair value through profit or loss may be reclassified if no longer held for the purpose of selling or repurchasing in the near term into:

- any financial asset category in rare circumstances; or
- the loans and receivables category if the instruments would have met the loans and receivables definition at initial recognition and the entity has the intent and ability to hold the asset for the foreseeable future or to maturity.

Such assets are reclassified at current fair value and differences between the fair values at the date of the reclassification and post reclassification may be amortized over the remaining life of the asset. Any fair value movements recognized in profit or loss before the reclassification may not be reversed.

17.4.15 Entities are permitted to reclassify assets classified as **available for sale** to loans and receivables provided:

- they would have met the definition of a loan or receivable at initial recognition; and
- the entity has the intent and ability to hold the asset for the foreseeable future or to maturity.

17.4.16 An entity may not classify any financial assets as **held to maturity:**

- if during the current year or preceding two years it sold or reclassified more than an insignificant amount of held-to-maturity investments before maturity; or
- unless the action is as a result of an unanticipated, nonrecurring, isolated event beyond its control.

Changes in intention regarding assets in this category will result in nonavailability of the category for a period of three years.

17.4.17 If the **held-to-maturity** category is discontinued, the assets in that category can be reclassified only as available for sale.

TABLE 17.3   Reclassifications by Category

Classification	Reclassification	Into
Fair value through profit or loss assets		
– held for trading		
* derivative instrument	Not allowed. Becoming and ceasing to be part of a hedging relationship is not considered to be a reclassification	
* nonderivative instrument	If no longer held for trading	Available for sale in rare circumstances Loans and receivables if the assets meet the loans and receivables definition and if there is intention and ability to hold for the foreseeable future
– designated at fair value	Not allowed	
Available for sale	Allowed	Loans and receivables if the assets meet the loans and receivables definition and if there is intention and ability to hold for the foreseeable future Held to maturity after the three-year tainting period
Loans and receivable	Not allowed	
Held to maturity	Not allowed, otherwise the classification is tainted	If tainted, all held-to-maturity assets must be reclassified as available-for-sale and for the next two years no classification as held to maturity allowed. After third year reclassify assets as held to maturity if they meet the requirements
Financial liabilities	Not allowed	

Note:
* Additional disclosures and factors must be considered for items reclassified out of held for trading and available-for-sale categories, as follows:
• differences between the previous fair values and the new carrying values which are being amortized over the remaining life of the asset, via other comprehensive income
• the amount reclassified into and out of each category
• the carrying amounts and fair values of all financial assets that have been reclassified in the current and previous reporting periods
• the effective interest rate and cash flows expected to recover

Hedging

17.4.18 Hedge accounting:

- is a methodology for accounting for gains and losses associated with hedging activities.
- is an **optional accounting choice**. (Even when a position is hedged, the entity does not have to use hedge accounting to account for the transaction.)
- is an **accounting, not a business decision**.
- is allowed only when a hedging instrument is a
  - derivative (but not if it is a written option);
  - written option only when used to hedge a purchased option; or
  - nonderivative financial asset or liability when used to hedge foreign currency risks.
- may not be designated for only a **portion** of the time period over which the instrument is outstanding.

17.4.19 Hedging means designating a derivative or nonderivative financial instrument as an offset to the change in fair value or cash flows of a hedged item. A hedging relationship qualifies for hedge accounting if the following criteria apply:

- At the inception of the hedge, there is formal **documentation** setting out the hedge details.
- The hedge is expected to be highly effective (prospective effectiveness).
- In the case of a forecasted transaction, the transaction must be highly probable.
- The effectiveness of the hedge is reliably measured.
- The hedge was effective *throughout* the period (retrospective effectiveness) (as described in table 17.4).

17.4.20 Hedge accounting (see table 17.4) recognizes symmetrically the offsetting effects on net profit or loss of changes in the fair values of the hedging instrument and the related item being hedged. Hedging relationships are of three types:

1. **Fair value hedge**—hedges the exposure of a recognized asset or liability or an unrecognized firm commitment (for example, changes in the fair value of fixed-rate bonds as a result of changes in market interest rates).
2. **Cash flow hedge**—hedges the exposure to variability in cash flows related to a recognized asset or liability (for example, future interest payments on a bond); or a forecasted Transaction (for example, an anticipated purchase or sale of inventories).
3. **Hedge of a net investment in a foreign operation**—hedges the exposure related to changes in foreign exchange rates.

17.4.21 The **gain or loss on a fair value hedge** should be recognized in net profit or loss, and the loss or the gain from adjusting the carrying amount of the hedged item should be recognized in net profit or loss. This applies even if the hedged item is accounted for at cost. If the hedged item is an unrecognized firm commitment, the gain or loss should be recognized as an asset or liability.

17.4.22 Profits and losses on cash flow hedges are treated as follows:

- The portion of the gain or loss on the hedging instrument deemed to be an **effective** hedge is recognized directly in other comprehensive income through the statement of comprehensive income. The ineffective portion is reported in net profit or loss.
- If the hedged forecasted transaction results in the recognition of a financial asset or liability, the associated gain or loss previously recognized in other comprehensive income should be recycled to profit or loss in the same period(s) that the asset or liability affects profit or loss.
- If the hedged forecasted transaction results in the recognition of a nonfinancial asset or liability, then the entity has an accounting policy election to either include the gains or loss previously recognized in other comprehensive income in the initial cost of the asset or liability, or to recycle the asset or liability to profit or loss in the same period(s) that the asset or liability affects profit or loss.
- If the hedged forecast transaction is no longer expected to occur, the gain or loss previously recognized in other comprehensive income is recycled.
- For cash flow hedges that do not result in an asset or liability, the gain or loss in other comprehensive income should be taken to profit or loss when the transaction occurs.

17.4.23 The portion of the **profits and losses on hedges of a net investment in a foreign entity** on the hedging instrument deemed to be an effective hedge is recognized directly in other comprehensive income through the statement of comprehensive income. The ineffective portion is reported in net profit or loss.

TABLE 17.4 Hedge Accounting Rules

	Recognize in profit or loss	Recognize in other comprehensive income	Recognize in initial measurement of asset/liability
Fair value hedge	All adjustments on hedging instrument and hedged item		
Cash flow hedge	Gain/loss on ineffective portion of hedging instrument[b] Gain/loss previously recognized in other comprehensive income when: • hedge does not result in asset/liability; • financial asset or liability affects profit or loss; and/or • forecast transaction no longer probable	Gain/loss on effective portion of the hedging instrument[a]	Gain/loss previously recognized in other comprehensive income if nonfinancial asset or liability and accounting policy elected
Hedge of net investment in foreign operation	Gain/loss on ineffective portion of hedging instrument[b] Gain/loss previously recognized in other comprehensive income when the foreign operation affects profit or loss	Gain/loss on the effective portion of hedging instrument	

Notes:
a. A hedge is normally regarded to be highly effective if, at inception and throughout the life of the hedge, the entity can expect changes in the fair values or cash flows of the hedged item to be almost fully offset by the changes in the hedging instrument, and actual results are in the range of 80 percent to 125 percent. For example, if the loss on a financial liability is 56 and the profit on the hedging instrument is 63, the hedge is regarded to be effective: $63 \div 56 = 112.5$ percent.
b. An ineffective hedge would be one where actual results of offset are outside the range mentioned above. Furthermore, a hedge would not be fully effective if the hedging instrument and the hedged item are denominated in different currencies, and the two do not move in tandem. Also, a hedge of interest-rate risk using a derivative would not be fully effective if part of the change in the fair value of the derivative is due to the counterparty's credit risk.

Financial Guarantees

17.4.24 Financial guarantees issued are within the scope of the standard unless the entity has specifically stated that such contracts are considered to be insurance contracts. Financial guarantees are defined as a contract that requires the issuer to make specified payments to reimburse the holder for a loss it incurs because a specified debtor fails to make payment when due in accordance with a debt instrument.

17.4.25 Financial guarantees are initially measured at fair value. Subsequent measurement is at the higher of the amount initially recognized amortized over the life of the guarantee or the amount determined per IAS 37 (see chapter 21).

17.5 PRESENTATION AND DISCLOSURE

17.5.1 Presentation issues are dealt with in IAS 32 (chapter 33).

17.5.2 Disclosure issues are dealt with in IFRS 7 (chapter 34).

17.6   **FINANCIAL ANALYSIS AND INTERPRETATION**

17.6.1 The analyst should obtain an understanding of management's policies for classifying securities.

17.6.2 Securities held for trading, designated fair value instruments, and available-for-sale securities are valued at fair value. However, the unrealized profits and losses on available-for-sale securities do not flow directly through profit or loss. Therefore, total return calculations need to reflect this.

17.6.3 Available-for-sale securities must also be marked-to-market (fair valued) and **unrealized** profits and losses taken directly to other comprehensive income (and not to profit or loss). Securities that are not held to maturity, but are also not held for trading, are classified as available for sale. These securities are valued in a similar way as trading securities: they are carried at fair value. However, only realized (actual sales) gains and losses arising from the sale or reclassification of investments or impairment below the original cost are recorded in profit or loss. Unrealized gains and losses are shown as a separate component of other comprehensive income.

17.6.4 The use of the available for sale category is a discretionary decision by entity management, and is therefore likely to be inconsistently applied across different entities. The standard requires that information relating to the profit and loss be separately disclosed in other comprehensive income, and it may be necessary for an analyst to use this disclosure to achieve comparability between entities.

17.6.5 There are sound reasons why it might be preferable to take **unrealized gains and losses** through profit or loss. The total return on the portfolio—including both coupon income and changes in price—is an accurate reflection of the portfolio performance. When there is an asymmetrical treatment of capital gains or losses and coupon income, it can lead to unsophisticated observers regarding investment income in a manner incompatible with the total return maximization objectives of modern portfolio management. By taking unrealized gains and losses through profit and loss, portfolio management will correctly focus on making portfolio decisions to maximize returns based on anticipated future relative returns, rather than on making decisions for short-term income effect.

17.6.6 Available-for-sale securities require sophisticated systems and accounting capacity. As stated in chapter 21, the treatment of foreign currency translation gains and losses adds to this complexity.

17.6.7 Held-to-maturity securities are most often purchased debt securities that management intends and is able to hold to maturity. These securities are recorded initially at cost and are valued on the Statement of Financial Position at amortized cost value. The book value of the marketable security is reported on the Statement of Financial Position, and the interest income as well as any amortization profits or losses and impairments losses are reported in profit or loss. The coupon receipt is recorded as an operating cash flow.

17.6.8 A key purpose of derivatives is to modify future cash flows by minimizing the entity's exposure to risks, by increasing risk exposure, or by deriving benefits from these instruments. An entity can readily adjust its positions in financial instruments to align its financing activities with operating activities and, thereby, improve its allocation of capital to accommodate changes in the business environment. All such activities, or their possible occurrence, should be transparent to financial statements' users. For example, not reporting significant interest rate or foreign currency swap transactions would be as inappropriate as not consolidating a significant subsidiary.

17.6.9 **Sensitivity analysis** is an essential element needed for estimating an entity's future expected cash flows; these estimates are needed in calculating the entity's valuation. Therefore, sensitivity analysis is an integral and essential component of fair value accounting and reporting. For example, many derivative instruments have significant statistical deviation from the expected norm, which affects future cash flows. Unless those potential effects are transparent in disclosures and analyses (for example, in sensitivity analyses or stress tests), the Statement of Financial Position representation of fair values for financial instruments is incomplete and cannot be used properly to assess risk-return relationships and to analyze management's performance.

17.7	**COMMENTARY**

17.7.1 IAS 39 has been the subject of considerable debate and controversy since its introduction. It deals with exceptionally complicated concepts and involves and requires a detailed understanding of financial instruments. The standard sets out to provide the preparer with the opportunity to reflect the economic outcome of managements' intention, but also sets out to prevent manipulation. These sometimes contradictory objectives have resulted in a standard which is complex, rule based, and incorporates a number of alternative choices.

17.7.2 The standard introduces a mixed measurement and a mixed classification model. The measurement model provides for measurement of financial instruments at amortized cost, fair value through profit or loss, or fair value through other comprehensive income. The classification model provides for classification of financial instruments based on various factors, for example the contractual terms of the instruments and management's intention and behavior with regards to that instrument. Additionally, the classification model contains certain anti-avoidance requirements and other specific classification rules. The mixed classification model can result in similar instruments being classified and measured differently within the same entity and by different entities. For example, a government bond can be held for trading by a bank's treasury department (classified as held for trading at fair value through profit or loss), held as part of the liquid asset portfolio (classified as available-for-sale), and held for investment purposes (classified as held to maturity). Hedge accounting, if applied, adds additional measurement and classification models.

17.7.3 The standard includes complex rules on derecognition, impairment, hedge accounting, and determining fair value among others, the details of which have not been addressed in this book. Significant judgment is required in various areas, for example determining whether the entity has transferred the significant risks and rewards of ownership of a financial asset or whether the fair value of the available-for-sale equity instrument indicates a significant or prolonged decline in fair value.

The hedge accounting requirements are very rules based and onerous to implement in practice. For example, a hedge has to be between 80–125 percent effective for hedge accounting to be allowed. If a hedge is 78 percent effective, hedge accounting is not allowed. Various other complex rules also exist, such as partial term hedging, hedging of a net position, and risks that may be hedged. Proving prospective and retrospective hedge effectiveness testing is a very onerous exercise. In many situations the requirements for applying hedge accounting are more onerous than beneficial, resulting in entities choosing not to apply it.

17.7.4 As a result of the global financial crisis during 2008 and 2009, the IASB has undertaken a fundamental reconsideration of reporting for financial instruments. The project has been divided into five phases:

- classification and measurement of financial assets;
- classification and measurement of financial liabilities, including the issue of movement in own credit risk;

- impairment;
- hedge accounting; and
- derecognition.

Classification and Measurement of Financial Assets

17.7.5 The classification and measurement of financial assets phase was completed in November 2009. Under the new model financial assets are classified and subsequently measured either at **amortized cost** or **fair value,** based on the entity's **business model** and the contractual cash flow characteristics.

17.7.6 A financial asset is measured at amortized cost if it is within a business model that holds the asset to collect contractual cash flows and the contractual cash flows are purely for principal and interest. All other assets are measured at fair value. The fair value option still exists whereby an entity can designate an asset on initial recognition as measured at fair value through profit or loss if the designation eliminates an accounting mismatch. The loans and receivables, available-for-sale, and held to maturity classifications have been deleted.

17.7.7 An embedded derivative attached to a financial host contract may not be bifurcated. The embedded derivative is considered in determining the amortized cost or fair value classification. An embedded derivative attached to a nonfinancial host is recognized in terms of the current requirements of IAS 39.

17.7.8 Reclassifications are allowed when the business model for managing financial assets changes.

17.7.9 Equity investments not held for trading purposes may be classified on initial recognition as fair value through other comprehensive income. The election is irrevocable. All fair value gains or losses are recognized in other comprehensive income and not recycled to profit or loss on sale of the asset. Dividends are recognized in profit or loss.

17.7.10 The requirements are effective for annual periods beginning on or after January 1, 2013, with retrospective application. Early application is permitted.

Other Phases

17.7.11 The other phases of the IASB project will be completed during the course of 2010. The current proposal is to change the current incurred loss model to an expected loss model that is applicable to all financial assets measured at amortized cost. Financial assets measured at fair value will not be impaired. The requirements of the hedge accounting and derecognition models have not been clarified.

Resource and Skill Requirements

17.7.12 Application of the standard requires a detailed understanding of these specific rules, and a detailed understanding of the underlying financial instruments. Proper and considered judgment is needed when classifying assets and liabilities in the context of management intention and the entity's ability to hold assets. The proper structure of hedging relationships, their documentation and measurement, and the ongoing testing requirement also require specialist skills.

17.8	**IMPLEMENTATION DECISIONS**

Strategic Decisions

17.8.1 IAS 39 allows an entity to designate financial instruments at fair value through profit or loss. In making this decision, consideration should be given to how the instruments are managed and whether such designation reduces an accounting mismatch.

17.8.2 Under very rare circumstances, an entity may reclassify financial instruments. IAS 39 requires disclosure of this reclassification. In reaching this decision, an entity should take account of market conditions, industry practice, and the potential reputational risk associated with a reclassification.

Tactical Decisions

17.8.3 Decisions need to be taken about which fees and costs are considered to be part of the effective interest rate.

17.8.4 A decision needs to be taken as to whether hedge accounting will be applied by the entity. When a hedging relationship is identified, the necessary documentation must be completed and must be in line with management's overall risk management framework.

17.8.5 Management will need to ensure that there are processes in place to identify embedded derivatives.

17.8.6 Management may need to determine whether it is appropriate to reclassify a financial instrument.

Problems to Overcome

17.8.7 Fair value measurement by its nature will result in more volatile profit and loss results. These may have to be explained to analysts and investors.

17.8.8 In smaller markets there are often many instruments for which there is no active market or for which there are not regular market transactions. Information required to determine the fair value of these types of instruments may be more difficult to obtain. The fair value of these instruments will obviously be more subjective than the fair value of an instrument for which there is a market price or for which other market information is available.

17.8.9 The requirements to apply hedge accounting are onerous. Extensive documentation is required at the inception of the hedge and at inception and throughout the life of the hedge the effectiveness must be tested.

17.8.10 If the requirements are not met in any reporting period hedge accounting will be prohibited. Therefore it is important for entities to have a system in place that monitors all hedges for compliance with the hedging requirements.

17.8.11 Embedded derivatives are often difficult to spot; they may go unnoticed, if there is not a specific process in place to identify them.

17.8.12 Determining whether an embedded derivative is closely related to the host contract may require some judgment.

17.8.13 Impairment losses for instruments designated as available for sale are calculated differently from those that are classified as loans and receivables and held to maturity.

EXAMPLES: FINANCIAL INSTRUMENTS—RECOGNITION AND MEASUREMENT

EXAMPLE 17.1

An entity receives $100 million equity in cash on July 1, 20X5.

It invests in a bond of $100 million par at a clean price of $97 million **and** a 5 percent fixed coupon on July 1, 20X5.

Coupons are paid annually, and the bond has a maturity date of June 30, 20X7. The yield to maturity is calculated as 6.6513 percent.

On June 30, 20X6, the entity receives the first coupon payment of $5 million. The clean market value of the security has increased to $99 million at June 30, 20X6. The security has not been impaired and no principal has been repaid.

Using the effective interest method, the $3 million discount is amortized $1.45 million in year 1 and $1.55 million in year 2.

17.1.A   Illustrate how this situation will be portrayed in the entity's Statement of Financial Position, as well as its Statement of Comprehensive Income—under each of the following three accounting policies for marketable securities: assets held for trading purposes, assets available for sale, assets held to maturity.

17.1.B   Discuss the treatment of discounts or premiums on securities purchased in the financial statements of the entity.

17.1.C   If these securities were denominated in a foreign currency, how would translation gains and losses be treated in the financial statements of the entity?

Source: Hamish Flett—Treasury Operations, World Bank.

EXPLANATIONS

17.1.A Financial Statements

Statement of Financial Position as of December 31, 20X6	Held-to-Maturity Portfolio	Trading Portfolio	Available-for-Sale Portfolio
Assets	8.00	8.00	8.00
Cash	98.45	99.00	99.00
Securities	106.45	107.00	107.00
Analysis of Securities			
Cost of securities	97.00	97.00	97.00
Amortization of discount/premium	1.45	–	1.45
Unrealized profit/loss	–	2.00	0.55
	98.45	99.00	99.00
Liabilities			
Equity	100.00	100.00	100.00
Unrealized profit/loss on securities	–	–	0.55
Net income	6.45	7.00	6.45
	106.45	107.00	107.00
Statement of Comprehensive Income for year ending December 31, 20X6			
Interest income	5.00	5.00	5.00
Amortization of discount/premium	1.45	–	1.45
Unrealized profit/loss on securities	–	2.00	–
Realized profit/loss net income	6.45	7.00	6.45

17.1.B

a. With the trading portfolio, the amortization of discount/premium is effectively accounted for in the mark-to-market adjustment. As the amortization of discount/premium, realized profit and loss (P&L), and unrealized P&L for a trading portfolio are all recorded in profit or loss, it is not necessary to separate the discount/premium amortization element from the mark-to-market adjustment. However, it may be desirable to record any discount/premium amortization separately, even for a trading portfolio, to provide additional management information on the performance of traders.

b. If the trading security were subsequently sold, the clean sale proceeds would be compared to its clean cost to determine the realized P&L.

c. If the available-for-sale security were subsequently sold, the clean sale proceeds would be compared to its amortized cost to determine the realized P&L, as amortization is already reflected.

d. Following is the interest amortization table:

	Amortized cost	Effective interest rate	Effective interest	Coupon payment	Amortization premium/ discount
End of Period	97.000	6.651%	6.45	5.00	1.452
1	98.452	6.651%	6.55	5.00	1.548
2	100.00				3.00

17.1.C All foreign currency translation adjustments on equity securities (see IAS 21) should be reflected in other comprehensive income. In the case of available-for-sale debt securities, the mark-to-market adjustment portion of the foreign currency translation should be reflected in other comprehensive income in line with the normal treatment of fair value adjustments for available-for-sale securities. Note, however, that the foreign currency adjustment related to the principal amount of an available-for-sale debt security is taken directly to profit or loss.

EXAMPLE 17.2

The following example illustrates the accounting treatment for a hedge of the exposure to variability in cash flows (cash flow hedge) that is attributable to a forecast transaction.

The Milling Co. is reviewing its maize purchases for the coming season. It anticipates purchasing 1,000 tons of maize in two months. Currently, the two-month maize futures are selling at $600 per ton, and Milling Co. will be satisfied with purchasing its maize inventory at this price by the end of May.

As renewed drought is staring the farmers in the face, Milling Co. is afraid that the maize price might increase. It therefore hedges its anticipated purchase against this possible increase in the maize price by going long (buying) on two-month maize futures at $600 per ton for 1,000 tons. The transaction requires Milling Co. to pay an initial margin of $30,000 into its margin account. Margin accounts are updated twice every month.

The following market prices are applicable:

Date	Futures price (per ton)
April 1	$600
April 15	$590
April 30	$585
May 15	$605
May 31	$620 (spot)

The maize price in fact increased because of the drought, and Milling Co. purchases the projected 1,000 tons of maize at the market (spot) price of $620 per ton on May 31.

The calculation of variation margins is as follows:

April 15 (600 − 590) × 1,000 tons = $10,000 (payable)
April 30 (590 − 585) × 1,000 tons = $5,000 (payable)
May 15 (605 − 585) × 1,000 tons = $20,000 (receivable)
May 31 (620 − 605) × 1,000 tons = $15,000 (receivable)

The accounting entries will be as follows:

	Dr ($)	Cr ($)
April 1		
Initial Margin Account (B/S)	30,000	
Cash		30,000
(Settlement of initial margin)		
April 15		
Hedging Reserve (Equity)	10,000	
Cash Payable (variation margin)		10,000
(Account for the loss on the futures contract—cash flow hedge)		
April 30		
Hedging Reserve (Equity)	5,000	
Cash Payable (variation margin)		5,000
(Account for the loss on the futures contract—cash flow hedge)		
May15		
Cash Receivable (variation margin)	20,000	
Hedging Reserve (Equity)		20,000
(Account for the profit on the futures contract—cash flow hedge)		
May 31		
Cash Receivable (variation margin)	15,000	
Hedging Reserve (Equity)		15,000
(Account for the profit on the futures contract—cash flow hedge)		
May 31		
Inventory	620,000	
Cash		620,000
(Purchase the inventory at spot—1,000 tons @ $620 per ton)		
May 31		
Cash	30,000	
Margin Account		30,000
(Receive initial margin deposited)		
May 31		
Hedging Reserve (Equity) Inventory	20,000	20,000

The gain or loss on the cash flow hedge should be removed from other comprehensive income, and the value of the underlying asset recognized should be adjusted, if that is the accounting policy elected by the entity. Alternatively the gain or loss remains in other comprehensive income until the underlying asset affects profit or loss, at which point it is recycled to profit or loss.

It is clear from this example that the value of the inventory is adjusted with the gain on the hedging instrument, resulting in the inventory being accounted for at the hedged price or futures price.

If the futures contract did not expire or was not closed out on May 31, the gains or losses calculated on the futures contract thereafter would be accounted for in profit or loss, because the cash flow hedge relationship no longer exists.

EXAMPLE 17.3

This example concerns short-term money market instruments not marked-to-market (held in a held-to-maturity portfolio).

A company buys a 120-day Treasury bill with a face value of $1 million for $996,742. When purchased, the recorded book value of the bill is this original cost.

EXPLANATION

Held-to-maturity instruments are recognized at amortized cost on the Statement of Financial Position using the effective interest rate method. The effective interest rate takes into account any premium or discount. The interest income is reported in profit or loss. The discount earned is recorded as an operating cash flow. Following is the entry to record the purchase of the bill:

	Dr ($)	Cr ($)
Short-term Investments	996,742	
Cash		996,742

If 60 days later the company is constructing its financial statements, the Treasury bill must be marked up to its amortized cost using the following adjusting entry:

	Dr ($)	Cr ($)
Short-term Investments	1,629	
Interest Income		1,629[1]

$$\text{Interest income} = (P_m - P_o)\ 1/t_m$$
$$= \$1,000,000 - 996,742\ (60/120)$$
$$= \$1629$$

where P_m is the value of the bill at maturity.

P_o is the value of the bill when purchased.

t is the number of days the bill has been held.

t_m is the number of days until the bill matures from when purchased.

The Treasury bill will be recorded on the Statement of Financial Position as a short-term investment valued at its adjusted cost of $998,371 ($996,742 + $1,629), whereas the $1,629 discount earned will be reported as interest income in profit or loss.

When the Treasury bill matures, the entry is as follows:

	Dr ($)	Cr ($)
Cash	1,000,000	
Short-term Investments		998,371
Interest Income		1,629*

*Assumes 60 days of interest on a straight-line basis as an approximation of effective interest rate.

EXAMPLE 17.4

This is an example of accounting for trading securities—marked-to-market and unrealized profits taken through profit or loss.

On November 30, 20X3, a company buys 100 shares of Amazon for $90 per share and 100 shares of IBM for $75 per share.

The securities are classified as trading securities (current assets) and are valued at fair value (market value).

EXPLANATION

Any increase or decrease in the value is included in net income in the year in which it occurs. Also, any income received from the security is recorded in net income.

To record the initial purchases, the entry is

	Dr ($)	Cr ($)
Traded Equities	16,500 (100 × $90 + 100 × $75)	
Cash		16,500

One month later, the company is preparing its year-end financial statements. On December 31, 20X3, Amazon's closing trade was at $70 per share, and IBM's was at $80 per share. Thus, the company's investment in these two firms has fallen to $15,000 (100 × $70 + 100 × $80). The traded securities account is adjusted as follows:

	Dr ($)	Cr ($)
Unrealized Gains/Loss on Investments	1,500	
Traded Equities		1,500

Notice that the loss on Amazon and gain on IBM are netted. Thus, a net loss is recorded, which reduces the firm's income. This is an unrealized loss, as the shares have not been sold, so the firm has not actually realized a loss, but this is still recorded in profit or loss.

In mid-January 20X4, the firm receives a dividend of $0.16 per share on its IBM stock. The entry is as follows:

	Dr ($)	Cr ($)
Cash	16 ($0.16 × 100)	
Investment Income		16

Finally, on January 23, 20X4, the firm sells both stocks. It receives $80 per share for Amazon and $85 per share for IBM. The entry is as follows:

	Dr ($)	Cr ($)
Cash	16,500 (100 × $80 + 100 × $85)	
Traded Equities		15,000
Unrealized Gains/Loss on Investments		1,500

By consistently recording fair value adjustments to an unrealized gain/loss account, that account is cleared when the security is sold.

EXAMPLE 17.5

This example shows calculation of the effective interest rate when there is a premium or a discount.

An entity acquires a bond with a nominal value of $1 million at a discount and pays $800,000. The bond accrues interest at 5 percent and has a maturity date of five years from the date of issue. In five years the bond will be redeemed for its nominal value and interest is payable annually.

The bond is not quoted in an active market and therefore is classified as loans and receivables and is measured at amortized cost.

When accounting for this bond the entity will first have to determine the effective interest rate, that is, the rate that exactly discounts the cash flows on the bond to $0.

The following cash flows are relevant:

Period	Cash flow $
0	(800,000)
1	50,000
2	50,000
3	50,000
4	50,000
5	1,050,000

These cash flows result in an effective interest rate of 10.32 percent when calculated on a financial calculator.

The following amortization schedule is applicable:

	Opening balance	Payment	Interest for the period	Capital repaid	Closing balance
Period 1	$800,000	$50,000	$82,552	–$32,552	$832,552
Period 2	$832,552	$50,000	$85,911	–$35,911	$868,463
Period 3	$868,463	$50,000	$89,617	–$39,617	$908,080
Period 4	$908,080	$50,000	$93,705	–$43,705	$951,785
Period 5	$951,785	$1,050,000	$98,215	$951,785	—

Therefore the following accounting journals will be recorded at each period:

Period 0

Dr Investment in bond	$800,000
Cr Bank	$800,000
Acquisition of bond	

Period 1

Dr Bank	$50,000
Dr Investment in bond	$32,552
Cr Interest income	$82,552
Recognition of interest earned and received	

Period 2

Dr Bank	$50,000
Dr Investment in bond	$35,911
Cr Interest income	$85,911
Recognition of interest earned and received	

Period 3

Dr Bank	$50,000
Dr Investment in bond	$39,617
Cr Interest income	$89,617
Recognition of interest earned and received	

Period 4

Dr Bank	$50,000
Dr Investment in bond	$43,705
Cr Interest income	$93,705
Recognition of interest earned and received	

Period 5

Dr Bank	$1,050,000
Cr Investment in bond	$951,785
Cr Interest income	$98,215
Recognition of interest earned and received	

CHAPTER 18

Financial Instruments
(IFRS 9)

18.1 | **OBJECTIVE**

IAS 39 has been criticized for being rule based, too complex, and permitting too many alternatives in respect of recognition and measurement of financial instruments. The IASB has undertaken a project to rewrite IAS 39 into a more principles-based standard with fewer alternatives. In order to complete the rewrite in the most efficient and effective manner the IASB has split the project into phases. IFRS 9 as it stands is the first phase of the IAS 39 rewrite, dealing with the classification of financial assets. Phases that have yet to be completed include financial liabilities, impairment, derecognition, and hedge accounting. It is expected that all of these will be completed by the end of 2010. Until these phases have been completed the requirements of IAS 39 for financial instruments remain in place (see chapter 17).

18.2 | **SCOPE**

IFRS 9 applies to all financial assets that are in the scope of IAS 39. Refer to chapter 17 for detailed rules in IAS 39.

18.3 | **KEY CONCEPTS**

IFRS 9 does not contain any definitions and relies on the current definitions of financial assets, derivatives, and embedded derivatives contained in IAS 39 and IAS 32. Refer to chapters 17 and 32 respectively for the accounting rules contained in these standards.

18.4 | **ACCOUNTING TREATMENT**

18.4.1 An entity shall recognize a financial asset in its statement of financial position when it becomes party to the contractual provisions of the instrument. The guidance relating to the initial recognition of a financial asset as contained in IAS 39 remains applicable to all financial assets. On initial recognition the financial asset should be classified as either amortized cost or fair value based on the requirements in IFRS 9.

18.4.2 A financial asset may be measured at amortized cost only if both of the following requirements are met:

- it is held within a business model whose objective is to hold assets in order to collect contractual cash flows; and
- the contractual terms of the financial asset give rise on specified dates to cash flows that are solely payments of principal and interest on the principal outstanding.

18.4.3 For the purposes of applying IFRS 9, interest must represent the consideration for the time value of money and for the credit risk associated with the principal amount outstanding during a particular period of time.

18.4.4 All financial instruments that are not measured at amortized cost must be measured at fair value. An instrument that meets the requirements of IFRS 9 to be measured at amortized cost may be designated at fair value if that designation eliminates or significantly reduces a measurement or recognition inconsistency.

18.4.5 If a hybrid contract that contains an embedded derivative is in the scope of IFRS 9 the classification requirements are applied to the entire hybrid contract. Embedded derivatives may not be separated; instead, the entire instrument will be measured at either fair value or amortized cost based on the classification criteria in IFRS 9. These rules only apply to hybrid contracts where the host contract is a financial asset. For instruments where the host contract is a financial liability or a nonfinancial instrument the current IAS 39 rules remain applicable.

18.4.6 Reclassification of financial instruments is possible only when an entity changes its business model for managing financial assets. Such changes are expected to be very infrequent and must be significant to the entity's operations and demonstrable to external parties. The reclassification will be applied prospectively from the first day of the reporting period following the change in business model. For example, if an entity has a financial year from April 1, X1 to March 31, X2 and the entity has a change in business model on February 15, X2, the reclassification will take effect from April 1, X2.

18.4.7 Initially financial assets must be measured at fair value, and for financial assets not measured at fair value through profit or loss, fair value plus transaction costs.

18.4.8 Subsequent to initial recognition, financial assets measured at amortized cost must be measured in line with the IAS 39 requirements for determining amortized cost. All financial assets measured at fair value must be measured at fair value in line with the IAS 39 requirements for determining fair value.

18.4.9 At initial recognition an entity may make an irrevocable election to present in other comprehensive income subsequent changes in the fair value of an investment in an equity instrument that is not held for trading. Dividends on these investments are recognized in profit or loss in accordance with IAS 18 when the entity's right to receive payment is established.

18.4.10 Gains or losses on financial assets measured at amortized cost that are not part of a hedging relationship are recognized in profit or loss. Gains or losses on financial assets measured at fair value that are not part of a hedging relationship are recognized in profit or loss. The only exception is for equity instruments where the entity has elected to present gains and losses on that instrument in other comprehensive income as per irrevocable election discussed in 18.4.9 above.

Figure 18.1 **Transitional Provisions of IFRS 9**

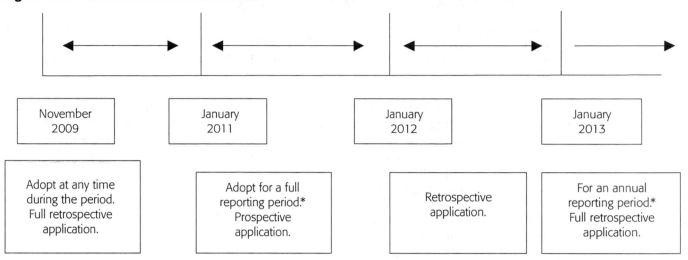

November 2009	January 2011	January 2012	January 2013
Adopt at any time during the period. Full retrospective application.	Adopt for a full reporting period.* Prospective application.	Retrospective application.	For an annual reporting period.* Full retrospective application.

* Wording per the standard. Unclear what the difference is between a full reporting period and an annual reporting period. A reporting period could be an interim period.

18.4.11 IFRS 9 is mandatorily applicable for annual periods beginning on or after January 1, 2013 with full retrospective application. If an entity adopts this IFRS before January 1, 2011, then the application date can be at any time and need not be at the beginning of the reporting period. However, full retrospective application will be required. If IFRS 9 is adopted for reporting periods beginning before January 1, 2012, the entity need not restate prior year numbers. These options are set out in figure 18.1 above.

18.4.12 The following transitional provisions apply:

- The classification will depend on the facts and circumstances at the date of initial application.
- The fair value of a hybrid contract that has not been accounted for as a single contract in the past shall be the sum of the fair value of the host contract and the fair value of the derivative. Any differences between the fair value at initial application and the sum of the fair value of the host and derivative should be recognized in opening retained earnings.
- The previous designation at fair value through profit or loss may be revoked if the financial asset meets the criteria to be measured at amortized cost.
- If it is impracticable to apply the effective interest rate method retrospectively, then the fair value of the asset in the comparative periods will be treated as amortized cost of the asset.
- Any unquoted equities or derivatives on these equities that were measured at cost in terms of IAS 39 will be measured at fair value and any difference between cost and fair value will be recognized in opening retained earnings.

18.5   PRESENTATION AND DISCLOSURE

18.5.1 The current presentation and disclosure requirements in IAS 32 and IFRS 7 are applied to all financial assets. Details of these requirements are set out in chapters 32 and 33 respectively.

18.6

FINANCIAL ANALYSIS AND INTERPRETATION

18.6.1 The choices for the classification and measurement of financial assets have been reduced significantly from IAS 39 to IFRS 9. Therefore, it should be easier for users to understand the financial assets recognized by an entity and the cash flows associated with those financial assets.

18.6.2 Until such time as IAS 39 has been replaced in its entirety there may be a mixed model for reporting financial instruments. Some aspects may be accounted for in terms of IAS 39 and other aspects under IFRS 9. This may increase complexity and reduce the understandability of financial statements in the short term. There could also be a mixed model between different entities as some entities would early adopt portions of IFRS 9 while others will continue applying IAS 39. Until IFRS 9 is finalized, users of financial statements should be aware of the possibly mixed accounting model when assessing the nature, amount, and uncertainty of cash flows associated with financial instruments and comparing the financial statements of different entities.

18.7

COMMENTARY

18.7.1 IFRS 9 provides a much simpler approach to classifying and measuring financial assets, including those that contain embedded derivatives. That said, the classification of financial instruments still will require significant judgment to be applied, particularly for instruments that have more complex cash flows.

18.7.2 The measurement requirements are not significantly impacted by this phase of the project as the method for determining fair value and amortized cost remains as per IAS 39. The fact that impairment is only calculated for instruments measured at amortized cost is a significant simplification, because the impairment of available-for-sale assets involved judgment and arbitrary rules regarding recognition and reversals.

18.7.3 The reclassification requirements prevent an entity from manipulating numbers by reclassifying financial assets in the current year. The benefit of the reclassification will only be effective in the following financial year.

18.7.4 It was hoped that the remaining four phases of IFRS 9 (accounting for financial liabilities, impairment, derecognition, and hedging) would be completed in 2010, and that IFRS 9 would entirely replace IAS 39 by the end of 2010. However, this goal may no longer be achievable. IASB probably will need to investigate whether decisions made in later stages of the project affect earlier conclusions about financial assets, and whether any changes are required to the principles that have been established.

18.7.5 In November 2009 the IASB issued an exposure draft that set out the proposals for including credit loss expectations in the amortized cost measurement of financial assets. The exposure draft defines amortized cost measurement as a measurement basis that "*provides information about the effective return on a financial asset or financial liability by allocating interest revenue over the expected life of the instrument.*" As such the exposure draft proposes that for instruments measured at amortized cost the effective interest rate is calculated at inception based on the expected cash flows over the life of the instrument. At each measurement date the current expected cash flows are to be discounted to the present value based on the effective interest rate calculated at inception. To the extent that the actual cash flows are in line with the expected cash flows no additional impairments will need to be recognized and the impairment allowance will be created through the effective interest rate being lower than the contractual interest rate. To the extent that the actual cash flows differ from the expected cash flows a change in estimate will be recognized immediately in profit or loss to bring the value of the instrument in line with the expected cash flows at the measurement date.

18.7.6 In May 2010 the IASB issued an exposure draft on the fair value option for financial liabilities. The exposure draft proposes allowing entities to designate a financial liability at fair value on the same basis as the current IAS 39. IAS 39 allows a fair value designation if it reduces an accounting mismatch, if the instrument is managed on a fair value basis, or if the instrument is a hybrid instrument that contains an embedded derivative and the entire hybrid contract has been designated at fair value. For instruments so designated the exposure draft proposes that all fair value movements be included in profit or loss. However, fair value movements related to own credit risk should be reversed out of profit or loss and recognized in other comprehensive income. This results in the value of such financial liabilities on the statement of financial position being full fair value, including the effect of own credit risk, whereas net profit or loss for the period is not affected by an entity's own credit risk.

18.8   IMPLEMENTATION DECISIONS

The following table sets out some of the strategic and tactical decisions that should be considered when applying IFRS 9.

Strategic decisions	Tactical decisions	Problems to overcome
Determine the most appropriate date for adoption of the standard.	Determine whether comparative information will be required for the period in which the standard is adopted and determine how the comparative information is going to be obtained, if necessary.	Historical fair value or amortized cost information may not have been maintained for instruments that now need to be measured at either fair value or amortized cost. A new system may be needed to record and measure certain instruments differently.
Define how business models will be identified and the level of granularity that will be applied in determining the business models.	Once the business models have been identified, determine those business models whose objective it is to collect contractual cash flows outstanding. Financial assets within the business model that the entity wishes to measure at amortized cost should be separately identified.	The business models used to collect the contractual cash flows outstanding on financial assets will need to determine whether those flows represent the repayment of principal and interest (where interest is determined to be compensation for the time value of money adjusted for credit risk).
Identify equity investments that are in the scope of IFRS 9 and that are held for strategic purposes.	For equity instruments held for strategic purposes, management should decide whether the fair value changes should be reflected in profit or loss or other comprehensive income.	The systems should be able to identify the fair value movements on these instruments separately from fair value movements on other instruments.

18.9   EXAMPLES

EXAMPLE 18.1

An entity holds investments to collect their contractual cash flows but would sell an investment in particular circumstances. Would a sale contradict the entity's objective to hold the asset to collect contractual cash flows and therefore prohibit amortized cost classification?

EXPLANATION

Although an entity may consider (among other financial information) the financial assets' fair values from a liquidity perspective, the entity's objective is to hold the financial assets and collect the contractual cash flows. Some sales would not contradict that objective and the investment could be classified at amortized cost.

EXAMPLE 18.2

An entity holds a bond with a stated maturity date that pays a variable market interest rate. That variable interest rate is capped. Are the cash flows on the bond solely for payments of interest and principal and therefore meet the requirement to be classified at amortized cost?

EXPLANATION

The contractual cash flows of the bond comprise both those cash flows associated with an instrument that has a fixed rate and an instrument that has a variable rate. These cash flows may be the payments of principal and interest as long as the interest reflects the consideration for the time value of money and for the credit risk associated with the instrument during the term of the instrument. The fact that the interest rate is capped reduces the variability in the cash flows as a variable rate becomes fixed but does not change the fact that the cash flows are solely for interest and principal. The bond could therefore be classified at amortized cost.

CHAPTER 19

Noncurrent Assets Held for Sale and Discontinued Operations
(IFRS 5)

19.1   **OBJECTIVE**

The objective of IFRS 5 is to specify how noncurrent assets and disposal groups that are held for sale should be measured and presented in financial statements. It further specifies how a discontinued operation should be presented and disclosed in financial statements.

19.2   **SCOPE OF THE STANDARD**

IFRS 5 presentation requirements apply to:

- all noncurrent assets and disposal groups (including the associated liabilities) held for sale; and
- discontinued operations.

Assets classified as noncurrent in accordance with IAS 1 should not be reclassified as current assets until they meet the criteria to be classified as held for sale.

Assets of a class that an entity would normally regard as noncurrent that are acquired exclusively with a view to resale should not be classified as current unless they meet the criteria to be classified as held for sale.

The measurement provisions of this IFRS do not apply to the following assets, either individually or as part of a disposal group, and the measurement provisions in the respective standard should be applied:

- deferred tax assets (IAS 12);
- assets arising from employee benefits (IAS 19);
- financial assets within the scope of IAS 39;
- noncurrent assets that are accounted for in accordance with the fair value model in IAS 40;
- noncurrent assets that are measured at fair value less estimated point-of-sale costs (IAS 41); and
- contractual rights under insurance contracts as defined in IFRS 4.

19.3   KEY CONCEPTS

19.3.1 An **operation** is **discontinued** at the date the operation meets the criteria to be classified as held for sale or when the entity has disposed of the operation and:

- is a separate major line of business or geographical area (the rule of thumb is if the operation is a reportable segment in terms of IFRS 8);
- is part of a single coordinated disposal plan; or
- is a subsidiary acquired exclusively with a view to resale.

19.3.2 A **disposal group** is a group of assets (and associated liabilities) to be disposed of, by sale or otherwise, in a single transaction.

19.4   ACCOUNTING TREATMENT

Recognition

19.4.1 An entity should classify a noncurrent asset or disposal group as held for sale if its carrying amount will be recovered principally through a sale transaction rather than through continuing use.

19.4.2 **An asset or disposal group** should be **classified** as held for sale in a period in which all the following criteria are met:

- The asset or disposal group is available for immediate sale in its present condition.
- A sale is highly probable and expected to be completed within one year. A sale is highly probable if:
  - management commits to a plan to sell;
  - an active program and other actions exist to locate a buyer;
  - a sale is expected to be completed within one year of date of classification;
  - the asset or disposal group is actively marketed at a reasonable price; and
  - it is unlikely that there will be significant changes to the marketing plan or that management will consider withdrawing its plan to sell.

19.4.3 Classification as held for sale could still be appropriate after one year if the delay is caused by events or circumstances beyond the entity's control and there is sufficient evidence that the entity remains committed to the plan to sell.

19.4.4 When an entity acquires a noncurrent asset (or disposal group) exclusively with a view to its subsequent disposal, it should **classify** the noncurrent asset (or disposal group) as **held for sale** at the acquisition date only if the one-year requirement in this IFRS is met (except in circumstances beyond the entity's control). If any other criteria are not met at that date, it must be highly probable that these criteria will be met within a short period following the acquisition (usually within three months). If the entity's plans for sale change, classification as a discontinued operation must cease immediately due to the requirements of 19.3.1.

19.4.5 A noncurrent asset (or disposal group) is classified as held for distribution to owners when the entity is committed to distribute the asset (or disposal group) to its owners. For this to be the case, the assets must be available for immediate distribution in their present condition and the distribution must be highly probable (see 19.4.2 for requirements of highly probable). The probability of shareholders' approval (if required in the jurisdiction) should be considered as part of the assessment of whether the distribution is highly probable.

19.4.6 A noncurrent asset that is to be abandoned should not be classified as held for sale as the carrying amount will not be recovered through sale. The abandonment is however likely to be an indication of impairment and the measurement and disclosure requirements of IAS 36 should be considered.

Initial Measurement

19.4.7 Noncurrent assets held for sale

- should be **measured** at the lower of carrying amount or fair value less cost to sell; and
- should not be depreciated from the date of classification.

Subsequent Measurement

19.4.8 An entity should recognize an **impairment loss** for any initial or subsequent write-down of the noncurrent asset held for sale (or disposal group) to fair value less costs to sell.

19.4.9 An entity should recognize a **gain** for any subsequent increase in fair value less costs to sell of an asset, but not in excess of the cumulative impairment loss that has been previously recognized.

19.4.10 When a sale is expected to occur beyond one year (see 19.4.3), the entity should measure the costs to sell at their present value. Any increase in the present value of the costs to sell that arises from the passage of time should be presented in profit or loss as a financing cost.

Derecognition

19.4.11 An entity should cease to classify an asset (or disposal group) as held for sale when it no longer meets the criteria in 19.4.2 or when the sale has taken place.

19.5   **PRESENTATION AND DISCLOSURE**

Presenting Discontinued Operations

19.5.1 **The Statement of Comprehensive Income and notes** should disclose (after the net profit for the period):

- the amounts and analyses of revenue, expenses, and pretax profit or loss attributable to the discontinued operation; and
- the amount of any gain or loss that is recognized on the disposal of assets or settlement of liabilities attributable to the discontinued operation and the related income tax expense.

19.5.2 The **cash flow statement** should disclose the net cash flows attributable to the operating, investing, and financing activities of the discontinued operation.

Presentation of a Noncurrent Asset or Disposal Group Classified as Held for Sale

19.5.3 An entity should present and disclose information that enables users of the financial statements to evaluate the financial effects of discontinued operations and disposals of noncurrent assets (or disposal groups).

19.5.4 Noncurrent assets held for sale and assets and liabilities (held for sale) of a disposal group should be presented separately from other assets and liabilities in the Statement of Financial Position in the year of classification.

19.5.5 An entity should disclose the following information in the **notes to the financial statements** in the period in which a noncurrent asset or disposal group has been either classified as held for sale or sold:

- a description of the noncurrent asset or disposal group;
- a description of the facts and circumstances of the sale, or leading to the expected disposal, and the expected manner and timing of that disposal;
- the gain, loss, or impairment recognized and, if not separately presented on the face of the Statement of Comprehensive Income, under the caption in the Statement of Comprehensive Income that includes that gain or loss;
- the segment in which the noncurrent asset or disposal group is presented (IFRS 8); and
- in the period of the decision to **change the plan** to sell the noncurrent asset or disposal group, a description of the facts and circumstances leading to the decision and the effect of the decision on the results of operations for the period and any prior periods presented.

19.5.6 An entity should not reclassify or represent amounts presented for noncurrent assets or for the assets and liabilities of disposal groups classified as held for sale in the statements of financial position for prior periods. The comparative period remains unadjusted as classification is prospective.

19.6   FINANCIAL ANALYSIS AND INTERPRETATION

19.6.1 The requirements related to discontinued operations assist the analyst in distinguishing between ongoing or sustainable operations and future profitability, based on operations that management plans to continue.

19.6.2 IFRS requires that gains or losses on the disposal of depreciable assets be disclosed in the Statement of Comprehensive Income. If, however, the operations of a business are sold, abandoned, spun off, or otherwise disposed of, then this IFRS requires that the results of continuing operations be reported separately from discontinued operations to facilitate analysis of core business areas.

19.6.3 To facilitate analysis of profitability, any gain or loss from disposal of an entire business or segment should also be reported with the related results of discontinued operations as a separate item on the Statement of Comprehensive Income below income from continuing operations.

19.7   COMMENTARY

19.7.1 Held for sale is the balance sheet presentation and discontinued operations is the comprehensive income and statement of cash flows presentation. Held for sale is a current year classification and the prior year numbers are not impacted whereas the prior year numbers are reclassified for discontinued operations.

19.7.2 On September 25, 2008 the IASB published for comment an exposure draft of proposed amendments to the standard. The exposure draft aims to revise the definition of discontinued operations and require additional disclosure about components of an entity that have been disposed of or are classified as held for sale. The proposed amendments are the result of a joint project by the IASB and the FASB to develop a common definition for discontinued operations and require common disclosures.

19.7.3 This exposure draft proposes changing the definition so that a discontinued operation is a component of an entity that:

▒ is an operating segment as defined in IFRS 8 and either has been disposed of or is classified as held for sale; or

▒ is a business as defined in IFRS 3 (revised in 2008) that meets the criteria to be classified as held for sale on acquisition.

19.7.4 The exposure draft proposes that an entity should determine whether the component of an entity meets the definition of an operating segment regardless of whether it is required to apply IFRS 8. The proposal is aimed at entities that do not apply IFRS 8 because they fall outside the scope of the standard but require a measure to determine whether the discontinued operation is a component of the entity.

19.7.5 The proposed change in definition could result in fewer items being recognized in financial statements as discontinued operations than at present. However, the additional disclosures would give information about components of an entity that have been disposed of or are held for sale but do not meet the definition of a discontinued operation.

19.8 IMPLEMENTATION DECISIONS

The following table sets out some of the strategic and tactical decisions that should be considered when applying IFRS 5.

Strategic decisions	Tactical decisions	Problems to overcome
Noncurrent assets held for sale should be identified.	Management should put processes in place to identify decisions taken that would result in noncurrent assets or disposal groups being classified as held for sale.	Assess whether the noncurrent asset for sale meets all the criteria for classification as held for sale. Determine if there are potential disclosure problems For example, if a subsidiary or division is held for sale, disclosing information may be sensitive and compromise the negotiation process.
Noncurrent assets held for sale should be measured at the lower of carrying amount and fair value less cost to sell.	The methodology to determine fair value should be decided on. For example if a market price is not available, choose whether a discounted cash flow model should be used, what the discount rate would be, etc.	It may be difficult to determine the fair value of noncurrent asset.
Identify the assets scoped out of the measurement requirements of this standard and measure them with the appropriate standard.	Processes should be in place to identify assets scoped out of the measurement requirements of the standard.	The identification of assets is generally straightforward and does not result in significant complexity.

EXAMPLE: DISCONTINUED OPERATIONS

EXAMPLE 19.1

Outback Inc. specializes in camping and outdoor products and operates in three divisions: food, clothes, and equipment. Because of the high cost of local labor, the food division has incurred significant operating losses. Management has decided to close down the division and draws up a plan of discontinuance.

On May 1, 20X9, the board of directors approved and immediately announced the formal plan. The following data were obtained from the accounting records for the current and prior year ending June 30:

	20X9 ($'000)			20X8 ($'000)		
	Food	**Clothes**	**Equip.**	**Food**	**Clothes**	**Equip.**
Revenue	470	1,600	1,540	500	1,270	1,230
Cost of sales	350	500	510	400	400	500
Distribution costs	40	195	178	20	185	130
Administrative expenses	70	325	297	50	310	200
Other operating expenses	30	130	119	20	125	80
Taxation expenses or (benefit)	(6)	137	124	3	80	90

The following additional costs, which are directly related to the decision to discontinue, are not included in the table above.

Incurred between May 1, 20X9, and June 30, 20X9:

■ Severance pay provision $85,000 (not tax deductible)

Budgeted for the year ending June 30, 20X0:

■ Other direct costs $73,000
■ Severance pay $12,000
■ Bad debts $4,000

A proper evaluation of the recoverability of the assets in the food division, in terms of IAS 36, led to the recognition of an impairment loss of $19,000, which is included in the other operating expenses above and is fully tax deductible.

Apart from other information required to be disclosed elsewhere in the financial statements, the Statement of Comprehensive Income for the year ending June 30, 20X9, could be presented as follows: Outback Inc.

Outback, Inc.

Statement of Comprehensive Income for the Year Ended June 30, 20X9

	20X8 $'000	20X9 $'000
Continuing Operations (Clothes and Equipment)		
Revenue	3,140	2,500
Cost of sales	(1,010)	(900)
Gross profit	2,130	1,600
Distribution costs	(373)	(315)
Administrative expenses	(622)	(510)
Other operating expenses	(249)	(205)
Profit before Tax	886	570
Income tax expense	(261)	(170)
Net Profit for the Period	625	400
Discontinued Operation (Food)	(99)	7
Total Entity Net Profit for the Period	526	407
Detail in the Notes to the Financial Statement		
Discontinued Operations		
Revenue	470	500
Cost of sales	(350)	(400)
Gross profit	120	100
Distribution costs	(40)	(20)
Administrative expenses	(70)	(50)
Other operating expenses (30–19)	(11)	(20)
Impairment loss	(19)	–
Severance pay	(85)	–
(Loss) or Profit before Tax	(105)	10
Income tax benefit or (expense)	6	(3)
Net (Loss) or Profit for the Period	(99)	7

EXAMPLE 19.2

XYZ Inc is planning to sell a business. The business consists of intangible assets, advances, and inventory. The example below illustrates how the fair value of the disposal group is allocated to the individual assets making up the disposal group held for sale, taking into account the assets that are excluded from the measurement scope of IFRS 5.

Assets	Carrying value on November 4, 2009	Fair value less costs to sell on November 5, 2009	Income statement on initial classifi- cation	Fair value less costs to sell on December 31, 2009	Carrying amount of disposal group at December 31, 2009	Income statement at December 31, 2009	
Intangible assets	200,000		(200,000)*		—†		
Advances^	300,000				330,000	30,000	IAS 39 effective interest
Inventory^	50,000				40,000	(10,000)	IAS 2 impairment to NRV
Total	550,000	350,000	(200,000)	390,000	330,000	160,000	Total income statement effect
						20,000	IFRS 5 gain in the income statement; otherwise the 30,000 and 20,000 are double counted.

* Allocate the impairment first to goodwill and then pro rate the other assets of the disposal group that fall within the scope of IFRS 5.
^ Assets that fall outside the measurement scope of IFRS 5 and therefore remeasured according to the appropriate IFRS.
† Amortisation ceases on classification as held for sale date.

Carrying value on November 4, 2009	550,000
Fair value less costs to sell on December 31, 2009	390,000
Total movement	(160,000)
IFRS 5 impairment recognized on November 5, 2009	(200,000)
IAS 39 interest recognized on December 31, 2009	30,000
IAS 2 impairment on December 31, 2009	(10,000)
IFRS 5 gain recognized on December 31, 2009	20,000‡

‡ The amount recognizable as a gain is restricted.

CHAPTER 20

Exploration for and Evaluation of Mineral Resources (IFRS 6)

| 20.1 | **OBJECTIVE** |

This standard was issued because there were different views in practice on how exploration and evaluation expenditures should be accounted for and there was no specific guidance dealing with this issue. IFRS 6 provides guidance for entities that recognize assets used in the exploration for and evaluation of mineral resources. The key issues are the initial recognition criteria and the measurement basis for these assets, measurement subsequent to initial recognition, and the tests for impairment of such assets in accordance with IAS 36 (see chapter 26).

| 20.2 | **SCOPE OF THE STANDARD** |

An entity should apply this IFRS to exploration and evaluation expenditures that it incurs.

IFRS 6 is specifically concerned with the initial recognition criteria for exploration and evaluation expenditure, the measurement basis thereafter (cost or revaluation model), the testing for any subsequent impairment of asset value, and the disclosures of amounts in financial statements arising from exploration for and evaluation of mineral resources. This standard does not address other aspects of accounting by entities engaged in the exploration for and evaluation of mineral resources.

An entity that has exploration and evaluation assets can test such assets for impairment on the basis of a cash-generating unit for exploration and evaluation assets, rather than on the basis of the cash-generating unit that might otherwise be required by IAS 36.

Entities with exploration and evaluation assets should disclose information about those assets, the level at which such assets are assessed for impairment, and any impairment losses recognized.

| 20.3 | **KEY CONCEPTS** |

20.3.1 A **cash-generating unit** is the smallest identifiable group of assets that generates cash inflows from continuing use that are largely independent of the cash inflows from other assets or groups of assets.

20.3.2 A cash-generating unit for exploration and evaluation assets should be no larger than an operating **segment** determined in accordance with IFRS 8 (see chapter 35). An entity should perform impairment tests of those assets under the accounting policies applied in its most recent annual financial statements.

20.3.3 Exploration and evaluation assets are expenditures for exploration and evaluation of mineral resources that are recognized as assets.

20.3.4 Exploration and evaluation expenditures are expenditures incurred by an entity in connection with the exploration for and evaluation of mineral resources.

20.3.5 Exploration for and evaluation of mineral resources is the search for mineral resources as well as the determination of the technical feasibility and commercial viability of extracting the mineral resource before the decision is made to develop the mineral resource.

20.4   ACCOUNTING TREATMENT

Initial Measurement

20.4.1 Exploration and evaluation assets should be measured at cost.

20.4.2 Expenditures related to the following activities are **potentially includable** in the initial measurement of exploration and evaluation assets:

- acquisition of exploration rights;
- topographical, geological, geochemical, and geophysical studies;
- exploratory drilling;
- trenching;
- sampling; and
- evaluating the technical feasibility and commercial viability of extracting mineral resources.

20.4.3 Expenditures **not to be included** in the initial measurement of exploration and evaluation assets are:

- the development of a mineral resource once technical feasibility and commercial viability of extracting a mineral resource have been established; and
- administration and other general overhead costs.

20.4.4 Any obligations for removal and restoration that are incurred during a particular period as a consequence of having undertaken the exploration for and evaluation of mineral resources are recognized in terms of IAS 37 (see chapter 21).

Subsequent Measurement

20.4.5 After recognition, an entity should apply either the **cost model** or the **revaluation model** to its exploration and evaluation assets. If the revaluation model is applied (either the model in IAS 16 or IAS 38), then the classification should be consistent with the classification of the assets as either tangible or intangible assets depending on the nature of the assets.

20.4.6 An entity that has recognized exploration and evaluation assets should assess those assets for **impairment** when facts and circumstances suggest that the carrying amount may exceed its recoverable amount and should measure, present, and disclose any resulting impairment loss in accordance with IAS 36.

20.4.7 One or more of the facts and circumstances below may indicate impairment:

- The period for which the entity has the right to explore in the specific area has expired during the accounting period or will expire in the near future, and is not expected to be renewed.
- Further exploration for and evaluation of mineral resources in the specific area are neither budgeted nor planned in the near future.
- Significant changes have occurred with an adverse effect on the main accounting assumptions, including prices and foreign exchange rates, underlying approved budgets, or plans for further exploration for and evaluation of mineral resources in the specific area.
- The decision not to develop the mineral resource in the specific area has been made.
- The entity plans to dispose of the asset at an unfavorable price.
- The entity does not expect the recognized exploration and evaluation assets to be reasonably recoverable from a successful development of the specific area or by the sale of the assets.

20.5 PRESENTATION AND DISCLOSURE

20.5.1 An entity should disclose information that identifies and explains the amounts recognized in its financial statements that arise from the exploration for and evaluation of mineral resources.

20.5.2 An entity should also disclose:

- its **accounting policies** for exploration and evaluation **expenditures**;
- its **accounting policies** for the **recognition** of exploration and evaluation **assets**;
- the **amounts** of assets; liabilities; income; expense; and, if it presents its cash flow statement using the direct method, cash flows arising from the exploration for and evaluation of mineral resources; and
- the level at which the entity assesses exploration and evaluation assets for **impairment**.

20.6 FINANCIAL ANALYSIS AND INTERPRETATION

20.6.1 The **allocation over time of the original cost** of acquiring and developing natural resources is called **depletion**. It is similar to depreciation.

20.6.2 **Depletion** is the means of expensing the costs incurred in acquiring and developing natural resources. When depletion is accounted for using the units-of-production method, the formula appears as follows:

$$\text{Depletion Rate} = \frac{\text{Capitalized Cost of the Natural Resource Asset}}{\text{Estimated Number of Extractable Units}}$$

20.6.3 If, for example, a company buys oil and mineral rights for $5 million on a property that is believed to contain 2 million barrels of extractable oil, every barrel of oil extracted from the property is recorded as $2.50 of depletion expense on the Statement of Comprehensive Income, until the $5 million is written off. From the above formula, the depletion rate is

$$\text{Depletion Rate} = \frac{\$5,000,000}{2,000,000 \text{ bbls.}} = \$2.50/\text{bbl.}$$

20.6.4 Companies in some accounting jurisdictions might choose to capitalize only those costs that are associated with a successful discovery of a natural resource. Costs associated with unsuccessful efforts (that is, when the natural resources sought are not found) are expensed against income. This could be in line with paragraph 20.4.2 above, with the exception that an impairment test should determine which costs are not recoverable through depletion (depreciation). This is the more conservative method of accounting for acquisition and development costs, because it usually results in higher expenses and lower profits.

20.6.5 A company might buy, for example, oil and mineral rights on two properties for $6 million and $4 million, respectively. Ultimately, the company finds no oil on the first property and finds that the second property contains an estimated 2 million barrels of oil. Under the successful-efforts method, the accounting is as follows:

- At the time property rights are purchased:

	Dr	Cr
Oil and Mineral Rights (Statement of Financial Position Asset)	10,000,000	
Cash		10,000,000

- At the time when the first property is found to contain no oil, its cost is written off and the loss is taken immediately:

	Dr	Cr
Loss on Oil and Mineral Rights (Statement of Comprehensive Income)	6,000,000	
Oil and Mineral Rights (Statement of Financial Position)		6,000,000

20.6.6 Suppose, during the next year, 300,000 barrels of oil are extracted from the second property. This process is repeated every year until the Statement of Financial Position natural resource asset, Oil and Mineral Rights, is written down to zero:

	Dr*	Cr
Depletion Expense (Statement of Comprehensive Income)	600,000	
Oil and Mineral Rights (Statement of Financial Position)		600,000

$$\text{Depletion Expense} = \left(\frac{\$4,000,000}{2,000,000 \text{ bbls}}\right) 300,000 \text{ bbls} = \$600,000$$

20.6.7 For the following reasons, larger firms are more likely to expense as many costs as possible:

- Larger firms tend to hold reported earnings down, thereby making the firm less vulnerable to taxes and to political charges of earning windfall profits.

- The earnings volatility associated with this method is less harmful to large firms that engage in many more activities than just exploration.

- The negative impact on earnings is not severe for integrated oil companies that make substantial profits from marketing and refining activities, rather than just exploration activities.

20.7 COMMENTARY

20.7.1 The concerns that have been raised in practice relate to the limitation of the scope of IFRS 6 to exploration and evaluation activities. The IFRIC confirmed that the scope of IFRS 6 is limited to exploration and evaluation activities and does not extend to activities outside the exploration and evaluation. The IASB is however working on a comprehensive research project with the objective of developing an IFRS that will supersede IFRS 6. This IFRS for extractive activities will include but not be limited to exploration and evaluation activities. The main focus of this project is to give guidance on the definition, recognition, initial and subsequent measurement, and disclosure of reserves and resources. The IASB plans to publish a discussion paper for public comment during 2010.

20.7.2 The IFRIC is in the process of drafting an interpretation that applies to waste removal costs that are incurred in surface mining activity, during the production phase of the mine.

20.8 STRATEGIC AND TACTICAL POLICY DECISIONS

The following table sets out some of the strategic and tactical decisions that should be considered when applying IFRS 6.

Strategic decisions	Tactical decisions	Problems to overcome
Whether the cost or revaluation model should be applied in measuring the exploration asset.	If the revaluation model is selected a decision should be taken as to how frequently the revaluation should take place and what methodology should be used.	Determining the value of exploration and evaluation asset might be difficult and might require specialized valuation knowledge.

EXAMPLES: MINERAL RESOURCES

EXAMPLE 20.1

Rybak Petroleum purchases an oil well for $100 million. It estimates that the well contains 250 million barrels of oil. The oil well has no salvage value. If the company extracts and sells 10,000 barrels of oil during the first year, how much depletion expense should be recorded?

a. $4,000
b. $10,000
c. $25,000
d. $250,000

EXPLANATION

Choice a. is correct. Depletion expense is:

$$\text{Depletion rate} \quad = \quad \frac{\text{Current period production}}{\text{Total barrels of production}}$$

$$= \quad \frac{10,000}{250,000,000}$$

$$= \quad 0.00004$$

$$\text{Depletion expense} \quad = \quad \text{Purchase price x Depletion rate}$$

$$= \quad 100,000,000 \times 0.00004$$

$$= \quad \$4,000$$

Choice b. is incorrect. The choice incorrectly uses the depletion rate multiplied by the total barrels of oil in the well rather than the depletion rate multiplied by the purchase price.

Choice c. is incorrect. The choice incorrectly divides current production of 10,000 barrels by the purchase price, and then multiplies this incorrect depletion rate by the total number of barrels of oil in the well.

Choice d. is incorrect. The choice incorrectly assumes a 0.001 depletion rate multiplied by the total number of barrels of oil in the well.

EXAMPLE 20.2

SunClair Exploration Inc. has just purchased new offshore oil drilling equipment for $35 million. The company's engineers estimate that the new equipment will produce 400 million barrels of oil over its estimated 15-year life, and has an estimated parts salvage value of $500,000. Assuming that the oil drilling equipment produced 22 million barrels of oil during its first year of production, what amount will the company record as depreciation expense for this equipment in the initial year using the units-of-production method of depreciation?

a. $2,300,000
b. $1,897,500
c. $1,925,000
d. $2,333,333

EXPLANATION

Choice b. is correct. Depreciation expense using units-of-production method is

$$\text{Depreciation rate per unit} \quad = \quad \frac{(\text{Original cost} - \text{Salvage value})}{\text{Est. production over useful life}}$$

$$= \quad \frac{(\$35,000,000 - \$500,000)}{400,000,000 \text{ barrels}}$$

$$= \quad 0.0863 \text{ expense}$$

$$\text{Depreciation expense} \quad = \quad \text{Depreciation rate x Unit produced}$$

$$= \quad 0.0863 \times 22,000,000$$

$$= \quad \$1,897,500$$

Choice a. is incorrect. Units produced were multiplied by a useful life of 15 years, and the resulting number was then incorrectly used as the denominator of the depreciation rate calculation, rather than using the estimated 400 million–barrel estimated production over the useful life.

Choice c. is incorrect. This choice fails to subtract salvage value from original cost in the depreciation rate per unit calculation.

Choice d. is incorrect. This choice fails to subtract salvage value from the original cost in the depreciation rate per unit calculation, and incorrectly multiplies units produced by a useful life of 15 years as the denominator of the depreciation rate calculation.

CHAPTER 21

Provisions, Contingent Liabilities, and Contingent Assets (IAS 37)

21.1   OBJECTIVE

The main objective of IAS 37 is to provide guidance for recognition of provisions and the disclosure of contingent liabilities. Provisions are recognized only when established criteria of reliability of the obligation are met. In contrast, contingent liabilities and assets are not recognized but should be disclosed so that such information is available in the financial statements.

21.2   SCOPE OF THE STANDARD

IAS 37 prescribes the appropriate accounting treatment as well as the disclosure requirements for all provisions, contingent liabilities, and contingent assets to enable users to understand their nature, timing, and amount.

The standard sets out the conditions that must be fulfilled for a provision to be recognized.

It guides the preparers of financial statements to decide when, with respect to a specific obligation, they should:

- provide for it (recognize it);
- only disclose information; or
- disclose nothing.

IAS 37 is applicable to all entities when accounting for provisions and contingent liabilities or assets, except those resulting from:

- financial instruments carried at fair value (IAS 39, see chapter 17);
- executory contracts (for example, contracts under which both parties have partially performed their obligations to an equal extent)
- insurance contracts with policyholders (IFRS 4, see chapter 38); and
- events or transactions covered by any another IAS (for example, income taxes and lease obligations).

21.3   **KEY CONCEPTS**

21.3.1 **A provision** is a liability of **uncertain timing** or **amount**. Provisions can be distinguished from other liabilities such as trade payables and accruals because there is uncertainty about the timing or amount of the future expenditure required in settlement.

21.3.2 **A liability** is defined in the framework as a **present obligation** of the entity arising from past events, the settlement of which is expected to result in an outflow from the entity of resources embodying economic benefits.

21.3.3 **A contingent liability** is either:

- a **possible obligation**, because it has yet to be confirmed whether the entity has a present obligation that could lead to an outflow of resources embodying economic benefits; or
- a **present obligation** that does not meet the recognition criteria, either because an outflow of resources embodying economic benefits probably will not be required to settle the obligation, or because a sufficiently reliable estimate of the amount of the obligation cannot be made.

21.3.4 **Contingent** liabilities are not recognized because:

- their existence will be confirmed by uncontrollable and uncertain future events (that is, not liabilities); or
- they do not meet the recognition criteria.

21.3.5 **A contingent asset** is a possible asset that arises from past events and whose existence will be confirmed only by uncertain future events not wholly within the control of the entity (for example, the entity is pursuing an insurance claim whose outcome is uncertain).

21.4   **ACCOUNTING TREATMENT**

Provisions

21.4.1 A provision should be **recognized** only when:

- an entity has a present obligation (legal or constructive) as a result of a past event (obligating event);
- it is probable that an outflow of resources embodying economic benefits will be required to settle the obligation; and
- a reliable estimate can be made of the amount of the obligation.

21.4.2 A past event is deemed to give rise to a present obligation if it is more likely than not that a present obligation exists at Statement of Financial Position date.

21.4.3 **A legal** obligation normally arises from a contract or legislation. A **constructive** obligation arises only when **both** of the following conditions are present:

- The entity has indicated to other parties, by an established pattern of past practice, published policies, or a sufficiently specific current statement, that it will accept certain responsibilities.
- As a result, the entity has created a valid expectation on the part of those other parties that it will discharge those responsibilities.

21.4.4 **The amount recognized** as a provision should be the best estimate of the expenditure required to settle the present obligation at the Statement of Financial Position date.

21.4.5 **Some** or all of the expenditure required to settle a provision might be expected to be reimbursed by another party (for example, through insurance claims, indemnity clauses, or suppliers' warranties). These reimbursements are treated as follows:

▪ Recognize a **reimbursement** when it is virtually certain that the reimbursement will be received if the entity settles the obligation. The amount recognized for the reimbursement should not exceed the amount of the provision.

▪ Treat the reimbursement as a separate asset.

▪ The entity may choose to present the expense relating to a provision net of the amount recognized for a reimbursement in the Statement of Comprehensive Income.

21.4.6 **Provisions** should be reviewed at each Statement of Financial Position date and adjusted to reflect the current best estimate.

21.4.7 **A provision** should be used only for expenditures for which the provision was originally recognized.

21.4.8 **Recognition and measurement** principles for (a) future operating losses, (b) onerous contracts, and (c) restructurings should be applied as follows:

a. **Provisions** should not be recognized for **future operating losses.** An expectation of future operating losses is an indication that certain assets of the operation could be impaired. IAS 36, Impairment of Assets, would then be applicable (see chapter 26).

b. The present obligation under an **onerous contract** should be recognized and measured as a provision. An onerous contract is one in which the unavoidable costs of meeting the contract obligations exceed the economic benefits expected to be received under it.

c. A **restructuring** is a program planned and controlled by management that materially changes either the scope of business or the manner in which that business is conducted. A provision for restructuring costs is recognized when the normal recognition criteria for provisions are met. A constructive obligation to restructure arises only when an entity:

▪ has a detailed formal plan for the restructuring; *and*

▪ has raised a valid expectation in those affected that it will carry out the restructuring by starting to implement that plan or announcing its main features to those affected by it.

Where a restructuring involves the sale of an operation, no obligation arises for the sale until the entity is committed by a binding sale agreement.

Contingent Liabilities

21.4.9 An entity should *not* recognize a contingent liability. An entity should disclose a contingent liability, but only when:

▪ an entity has a present obligation (legal or constructive) as a result of a past event (obligating event);

▪ it is possible, but not probable that an outflow of resources embodying economic benefits will be required to settle the obligation; and

▪ the possibility of an outflow of resources embodying economic benefits is not remote.

21.4.10 Contingent liabilities are assessed continually to determine whether an outflow of resources embodying economic benefits has become probable. When such an outflow becomes probable for an item previously dealt with as a contingent liability, a provision is recognized.

Contingent Assets

21.4.11 An entity should not recognize a contingent asset since this may result in the recognition of income that may be never be realized. However, when the realization of income is virtually certain, then the related asset is not a contingent asset and its recognition is appropriate under the framework.

21.4.12 A contingent asset should be disclosed where an inflow of economic benefits is probable.

21.5   PRESENTATION AND DISCLOSURE

21.5.1 **Provisions:** Disclose the following for *each* class separately:

- a detailed itemized reconciliation of the carrying amount at the beginning and end of the accounting period (comparatives are not required);
- a brief description of the nature of the obligation and the expected timing of any resulting outflows of economic benefits;
- an indication of the uncertainties about the amount or timing of those outflows; and
- the amount of any expected reimbursement, stating the amount of any asset that has been recognized for that expected reimbursement.

21.5.2 **Contingent liabilities:** Disclose the following for *each* class separately:

- brief description of the nature of the liability;
- estimate of the financial effect;
- indication of uncertainties relating to the amount or timing of any outflow of economic benefits; and
- the possibility of any reimbursement.

21.5.3 **Contingent assets:** Disclose the following for *each* class separately:

- brief description of the nature of the asset; and
- estimate of the financial effect.

21.5.4 **Exceptions** allowed are as follows:

- If any information required for contingent liabilities or assets is not disclosed because it is not practical to do so, it should be so stated.
- In extremely rare cases, disclosure of some or all of the information required can be expected to seriously prejudice the position of the entity in a dispute with other parties regarding the provision, contingent liability, or contingent asset. In such cases, the information need not be disclosed; however, the general nature of the dispute should be disclosed, along with an explanation of why the information has not been disclosed.

21.5.5 Figure 21.1 summarizes the main requirements of IAS 37.

FIGURE 21.1   Decision Tree for Identifying Provisions, Contingent Liabilities, and Contingent Assets

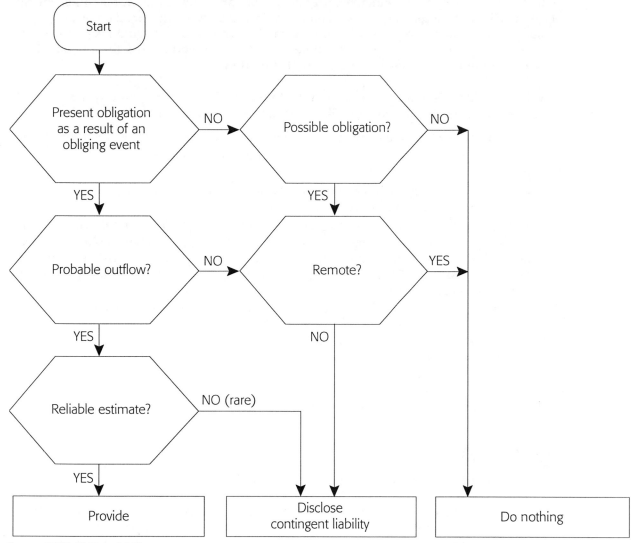

Source: IASCF, 2008, p. 1,849.

21.6   **COMMENTARY**

21.6.1 This standard, although relatively simple, is often not easy to apply in practice, mainly because of the subjectivity relating to the identification and measurement of provisions and contingent liabilities. The following judgments are required in practice:

▨ the identification of constructive obligations;

▨ the identification and measurement of onerous contracts; and

▨ the probability of an inflow or outflow occurring.

21.6.2 In 2005, the IASB issued an exposure draft of a standard to replace IAS 37. After reviewing the responses to this exposure draft, the IASB reached a decision on most of the principles to be included in the new standard. However, in the light of comments received, the IASB re-exposed one section in January 2010. This exposure draft proposes that the measurement should be the amount that the entity would rationally pay at the measurement date to be relieved of the liability. This amount would normally be the estimate of the present value of the resources required to fulfill the liability. The estimate would take into account the expected outflows of resources, the time value of money, and the risk that the actual outflows might ultimately differ from the expected outflows.

21.6.3 The IASB is aiming to issue an IFRS to replace IAS 37 in the third quarter of 2010. Some of the issues that the new IAS 37 will seek to address are as follows:

- removing the probability-driven recognition criterion for recognizing IAS 37 liabilities;
- removing the term "contingent liability" and updating guidance on identifying liabilities;
- improving the general guidance on identifying constructive obligations, and hence, the specific requirements for restructuring liabilities;
- making a range of other minor improvements—for example removing the outdated terminology (such as "provisions"), clarifying that IAS 37 applies to all liabilities that are not within the scope of other standards (such as liabilities to decommission assets and liabilities arising from legal disputes), and adding guidance on identifying and measuring onerous contracts; and
- incorporating into the standard guidance contained in IFRIC 1 (*Changes in Existing Decommissioning, Restoration and Similar Liabilities*), IFRIC 5 (*Rights to Interests Arising from Decommissioning, Restoration and Environmental Funds*), and IFRIC 6 (*Liabilities Arising from Participating in a Specific Market—Waste Electrical and Electronic Equipment*).

EXAMPLE: PROVISIONS, CONTINGENT LIABILITIES, AND CONTINGENT ASSETS

EXAMPLE 21.1

The following scenarios relate to provisions and contingencies:

A. The Mighty Mouse Trap Company has just started to export mousetraps to the United States. The advertising slogan for the mousetraps is, "A girl's best friend." The Californian Liberation Movement is claiming $800,000 from the company because the advertising slogan allegedly compromises the dignity of women. The company's legal representatives believe that the success of the claim will depend on the judge who presides over the case. They estimate, however, that there is a 70 percent probability that the claim will be thrown out and a 30 percent probability that it will succeed.

B. Boss Ltd. specializes in the design and manufacture of an exclusive sports car. During the current financial year, 90 sports cars have been completed and sold. During the testing of the sports car, a serious defect was found in its steering mechanism.

All 90 clients were informed by letter of the defect and were told to bring their cars back to have the defect repaired at no charge. All the clients have indicated that this is the only remedy that they require. The estimated cost of the recall is $900,000.

The manufacturer of the steering mechanism, a listed company with sufficient funds, has accepted responsibility for the defect and has undertaken to reimburse Boss Ltd. for all costs that it might incur in this regard.

EXPLANATION

The matters above will be treated as follows for accounting purposes:

A. **Present obligation as a result of a past event:** The available evidence provided by the experts indicates that it is more likely that no present obligation exists at Statement of Financial Position date; there is a 70 percent probability that the claim will be thrown out. No obligating event has taken place.

Conclusion: No provision is recognized. The matter is disclosed as a contingent liability unless the 30 percent probability is regarded as being improbable.

B. **Present obligation as a result of a past event:** The constructive obligation derives from the sale of defective cars.

Conclusion: The outflow of economic benefits is beyond any reasonable doubt. A provision is therefore recognized. However, as it is virtually certain that all of the expenditures will be reimbursed by the supplier of the steering mechanism, a separate asset is recognized in the Statement of Financial Position. In the Statement of Comprehensive Income, the expense relating to the provision can be shown net of the amount recognized for the reimbursement.

CHAPTER 22

The Effects of Changes in Foreign Exchange Rates (IAS 21)

22.1	## OBJECTIVE

Investments or balances in a foreign currency or ownership in a foreign operation exposes an entity to foreign exchange gains or losses. Foreign currency movements are volatile and sensitive to the global conditions and could have a significant effect on the profits of an entity that has entered into such transactions. In order to assess this risk and the related impact, an entity has to accurately account for foreign currency transactions and balances.

The objective of IAS 21 is to establish principles for the accounting treatment of foreign currency transactions, balances, and foreign operations. The principal aspects addressed are:

- **exchange rate differences** and their effect on transactions in financial statements; and
- **translation** of the financial statements of foreign operations (where the presentation currency differs from the functional currency).

22.2	## SCOPE OF THE STANDARD

This standard prescribes the accounting treatment in relation to:

- accounting for transactions and balances in foreign currencies;
- translating the results and financial position of foreign operations included in the financial statements of an entity;
- translating the results and financial position of an entity into its presentation currency; and
- the treatment of monetary and nonmonetary gains and losses related to foreign currency transactions, balances, and translations.

IAS 21 does not apply to derivative transactions and balances or hedge accounting, which fall within the scope of IAS 39. Nor does it apply to the presentation in the statement of cash flows of cash flows arising from foreign currency transactions.

However, the standard does apply to the translation of amounts relating to derivatives from functional to presentation currency.

22.3

KEY CONCEPTS

22.3.1 **Foreign currency transactions** are transactions denominated in or requiring settlement in a currency other than the functional currency of the entity, including:

- buying or selling goods or services where the prices are in foreign currency;
- borrowing or lending funds resulting in a payable or receivable in foreign currency;
- acquiring or disposing of assets in a foreign currency;
- incurring or settling liabilities in a foreign currency; and
- foreign bank accounts with deposits, payments, charges, and interest in a foreign currency.

22.3.2 A **foreign operation** is a subsidiary, associate, joint venture, or branch of the reporting entity, the activities of which are based or conducted in a country other than the country of the reporting entity.

22.3.3 The **functional currency** is the currency of the primary economic environment in which an entity operates. It is used to measure items in financial statements. It need not be the local currency of an entity. It is the currency in which an entity primarily generates and expends cash, for example:

- the currency that mainly influences sales prices (invoice and settlement currency);
- the currency of the country whose competitive forces and regulations determine the sales prices of goods and services; or
- the currency that influences labor, material, and other costs of providing goods and services.

When the functional currency of an entity is not obvious, management must use judgment to determine the functional currency by looking at other available indicators such as the currency in which the entity is financed.

Once the functional currency has been decided on it is not changed unless the underlying transactions and operations change. This change should be prospectively applied.

22.3.4 The **functional currency of a foreign operation** is the **same** as the reporting entity's functional currency when:

- the activities of the foreign operation are an extension of the reporting entity, that is, without a significant degree of autonomy;
- a high proportion of the foreign operation's transactions are with the reporting entity;
- the cash flows of the foreign operation directly affect those of the reporting entity;
- the foreign operation's cash flows are available for remittance to the reporting entity; and
- the foreign operation's cash flows are insufficient to service existing and normal debt obligations.

22.3.5 The **presentation currency** of an entity is the currency in which the financial statements are presented. It might be any currency, although many jurisdictions require the use of the **local currency**.

- The **functional currency of the parent** (or major) entity usually will determine the presentation currency.
- If the presentation currency is different from the functional currency, **translation** of financial statements from the functional currency to the presentation currency will be required.

22.3.6 The **closing rate** is the spot exchange rate at the end of the reporting period used for the translation of monetary items at that date.

22.3.7 The **spot exchange rate** is the exchange rate for immediate delivery on any particular day. The spot rate is used on the date of a transaction to recognize the initial amounts. The selling spot rate is the rate used for imports and the buying spot rate is the rate used for exports.

22.3.8 The **average exchange rate** is the average of spot rates over a period of time (such as a week or month). This rate can be used instead of the spot rate on the date of the transaction but only if the spot rate does not fluctuate significantly during that relevant period.

22.3.9 **Exchange differences** are the differences that arise on translating an amount of one currency into another currency at different exchange rates, for example translating the financial statements from a functional currency to a different presentation currency.

22.3.10 Assets and liabilities are classified as follows to determine the rates at which items are measured **subsequent** to the initial transaction date:

- **Monetary items** are units of currency held and assets and liabilities to be received or paid in a fixed or determinable number of units of currency. The essential feature of a monetary item is a right to receive (or an obligation to deliver) a fixed or determinable number of units of currency. Monetary items include cash, receivables, loans, payables, long-term debt, provisions, employee benefit liabilities, and deferred tax assets and liabilities.
- **Nonmonetary items** include equity securities, inventories, prepaid expenses, property, plant, equipment and related accounts, goodwill, and intangible assets.

22.4   ACCOUNTING TREATMENT

Foreign Currency Transactions

Recognition and Initial Measurement

22.4.1 For purposes of **recognition,** determine for **each entity** whether it is:

- a stand-alone entity;
- an entity with foreign operations (parent); or
- a foreign operation (subsidiary or branch).

22.4.2 On **initial recognition**, a foreign currency transaction should be reported in the functional currency by applying to the foreign currency amount the **spot exchange rate** between the functional currency and the foreign currency. Use the spot exchange rate on the transaction date, which is the date the item first qualifies for recognition per the relevant standard.

Subsequent Measurement

22.4.3 At each reporting date, **subsequent measurement** takes place as follows:

- **Monetary items** that remain unsettled are translated using the **closing rate** (the spot exchange rate on the date of the Statement of Financial Position).
- **Nonmonetary items** are carried using the following measurements:
  - **Historical cost items** are reported using the exchange rate at the **date of the transaction**. Approximate or average rates may be more appropriate for inventories or cost of sales, which affect the statement of comprehensive income.
  - **Fair value items** are reported using the exchange rate at the **date when the fair value** was determined.

22.4.4 **Exchange differences on monetary items** are included in profit or loss in the period in which they arise, regardless of whether they arise on **settlement** or **translation** at rates different from those at which they were translated on initial recognition.

22.4.5 The following exchange differences are **included in other comprehensive income until disposal** of the related asset or liability, when they are transferred to profit or loss:

- **Mark-to-market** gains or losses on available-for-sale financial assets. Translation differences on nonmonetary items classified as available for sale, for example equity instruments, are included in other comprehensive income. However, translation gains and losses on monetary items classified as available-for-sale, for example bonds, are included in profit or loss.

- **Nonmonetary item gains and losses** (for example gains on property, plant, and equipment, revalued in terms of IAS 16).

- **Inter-group monetary items** that form part of an entity's net investment in a foreign entity. These differences are recognized in profit or loss in the stand-alone financial statements of the parent but are included in other comprehensive income in its consolidated financials until the investment is disposed of.

- A **foreign liability** that is accounted for as a **hedge** of an entity's net investment in a foreign entity (IAS 39 criteria, see chapter 17).

Presentation Currency: Translation from Functional Currency

22.4.6 An entity can present its financial statements in any currency. If this presentation currency is not the same as the functional currency, the entity must translate the results and financial position into its presentation currency at the reporting date. For consolidation purposes the group financial statements must be presented in the presentation currency of the parent.

22.4.7 When the functional currency of an entity is **not that of a hyperinflationary economy**, the translation into the presentation currency is as follows:

- Translate **assets and liabilities** using the **closing rate** at the reporting date.
- Translate **income and expenses** using the **spot rates** at the dates of transactions or the **average rates** for the period if more practical.

  All resulting **exchange differences** are recognized in other comprehensive income.

22.4.8 When the functional currency of an entity or a foreign operation is the currency of a **hyperinflationary economy**, the translation into presentation currency is as follows:

- First apply IAS 29 to restate both the current and comparative figures for price changes.
- Restate all the items in the financial statements at the **closing rate** at the date of the most recent financial statements.

Foreign Operations

22.4.9 When an entity holds an investment in a foreign operation, a net investment in the foreign operation is included in the financial statements of the parent and must be translated at each reporting date. The results and financial position of the operation are incorporated into the parent's financial statements per the normal consolidation procedures. Intra-group monetary items cannot be eliminated without recognizing the related exchange differences.

22.4.10 The accounting treatment of the investment in a foreign operation is as follows:

- On acquiring the investment, the financial statements of the foreign entity should be translated into the functional currency of the parent based on the above rules for the translation of monetary and nonmonetary items. The net investment can then be calculated and recognized in the parent's financial statements per IFRS 3.

▪ Goodwill on the acquisition of the foreign operation and any fair value adjustments to the carrying amounts of assets and liabilities at acquisition date are treated as assets of the foreign operation and are therefore carried in the functional currency of the foreign operation and translated at the closing rate each year.

▪ At each reporting date until settlement, any monetary items included as part of the net investment in the foreign operation are translated at the closing rate. The resulting exchange difference is recognized in profit or loss in the separate financial statements of the parent, and in other comprehensive income of its consolidated financial statements.

▪ On disposal of the foreign operation, the cumulative exchange differences recognized in other comprehensive income are transferred to profit or loss when the gain or loss on disposal is recognized. If it is only a partial disposal, only the proportionate share of exchange differences is realized and transferred to profit or loss.

▪ On impairment of the net investment in the foreign operation, no portion of the exchange differences in other comprehensive income is realized in profit or loss.

| 22.5 | **PRESENTATION AND DISCLOSURE** |

22.5.1 An entity should make the following disclosures:

▪ the amount of exchange differences recognized in profit or loss, **except** for differences arising on financial instruments measured at fair value through profit or loss in accordance with IAS 39; and

▪ the net exchange differences classified in other comprehensive income as a separate component of equity (a foreign exchange reserve), and a reconciliation of the amount of such exchange differences at the beginning and end of the period.

22.5.2 The **difference between the presentation and functional currency** should be stated, together with disclosure of the functional currency and the reason for using a different presentation currency.

22.5.3 Any **change** in the functional currency of an entity, and the reason for the change, should be disclosed.

22.5.4 When an entity presents its financial statements in a **currency that is different from its functional currency,** the entity should describe the financial statements as complying with IFRS only if the statements comply with all the requirements of each applicable standard and interpretation.

| 22.6 | **FINANCIAL ANALYSIS AND INTERPRETATION** |

22.6.1 Changes in the value of assets and liabilities resulting from exchange rate movements are treated in one of two ways. Gain or losses from individual transactions are recognized in profit or loss, whereas changes in the assets and liabilities of foreign operations are reported in other comprehensive income.

22.6.2 Foreign currency–denominated monetary assets such as cash reflect a gain when the value of that currency rises relative to the functional currency, and a loss when the value of that currency falls. Inversely, foreign currency denominated–liabilities reflect a loss when the value of the foreign currency rises and a gain when it falls. Where an entity holds both monetary assets and liabilities, the effect will depend on the net position. These movements have a direct impact on profit and loss.

22.6.3 The reported net income from the foreign operations of an entity consists of three parts:

1. **Operational effects,** which is the net income that the entity would have reported in the reporting currency if exchange rates had not changed from their weighted average levels of the previous years.
2. **Flow effects,** which is the impact on the amount of revenues and expenses reported on the Statement of Comprehensive Income as a consequence of changes in average exchange rates, and which can be calculated as a residual.
3. **Holding gain (loss) effects,** which is the impact on the values of assets and liabilities reported on the Statement of Financial Position, as a consequence of changes in spot exchange rates.

22.6.4 The impact of the translation from functional currency to presentation currency is recorded in the equity portion of the Statement of Financial Position, and not on the Statement of Comprehensive Income. As a consequence, the net income and earnings per share of an entity with a foreign operation will not be impacted as significantly as an entity with foreign balances. However, the net worth (or equity) shown on the Statement of Financial Position will still reflect the full impact of the foreign currency translation.

22.7   **IMPLEMENTATION DECISIONS**

The following table sets out some of the strategic and tactical decisions that should be considered when applying IAS 21.

Strategic decisions	Tactical decisions	Problems to overcome
The functional and presentation currency of the entity should be determined.	Management must consider other entities in the group and ensure that currencies are consistent. The jurisdictions in which the entity operates must be considered.	Complexities could arise where different currencies are selected for operations and for presentation and between entities in the group. Translations will have to be made and foreign exchange differences will have to be accounted for, which could negatively impact profits.

EXAMPLE: THE EFFECTS OF CHANGES IN FOREIGN EXCHANGE RATES

EXAMPLE 22.1

Bark Inc. (whose functional currency is the U.S. dollar) purchased manufacturing equipment from the United Kingdom. The transaction was financed by a loan from a commercial bank in England.

Equipment costing £400,000 was purchased on January 2, 20X7, and the amount was paid over by the bank to the supplier on that same day. The loan must be repaid on December 31, 20X8, and interest is payable at 10 percent biannually in arrears. The reporting date is December 31.

The following exchange rates apply:

	£1 = $
January 2, 20X7	1.67
June 30, 20X7	1.71
December 31, 20X7	1.75
June 30, 20X8	1.73
December 31, 20X8	1.70

EXPLANATION

The **interest payments** would be recorded at the spot rates applicable on the dates of payment in the following manner:

	$
June 30, 20X7 (£20,000 × 1.71)	34,200
December 31, 20X7 (£20,000 × 1.75)	35,000
Total interest for 20X7	69,200
June 30, 20X8 (£20,000 × 1.73)	34,600
December 31, 20X8 (£20,000 × 1.70)	34,000
Total interest for 20X8	68,600

The **loan** is initially recorded on January 2, 20X7, and restated at the spot rate on December 31, 20X7, as well as December 31, 20X8, after which it is repaid at the spot rate. The movements in the balance of the loan are reflected as follows:

	$
Recorded at January 2, 20X7 (£400,000 × 1.67)	668,000
Foreign currency loss on restatement of loan	32,000
Restated at December 31, 20X7 (£400,000 × 1.75)	700,000
Foreign currency profit on restatement of loan	(20,000)
Restated and paid at December 31, 20X8 (£400,000 × 1.70)	680,000

The loan will be stated at an amount of $700,000 in the **Statement of Financial Position** on December 31, 20X7.

The manufacturing equipment remains at its historical spot rate of $668,000.

The following amounts will be recognized in the **Statement of Comprehensive Income**:

	20X7 $	20X8 $
Interest	68,600	69,200
Foreign currency loss (profit)	(20,000)	32,000

Part IV

Statement of Comprehensive Income/ Income Statement

CHAPTER 23

Revenue (IAS 18)

23.1 **OBJECTIVE**

IAS 18 defines revenue as the inflow of economic benefits that derive from activities in the ordinary course of business. Key issues in IAS 18 are the definition of revenue, criteria for revenue recognition, and the distinction between revenue and other income (for example, gains on disposal of noncurrent assets or on translating foreign balances). The purpose of IAS 18 is to determine when and how revenue should be recognized.

23.2 **SCOPE OF THE STANDARD**

This standard describes the accounting treatment of revenue. The following aspects are addressed:

- Revenue is distinguished from income. (Income includes both revenue and gains.)
- Recognition criteria for revenue are identified.
- Practical guidance is provided on the
  - timing of recognition;
  - amount to be recognized; and
  - disclosure requirements.

This standard deals with the accounting treatment of revenue that arises from:

- sale of goods;
- rendering of services;
- use by others of entity assets yielding interest (see also IAS 39);
- royalties; and
- dividends (see also IAS 39).

The standard does not deal with revenue arising from:

- lease income (IAS 17);
- equity method investments (IAS 28);
- insurance contracts (IFRS 4);
- changes in fair value of financial assets and liabilities (IAS 39); and
- initial recognition and changes in fair value on biological assets (IAS 41).

23.3

KEY CONCEPTS

23.3.1 Revenue is defined as the gross inflow of economic benefits

- during the period;
- arising in the ordinary course of activities; and
- resulting in increases in equity, but specifically excluding contributions by equity participants.

23.3.2 Revenue excludes amounts collected on behalf of third parties, for example, a value-added tax or where the entity acts as an agent.

23.3.3 Fair value is the amount for which an asset could be exchanged, or a liability settled, between knowledgeable, willing parties in an arm's-length transaction.

23.3.5 Effective yield on an asset is the rate of interest required to discount the stream of future cash receipts expected over the life of the asset, to equal the initial carrying amount of the asset.

23.3.6 The standard is generally applied on a transaction basis. In certain circumstances the transaction has to be split into its separately identifiable components and revenue recognized separately for each component. Customer awards are an example of a transaction that has to be split into components. The converse would also apply when separate contracts in substance amount to a single transaction.

23.4

ACCOUNTING TREATMENT

Recognition

23.4.1 Revenue cannot be recognized when related expenses cannot be **measured reliably.** Consideration already received for the sale is **deferred** as a liability until revenue recognition can take place.

23.4.2 When goods or services are exchanged for goods or services that are of a **similar nature** and value, no revenue recognition occurs. (Commercial substance of the transaction should govern.)

23.4.3 Revenue recognition from the **sale of goods** takes place when:

- significant risks and rewards of ownership of the goods are transferred to the buyer;
- the entity retains neither continuing managerial involvement of ownership nor effective control over the goods sold;
- the amount of revenue can be measured reliably;
- it is probable that the economic benefits of the transaction will flow to the entity; and
- the costs of the transaction can be measured reliably.

23.4.4 Revenue recognition of **services** takes place as follows (similar to IAS 11, Construction Contracts):

- When the outcome (amount of revenue, stage of completion, and costs) of the transaction can be estimated reliably, revenues are recognized according to the stage of completion at the reporting date.
- When the outcome of the transaction cannot be estimated reliably, recoverable contract costs will determine the extent of revenue recognition.

23.4.5 Other revenues are recognized as follows:

- **Royalties** are recognized on an accrual basis (substance of the relevant agreements).
- **Dividends are** recognized when the right to receive payment is established (which is normally the "last day to register" for the dividend).
- **Repurchase agreements** arise when an entity sells goods and immediately concludes an agreement to repurchase them at a later date; the substantive effect of the transaction is negated, and the two transactions are dealt with as one.
- **Sales plus service** refers to when the selling price of a product includes an amount for subsequent servicing, and the service revenue portion is deferred over the period that the service is performed.

Initial Measurement

23.4.6 Revenue should be measured at the **fair value** of the consideration received or **receivable**:

- **Trade (cash) discounts** and **volume rebates** are deducted to determine fair value. However, payment discounts are nondeductible.
- When the inflow of cash is deferred (for example, the provision of interest-free credit), it effectively constitutes a financing transaction. The imputed rate of interest should be determined and the present value of the inflows calculated. The difference between the fair value and nominal amount of the consideration is separately recognized and disclosed as interest.
- When goods or services are rendered in exchange for dissimilar goods or services, revenue is measured at the fair value of the goods or services received. When the fair value of the goods or services received cannot be measured reliably, the revenue is measured at the fair value of the goods or services given up.
- Revenue only includes inflows received by the entity on its own account. Amounts collected on behalf of third parties are excluded from revenue, for example agency relationships and certain taxes.

23.4.7 Interest income should be recognized on a time-proportion basis that:

- takes into account the effective yield on the asset (the effective interest rate method—see IAS 39); and
- includes amortization of any discount, premium, transaction costs, or other differences between initial carrying amount and amount at maturity.

Subsequent Measurement and Special Circumstances

23.4.8 Financial service fees are recognized as follows:

- Financial service fees that are an integral part of the effective yield on a financial instrument (such as an equity investment) carried at fair value are recognized immediately as revenue.
- Financial service fees that are an integral part of the effective yield on a financial instrument carried at amortized cost (for example, a loan) are recognized as interest revenue over the life of the asset as part of the application of the effective interest rate method.
- Origination fees on creation or acquisition of financial instruments carried at amortized cost, such as a loan, are deferred and recognized as adjustments to the effective interest rate.
- Most commitment fees to originate loans are deferred and recognized as adjustments to the effective interest rate or recognized as revenue on earlier expiration of the commitment.

■ Financial services fees earned for the performance of a significant act—for example loan syndication, arrangement or structuring fees, or commission on the allotment of shares—are recognized when the significant act is completed.

23.4.9 If an entity grants customer loyalty awards to its customers, IFRIC 13 determines that revenue should be recognized as follows:

■ Where the entity itself supplies the awards, the amount receivable should be allocated between the award credits and the other goods or services. The portion of the revenue relating to the awards may only be recognized as revenue when the awards are redeemed.

■ Where a third party supplies the awards it must assess whether it receives the consideration on behalf of a third party or not—that is, on behalf of an agent or a principle. The gross or net consideration should be recognized when the entity fulfils its obligation in respect of the awards.

Derecognition

23.4.10 Uncertainty about the collectability of an amount already included in revenue is treated as an expense rather than as an adjustment to revenue.

23.4.11 To determine the amount of an **impairment loss,** use the rate of interest that is used to discount cash flows.

23.5   PRESENTATION AND DISCLOSURE

23.5.1 Disclose the following **accounting policies:**

■ revenue measurement bases used;
■ revenue recognition methods used; and
■ stage of completion method for services.

23.5.2 The Statement of Comprehensive Income and notes should include the following:

■ amounts of significant revenue categories, including:
    – sale of goods;
    – rendering of services;
    – interest;
    – royalties; and
    – dividends;
■ amount of revenue recognized from the exchange of goods or services; and
■ the methods adopted to determine the stage of completion of transactions involving the rendering of services.

23.6   FINANCIAL ANALYSIS AND INTERPRETATION

23.6.1 Accounting income is generated when revenues and their associated expenses are recognized on a Statement of Comprehensive Income. The recognition and matching principles determine when this occurs. IAS 18 sets out the criteria that must be met before revenue is earned (and hence recognized) in IFRS financial statements.

23.6.2 When a company intentionally distorts its financial results, financial condition, or both, it is engaging in financial manipulation. Generally, companies engage in such activities to hide operational problems. When they are caught, the company faces outcomes such as investors losing faith in management and a subsequent fall in the company's stock price. The two basic strategies underlying all accounting manipulation are:

■ to inflate current-period earnings through overstating revenues and gains or understating expenses; and

■ to reduce current-period earnings by understating revenues or overstating expenses. A company is likely to engage in this strategy to shift earnings to a later period when they might be needed.

23.6.3 Financial manipulation involving revenue can generally be grouped under four headings.

1. **Recording questionable revenue or recording revenue prematurely:**
   ■ recording revenue for services that have yet to be performed;
   ■ recording revenue prior to shipment or before the customer acquires control of the products;
   ■ recording revenue for items for which the customer is not required to pay;
   ■ recording revenue for contrived sales to affiliated parties; and
   ■ engaging in quid pro quo transactions with customers.

2. **Recording fictitious revenue:**
   ■ recording revenue for sales that lack economic substance;
   ■ recording revenue that is, in substance, a loan;
   ■ recording investment income as revenue;
   ■ recording supplier rebates that are tied to future required purchases as revenue; and
   ■ reporting revenue that was improperly withheld prior to a merger.

3. **Recording one-time gains to boost income:**
   ■ deliberately undervaluing assets, resulting in the recording of a gain on sale;
   ■ recording investment gains as revenue;
   ■ recording investment income or gains as a reduction in expenses; and
   ■ reclassifying Statement of Financial Position accounts to create income.

4. **Shifting revenues to future periods:**
   ■ creating reserves that are reversed (reported as income) in later periods; and
   ■ withholding revenues before an acquisition and then releasing these revenues in later periods.

23.6.4 Not all manipulations are of equal importance to investors. It is sometimes argued that inflation of revenues is more serious than manipulations that affect expenses, because consistent revenue growth is important to many investors in assessing a company's prospects. Therefore, identifying inflated revenues is of critical importance. However, manipulation is manipulation and can never be justified, regardless of how "serious" it is or is not.

23.6.5 Early warning signs that will help identify problem companies include:

■ few or no independent members on the board of directors;
■ an incompetent external auditor or lack of auditor independence; and
■ highly competitive pressures on management.

23.7	**COMMENTARY**

23.7.1 Financial services fees that are an *integral* part of the effective interest rate of a financial instrument (such as origination fees) may instead be recognized as an *adjustment* to the effective interest rate. This results in the deferral of the recognition of revenue items that historically may have been recognized when received. This has a particularly big impact on financial institutions when IFRS is adopted.

23.7.2 The application of IFRIC 13 regarding customer loyalty programs could also result in the deferral of the recognition of a significant portion of revenue that historically has been recognized when the amounts are received. For example, airlines and retail stores are required under IFRIC 13 to defer a portion of their revenue until the customer awards are redeemed. Determining the fair value of the award could be complex and require system development and management judgment.

23.7.3 The IASB issued a discussion paper on December 19, 2008 titled "Preliminary Views on Revenue Recognition in Contracts with Customers." The discussion paper is a consequence of the IASB's efforts to develop a single conceptual model for revenue recognition to ensure comparability between industries. The paper proposes a single contract-based revenue recognition model that would apply broadly to contracts with customers, although contracts in the areas of financial instruments, insurance, and leasing may be excluded. In the proposed model, revenue is recognized when a contract asset increases or a contract liability decreases (or some combination of the two). This occurs when an entity satisfies an obligation in the contract with the customer.

23.7.4 In accordance with the IASB project timetable, the final IFRS is expected to be issued in the first half of 2011. If the final standard adopts the principles addressed in the discussion paper, entities could be required to apply significantly different revenue recognition principles. The Statement of Financial Position and Statement of Comprehensive Income would then present amounts that are very different from the current approach.

EXAMPLES: REVENUE

EXAMPLE 23.1

Sykes and Anson, a high-tech company, is having a very poor year as a result of weak demand in the technology markets. The entity's controller has determined that much of the inventory on hand is worth far less than the value recorded on the entity's books. He decides to write off this excess amount, which totals $10 million. Furthermore, he is worried that the inventory will fall in value next year and decides to take a further write-down of $5 million. Both of these write-offs occur in the current year.

Which of the following statements is true?

a. The company has engaged in a technique known as recording "sham" revenue.
b. The company has overstated its income in the current period.
c. The company has engaged in a technique that shifts future expenses into the current period.
d. The company should be applauded for being so conservative in its accounting for inventories.

EXPLANATION

Choice c. is correct. The company has overstated the amount of the current charge by $5 million. This expected decline in value should not be written off until it occurs. It is conceivable that the market for Sykes and Anson's products will rebound and that the write-off was not needed. Effectively, the company has brought forward a potential future expense to the current period. The $10 million write-off is however, appropriate.

Choice a. is incorrect. The facts do not support any issue concerning sham revenues.

Choice b. is incorrect. The company's income is understated, not overstated, in the current period, as a result of the excess $5 million write-off.

Choice d. is incorrect. Whereas conservative accounting is desirable, the entity has gone too far and is reporting results that are incorrect.

EXAMPLE 23.2

The information below comes from the 20X0 financial statements of Bear Corp. and Bull Co., both of which are based in Europe.

	Bear Corp.	**Bull Co.**
Acquisition accounting	The excess of acquisition cost over net fair value of assets acquired is charged to goodwill and written off over 10 years.	The excess of acquisition cost over net fair value of assets acquired is recorded as goodwill and written off over 20 years.
Soft costs	In anticipation or hope of future revenues, the company incorrectly defers certain costs incurred and matches them against future expected revenues.	The company expenses all costs incurred unless paid in advance and directly associated with future revenues.

Which company has a higher quality of earnings, as a result of its accounting for its soft costs?

a. Bull Co.
b. Bear Corp.
c. They are equally conservative.
d. Cannot be determined.

EXPLANATION

Choice a. is correct. Bull Co. is more conservative with soft cost reporting because it expenses all soft costs unless they are directly tied to future revenue.

Choice b. is incorrect. Bear Corp. is less conservative than Bull Co. with soft cost reporting because it defers costs in anticipation of matching them with future revenues.

Choice c. is incorrect. Bull Co.'s method of expensing all soft costs unless directly tied to future revenue is clearly more conservative.

Choice d. is incorrect.

Comment: Neither company is complying with IFRS with respect to goodwill. Goodwill should be tested for impairment on an annual basis and should not be amortized.

EXAMPLE 23.3

A generous benefactor donates raw materials to an entity for use in its production process. The materials had cost the benefactor $20,000 and had a market value of $30,000 at the time of donation. The materials are still on hand at the Statement of Financial Position date. No entry has been made in the books of the entity. Should the entity recognize the donation as revenue in its books?

EXPLANATION

The proper accounting treatment of the above matter is as follows:

- The accounting standard that deals with inventories, IAS 2, provides no guidance on the treatment of inventory acquired by donation. However, donations received meet the definition of revenue in IAS 18 (that is, the gross inflow of economic benefits during the period arising in the course of ordinary activities when those inflows result in increases in equity, other than increases relating to contributions from equity participants). It could be argued that receiving a donation is not part of the ordinary course of activities. In that case, the donation would be regarded as a capital gain. For purposes of this case study, the donation is regarded as revenue.

- The donation should be recorded as revenue measured at the fair value ($30,000) of the raw materials received (because that is the economic benefit).

- The raw materials received clearly meet the framework's definition of an asset, because the raw materials (resource) are now owned (controlled) by the corporation as a result of the donation (past event) from which a profit can be made in the future (future economic benefits). The recognition criteria of the framework, namely those of measurability and probability, are also satisfied.

- Because the raw materials donated relate to trading items, they should be disclosed as inventory, with the fair value of $30,000 at the acquisition date being treated as the cost thereof.

CHAPTER 24

Construction Contracts (IAS 11)

24.1   OBJECTIVE

The primary challenge in accounting for construction contracts is to allocate contract revenue and costs to the correct accounting periods. The objective of this standard is to give guidance on the appropriate criteria for recognition of construction contract revenue and costs, with a focus on the allocation of contract revenue and costs to the accounting periods in which construction work is performed.

24.2   SCOPE OF THE STANDARD

This standard applies to accounting for construction contracts in the financial statements of contractors.

24.3   KEY CONCEPTS

24.3.1 A **construction contract** is a contract negotiated specifically for the construction of an asset or a combination of assets that are closely interrelated or interdependent in terms of their design, technology, and function, or in terms of their ultimate purpose or use. Construction contracts include those for the construction or restoration of assets and the restoration of the environment.

24.3.2 A **fixed-price contract** is a construction contract in which the contractor agrees to a fixed contract price, or a fixed rate per unit of output, which in some cases is subject to cost-escalation clauses.

24.3.3 A **cost-plus contract** is a construction contract in which the contractor is reimbursed for allowable or otherwise defined costs, plus a percentage of these costs or a fixed fee.

24.4   ACCOUNTING TREATMENT

Recognition and Initial Measurement

24.4.1 **Contract revenue** is measured at the fair value of the consideration received or receivable. The measurement of contract revenue is affected by a variety of uncertainties that depend on the outcome of future events. The estimates often need to be revised as events occur and uncertainties are resolved. Therefore, the amount of contract revenue may increase or decrease from one period to the next.

24.4.2 **Contract revenues** comprise:

- the initial agreed contract amount; and
- variations, claims, and incentive payments to the extent that it is probable that these will result in revenue and are capable of being reliably measured.

24.4.3 **Contract costs** comprise:

- direct contract costs (for example materials, site labor, or depreciation of plant and equipment used on the contract);
- general contract costs (for example insurance, costs of design, or construction overheads); and
- costs specifically chargeable to the customer in terms of the contract (for example administrative costs or selling costs).

Subsequent Measurement

24.4.4 When the outcome of a construction contract can be reliably estimated, contract revenue and contract costs should be recognized as revenue and expenses respectively by reference to the stage of completion of the contract activity at the end of the reporting period.

24.4.5 The stage of completion can be determined by reference to:

- the portion of costs incurred in relation to estimated total costs;
- surveys of work performed; and
- the physical stage of completion.

24.4.6 In the case of a fixed-price contract, the outcome of a construction contract can be estimated reliably when all the following conditions are met:

- total contract revenue can be measured reliably;
- it is probable that the economic benefits associated with the contract will flow to the entity; and
- the costs attributable to the contract can be clearly identified and measured reliably so that actual contract costs incurred can be compared with prior estimates.

24.4.7 In the case of a cost-plus contract, the outcome of a construction contract can be estimated reliably when all the following conditions are satisfied:

- it is probable that the economic benefits associated with the contract will flow to the entity; and
- the contract costs attributable to the contract, whether or not specifically reimbursable, can be clearly identified and measured reliably.

24.4.8 When the outcome of a contract cannot be reliably estimated, revenue should be recognized to the extent that recovery of contract costs is probable. The contract costs should be recognized as an expense in the period in which they are incurred.

24.4.9 When the uncertainties that prevented the outcome of the contract being estimated reliably no longer exist, revenue and expenses associated with the construction contract should be recognized as in 24.4.8.

24.4.10 Any expected excess of *total* contract costs over *total* contract revenue (expected loss) is recognized as an expense immediately.

24.4.11 The principles of IAS 11 are normally applied separately to each contract negotiated specifically for the construction of:

- an asset (for example, a bridge); or
- a combination of assets that are closely interrelated or interdependent in terms of their design, technology, function, or use (for example, specialized production plants).

24.4.12 A group of contracts should be treated as a *single* construction contract if it was negotiated as a single package.

24.4.13 The following contracts should be treated as *separate* construction contracts:

- a contract for a number of assets if separate proposals have been submitted for each asset; and
- an additional asset constructed at the option of the customer that was not part of the original contract.

24.4.14 The IFRIC issued IFRIC 15 in July of 2008, which clarifies how companies that construct real estate should recognize their revenue and expenses in terms of this standard or in terms of IAS 18 (chapter 23). If the contract is for the sale of goods, apply IAS 18; if it is for the construction of real estate, apply IAS 11. The main expected change in practice is a shift for some entities from recognizing revenue using the percentage-of-completion method (that is, as construction progresses, with reference to the stage of completion of the development) to recognizing revenue at a single point in time (that is, at completion upon or after delivery).

24.5 PRESENTATION AND DISCLOSURE

24.5.1 The Statement of Financial Position and notes include:

- amount of advances received;
- amount of retention monies;
- contracts in progress being costs-to-date-plus-profits or costs-to-date-less-losses;
- gross amount due from customers (assets);
- gross amount due to customers (liabilities); and
- contingent assets and contingent liabilities (for example claims).

24.5.2 The Statement of Comprehensive Income includes:

- amount of contract revenue recognized.

24.5.3 Accounting policies include:

- methods used for revenue recognition; and
- methods used for stage of completion.

24.6 FINANCIAL ANALYSIS AND INTERPRETATION

24.6.1 The use of the **percentage-of-completion method** requires that the total cost and total profit of a project be estimated at each reporting date. A pro rata proportion of the total estimated profit is then recognized in each accounting period during the performance of the contract. The pro rata proportion is based on the stage of completion at the end of the reporting period and reflects the work performed during the period from an engineering perspective. (Production is the critical event that gives rise to income.)

24.6.2 At each reporting date, the percentage-of-completion method is applied to up-to-date estimates of revenue and costs so that any adjustments are reflected in the current period and future periods. Amounts recognized in prior periods are not adjusted.

24.6.3 Table 24.1 summarizes how the choice of accounting method affects the Statement of Financial Position, Statement of Comprehensive Income, statement of cash flows, and the key financial ratios when accounting for long-term projects. The effects are given for the early years of the project's life.

TABLE 24.1   Impact of Percentage-of-Completion Method on Financial Statements

Item or ratio	Percentage-of-completion method (as opposed to a situation where the outcome of a contract cannot be reliably estimated)
Statement of Financial Position	Billings recorded but not received in cash are recorded as accounts receivable.
	Cumulative project expenses plus cumulative reported income less cumulative billings is recorded as a current asset if positive or a current liability if negative.
	Upon project completion, work-in-progress and advanced billings net to zero.
	Uncollected billings are accounts receivable.
Income Statement	Project costs are recorded as incurred.
	Revenues are recognized in proportion to the costs incurred during the period relative to the estimated total project cost.
	Reported earnings represent estimates of future operating cash flows.
	Estimated losses are recorded in their entirety as soon as a loss is estimated.
Statement of Cash Flows	Cash received from customers is reported as an operating cash inflow when received.
	Cash expended is recorded as an operating cash outflow when paid.
	Size of cash flow is the **same** because accounting choices have no effect on pretax cash flows.
Size of Current Assets	**Higher** if the cumulative work-in-progress (cumulative project costs and cumulative project income) exceeds cumulative billings.
	Same if cumulative billings equal or exceed work-in-progress.
Size of Current Liabilities	**Lower** as only receipts in excess of revenues are deferred as liabilities.
Net Worth	**Higher** because earnings are reported before the project is complete.
Profit Margin	**Higher** because earnings are reported during the project's life.
Asset Turnover	**Higher** because sales are reported during the project's life.
Debt or Equity	**Lower** because liabilities are lower and net worth is higher.
Return on Equity	**Higher** because earnings are higher percentage-wise than the higher equity.
Cash Flow	**Same** because accounting choices have no effect on cash flow.

24.7   **COMMENTARY**

24.7.1 Judgment is required when determining whether IAS 18 or IAS 11 should be applied to the revenue recognition. IFRIC 15 was issued to provide additional guidance.

24.7.2 There are no future developments planned on construction contracts.

24.8   **IMPLEMENTATION DECISIONS**

The following table sets out some of the strategic and tactical decisions that should be considered when applying IAS 11.

Strategic decisions	Tactical decisions	Problems to overcome
None	The methodologies to determine the percentage of completion should be chosen.	Determining the percentage of completion can be difficult and often will involve the use of experts (e.g., quantity surveyors).
None	Management should put measures in place to separate the costs between those relating to future activities and those that are not.	Judgment is required to determine at what point the expenses relate to future activities and past activities.

EXAMPLES: CONSTRUCTION CONTRACTS

EXAMPLE 24.1

A company undertakes a four-year project at a contracted price of $100 million that will be billed in four equal annual installments of $25 million over the project's life. The project is expected to cost $90 million, producing a $10 million profit. Over the life of the project, the billings, cash receipts, and cash outlays related to the project are as follows:

	1 ($'000)	Year 2 ($'000)	Year 3 ($'000)	Year 4 ($'000)
Billings	25,000	25,000	25,000	25,000
Cash receipts	20,000	27,000	25,000	28,000
Cash outlays	18,000	36,000	27,000	9,000

Financial statements and schedules must be produced under the percentage of completion contract method, showing:

A. the cash flows from the project each year;

B. the profit or loss for the project each year;

C. the Statement of Financial Position each year; and

D. the profit margin, asset turnover, debt to equity, return on assets, return on equity, and the current ratio.

A. The cash flow is simply the difference between the cash received and paid every year as given in the problem:

	Year 1 ($'000)	Year 2 ($'000)	Year 3 ($'000)	Year 4 ($'000)
Cash receipts	20,000	27,000	25,000	28,000
Cash outlays	18,000	36,000	27,000	9,000
Cash flow	2,000	(9,000)	(2,000)	19,000
Cumulative cash flow (on Statement of Financial Position)	2,000	(7,000)	(9,000)	10,000

B. The revenues recorded in profit or loss each year are calculated as

$$\text{Revenues in a Year} = \frac{\text{Costs Incurred in Year}}{\text{Total Project Cost}} \times \text{Total Estimated Project Price}$$

Assuming the cash paid each year is the cost incurred in the year, with a total project cost of $90 million and the estimated project profit of $10 million, the profit or loss schedule is as follows:

	Year 1 ($'000)	Year 2 ($'000)	Year 3 ($'000)	Year 4 ($'000)
$\text{Revenues} = \left(\dfrac{\text{Year's Expense}}{\$90,000,000}\right) \times \$100,000,000$	20,000	40,000	30,000	10,000
Expense (cash paid)	18,000	36,000	27,000	9,000
Income	2,000	4,000	3,000	1,000
Cumulative income (retained earnings)	2,000	6,000	9,000	10,000

C. In constructing the Statement of Financial Position, the following is required:

■ The difference between cumulative billings (to customers) and cumulative cash receipts (from customers) is recorded on the Statement of Financial Position as accounts receivable.

■ The sum of the cumulative expenses and the cumulative reported income is a work-in progress current asset.

■ Cumulative billings (to customers) are an advanced billings current liability.

■ The *net* difference between the work-in-progress current assets and the advanced billings current liabilities is recorded on the Statement of Financial Position as a net current asset if it is positive or as a net current liability if it is negative.

A schedule of these items is as follows:

	Year 1 ($'000)	Year 2 ($'000)	Year 3 ($'000)	Year 4 ($'000)
Cumulative billings	25,000	50,000	75,000	100,000
Cumulative cash receipts	20,000	47,000	72,000	100,000
Accounts receivable (on Statement of Financial Position)	5,000	3,000	3,000	0
Cumulative expenses	18,000	54,000	81,000	90,000
Cumulative income	2,000	6,000	9,000	10,000
Work-in-progress	20,000	60,000	90,000	100,000
Less Cumulative billings	25,000	50,000	75,000	100,000
Net asset (liability) on Statement of Financial Position	(5,000)	10,000	15,000	0

The Statement of Financial Position's cash equals the cumulative cash based on the previous cash flow schedule.

Cumulative income is reported as retained earnings on the Statement of Financial Position.

The Statement of Financial Position is as follows:

	Year 1 ($'000)	Year 2 ($'000)	Year 3 ($'000)	Year 4 ($'000)
Cash (cumulative cash from the cash flow schedule)	2,000	(7,000)	(9,000)	10,000
Accounts receivable	5,000	3,000	3,000	0
Net asset (0 in last year)	—	10,000	15,000	0
Total assets	7,000	6,000	9,000	10,000
Net liability (0 in last year)	5,000	—	—	0
Retained earnings (cumulative income from statement of comprehensive income)	2,000	6,000	9,000	10,000
Total liabilities and capital	7,000	6,000	9,000	10,000

D. The following illustrates the profit margin, asset turnover, debt-to-equity, return on assets, return on equity, and the current ratio:

Key financial ratios	Year 1	Year 2	Year 3	Year 4
Profit margin	10.0%	10.0%	10.0%	10.0%
Asset turnover	5.7x	6.2x	4.0x	1.1x
Debt-to-equity	2.5x	0.0x	0.0x	0.0x
Return on assets	57.1%	61.5%	40.0%	10.5%
Return on equity	200.0%	100.0%	40.0%	10.5%
Current ratio	1.4x	—	—	—

EXAMPLE 24.2

When comparing the use of the percentage-of-completion method with the completed-contract method during a long-term project's life, the percentage-of-completion method will result in which of the following:

a. Earlier recognition of cash flows
b. A higher return on assets
c. A lower debt-to-equity ratio
d. A higher asset turnover

EXPLANATION

a. No. The choice of accounting method has no effect on cash flow.
b. Yes. Because the periodic earnings will be higher under the percentage of completion method, the return on assets ratio will be higher.
c. Yes. Because the percentage-of-completion method reports lowers liabilities and higher net worth, the debt-to-equity ratio will be lower.
d. Yes. The asset turnover ratio is higher under the percentage-of-completion method because sales are reported during the life of the project.

EXAMPLE 24.3

Omega Inc. started a four-year contract to build a dam. Activities commenced on February 1, 20X6. The total contract price amounted to $12 million, and it was estimated that the work would be completed at a total cost of $9.5 million. In the construction agreement the customer agreed to accept increases in wage tariffs additional to the contract price.

The following information refers to contract activities for the financial year ending December 31, 20X6:

1. Costs for the year:

	$'000
Material	1,400
Labor	800
Operating overhead	150
Subcontractors	180

2. Current estimate of total contract costs indicates the following:
▪ Materials will be $180,000 higher than expected.
▪ Total labor costs will be $300,000 higher than expected. Of this amount, only $240,000 will be the result of increased wage tariffs. The remainder will be caused by inefficiencies.
▪ A savings of $30,000 is expected on operating overhead.

3. During the current financial year the customer requested a variation to the original contract, and it was agreed that the contract price would be increased by $900,000. The total estimated cost of this extra work is $750,000.

4. By the end of 20X6, certificates issued by quantity surveyors indicated a 25 percent stage of completion.

Determine the profit to date, based on:

- Option 1—contract costs in proportion to estimated contract costs
- Option 2—percentage of the work certified

EXPLANATION

Contract profit recognized for the year ending December 31, 20X6, is as follows:

	Option 1 $'000	Option 2 $'000
Contract revenue (Calculation d)	3,107	3,285
Contract costs to date (Calculation a)	(2,530)	(2,530)
	577	755

Calculations	**$'000**	**$'000**
a. **Contract costs to date**		
Materials	1,400	
Labor	800	
Operating overhead	150	
Subcontractors	180	
	2,530	
b. **Contract costs (revised estimated total costs)**		
Original estimate	9,500	
Materials	180	
Labor	300	
Operating overhead	(30)	
Variation	750	
	10,700	
c. **Contract revenue (revised estimate)**		
Original amount	12,000	
Labor (wage increases added to contract price)	240	
Variation	900	
	13,140	
d. **Stage of completion**	Option 1	Option 2
Based on contract costs in proportion to estimated total contract costs:		
2,530 + 10,700 × 13,140 (rounded off)	3,107	
Based on work certified: 25% × 3,140		3,285

CHAPTER 25

Employee Benefits (IAS 19)

25.1	**OBJECTIVE**

IAS 19 requires entities to identify and recognize all the benefits that they are obliged to provide to employees, regardless of the form or timing of the benefits. While some employee benefits such as salaries are paid to employees as they render the services to the entity, other benefits such as long service awards and retirement benefits are only paid to employees after the services have been rendered to the entity. IAS 19 provides guidance on how to recognize and measure all types of benefits. The goal is that the entity recognizes the related expenses as the employee renders the service rather than when they receive payment for the services rendered.

25.2	**SCOPE OF THE STANDARD**

IAS 19 applies to all employee benefits, including benefits provided under formal arrangements, legislative requirements, and informal practices. The standard does not cover equity compensation benefits, which are within the scope of IFRS 2.

The standard identifies five types of employee benefits:

1. short-term employee benefits (for example, bonuses, wages, and social security);
2. postemployment benefits (for example, pensions and other retirement benefits);
3. long-term employee benefits (for example, long-service leave and, if not due within 12 months, profit sharing, bonuses, and deferred compensation);
4. termination benefits; and
5. equity compensation benefits (for example, employee share options per IFRS 2).

Employee benefits include benefits that are payable to dependants of employees. Furthermore, "employees" includes all employees employed on any basis—full time, part time, permanent, temporary, or casual.

25.3   **KEY CONCEPTS**

25.3.1 Employee benefits can be provided in terms of either:

- **legal obligations,** which arise from the operation of law (for example, agreements and plans between the entity and employees or their representatives); or
- **constructive obligations,** which arise from informal practices that result in an obligation whereby the entity has no realistic alternative but to pay employee benefits (for example, the entity has a history of increasing benefits for former employees to keep pace with inflation even if there is no legal obligation to do so).

25.3.2 Employee benefits are all forms of consideration given by an entity in exchange for services rendered by employees.

25.3.3 Short-term employee benefits are employee benefits (other than termination benefits) that fall due wholly within 12 months after the end of the period in which the employees render the related service.

25.3.4 Postemployment benefits are employee benefits (other than termination benefits) that are payable after the completion of the employment.

25.3.5 Equity compensation plans are formal or informal arrangements under which an entity provides equity compensation benefits for one or more employees. These are accounted for in terms of IFRS 2 and not IAS 19.

25.3.6 Vested employee benefits are employee benefits that are not conditional on future employment.

25.3.7 Defined contribution plans are postemployment benefit plans under which an entity pays fixed contributions into a separate entity. The reporting entity has no legal or constructive obligation if the fund does not hold sufficient assets to pay all employee benefits relating to employee service in the current and prior periods.

25.3.8 Defined benefit plans are postemployment benefit plans other than defined contribution plans.

25.3.9 Present value of a defined benefit obligation is the present value, without deducting any plan assets, of expected future payments required to settle the obligation resulting from the employee service in the current and prior periods.

25.3.10 Plan assets comprise assets held by the long-term employee benefit fund and qualifying insurance policies.

25.3.11 Return on plan assets comprises interest, dividends, and other revenue derived from the plan assets, together with realized and unrealized gains or losses on the plan assets, less any costs of administering the plan and less any tax payable by the plan itself.

25.3.12 Actuarial gains and losses comprise experience adjustments (the effects if differences between the previous actuarial assumptions and what has actually occurred) and the effects of changes in actuarial assumptions.

25.3.13 Past service cost is the increase in the present value of the defined benefit obligation for employee service in prior periods, resulting in the current period from the introduction of, or changes to, postemployment benefits or other long-term employee benefits. Past service cost may be either positive (where benefits are introduced or improved) or negative (where existing benefits are reduced).

25.3.14 **Termination benefits** are payable as a result of either an entity's decision to terminate an employee's employment before the normal retirement date or the employee's decision to accept voluntary redundancy in exchange for those benefits.

25.3.15 **Other long-term employee benefits** are employee benefits (other than postemployment benefits and termination benefits) which do not fall due wholly within the 12 months after the end of the period in which the employees render the related service.

25.4	**ACCOUNTING TREATMENT**

Recognition

25.4.1 **Short-term employment benefits.** These include wages; salaries; short-term compensated absences; profit sharing or bonuses payable within 12 months; and nonmonetary benefits, for example medical benefits, for current employees. When the employee has rendered the service to an entity during an accounting period the entity must recognize the undiscounted amount of short-term employee benefits expected to be paid in exchange for that service as an expense. A liability should be recognized to the extent that these benefits have not been paid in cash.

25.4.2 **Other long-term employee benefits.** These include long-term compensated absences, long service benefits, long-term disability benefits, bonuses or profit sharing payable after 12 months, and deferred compensation. IAS 19 requires the projected unit credit method to be applied to the measurement of other long-term benefits, as for defined benefit plans. However, a long-term benefit is not subject to the same degree of estimation uncertainty as a defined benefit retirement plan. Therefore, simplified rules for actuarial gains or losses and past service costs are applicable. In terms of these simplified rules all actuarial gains and losses and past service costs are recognized immediately.

25.4.3 **Termination benefits.** When the event that results in an obligation is termination rather than employee service, an entity should recognize the benefits due only when it is demonstrably committed through a detailed formal plan to either:

■ terminate the employment of an employee or group of employees before the normal retirement date; or
■ provide termination benefits to encourage voluntary redundancy.

Termination benefits falling due more than 12 months after the reporting date should be discounted.

25.4.4 **Postemployment benefits—defined contribution plans.** An entity recognizes contributions to a defined contribution plan as an expense when an employee has rendered services in exchange for those contributions. When the contributions do not fall due within 12 months after the accounting period that services were rendered, they should be discounted. To the extent that contributions have not been paid a liability should be recognized.

25.4.5 **Postemployment benefits—defined benefit plans.** The following rules are applicable to the accounting for defined benefit plans:

■ An entity should use the projected unit credit method to measure the present value of its defined benefit obligations and related current- and past-service costs. This method sees each period of service as giving rise to an additional unit of benefit entitlement and measures each unit separately to build up the final obligation.

- Unbiased and mutually compatible actuarial assumptions about demographic variables (for example, employee turnover and mortality) and financial variables (for example, future increases in salaries and certain changes in benefits) should be used in determining the present value of the liability.

- To determine the amount to be included in the statement of financial position the present value of the liability should be increased for any unrecognized actuarial gains, reduced for unrecognized actuarial losses and past service cost not recognized. Furthermore, the fair value of the plan assets should be deducted. The net amount is then recognized as a liability or asset.

- When it is virtually certain that another party will reimburse some or all of the expenditure required to settle a defined benefit obligation, an entity should recognize its right to reimbursement as a separate asset.

- Offsetting assets and liabilities of different plans is not allowed.

- The amount recognized in profit or loss is the net total of current-service cost, interest cost, expected return on plan assets, any reimbursement rights, recognized actuarial gains and losses, and recognized past-service cost. The effect of any plan curtailments or settlements should be recognized as expense or income.

- Past-service costs are recognized on a straight-line basis over the average period until the amended benefits become vested.

- Gains or losses arising on the curtailment or settlement of a defined benefit plan are recognized when the curtailment or settlement occurs.

- Actuarial gains or losses may be recognized in one of three ways:
  1. the full amount is recognized in other comprehensive income as it arises;
  2. the full amount is recognized in profit or loss as it arises;
  3. the gains or losses are only recognized to the extent that the cumulative unrecognized gains or losses exceed the *greater* of
     - 10 percent of the present value of the defined benefit obligation (before deducting plan assets), and
     - 10 percent of the fair value of any plan assets at the end of the previous reporting period (the corridor approach).

In terms of the corridor approach the minimum amount to be recognized for each defined benefit plan is the excess outside of the 10 percent corridor at the previous reporting date, divided by the expected average remaining working lives of the employees participating in that plan.

25.4.6 IFRIC 14 was issued to provide guidance on the interaction between minimum funding requirements and the limit on the defined benefit asset. The IFRIC gives guidance on how the existence of a minimum funding requirement may limit the amount of refunds or reductions in future contributions available to the entity and consequently the amount of any asset that can be recognized in terms of IAS 19. Furthermore, the extent to which contributions in respect of a minimum funding requirement will not be available as a refund or reduction after they have been paid into the fund will result in a liability when the obligation arises.

The decision tree below (figure 25.1) illustrates the principles set forth in IFRIC 14.

FIGURE 25.1 Interaction between Minimum Funding Requirements and the Defined Benefit Asset

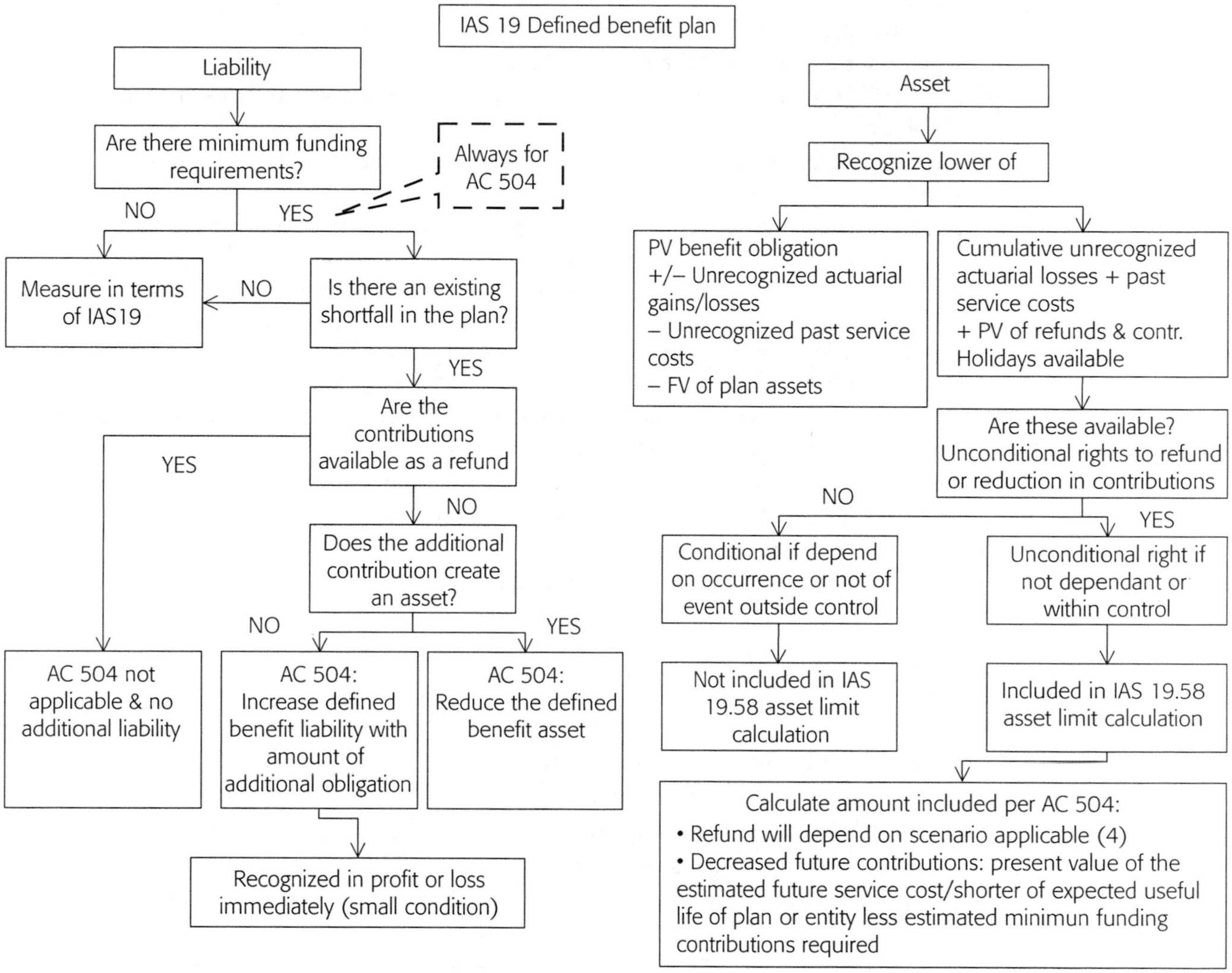

25.5 PRESENTATION AND DISCLOSURE

25.5.1 Short-term employee benefits. IAS 19 does not provide specific disclosure requirements for these types of plans, although IAS 1 requires disclosure of the employee benefits expense. Furthermore, IAS 24 requires specific disclosures in respect of amounts paid to key management personnel.

25.5.2 Other long-term employee benefits. IAS 19 has no specific requirements although the requirements of IAS 1 and IAS 24 in respect of employee benefits and key management personnel will be applicable.

25.5.3 Termination benefits. Where there is uncertainty about the number of employees who will accept the offer, a contingent liability exists. IAS 37 requires certain disclosures in respect of contingent liabilities that must be applied to the termination benefits. In accordance with IAS 1 if the expense is material it should be separately disclosed and IAS 24 requires disclosure of termination benefits paid to key management personnel.

25.5.4 Postemployment defined contribution plans. An entity shall disclose the amount recognized as an expense for defined contribution plans.

25.5.5 Postemployment defined benefit plans. IAS 19 requires an entity to disclose information that enables the users of financial statements to evaluate the nature of defined benefit plans and the financial effects of changes in those plans during the period. Information to be disclosed should include the following:

- accounting policies for recognizing actuarial gains or losses;
- a general description of the type of plan;
- a reconciliation between the opening and closing balances of the present value of the obligation;
- a reconciliation between the opening and closing balances of the fair value of the plan assets;
- a reconciliation between the defined benefit obligation, fair value of the plan assets, and the net amount recognized on the statement of financial position;
- the total expense recognized in profit or loss, showing separate line items such as current service cost, interest cost, expected return on plan assets, expected return on reimbursement rights, actuarial gains or losses, past service costs, the effect of any curtailments, and the effect of any limitation on the net asset recognized;
- the amount of actuarial gains or losses recognized in other comprehensive income if that is the entity's accounting policy;
- the major categories of plan assets, for example debt, equities, or property;
- amounts included in the fair value of plan assets with respect to:
  - the entity's own financial instruments; or
  - property occupied or assets used by the entity;
- a description of how the expected return on plan assets is determined;
- the actual return on plan assets;
- the principal actuarial assumptions;
- the amounts for the current annual period and previous four annual periods of:
  - the present value of the obligation;
  - the fair value of the plan assets;
  - the surplus or deficit in the plan; and
  - the experience adjustments; and
- the best estimate of the contributions to be paid in the next annual period.

25.6   FINANCIAL ANALYSIS AND INTERPRETATION

25.6.1 The accounting for short-term and termination benefits is relatively straightforward as there are limited assumptions required for these valuations. Some long-term employee benefits are subject to a degree of estimation uncertainty. However this is not as extensive as for postemployment benefits.

25.6.2 The complexity of the accounting requirements applicable to postemployment benefits contributes to the wide range of differences among the companies offering these plans. As a result of this complexity and the fundamental differences in the two types of plans described below, analysts have a difficult time discerning the underlying economic substance of a firm's reported pension and other retirement benefits.

- **Defined contribution plans** require the employer to contribute a specific amount to a pension plan each year. The employee's retirement income is largely determined by the performance of the portfolio in which the contributions were invested.
- **Defined benefit plans** require the employer to pay specified pension benefits to retired employees. The investment risk is borne by the employer.

25.6.3 For **defined contribution plans,** the employer's annual pension expense is the amount that the company plan must contribute to the plan each year according to the contribution formula. Pension expense and cash outflow are the same, and there are no assets or liabilities recorded by the employer. A defined contribution pension plan obliges the employer only to make annual contributions to the pension plan based on a prescribed formula. When the contributions are made, the company has no further obligation that year. These plans are not subject to estimation uncertainty and the employer's contribution is recognized as an expense as incurred.

25.6.4 Defined benefit plans are subject to much estimation uncertainty, including assumptions regarding mortality rates of plan participants, staff turnover rates, future salary levels, discount rates, and rates of return on plan assets. Benefits promised to participants are defined by a specific formula that reflects these estimated future events. The estimated benefits are allocated to the years of service worked by employees to develop the annual pension expense. Companies with defined benefit pension plans accrue obligations to pay benefits, according to the benefit formula, as the employee performs work; therefore the expense is recognized on an accrual basis as earned by the employee. However, these obligations are not discharged until after the employee retires.

25.6.5 As described above, the accounting for defined benefit plans is subject to a significant amount of estimation uncertainty. The main actuarial assumptions include:

- the discount rate;
- the salary growth rate;
- staff turnover rates;
- the expected return on plan assets;
- the age distribution of the workforce;
- the average service life of employees; and
- mortality rates.

25.6.6 In **analyzing the actuarial assumptions,** analysts need to determine whether the current assumptions are appropriate, particularly when comparing to the entity's competitors. In addition, if the assumptions have been changed, analysts need to determine the effect of a change in the following parameters on the financial statements:

- **Discount rate assumption.** If the discount rate is increased, the pension obligations will decrease, producing an actuarial gain for the year. If the discount rate is decreased, however, the pension obligation will increase, resulting in an actuarial loss for the year.
- **Salary growth rate assumption.** The wage growth rate assumption directly affects pension obligations and the service cost component of the reported pension expense. Therefore, a higher (lower) wage growth rate assumption will result in a higher (lower) pension obligation and a higher (lower) service cost component of the reported pension expense.
- **Expected rate of return on fund assets.** Because all funds should earn the same risk-adjusted return in the long run (if the market is efficient), deviations in this assumption from the norm that are unrelated to changes in a pension portfolio's asset mix might suggest that the pension expense is overstated or understated. In general, if the expected return on plan assets is too high, the pension expense is understated, increasing reported earnings; if the expected return on plan assets is too low, the pension expense is overstated, reducing reported earnings. Again, manipulating the expected return on plan assets will manipulate reported earnings and can be used to smooth earnings per share.

25.7   COMMENTARY

25.7.1 Due to the fact that limited assumptions are required for the accounting for short-term and termination benefits there is little controversy around the accounting treatment for these items. Other long-term benefits require some estimation but the accounting for these is also generally uncontroversial.

25.7.2 There is much controversy around the accounting for postemployment benefits, particularly defined benefit plans. Much of the controversy relates to the differentiation between defined benefit plans and defined contribution plans, complex valuation rules, and the choice of policies for the recognition of actuarial gains and losses. Many users and preparers have indicated that the current requirements don't provide high-quality, transparent information about postemployment plans.

25.7.3 Of particular concern is the deferral of actuarial gains and losses, which results in misleading information being presented in the Statement of Financial Position because liabilities could be significantly understated.

25.7.4 In response to criticism of the current accounting for postemployment benefits, the IASB has embarked on a long-term project with the FASB to produce a single, high-quality accounting standard for these benefits. The project is likely to take some time.

25.7.5 However, the IASB believes that while the long-term project is progressing the standard can be improved in the medium term. In March 2008 the IASB issued a discussion paper setting out these proposed improvements on the following topics:

- the deferral of certain gains or losses arising from defined benefit plans;
- the presentation of defined benefit liabilities;
- accounting for benefits that are based on contributions plus a promised return; and
- accounting for benefit promises with a "higher of" option.

25.7.6   The IASB issued an exposure draft for these amendments in April 2010 with a standard to be issued in 2011. At this stage there is no timetable for completion of the longer-term project with the FASB.

25.8   **IMPLEMENTATION DECISIONS**

The following table sets out some of the strategic and tactical decisions that should be considered when applying IAS 19.

Strategic decisions	Tactical decisions	Problems to overcome
The kind and type of employee benefits and benefit plans needs to be decided on by management.	Specific aspects of employee benefits to be decided on include: • salaries and wages; • other benefits and allowances, for example, medical and travel allowances; • leave policies; • postemployment benefits; • long-term benefits; and • termination benefits. The entity should determine whether it has the skills internally for the more complex accounting, especially relating to defined benefit plans. If the entity does not have the internal know-how, it can be obtained from the pension administrator, in which case the entity should ensure that the information is accurate and timely.	The complexity of employee benefits often leads to complex accounting. Defined benefit plans and long-term employee benefits often result in the most significant accounting challenges.
If a defined benefit plan is chosen as the preferred postemployment compensation plan for the entity, then there will be accounting policy elections, a number of accounting complexities, and significant disclosure.	The accounting policy for actuarial gains and losses should be selected as one of the following: • the deferral of all gains and losses within the corridor; • the recognition of all gains or losses in profit or loss when they arise; or • the recognition of all gains or losses in other comprehensive income when they arise.	Significant actuarial involvement is required to determine the value of the defined benefit plan and the related income statement impact.

EXAMPLE: EMPLOYEE BENEFITS

EXAMPLE 25.1

On December 31, 20X0, an entity's Statement of Financial Position includes a defined benefit plan liability of $12 million. Management has decided to adopt IAS 19 as of January 1, 20X1, for the purpose of accounting for employee benefits. At that date, the present value of the obligation under IAS 19 is calculated at $146 million, and the fair value of the plan assets is determined to be $110 million. On January 1, 19X1, the entity had improved pension benefits. (The cost for nonvested benefits amounted to $16 million, and the average remaining period until vesting was eight years.)

EXPLANATION

The transitional liability is calculated as follows:

	$'000
Present value of the obligation	146,000
Fair value of plan assets	(110,000)
Past-service cost to be recognized in later periods ($16 × 3/8)	(6,000)
Transitional liability	30,000
Liability already recognized	12,000
Increase in liability	18,000

The entity might (in terms of the transitional provisions of IAS 19) choose to either recognize the transitional liability of $18 million immediately or recognize it as an expense on a straight-line basis for up to five years. The choice is irrevocable. Subsequently, transitional arrangements are dealt with by IFRS 1.

EXAMPLE 25.2

Smith is analyzing three companies in the utilities industry: Northern Lights, Southeast Power, and Power Grid. After reviewing each company's defined benefit plan disclosures, Smith made the following notes:

Assumption	Northern Lights 20X0	Northern Lights 20X1	Southeast Power 20X0	Southeast Power 20X1	Power Grid 20X0	Power Grid 20X1
Discount Rate	6.0%	5.5%	6.5%	6.5%	6.2%	6.0%
Assumed Rate of Salary Growth	3.5%	3.5%	2.5%	3.0%	3.3%	3.0%
Expected Return on Plan Assets	7.0%	7.0%	7.5%	7.2%	8.0%	8.5%

Issue 1: If Power Grid had left its expected rate of return on plan assets at 8 percent instead of raising it to 8.5 percent, what would the company have reported in 20X1?

    a. A lower accumulated benefit obligation

    b. A higher projected benefit obligation

    c. A larger deficit

    d. Higher pension expense

EXPLANATION

Choice d. is correct. The expected rate of return on plan assets is a direct (negative) component in the computation of defined benefit expense. A lower rate would thus result in a higher pension expense. However, the value of the obligation (both accumulated and projected) and the size of the deficit are not affected by the expected return on plan assets.

Choice a. is incorrect. Only pension expense is affected by changes in the expected rate of return on plan assets. Therefore, there will not be a change in the accumulated benefit obligation (ABO).

Choice b. is incorrect. Only pension expense is affected by changes in the expected rate of return on plan assets. Therefore, there will not be a change in the projected benefit obligation (PBO).

Choice c. is incorrect. Only pension expense is affected by changes in the expected rate of return on plan assets. Therefore, there will not be a change in the funded status.

Issue 2: Based on the statistics and assumptions provided, which company has the most conservative pension accounting (that is, the one that will produce the highest obligation, and pension expense)?

    a. Northern Lights
    b. Southeast Power
    c. Power Grid
    d. Cannot be determined

EXPLANATION

Choice a. is correct. Northern Lights has the most conservative pension plan assumptions, including the lowest discount rate, highest compensation growth, and the lowest expected return on plan assets. These assumptions result in a higher obligation, as well as higher pension expense than either Southeast Power or Power Grid.

Choice b. is incorrect. All of Southeast Power's assumptions are more aggressive than the assumptions made by Northern Lights.

Choice c. is incorrect. All of Power Grid's assumptions are more aggressive than the assumptions made by Northern Lights.

Choice d. is incorrect. Enough information was provided in the table above to determine that the assumptions made by Northern Lights are the most conservative, resulting in a higher ABO, PBO, and pension expense than either Southeast Power or Power Grid.

Issue 3: When Power Grid lowers its discount rate in 20X1 to 6 percent from 6.2 percent in 20X0, what will be the effects on the obligation, accumulated and projected?

	Projected	Accumulated
a.	Increase	Increase
b.	Decrease	Increase
c.	Decrease	Decrease
d.	Increase	Decrease

EXPLANATION

Choice a. is correct. The discount rate is used to calculate the present value of the benefits owed, both accumulated and projected. Therefore, a decrease in the discount rate will increase both the accumulated and projected benefits.

Choice b. is incorrect. The PBO will not decrease when the discount rate decreases, because the discount rate is used to calculate the present value of future benefits.

Choice c. is incorrect. The discount rate is used to calculate the present value of future benefits. Therefore, a decrease in the discount rate will not decrease either the PBO or the ABO.

Choice d. is incorrect. The ABO will not decrease when the discount rate decreases, because the discount rate is used to calculate the present value of future benefits.

CHAPTER 26

Impairment of Assets (IAS 36)

26.1   **OBJECTIVE**

The purpose of this standard is to provide entities with guidance to determine whether an asset is impaired and how the impairment should be recognized. The key concept is the identification and recognition of movements in asset value subsequent to initial recognition when such movements result in a reduction of asset value.

The principles in this standard apply to all assets where impairment is not specifically addressed in another standard. (For example, property, plant, and equipment and intangible assets are addressed in other standards.)

26.2   **SCOPE OF THE STANDARD**

IAS 36 prescribes:

- the circumstances in which an entity should calculate the recoverable amount of its assets, including internal and external indicators or impairment;
- the measurement of recoverable amounts for individual assets and cash-generating units; and
- the recognition and reversal of impairment losses.

This standard covers most noncurrent assets, with the exception of financial assets and noncurrent assets classified as held for sale.

26.3   **KEY CONCEPTS**

26.3.1 An **impairment loss** is the amount by which the carrying amount of an asset or a cash-generating unit exceeds its recoverable amount.

26.3.2 The **recoverable amount** of an asset or a cash-generating unit is the higher of its fair value less costs to sell and its value in use.

26.3.3 **Value in use** is the present value of the future cash flows expected to be derived from an asset or a cash-generating unit.

26.3.4 Fair value less costs to sell is the amount obtainable from the sale of an asset or a cash-generating unit in an arm's-length transaction between knowledgeable, willing parties less the costs of disposal.

26.3.5 If either the net selling price or the value in use of an asset exceeds its carrying amount, the asset is not impaired.

26.4   ACCOUNTING TREATMENT

26.4.1 The **recoverable amount** of an asset should be estimated if, at the reporting date, there is an indication that the asset could be impaired. The recoverable amount of the following assets should also be determined annually, irrespective of whether there is an indication of impairment:

- intangible assets with an indefinite useful life;
- intangible assets not yet ready for use; and
- goodwill.

26.4.2 In assessing whether there is any indication that an asset may be impaired, at a minimum, an entity should consider the following:

- **external sources of information,** for example, decline in an asset's market value, significant changes that have an adverse effect on the entity, increases in market interest rates, and whether the carrying amount of the net assets of the entity is more than its market capitalization; and
- **internal sources of information,** for example, evidence of obsolescence or physical damage, significant changes in the extent to which or the manner in which the assets are used or are expected to be used, or evidence from internal reporting indicating an asset is performing worse than expected.

26.4.3 The best evidence of an asset's fair value less costs to sell is a price in a binding sale agreement in an arm's length transaction, adjusted for incremental costs that would be directly attributable to the disposal of the asset.

26.4.4 The calculation of value in use should reflect the following elements:

- an estimate of the future cash flows the entity expects to derive from the asset;
- expectations about possible variations in the amount or timing of those future cash flows;
- the time value of money, represented by the current market risk-free rate of interest;
- the price for bearing the uncertainty inherent in the asset; and
- other factors, such as illiquidity, that market participants would reflect in pricing the future cash flows the entity expects to derive from the asset.

26.4.5 In determining the **value in use** of an asset, an entity should use pretax cash flow projections and a pretax discount rate.

26.4.6 Cash flow projections (before income taxes and finance costs) for the asset or cash-generating unit in its current condition should be based on reasonable and supportable assumptions that:

- reflect management's best estimate of the range of economic conditions that will exist over the remaining useful life of the asset;

- are based on the most recent financial budgets and forecasts approved by management for a maximum period of five years; and
- base any projections beyond the period covered by the most recent budget and forecasts on budgets and forecasts that use a steady or declining growth rate, unless an increasing rate can be justified.

26.4.7 The pretax discount rate must reflect current market assessments of the time value of money and the risks specific to the asset or cash-generating unit. The discount rate should not reflect risks for which future cash flows have been adjusted.

26.4.8 If the recoverable amount of an asset is less than its carrying amount, the carrying amount of the asset shall be reduced to its recoverable amount. That reduction is an impairment loss.

26.4.9 An impairment loss should be recognized in **profit or loss** unless the asset is carried at the revalued amount in accordance with IAS 16 (see chapter 10) or IAS 38 (see chapter 13), in which case it should be dealt with as a revaluation decrease. After recognition of the impairment loss, the depreciation charge for subsequent periods is based on the revised carrying amount.

26.4.10 An entity should reassess at each reporting date whether there is any indication that an impairment loss recognized in a prior period no longer exists or has decreased. If any such indication exists, the entity should estimate the recoverable amount of that asset. An impairment loss recognized in prior periods should be **reversed** if, and only if, there has been a change in the estimates used to determine recoverable amount since the last impairment loss was recognized. If that is the case, the carrying amount of the asset should be increased to its recoverable amount, but only to the extent that it does not increase the carrying amount of the asset above the carrying amount that would have been determined for the asset (net of amortization or depreciation) if no impairment loss had been recognized in prior years.

26.4.11 For the purpose of **impairment testing,** goodwill should be allocated to each of the acquirer's cash-generating units or groups of cash-generating units that are expected to benefit from a combination, regardless of whether other assets or liabilities of the acquiree are allocated to that unit or those units. A cash-generating unit is the smallest identifiable group of assets that generates cash inflows from continuing use that are largely independent of the cash inflows from other assets or groups of assets.

26.4.12 A recoverable amount should be estimated for an individual asset. If it is not possible to do so, an entity should determine the recoverable amount for the **cash-generating unit** to which the asset belongs. The recoverable amount of a cash-generating unit is determined in the same way as that of an individual asset. The entity should identify all the corporate assets that relate to the cash-generating unit under review. When corporate assets cannot be allocated to cash-generating units on a reasonable and consistent basis, the entity should identify the units to which the corporate assets can be allocated on a reasonable and consistent basis and perform the impairment test for those units.

26.4.13 An impairment loss for a cash-generating unit should be allocated to reduce the carrying amount of the assets of the unit in the following order:

- goodwill, and
- other assets in the cash-generating unit on a pro rata basis.

The carrying amount of any asset in the cash-generating unit should not be reduced below its recoverable amount, which is the highest of its fair value less costs to sell or its value in use and zero.

26.4.14 A reversal of an impairment loss should be recognized in **profit or loss** unless the asset is carried at the revalued amount in accordance with IAS 16 or IAS 38, in which case the reversal is treated as a revaluation increase in accordance with that standard.

26.4.15 An **impairment loss for goodwill** may never be reversed.

26.5   PRESENTATION AND DISCLOSURE

26.5.1 The following should be disclosed for *each* class of assets and for *each* IFRS 8 reportable segment:

- amount recognized in the statement of comprehensive income for
  - impairment losses; and
  - reversals of impairment losses;
- amount recognized directly in comprehensive income for
  - impairment losses; and
  - reversals of impairment losses.

26.5.2 If an impairment loss for an individual asset or a cash-generating unit is recognized or reversed, the following should be disclosed:

- events and circumstances that led to the loss being recognized or reversed;
- amount recognized or reversed;
- details about the nature of the asset or the cash-generating unit and the reportable segments involved;
- whether the recoverable amount is the net selling price or value in use; and
- the basis used to determine the net selling price *or* the discount rate used to determine value in use, and any previous value in use.

26.5.3 Where the recoverable amount of a cash-generating unit is used to determine impairment, detailed disclosure is required, the most significant being:

- A description of the cash-generating unit
- The goodwill allocated to the unit
- The impairment loss recognized or reversed by class of asset in the cash-generating unit
- The basis on which the recoverable amount has been determined

26.5.4 If the recoverable amount is based on value in use, disclose:

- a description of the key assumptions;
- a description of the approach to determine the values assigned to each assumption;
- the period over which the cash flow has been projected;
- the growth rate; and
- the discount rate.

26.5.5 If the recoverable amount is based on fair value less cost to sell, disclose:

- a description of the key assumptions; and
- a description of the approach to determine the values assigned to each assumption.

26.6

FINANCIAL ANALYSIS AND INTERPRETATION

26.6.1 An **impaired asset** is an asset that will be retained by the entity and whose book value, prior to recognizing any impairment charges, is not expected to be recovered from future operations. Lack of recoverability is indicated by such factors as:

- a significant decrease in market value, physical change, or use of the asset;
- adverse changes in the legal or business climate;
- significant cost overruns; and
- current, historical, and probable future operating or cash flow losses from the asset.

26.6.2 Management makes the decisions about whether or not an asset's value is impaired by reference to internal and external sources of information, using cash flow projections based on reasonable and supportable assumptions and its own most recent budgets and forecasts. In IFRS financial statements, the need for a write-down, the size of the write-down, and the timing of the write-down are determined by objective and supportable evidence rather than at management's discretion. Impairment losses, therefore, cannot be used in IFRS financial statements to smooth or manipulate earnings in some other way. The discount rate used to determine the present value of future cash flows of the asset in its recoverability test must be determined objectively, based on market conditions.

26.6.3 From an external analyst's perspective, it is difficult to forecast impairment losses. However, the impairment losses themselves and the related disclosures provide the analyst with useful information about management's projections of future cash flows.

26.6.4 When impairment losses are recognized the financial statements are affected in several ways:

- The carrying amount of the asset is reduced by the impairment loss. This reduces the carrying amount of the entity's total assets.
- The deferred tax liability is reduced and deferred tax income is recognized if the entity cannot take a tax deduction for the impairment loss until the asset is sold or fully used.
- Retained earnings and, hence, shareholders' equity is reduced by the difference between the impairment loss and any associated reduction in the deferred tax liability.
- Profit before tax is reduced by the amount of the impairment loss.
- Profit is reduced by the difference between the impairment loss and any associated reduction in deferred tax expense.

26.6.5 In addition, the impairment loss affects the following financial ratios and elements:

- **Asset turnover** ratios increase because of the lower asset base.
- The **debt-to-equity** ratios rise because of the lower equity base.
- **Profit margins** suffer a one-time reduction because of the recognition of the impairment loss.
- The **book value** (shareholders' equity) of the entity is reduced because of the reduction in equity.
- **Future depreciation or amortization charges** are reduced because the carrying amount of the depreciable or amortizable asset is reduced.
- Lower future depreciation charges tend to cause the **future profitability** of the firm to increase (because the losses are taken in the current year).
- Higher future profitability and lower asset values tend to increase **future returns on assets.**
- Higher future profitability and lower equity values tend to increase **future returns on equity.**

26.6.6 Impairment losses do not directly affect cash flows because the cash outflows for the asset have already occurred; tax deductions, and hence tax payments, might not be affected. However, the impairment loss is an indicator that future operating cash flows could be lower than previously forecast.

26.7   COMMENTARY

26.7.1 In practice, there is some difficulty implementing IAS 36 in regards to cash-generating units. It is difficult to determine the following:

- the identification of the cash-generating units and the allocation of the goodwill to the cash-generating units; and
- the value in use, specifically expected cash flows, growth rates, and discount rates. When determining the growth rate, the entity should consider whether it should be in line with industry growth or the entity's own estimated growth. When determining the discount rate, pretax rates should be used. The entity should also consider, for example, whether the *weighted average cost of capital* (WACC) should be a group- or entity-specific value, or whether it should be a country-specific value.

26.7.2 There have been no recent amendments to IAS 36 and the IASB has not indicated any future project regarding the standard.

26.8   IMPLEMENTATION DECISIONS

The following table sets out some of the strategic and tactical decisions that should be considered when applying IAS 36.

Strategic decisions	Tactical decisions	Problems to overcome
Identifying cash-generating units that exist within the entity.		Allocating the assets and specifically goodwill to relevant cash-generating units.
	The valuation methodology for determining value in use and fair value less costs to sell.	Consistent application of growth rates and discount rates and methodologies across the entity/group.

EXAMPLE: IMPAIRMENT OF ASSETS

EXAMPLE 26.1

The following information relates to individual equipment items of an entity on the reporting date:

	Carrying amount $	Fair value less costs to sell $	Value in use $
Item #1	119,000	121,000	114,000
Item #2 (note 1)	237,000	207,000	205,000
Item #3 (note 1)	115,000	117,000	123,000
Item #4	83,000	75,000	79,000
Item #5 (note 2)	31,000	26,000	–

Notes

1. Items #2 and #3 are carried at revalued amounts, and the cumulative revaluation surpluses included in other comprehensive income for the items are $12,000 and $6,000, respectively. Both items are manufacturing equipment.

2. Item #5 is a bus used for transporting employees in the mornings and evenings. It is not possible to determine the value in use of the bus separately because the bus does not generate cash inflows from continuing use that are independent of the cash flows from other assets.

EXPLANATION

The major issues related to the possible impairment of the above-mentioned items can be analyzed as follows:

Item #1
The recoverable amount is defined as the **higher** of an asset's net selling price and its value in use. No impairment loss is recognized because the recoverable amount of $121,000 is higher than the carrying amount of $119,000.

Item #2
Item #2 is impaired because its recoverable amount ($207,000) is lower than its carrying amount ($237,000), giving rise to an impairment loss of $30,000. According to IAS 36 (paragraph 60), the loss should be treated as a revaluation decrease. Therefore, $12,000 of the loss is debited to revaluation surplus in other comprehensive income, and the balance of the loss ($18,000) is recognized in profit or loss.

Item #3
Item #3 is not impaired.

Item #4
Item #4 is impaired because its recoverable amount ($79,000) is lower than its carrying amount ($83,000), giving rise to an impairment loss of $4,000, which is recognized as an expense in profit or loss.

Item #5
The recoverable amount of the bus cannot be determined because the asset's value in use cannot be estimated to be close to its net selling price, and it does not generate cash inflows from continuing use that are largely independent of those from other assets. Therefore, man-

agement must determine the cash-generating unit to which the bus belongs and estimate the recoverable amount of this unit as a whole. If this unit consists of items #1 to #5, the carrying amount of the cash-generating unit (after recognizing the impairment losses on items #2 and #4) is $551,000. The fair value less costs to sell of the cash-generating unit is $546,000 (assuming that the assets could not be sold for more than the aggregate of their individual fair values). The value in use of the cash-generating unit is $521,000 (assuming, again, that the assets do not collectively produce cash flows that are higher than those used in the determination of their individual values in use). Therefore, the recoverable amount of the cash-generating unit is $546,000 giving rise to a further impairment loss of $5,000. The loss should be allocated on a pro rata basis to items #1, #3, and #5, provided that the carrying amount of each item is not reduced below the highest of its fair value less costs to sell and value in use. This means, in practice, that the whole of the loss is allocated to item #5, the bus.

CHAPTER 27

Borrowing Costs (IAS 23)

27.1	**OBJECTIVE**

The acquisition, construction, or production of certain assets can take longer than one accounting period. If borrowing costs incurred during a period are directly attributable to specific qualifying assets, under certain circumstances it will be legitimate to regard these costs as forming part of the costs of getting such assets ready for their intended use or sale.

IAS 23 defines a qualifying asset and provides guidance on which borrowing costs should be capitalized and included in the carrying amount of a qualifying asset. This guidance addresses instances in which the funds are specifically borrowed to obtain a qualifying asset and where the entity utilizes funds from their general borrowings.

27.2	**SCOPE OF THE STANDARD**

IAS 23 is to be applied in accounting for all **borrowing costs**, which are defined as interest and other costs incurred by an entity in connection with the borrowing of funds.

IAS 23 is not applicable to borrowing costs that are directly attributable to qualifying assets measured at fair value or inventories that are produced in large quantities on a repetitive basis over a short period of time.

27.3	**KEY CONCEPTS**

27.3.1 Borrowing costs are interest and other costs that an entity incurs in connection with the borrowing of funds. The costs include:

- interest calculated using the effective interest rate method as described in IAS 39;
- finance charges in respect of finance leases as set out in IAS 17; and
- exchange differences arising from foreign currency borrowings to the extent that they are regarded as an adjustment to interest cost.

27.3.2 Qualifying assets are those assets that require a substantial time to bring to their intended use or saleable condition, for example:

- inventories requiring a substantial period to bring them to a saleable condition; and
- manufacturing plants, power generation facilities, and investment properties.

27.4

ACCOUNTING TREATMENT

Recognition

27.4.1 Borrowing costs that are directly attributable to the acquisition, construction, or production of a qualifying asset should be **capitalized** when:

■ it is **probable** that they will result in future economic benefits to the entity; and

■ the costs can be **measured reliably** (see effective interest rate method per IAS 39).

27.4.2 Other borrowing costs are recognized as an expense in the period in which they are incurred.

27.4.3 Capitalization **commences** when all of the following conditions have been met:

■ expenditures on a qualifying asset are being incurred;

■ borrowing costs are being incurred; and

■ activities necessary to prepare the asset for its intended sale or use are in progress.

27.4.4 Capitalization should be **suspended** during extended periods in which the active development of the asset is interrupted.

27.4.5 Capitalization should **not cease**:

■ when all of the components required before any part of the asset can be sold or used are not yet completed;

■ for brief interruptions in activities;

■ during periods when substantial technical and administrative work is being carried out; or

■ for delays that are inherent in the asset acquisition process (for example, wines that need long periods of maturity).

27.4.6 Capitalization should **cease** when:

■ the asset is materially ready for its intended use or sale; or

■ construction is completed in part and the completed part can be used independently.

Measurement

27.4.7 The **amount to be capitalized** is the borrowing costs that could have been **avoided** if the expenditure on the qualifying asset had not been made:

■ If funds are **specifically borrowed** to obtain a particular asset, the amount of borrowing costs qualifying for capitalization is the actual costs incurred during the period, less income earned on temporary investment of those borrowings.

■ If funds are **borrowed generally** and used to obtain an asset, the amount of borrowing costs to be capitalized should be determined by applying the weighted average of the borrowing costs to the expenditure on that asset. The amount capitalized during a period should not exceed the amount of borrowing costs incurred during that period.

27.4.8 When the **carrying value** of an asset, inclusive of capitalized interest, exceeds the net realizable value, the asset should be written down to the net realizable value.

27.5	**PRESENTATION AND DISCLOSURE**

The following should be disclosed:

- the amount of borrowing costs capitalized during the period; and
- the capitalization rate used to determine the amount of borrowing costs capitalized.

27.6	**FINANCIAL ANALYSIS AND INTERPRETATION**

27.6.1 Capitalized interest becomes a part of the historical cost of the asset. Included in capitalized interest are explicit interest costs and interest related to a finance lease. This capitalized interest requirement does not apply to:

- inventories routinely produced or purchased for sale or use;
- assets that are not being made ready for use; or
- assets that could be used immediately, whether or not they are actually being used.

27.6.2 The amount of interest cost to be capitalized is that portion of interest expense incurred during the asset's construction period that theoretically could have been avoided if the asset had been acquired ready to use. This includes any interest on borrowings that are made specifically to finance the construction of the asset, and any interest on the general debt of the company, up to the amount invested in the project. The capitalized interest cost cannot exceed the total interest expense that the entity incurred during the period.

27.6.3 Before the asset is operational, the interest portion should be included and recorded on the Statement of Financial Position as an **asset in course of construction.** That capitalized interest will subsequently be expensed over the life of the asset by means of depreciation of the asset.

27.6.4 The capitalization of interest expense that is incurred during the construction of an asset reduces interest expense during the period in which the interest was paid. As a result, capitalized interest causes accounting profit to be greater than cash flow.

27.6.5 For analytical purposes, especially when comparing two companies that do not have similar borrowing patterns, analysts often remove the capitalized interest expense from the asset portion of the Statement of Financial Position and treat that capitalized interest as an interest expense. If this adjustment is not made, analysts reason that important ratios—such as the interest coverage ratio—will be higher than those of comparable companies. However, IFRS no longer provides a choice of expensing interest and now requires capitalization of interest on qualifying assets. The financial statements of companies that have not capitalized such interest should therefore be adjusted.

27.7	**COMMENTARY**

27.7.1 Judgment could be required to determine what comprises general borrowings for the purposes of capitalizing borrowing costs and calculating the capitalization rate. IAS 23 paragraph 14 states that "the capitalization rate should be the weighted average of the borrowing costs applicable to the borrowings of the entity that are outstanding during the period, other than borrowings made specifically for the purpose of obtaining a qualifying asset." Different interpretations of what comprises general borrowings exist and are accepted in practice. One interpretation is that all borrowings, other than borrowings made specifically for the purpose of obtaining a qualifying asset, have to be taken into account when calculating the capitalization rate. Another interpretation is that the capitalization rate should be calculated by allocating amounts between general borrowings and other borrowings made specifically for the acquisition of other assets that do not meet the definition of qualifying assets.

27.7.2 Consequently, the application of IAS 23 for purposes of capitalization of borrowing costs is a matter of accounting policy requiring the exercise of judgment. IAS 1 (refer to chapter 3) requires clear disclosure of significant accounting policies and judgments that are relevant to an understanding of the financial statements.

27.7.3 The IASB issued the amended IAS 23 in March 2007. The revised IAS 23 requires the capitalization of borrowing costs. The amendment was made as part of the IASB's project to converge IFRSs with U.S. GAAP. The amendment eliminates the main difference in the fundamental accounting recognition principle between IFRSs and U.S. GAAP in this area, although significant measurement differences remain. The IASB's current project agenda does not include any future amendments to IAS 23.

27.8   IMPLEMENTATION DECISIONS

The following table sets out some of the strategic and tactical decisions that should be considered when applying IAS 23.

Strategic decisions	Tactical decisions	Problems to overcome
If an entity purchases or constructs an asset and incurs borrowing costs on this asset, management should determine whether it meets the definition of a qualifying asset (that is, it takes a substantial period of time to get the asset ready for its intended use or sale).	Management should ensure that capitalized borrowing costs meet the IAS 23 criteria for capitalization.	The specific facts and circumstances should be considered and judgment applied in order to determine whether the period required to get the asset ready for its intended use is substantial. IAS 23 does not define what is considered substantial.
Entities acquiring or constructing a qualifying asset should determine whether funds utilized to purchase or construct the assets will be borrowed specifically or whether they will utilize the entity's general borrowings.	If general borrowings are utilized, the entity should formulate a policy on how the amount of borrowing costs capitalized and the capitalization rate will be determined; that is, whether funds to obtain nonqualifying assets will be included or not when determining the capitalization rate. If specific borrowings are used, management should decide whether excess funds will temporarily be invested and investment income tracked.	When the entity utilizes funds from its general borrowings to construct or purchase a qualifying asset, management should apply judgment in order to determine the capitalization rate and the borrowing costs that are directly attributable to obtaining the qualifying asset.

Strategic decisions	Tactical decisions	Problems to overcome
The entity should formulate and implement a policy in line with IAS 23 to determine when capitalization of borrowing costs should commence, be suspended, and ceased.	When purchasing or constructing a qualifying asset, management should have a detailed project plan stipulating the following: • the date that expenses in respect of getting the asset ready for its intended use will commence; • the date that the funding will be obtained; • the intended use of the asset and the criteria that should be met before it will be ready for its intended use; • whether there will be periods that substantial technical and administrative work will be undertaken; and • delays that are considered to be inherent in getting the asset ready for use.	Judgment should be applied to distinguish whether the capitalization of borrowing costs should be suspended and ceased.

EXAMPLES: BORROWING COSTS

EXAMPLE 27.1

Morskoy Inc. is constructing a warehouse that will take about 18 months to complete. It began construction on January 1, 20X2. The following payments were made during 20X2:

	$'000
January 31	200
March 31	450
June 30	100
October 31	200
November 30	250

The first payment on January 31 was funded from the entity's pool of debt. However, the entity succeeded in raising a medium-term loan for an amount of $800,000 on March 31, 20X2, with simple interest of 9 percent per year, calculated and payable monthly in arrears. These funds were specifically used for this construction. Excess funds were temporarily invested at 6 percent per year monthly in arrears and payable in cash. The pool of debt was again used for a $200,000 payment on November 30, which could not be funded from the medium-term loan.

The construction project was temporarily halted for three weeks in May, when substantial technical and administrative work was carried out.

The following amounts of debt were outstanding at the Statement of Financial Position date, December 31, 20X2:

	$'000
Medium-term loan (see description above)	800
Bank overdraft	1,200
(The weighted average amount outstanding during the year was $750,000, and total interest charged by the bank amounted to $33,800 for the year.)	
A 10%, 7-year note dated October 1, 19x7, with simple interest payable annually at December 31	9,000

EXPLANATION

The amount to be capitalized to the cost price of the warehouse in 20X2 can be calculated as follows:

	$
Specific loan	
$800,000 × 9 percent × 9/12	54,000
Interest earned on unused portion of loan available during the year:	
April 1 to June 30 [(800,000 − 450,000) × 3/12 × 6%]	(5,250)
July 1 to October 31 [(800,000 − 550,000) × 4/12 × 6%]	(5,000)
November 1 to November 30 [(800,000 − 750,000) × 1/12 × 6%]	(250)
	43,500
General pool of funds	
Capitalization rate is 9.58 percent (Calculation a)	
Paid on January 31 (200,000 × 11/12 × 9.58%)	17,563
Paid on November 30 (200,000 × 1/12 × 9.58%)	1,597
	19,160
Total Amount to Be Capitalized	62,660

Note: Although the activities had been interrupted by technical and administrative work during May 20X2, capitalization is not suspended for this period according to IAS 23.

Calculation a	$
Capitalization rate for pool of debt	
Total interest paid on these borrowings	
Bank overdraft	33,800
7-year note (9,000,000 × 10%)	900,000
	933,800
Weighted average total borrowings	
Bank overdraft	750,000
7-year note	9,000,000
	9,750,000

Capitalization rate = 933,800 + 9,750,000
                     = 9.58% (rounded)

EXAMPLE 27.2

A company has a building under construction that is being financed with $8 million of debt, $6 million of which is a construction loan directly on the building. The rest is financed out of the general debt of the company. The company will use the building when it is completed. The debt structure of the firm is as follows:

	$'000
Construction loan @ 11%	6,000
Long-term debentures @ 9%	9,000
Long-term subordinated debentures @ 10%	3,000

The debentures and subordinated debentures were issued at the same time.

Issue 1: What is the interest payable during the year?

  a. $660,000
  b. $1,800,000
  c. $1,770,000
  d. $1,140,000

EXPLANATION

Choice c. is correct (0.11 ($6,000,000) + 0.09 ($9,000,000) + 0.10 ($3,000,000) = $1,770,000).

Issue 2: The capitalized interest cost to be recorded as an asset on the Statement of Financial Position, according to IAS 23, is

  a. $660,000
  b. $850,000
  c. $845,000
  d. $1,770,000

EXPLANATION

Choice c. is correct.

The effective interest rate on the construction loan is 11 percent. The effective average interest rate on the company's other debt is

$$\frac{9,000,000}{12,000,000} \times 9\% + \frac{3,000,000}{12,000,000} \times 10\% = 9.25\%$$

These two rates are used to calculate the capitalized interest:

Capitalized Interest = $6,000,000 (0.11) + 2,000,000 (0.0925)

$$= \$660,000 + 185,000 = \$845,000$$

Issue 3: What amount of interest expense should be reported on the Statement of Comprehensive Income?

a. $920,000

b. $1,140,000

c. $925,000

d. $1,770,000

EXPLANATION

Choice c. is correct ($1,770,000 − 845,000 = $925,000).

CHAPTER 28

Accounting for Government Grants and Disclosure of Government Assistance (IAS 20)

28.1   OBJECTIVE

IAS 20 deals with the accounting of grants and other forms of assistance from the government.

28.2   SCOPE OF THE STANDARD

This standard addresses the accounting and disclosures for government grants and other forms of government assistance, but does not deal with:

- the accounting for government grants reflecting the effects of changing prices;
- government assistance to an entity in the form of benefits that are available in determining taxable profit or tax loss, or are determined or limited on the basis of income tax liability (for example income tax holidays, investment tax credits, accelerated depreciation allowances, and reduced income tax rates);
- government participation in the ownership of the entity; and
- government grants covered by IAS 41, Agriculture.

28.3   KEY CONCEPTS

28.3.1 The term **government** refers to government, government agencies, and similar bodies, whether local, national, or international.

28.3.2 **Government grants** are transfers of resources from the government to an enterprise in return for past or future compliance with conditions relating to the operating activities. The two types of government grants are as follows:

- **Grants related to assets.** Enterprises qualifying for these grants should purchase, construct, or otherwise acquire long-term assets.
- **Grants related to income.** These are government grants other than those related to assets.

28.3.3 **Government assistance** is action by government to provide a specific economic benefit for an entity (or entities). It excludes benefits provided indirectly through action affecting general trading conditions (for example, provision of infrastructure).

28.3.4 Government assistance includes:

- free technical and marketing advice;
- provision of guarantees;
- government procurement policy that is responsible for a portion of the enterprise's sales; and
- loans at nil or low interest rates (the benefit is not quantified by the imputation of interest).

28.4

ACCOUNTING TREATMENT

Recognition

28.4.1 Government grants should be recognized as income on a systematic basis over the periods necessary to **match** them with related costs that they should compensate. Examples include the following:

- Grants used to acquire depreciable assets are recognized as income over the periods and in the proportions to which depreciation is charged by reducing costs, or by spreading income over the life of the assets.
- A grant of land can be conditional upon the erection of a building on the site. Income is normally then recognized over the life of the building.

28.4.2 A government grant as compensation for expenses or losses already incurred or immediate financial support with no future related costs is recognized as income of the period in which it becomes receivable.

28.4.3 Government grants, including nonmonetary grants at fair value, should be **recognized** only when there is reasonable assurance that:

- the enterprise will comply with the conditions attached to them; and
- the grants will be received.

A grant received in cash or as a reduction of a liability to government is accounted for similarly.

Initial Measurement

28.4.4 Nonmonetary grants (for example, land or other resources) is assessed and recorded at fair value.

28.4.5 A **forgivable loan** (where the lender undertakes to waive repayment of loans under prescribed conditions) is treated as a grant when there is reasonable assurance that the terms for forgiveness of the loan will be met. This conflicts with IAS 39, but it is not currently addressed in IFRS.

Subsequent Measurement

28.4.6 A repayment of a government grant is accounted for as a revision of an accounting estimate (refer to IAS 8) as follows:

▪ Repayment related to income is first applied against an unamortized deferred grant credit.

▪ Repayment in excess of a deferred grant credit is recognized as an expense.

▪ Repayment related to an asset is recorded by increasing the carrying amount of the asset or reducing a deferred income balance. Cumulative additional depreciation that would have been recognized to date is recognized immediately and the asset would then be subject to an impairment test.

28.5   PRESENTATION AND DISCLOSURE

28.5.1 Presentation is as follows:

▪ **Asset-related grants.** Present the grant in the **Statement of Financial Position** by either:
  - recording the grant as a deferred income liability or
  - deducting it from the carrying amount of the asset.

▪ **Income-related grants.** Present the grant in the **Statement of Comprehensive Income** as either:
  - a separate credit line item; or
  - a deduction from the related expense.

28.5.2 Disclosure is as follows:

▪ Describe the **accounting policies** related to method of presentation and method of recognition.

▪ Include the following in the **Statement of Comprehensive Income and notes:**
  - government grants (describe the nature, extent, and amount);
  - government assistance (describe the nature, extent, and duration);
  - unfulfilled conditions; and
  - contingencies attached to assistance.

28.6   COMMENTARY

28.6.1 Government assistance to entities can be aimed at encouragement or long-term support of certain industries or regions. The conditions for receiving the assistance do not necessarily relate to the operating activities of the entity. The issue has arisen in practice as to whether such government assistance is within the scope of IAS 20. The IASB issued SIC 10 clarifying that this government assistance meets the definition of a government grant and should be included in IAS 20.

28.6.2 The IASB has not indicated that any projects regarding IAS 20 are being planned.

28.7   IMPLEMENTATION DECISIONS

The following table sets out some of the strategic and tactical decisions that should be considered when applying IAS 20.

Strategic decisions	Tactical decisions	Problems to overcome
	The entity should choose an accounting policy, either: • presenting the grant as deferred income, which is then recognized as income on a systematic and rational basis over the useful life of the asset; or • deducting the grant in arriving at the carrying amount of the asset, in which case the grant is recognized as income over the life of a depreciable asset by way of a reduced deprecation charge.	Because of its nature it may be difficult to determine the fair value to place on nonmonetary grants.

EXAMPLE: ACCOUNTING FOR GOVERNMENT GRANTS AND DISCLOSURE OF GOVERNMENT ASSISTANCE

EXAMPLE 28.1

Jobworld Inc. obtained a grant of $10 million from a government agency for an investment project to construct a manufacturing plant costing at least $88 million. The principal term is that the grant payments relate to the level of capital expenditure. The secondary intention of the grant is to safeguard 500 jobs. The grant will have to be repaid pro rata if there is an underspending on capital. Twenty percent of the grant will have to be repaid if the jobs are not safeguarded until 18 months after the date of the last asset purchase.

The plant was completed on January 1, 20X4, at a total cost of $90 million. The plant has an expected useful life of 20 years and is depreciated on a straight-line basis with no residual value.

EXPLANATION

The grant should be recognized as income on a systematic basis over the periods that will match it with the related costs it is intended to compensate. Difficulties can arise where the terms of the grant do not specify precisely the expenditure to which it is intended to contribute. Grants might be intended to cover costs consisting of both capital and revenue expenditure. This would require a detailed analysis of the terms of the grant.

The employment condition should be seen as an additional condition to prevent replacement of labor by capital, rather than as the reason for the grant. This grant should therefore be regarded as an **asset-related grant.** IAS 20 allows two acceptable methods of presentation of such grants. The application of each method is demonstrated for the first three years of operation:

1. *Setting grant up as deferred income*

The plant would be reflected as follows in the Statement of Financial Position at December 31 of the years indicated:

	20×6 $'000	20×5 $'000	20×4 $'000
Plant	90,000	90,000	90,000
Historical cost	(13,500)	(9,000)	(4,500)
Accumulated depreciation	76,500	81,000	85,500
Carrying value	**10,000**	**10,000**	**10,000**
Deferred income	500	1,000	1,500

The following amounts would be recognized in the Statement of Comprehensive Income of the respective years:

	20×6 $'000	20×5 $'000	20×4 $'000
Depreciation (expense) (90,000,000 ÷ 20)	4,500	4,500	4,500
Government grant (income) (10,000,000 ÷ 20)	(500)	(500)	(500)

The above amounts are treated as separate Statement of Comprehensive Income items and should not be offset under this method of presentation.

2. *Deducting grant in arriving at carrying amount of asset*

The adjusted historical cost of the plant would be $80 million, which is the total cost of $90 million less the $10 million grant.

The plant would be reflected as follows in the Statement of Financial Position of the respective years:

Plant	**20×6 $'000**	**20×5 $'000**	**20×4 $'000**
Historical cost	80,000	80,000	80,000
Accumulated depreciation	(12,000)	(8,000)	(4,000)
	68,000	72,000	76,000

The Statement of Comprehensive Income would reflect an annual depreciation charge of $4 million ($80,000,000 ÷ 20). This charge agrees with the net result of the annual amounts recognized in the Statement of Comprehensive Income under the first alternative.

CHAPTER 29

Share-Based Payment (IFRS 2)

29.1	**OBJECTIVE**

Share-based payments are transactions where an entity settles an obligation in shares or incurs a cash obligation linked to the share price of the entity. IFRS 2 covers situations where the entity makes any share-based payment. IFRS 2 includes transactions where the obligation is settled in or referenced to the equity of the entity's parent entity, or any other entity under common control. The primary issues addressed by the standard relate to if and when a share-based payment should be recognized, when the transactions should be reflected as an expense in the Statement of Comprehensive Income, and how the amount should be measured.

29.2	**SCOPE OF THE STANDARD**

This IFRS should be applied to all share-based payment transactions. IFRS 2 covers both employee share-based payment arrangements and the issuance of shares (and rights to shares) in return for services and goods. The standard specifically covers:

- the criteria for defining a share-based payment; and
- the distinction and accounting for various types of share-based payments, specifically equity settled, cash settled, and transactions in which there is an option to settle the transaction in cash (or other assets) or by issuing equity instruments.

An entity should reflect in its profit and loss and financial position statements the effects of share-based payment transactions, including expenses associated with transactions in which employees receive share options.

29.3	**KEY CONCEPTS**

29.3.1 A **share-based payment transaction** is a transaction in which the entity receives goods or services as consideration for equity instruments of the entity, its parent entity, or another entity within the consolidated group (including shares or share options), or acquires goods or services by incurring liabilities to the supplier of those goods or services for amounts that are based on the price of the entity's shares or other equity instruments of the entity. Share-based payment transactions include transactions where the terms of the arrangement provide either the entity or the supplier of those goods or services with a choice of whether the entity settles the transaction in cash (or other assets) or through the issuance of equity instruments.

29.3.2 In an **equity-settled share-based payment transaction,** the entity receives goods or services as consideration for equity instruments (including shares or share options) of the entity, its parent, or another entity within the consolidated group. An **equity instrument** is a contract that evidences a residual interest in the assets of an entity after deducting all of its liabilities.

29.3.3 In a **cash-settled share-based payment transaction,** the entity acquires goods or services by incurring a liability to transfer cash or other assets to the supplier of those goods or services for amounts that are based on the price or value of the entity's shares or other equity instruments.

29.3.4 The **grant date** is the date at which the entity and another party (including an employee) agree to a share-based payment arrangement. At grant date, the entity confers on the counterparty the right to cash, other assets, or the entity's equity instruments, provided that the specified vesting conditions are met. If the transaction is subject to an approval process (for example by shareholders or the board), the grant date is the date that the necessary approval is obtained.

29.3.5 **Employees and others providing similar services** are individuals who render personal or similar services to the entity.

29.3.6 Under a share-based payment arrangement, a counterparty's right to receive the entity's cash, other assets, or equity instruments **vests** upon satisfaction of any specified vesting conditions. Vesting conditions include service conditions. The **vesting period** is the period during which all the specified vesting conditions of a share-based payment arrangement should be satisfied.

29.3.7 **Fair value** is the amount for which an asset could be exchanged, a liability settled, or an equity instrument granted between knowledgeable, willing parties in an arm's-length transaction.

29.3.8 **Intrinsic value** is the difference between the fair value of the shares to which the counterparty has the right to subscribe or which it has the right to receive, and the price the counterparty is required to pay for those shares.

29.3.9 **Market condition is** a condition that is related to the market price of the entity's equity instruments.

29.3.10 A **share option** is a contract that gives the holder the right but not the obligation to subscribe to the entity's shares at a fixed or determinable price for a specified period of time.

29.4 ## ACCOUNTING TREATMENT

29.4.1 Share-based payments could be:

- cash settled, that is, by a cash payment based on the value of equity instruments;
- equity settled, that is, by the issue of equity instruments; or
- cash or equity settled (at the option of the entity or supplier).

Recognition

29.4.2 An entity should recognize **the goods or services received or acquired** in a share-based payment transaction when it obtains the goods or as the services are received.

29.4.3 If the goods or services received do not meet the requirements to be recognized as an asset (for example, inventory), the entity shall recognize an expense (for example, services received or employee benefits).

Measurement

29.4.4 Share-based payment transactions should be measured at:

- the fair value of the goods or services received in the case of all third-party nonemployee transactions, unless it is not possible to measure the fair value of those goods or services reliably; or
- the fair value of the equity instruments in all other cases, including all employee transactions.

Equity-Settled Share-Based Payment Transactions
Recognition

29.4.5 An entity should recognize the goods or services received or acquired in a share-based payment transaction when it obtains the goods or as the services are received. For equity-settled share-based payment transactions, a corresponding increase should be recognized in equity.

Measurement

29.4.6 The fair value of the equity instruments issued or to be issued should be measured:

- at grant date for transactions with employees and others providing similar services; and
- at the date on which the entity receives the goods or the counterparty renders the services in all other cases.

29.4.7 The fair value of the equity instruments issued or to be issued should be based on market prices. The grant date fair value should take into account market vesting conditions (for example, market prices or reference to an index) but not nonmarket vesting conditions (for example, service periods). Listed shares should be measured at market price. Options should be measured:

- on the basis of the market price of any equivalent traded options;
- using an option pricing model in the absence of such market prices; or
- at intrinsic value when the options cannot be measured reliably on the basis of market prices or on the basis of an option pricing model.

29.4.8 In the rare cases where the entity is required to measure the equity instruments at their **intrinsic value,** it remeasures the instruments at each reporting date until final settlement and recognizes any **change in intrinsic value in profit or loss.**

29.4.9 The entity should recognize an asset or expense and a corresponding increase in equity:

- on grant date if there are no vesting conditions or if the goods or services have already been received;
- as the services are rendered if nonemployee services are rendered over a period; or
- over the vesting period for employee and other share-based payment transactions where there is a vesting period.

29.4.10 If the equity instruments granted do not **vest** until the counterparty completes a specified period of service, the amount recognized should be adjusted over any vesting period for changes in the estimate of the number of securities that will be issued (referred to as the true up calculation), but not for changes in the fair value of those securities. Therefore, on the vesting date, the amount recognized is the exact number of securities that can be issued as of that date, measured at the fair value of those securities at grant date.

29.4.11 If the entity **cancels or settles a grant** of equity instruments during the vesting period (other than a grant canceled by forfeiture when the vesting conditions are not satisfied), the following accounting requirements apply:

- The entity accounts for the cancellation or settlement as an acceleration of vesting by recognizing immediately the amount that otherwise would have been recognized over the remainder of the vesting period.
- The entity recognizes in equity any payment made to the employee on the cancellation or settlement to the extent that the payment does not exceed the fair value at the repurchase date of the equity instruments granted.
- The entity recognizes as an expense the excess of any payment made to the employee on the cancellation or settlement over the fair value at the repurchase date of the equity instruments granted.
- The entity accounts for new equity instruments granted to the employee as replacements for the cancelled equity instruments as a modification of the original grant. The difference between the fair value of the replacement equity instruments and the net fair value of the cancelled equity instruments at the date the replacement equity instruments are granted is recognized as an expense.

Cash-Settled Share-Based Payment Transaction
Recognition

29.4.12 An entity should recognize the goods or services received or acquired in a share-based payment transaction when it obtains the goods or as the services are received. For cash-settled share-based payment transactions, the corresponding credit should be recognized as a liability.

Measurement

29.4.13 The goods and services received and the liability incurred should be measured at the fair value of the liability. Until the liability is settled, the entity should remeasure the fair value of the liability at each reporting date and at the date of settlement, with any changes in fair value recognized in profit or loss for the period.

29.4.14 If the share-based payment granted does not **vest** until the counterparty completes a specified period of service, the amount recognized should be adjusted over any vesting period for changes in the estimate of the number of benefits expected to vest (referred to as the true up calculation) and for changes in the fair value of those securities.

29.4.15 If the entity **cancels or settles a grant** a cash-settled grant, the same principles as discussed in 29.4.11 should be applied.

Share-Based Payment Transactions with Cash Alternatives

29.4.16 For **share-based payment transactions** in which the terms of the arrangement provide either the entity or the counterparty with the choice of settlement either in cash (or other assets) or by issuing equity instruments, the following principles should be applied to the transaction:

- the transaction should be accounted for as cash-settled, if and to the extent that the entity has incurred a liability to settle in cash or other liabilities; or
- the transaction should be accounted for as equity-settled if and to the extent that no liability has been incurred.

Share-Based Payment Transactions That Provide the Counterparty with a Choice of Settlement

29.4.17 For share-based payment transactions in which the terms of the arrangement provide the counterparty with the choice of settlement, the entity has granted a compound financial instrument. The instrument has both a debt (the counterparty's right to demand cash) and an equity component (the counterparty's option to receive equity instruments rather than cash). Each component is accounted for separately, similar to the requirements of IAS 32 (refer to chapter 33).

Share-Based Payment Transactions That Provide the Entity with a Choice of Settlement

29.4.18 For share-based payment transactions in which the terms of the arrangement provide the entity with a choice of settlement it is necessary to determine whether the entity has a present obligation to settle in cash. The entity has a present obligation to settle in cash if:

- the choice of settlement has no commercial substance (for example when the entity is prohibited from issuing shares);
- the entity has a past practice or stated policy of settling in cash; or
- the entity generally settles in cash whenever the counterparty asks for cash settlement.

Share-Based Payment Transactions among Group Entities

29.4.19 The accounting treatment of share-based payment transactions within a group was previously addressed by IFRIC 11. The requirements of IFRIC 11 were clarified and incorporated in IFRS 2 during June 2009. This amendment to IFRS 2 is effective for financial years beginning on or after January 1, 2010.

29.4.20 When recognizing the share-based payments in its separate financial statements, the entity receiving the goods or services should measure them as either an equity-settled or cash-settled share-based payment transaction, by assessing the nature of the awards and its own rights and obligations.

29.4.21 The entity receiving the goods or services should measure them as an equity-settled share-based payment transaction when:

- the awards granted are its own equity instruments (that is, not the equity instruments of its parent or another entity within the group); or
- the entity has no obligation to settle the share-based payment transaction (that is, the parent or another entity within the consolidated group has the obligation to settle).

In all other circumstances, the entity receiving the goods or services should measure them as a cash-settled share-based payment transaction.

29.4.22 The entity settling a share-based payment transaction when another entity in the group receives the goods or services should recognize the transaction as an equity-settled share-based payment transaction only if it is settled in the entity's own equity instruments. Otherwise the transaction should be recognized as a cash-settled share-based payment transaction.

29.5 | **PRESENTATION AND DISCLOSURE**

29.5.1 An entity should disclose information that enables users of the financial statements to understand **the nature and extent** of share-based payment arrangements that existed during the period.

29.5.2 An entity should provide **a description** of:

- each type of share-based payment arrangement that existed at any time during the period; and
- the general terms and conditions of each arrangement, such as vesting requirements, the maximum term of options granted, and the method of settlement (for example, whether in cash or equity).

29.5.3 An entity should provide the **number and weighted average exercise prices** of share options for each of the following groups of options:

- outstanding at the beginning of the period;
- granted during the period;
- forfeited during the period;
- exercised during the period;
- expired during the period;
- outstanding at the end of the period; and
- exercisable at the end of the period.

29.5.4 For **share options granted** during the period, the weighted average fair value of those options at the measurement date and information on how that fair value was measured should be disclosed, including:

- the option pricing model used and the inputs to that model, including:
  - the weighted average share price;
  - exercise price;
  - expected volatility;
  - option life;
  - expected dividends;
  - the risk-free interest rate; and
  - any other inputs to the model, including the method used and the assumptions made to incorporate the effects of expected early exercise;
- how expected volatility was determined, including an explanation of the extent to which expected volatility was based on historical volatility; and
- whether and how any other features of the option grant were incorporated into the measurement of fair value, such as a market condition.

29.5.5 An entity should disclose information that enables users of the financial statements to understand how the **fair value of the goods or services received** or the fair value of the equity instruments granted during the period was determined.

29.5.6 For share **options exercised** during the period, an entity should disclose the weighted average share price at the date of exercise.

29.5.7 For share **options outstanding** at the end of the period, an entity should disclose the range of exercise prices and weighted average remaining contractual life.

29.5.8 For share-based payment arrangements that were modified during the period, an entity should disclose:

- an explanation of those modifications;
- the incremental fair value granted (as a result of those modifications); and
- information on how the incremental fair value granted was measured, consistent with the requirements set out above, where applicable.

29.5.9 An entity should disclose information that enables users of the financial statements to understand the effect of share-based payment transactions on the entity's profit or loss for the period and on its financial position. As a result the entity should disclose at least the following:

- the total expense recognized for the period arising from share-based payments, including separate disclosure of that portion of the total expense that arises from transactions accounted for as equity-settled share-based payment transactions;
- for liabilities arising from share-based payment transactions:
  - the total carrying amount at the end of the period; and
  - the total intrinsic value at the end of the period of liabilities for which the counterparty's right to cash or other assets had vested by the end of the period.

29.6   FINANCIAL ANALYSIS AND INTERPRETATION

29.6.1 Share-based payments complicate the analysis of various operating areas, in particular operating cash flow.

29.6.2 The variables used to measure the fair value of an equity instrument issued under IFRS 2 have a significant impact on that valuation, and the determination of these variables requires significant professional judgment. A minor change in a variable, such as volatility or expected life of an instrument, could have a quantitatively material impact on the fair value of the instruments granted. In the end, the selection of variables must be based on entity-specific information.

29.6.3 One of the most difficult issues in applying IFRS 2 will be determining the fair value of share-based payments, which requires numerous estimates and the application of careful judgment. Measurement difficulties may arise because the final value of the share-based payment transaction is determined when the transaction is settled at some point in the future but must be estimated at the date of grant.

29.6.4 The determination of the model an entity uses is an accounting policy choice and should be applied consistently to similar share-based payment transactions. Improvements to a model would be considered a change in estimate, and IAS 8 should be applied when an entity changes models (for example, from Black-Scholes to a binomial model).

29.6.5 The major strength of the Black-Scholes model is that it is a generally accepted method for valuing share options. It has gained wide acceptance from both regulators and users. Nearly all companies with share option plans use the Black-Scholes model to compute the fair value of their share options today. The consistent use of this model also enhances the comparability between entities.

29.6.6 Another strength of Black-Scholes is that the formula required to calculate the fair value is relatively straightforward and can be easily included in spreadsheets.

29.6.7 The binomial model is described as an "open form solution," as it can incorporate different values for variables (such as volatility) over the term of the option. The model can also be adjusted to take account of market conditions and other factors.

29.6.8 Many factors should be considered when estimating expected volatility. For example, the estimation of volatility might first focus on implied volatilities for the terms that were available in the market and compare the implied volatility to the long-term average historical volatility for reasonableness. In addition to implied and historical volatility, IFRS 2 suggests the following factors be considered in estimating expected volatility:

- the length of time an entity's shares have been publicly traded;
- appropriate and regular intervals for price observations; and
- other factors indicating that expected future volatility might differ from past volatility (for example, extraordinary volatility in historical share prices).

29.6.9 Typically, the shares underlying traded options are acquired from existing shareholders and therefore have no dilutive effect. Capital structure effects of nontraded options, such as dilution, can be significant and are generally anticipated by the market at the date of grant. Nevertheless, except in the most unusual cases, dilutive considerations should have no impact on the individual employee's decision. The market's anticipation will depend on, among other matters, whether the process of share returns is the same or is altered by the dilution and the cash infusion. In many situations the number of employee share options issued relative to the number of shares outstanding is not significant, and the effect of dilution on share price can therefore be ignored. IFRS 2 suggests that the issuer consider whether the possible dilutive effect of the future exercise of options granted has an effect on the fair value of those options at grant date by an adjustment to option pricing models.

29.6.10 Entities may elect to hedge their share-based payment schemes through holding the shares required to settle the scheme. The shares held in those instances meet the requirement of treasury shares in IAS 32 (refer to chapter 33) and are therefore treated as unissued for reporting purposes. For regulated entities that are required to maintain capital levels, this could have a significant impact as treasury shares decrease capital.

29.6.11 The amendments to IFRS 2 regarding group-settled schemes could result in different treatment of the schemes at the different consolidation levels. For example, if a subsidiary grants shares of the parent to its employees and the subsidiary has the obligation to acquire the shares to settle the obligation, then the subsidiary would account for the scheme as cash settled. However, because it is the shares of the parent, from the parent consolidated perspective it is equity settled.

29.7   **COMMENTARY**

29.7.1 There are a broad range of share-based payment schemes in operation and the application of IFRS 2 presents various challenges for the preparation of financial statements. The challenges include (but are not limited to) the following:

- determining whether conditions are vesting conditions or not and whether those conditions are market or nonmarket related;
- determining the fair value of awards with complex terms and conditions;
- the classification of transactions as cash or equity settled when there are settlement alternatives; and
- accounting for share-based payment arrangements in group situations.

29.7.2 As a result of these challenges, various interpretations have been issued by the IFRIC for application of requirements of IFRS 2. The interpretations include IFRIC 8, "Scope of IFRS 2," and IFRIC 11, "IFRS 2, Group and Treasury Share Transactions." IFRIC 8 clarifies that IFRS 2 applies to arrangements where an entity makes share-based payments for apparently nil or inadequate consideration, while IFRIC 11 addresses the accounting treatment of share-based payment transactions within a group. In June 2009 the IASB clarified the requirements of IFRIC 11 and incorporated these updated requirements in IFRS 2. The guidance contained in IFRIC 8 was also incorporated in IFRS 2. The amendments to IFRS 2 are effective for financial years beginning on or after January 1, 2010. IFRIC 8 and IFRIC 11 were withdrawn by the IASB.

29.7.3 The IFRIC is currently busy with a project to investigate the definitions of vesting and nonvesting and market and nonmarket conditions in an effort to eliminate the different interpretations and applications of these in the market.

29.8   IMPLEMENTATION DECISIONS

The following table sets out some of the strategic and tactical decisions that should be considered when applying IFRS 2.

Strategic decisions	Tactical decisions	Problems to overcome
Management should determine the nature of share-based payments to be issued to staff and the impact on earnings, reserves, capital, and profit or loss.		For schemes that have complex vesting conditions, it could be difficult to determine whether the conditions are vesting or nonvesting and market or nonmarket conditions. Building an appropriate valuation model and determining the inputs into the model.
Management needs to determine how they will manage their exposure to risks relating to share-based payments issued to employees, including, specifically, income volatility.	Management needs to consider whether employee share ownership trusts should be set up as vehicles for distributing shares to employees and how to mitigate the entity's risk to increases in their share price.	If management sets up an employee share ownership trust, management will need to consider whether these share trusts should be consolidated and should consider the relevant rights and obligations of the various parties as set out in the trust deed. If the trust holds equity instruments and the trust is consolidated, the shares held would meet the definition of treasury shares and could have an impact on the capital levels of the entity.

EXAMPLE: DISCLOSURE OF SHARE-BASED PAYMENT

EXAMPLE 29.1

Summary of Significant Accounting Policies

Share-based payments

On January 1, 20X5, the Group applied the requirements of IFRS 2 share-based payments. In accordance with the transition provisions, IFRS 2 was applied to all grants after November 7, 20X2, that were unvested as of January 1, 20X5.

The Group issues equity-settled and cash-settled share-based payments to certain employees. Equity-settled share-based payments are measured at fair value at the date of grant. The fair value determined at the grant date of the equity-settled share-based payments is expensed on a straight-line basis over the vesting period, based on the Group's estimate of shares that will eventually vest. A liability equal to the portion of the goods or services received is recognized at the current fair value determined at each Statement of Financial Position date for cash-settled share-based payments.

Fair value is measured by use of the Black-Scholes pricing model. The expected life used in the model has been adjusted, based on management's best estimate, for the effects of non-transferability, exercise restrictions, and behavioral considerations.

The Group also provides employees the ability to purchase the Group's ordinary shares at 85 percent of the current market value. The Group records an expense based on its best estimate of the 15 percent discount related to shares expected to vest on a straight-line basis over the vesting period.

Note XX: Share-based payments.

Equity-settled share option plan

The Group plan provides for a grant price equal to the average quoted market price of the Group shares on the date of grant. The vesting period is generally 3 to 4 years. If the options remain unexercised after 10 years from the date of grant, the options expire. Furthermore, options are forfeited if the employee leaves the Group before the options vest.

	20X4		20X5	
	Options	Weighted average exercise price in €	Options	Weighted average exercise price in €
Outstanding at the beginning of the period	42,125	64.26	44,440	65.75
Granted during the period	11,135	68.34	12,120	69.68
Forfeited during the period	(2,000)	65.67	(1,000)	66.53
Exercised during the period	(5,575)	45.32	(8,300)	53.69
Expired during the period	(1,245)	82.93	(750)	82.93
Outstanding at the end of the period	44,440	65.75	46,510	66.33
Exercisable at the end of the period	23,575	46.47	24,650	52.98

Source: Deloitte Touche Tohmatsu, IFRS 2: Share-based payments, pp. 61–63.

The weighted average share price at the date of exercise for share options exercised during the period was €53.69. The options outstanding at December 31, 20X5, had a weighted average exercise price of €66.33, and a weighted average remaining contractual life of 8.64 years. The inputs into the Black-Scholes model were as follows:

	20X4	20X5
Weighted average share price	68.34	69.68
Weighted average exercise price	68.34	69.68
Expected volatility	40%	35%
Expected life	3–8 years	4–9 years
Risk-free rate	3%	3%
Expected dividends	none	none

Expected volatility was determined by calculating the historical volatility of the Group's share price over the previous nine years. The expected life used in the model was adjusted, based on management's best estimate, for the effects of nontransferability, exercise restrictions, and behavioral considerations.

During 20X5, the Group repriced certain of its outstanding options. The strike price was reduced from €82.93 to the then-current market price of €69.22. The incremental fair value of €125,000 will be expensed over the remaining vesting period (two years). The Group used the inputs noted above to measure the fair value of the old and new shares.

The Group recognized total expenses of €775,000 and €750,000 related to equity-settled share-based payment transactions in 20X4 and 20X5, respectively.

Cash-settled share-based payments

The Group issues to certain employees share appreciation rights (SARs) that require the Group to pay the intrinsic value of the SAR to the employee at the date of exercise. The Group has recorded liabilities of €1,325,000 and €1,435,000 in 20X4 and 20X5, respectively. Fair value of the SARs is determined using the Black-Scholes model using the assumptions noted in the above table. The Group recorded total expenses of €325,000 and €110,000 in 20X4 and 20X5, respectively. The total intrinsic value at 20X4 and 20X5 was €1,150,000 and €1,275,000, respectively.

Other share-based payment plans

The employee share purchase plans are open to almost all employees and provide for a purchase price equal to the daily average market price on the date of grant, less 15 percent. The shares can be purchased during a two-week period each year. The shares so purchased are generally placed in the employee share savings plan for a five-year period. Pursuant to these plans, the Group issued 2,123,073 ordinary shares in 20X5 at a weighted average share price of €64.35.

Part V

Disclosure

CHAPTER 30

Events after the Reporting Period
(IAS 10)

30.1

OBJECTIVE

There will always be a time delay between the end of the reporting period and the date on which the financial statements are authorized for issue. During the delay, there will almost certainly be events that will take place and the question arises as to how those events should be accounted for in the financial statements. Some of these events might indicate the need for adjustments to the amounts recognized in the financial statements or require disclosure. IAS 10 addresses the effect of such events on the information that is provided in the financial statements.

30.2

SCOPE OF THE STANDARD

IAS 10 should be applied in the accounting for and disclosure of events after the reporting period.

Events after the reporting period are those events, favorable and unfavorable, that occur between the end of the reporting period and the date when the financial statements are authorized for issue. This standard prescribes the appropriate accounting treatment for such events and whether adjustments or simple disclosure is required.

This standard also requires that an entity should not prepare its financial statements on a going-concern basis if events after the reporting period indicate that the going-concern assumption is not appropriate.

30.3

KEY CONCEPTS

30.3.1 Events after the reporting period are those events that:

- provide evidence of conditions that existed at the end of the reporting period (that is, the origin of the event is in the current reporting period) and are **adjusting events**; and
- are indicative of conditions that arose after the reporting period and are **nonadjusting events**.

30.4   ACCOUNTING TREATMENT

30.4.1 Amounts recognized in the financial statements of an entity are **adjusted** for events occurring after the reporting period that provide additional information about conditions existing at the end of the reporting period, and therefore allow these amounts to be estimated more accurately. For example, adjustments could be required for a loss recognized on a trade debtor that is confirmed by the bankruptcy of a customer after the reporting period.

30.4.2 If events occur after the reporting period and the events do not affect the condition of assets and liabilities at the end of the reporting period, **no adjustment** is required. However, disclosure should be made of such events if they are of such importance that non-disclosure would affect decisions made by users of the financial statements. For example, it should be disclosed if an earthquake destroys a major portion of the manufacturing plant of the entity after the reporting period or an event were to alter the current or noncurrent classification of an asset at the end of the reporting period, per IAS 1.

30.4.3 Dividends or a liability for dividend should only be recognized if appropriately declared and authorized and thus are no longer at the discretion of the entity. Dividends that are proposed or declared after the end of the reporting period but before the approval of the financial statements should not be recognized as a liability at the end of the reporting period but should be disclosed in the notes to the financial statements.

30.4.4 An entity should not prepare financial statements on a going-concern basis if management determines after the reporting period that it intends to either liquidate the entity or cease trading (or that it has no realistic alternative but to do so). For example, if a fire destroys a major part of the business after the year-end, going-concern considerations would override all considerations (even if an event technically did not require disclosure) and the financial statements would be adjusted.

30.4.5 The process of **authorization** for issue of financial statements will depend on the form of the entity and its management structure. The date of authorization for issue would normally be the date on which the financial statements are authorized for release outside the entity.

30.5   PRESENTATION AND DISCLOSURE

30.5.1 Disclosure requirements related to the **date of authorization for issue** are as follows:

- the date when financial statements were authorized for issue;
- the name of the person who gave the authorization; and
- the name of the party (if any) with the power to amend the financial statements after issuance.

30.5.2 For **nonadjusting events** that would affect the ability of users to make proper evaluations and decisions, the following should be disclosed:

- the nature of the event;
- an estimate of the financial effect; and
- a statement if such an estimate cannot be made.

30.5.3 Disclosures that relate to conditions that existed at the end of the reporting period should be updated in light of any new information about those conditions that is received after the reporting period.

| 30.6 | **COMMENTARY** |

IAS 10 is a fairly simple standard that is easy to understand and apply in practice.

| 30.7 | **IMPLEMENTATION DECISIONS** |

The following table sets out some of the strategic and tactical decisions that should be considered when applying IAS 10.

Strategic decisions	Tactical decisions	Problems to overcome
On a case-by-case basis, decide whether an event occurring after the report date is an adjusting event or a nonadjusting event.	If the information is sensitive, management should consider the best way to disclose the information without jeopardizing its sensitive nature.	For some events, it is often not clear if the event relates to a condition that existed at the report date or not and judgment should be applied when making the decision.

EXAMPLE: EVENTS AFTER THE REPORTING PERIOD

EXAMPLE 30.1

Entity A exports a certain component to a manufacturer based in a foreign country. This foreign manufacturer uses this component supplied by Entity A in order to produce widgets. At the end of its reporting period (June 20X8), Entity A has unusually high levels of stock due to lower-than-expected orders from its foreign manufacture. On August 15, 20X8, before the financial statements of Entity A are authorized for issue, the government of the country where the manufacture is based announces that the components supplied by Entity A will only be procured within the country of the manufacturer (that is, the components will not be imported but instead will be acquired locally). Entity A does not have any alternative markets for the components. Is the announcement by the government an adjusting or a nonadjusting event?

EXPLANATION

The announcement by the government of the foreign country to impose restrictions on imports of the components supplied by Entity A is an **adjusting event** because it provides evidence of the conditions that existed at the end of the reporting period. The unusually high levels of inventory at the end of the reporting period indicated low demand. The announcement by the government confirmed that the inventory should be written down as there is no demand for it.

EXAMPLE 30.2

A corporation with a financial year end of June 30 has an amount of $20 million that is due from Debtor A as of June 30, 20X8. The corporation provided for impairment on June 30, 20X8 of $5 million against the gross value of $20 million due from Debtor A. On July 31, 20X8, before the financial statements were authorized for issue, Debtor A goes bankrupt and files for protections from its creditors. Is Debtor A's bankruptcy and filing for protection from its creditors an adjusting or nonadjusting event?

EXPLANATION

The bankruptcy and filing for protection from its creditors of Debtor A after the end of the reporting period provides evidence of the fact that the amount receivable from Debtor A was impaired at the end of the reporting period. This is an **adjusting event** and the corporation should impair the amount receivable from Debtor A as of June 30, 20X8.

EXAMPLE 30.3

Shortly after its financial year end of June 30, 20X8, but before the financial statements are authorized for issue, Entity B's inventory was destroyed by a fire which resulted in a loss of $2 million. Is this event an adjusting or a nonadjusting event?

EXPLANATION

This event is a **nonadjusting event** as it is indicative of a condition (fire) that arose after the end of the reporting period. Because this is a nonadjusting event, no adjustments will be made to the amounts recognized in the financial statements of Entity B's for the year ending June 30, 20X9. However, if the loss of $2 million is consequential enough that its nondisclosure would influence the economic decisions of the users of financial statements, disclosure of the nature of the event, the estimate of its financial effect, or a statement if such an estimate cannot be made, would be required.

EXAMPLE 30.4

A corporation with a financial year end of December 31 has a foreign long-term liability that is not covered by a foreign exchange contract. The foreign currency amount was converted at the closing rate on December 31, 20X4, and is shown in the accounting records at the local currency (LC) 2.0 million.

The local currency dropped significantly against the U.S. dollar on February 27, 20X5, resulting in a loss of LC4.0 million. On this date, management decided to hedge further exposure by taking out a foreign currency forward-exchange contract, which limited the eventual liability to LC6.0 million. If this situation were to apply at the end of the reporting period, it would result in the corporation's liabilities exceeding the fair value of its assets.

EXPLANATION

The situation above falls within the definition of **events after the reporting period** and specifically those events that refer to conditions arising *after* the reporting period.

The loss of LC4.0 million that arose in 20X5 must be recognized in the 20X5 Statement of Comprehensive Income. No provision with respect to the loss can be made in the financial statements for the year ending December 31, 20X4.

However, consideration should be given to whether it would be appropriate to apply the **going-concern** concept in the preparation of the financial statements. The date and frequency of repayment of the liability will have to be considered.

The following information should be **disclosed in a note** to the financial statements for the year ending December 31, 20X4:

- the nature of the events; and
- an estimate of the financial effect, in this case, a loss of LC4.0 million.

CHAPTER 31

Related-Party Disclosures (IAS 24)

31.1   **OBJECTIVE**

A related-party relationship between entities or individuals is unlike the more usual type between independent businesses. Related-party relationships and transactions can have an effect on the financial position and operating results of the reporting entity because the transactions may not always be on an arm's-length basis. The objective of this standard is to define related-party relationships and transactions and disclose their effects on an entity's financial position and performance.

31.2   **SCOPE OF THE STANDARD**

This IAS should be applied when identifying related-party relationships, transactions, and outstanding balances between related parties and the circumstances under which these aspects should be disclosed.

31.3   **KEY CONCEPTS**

31.3.1 **Related-party relationships** include any of the following:

- an entity that directly or indirectly
  - controls or is controlled (or under common control) by another entity;
  - has significant influence;
  - has joint control;
- entities that are subsidiaries of the reporting entity per IAS 27;
- entities that are associates of the reporting entity per IAS 28;
- entities that are joint ventures of the reporting entity per IAS 31;
- relationships between key management personnel (including any directors and officers of the reporting entity and any close family members of these directors and officers) responsible for planning, directing, and controlling the activities of the reporting entity;
- entities in which a substantial interest in the voting power is held, either directly or indirectly, by individuals (key management personnel or their close family members), including subsidiaries, associates, or joint ventures; and
- postemployment benefit plans for employees of the reporting entity, or for any entity that is a related party to the reporting entity.

31.3.2 A **related-party transaction** is a transfer of resources, services, or obligations between related parties, regardless of whether a price is charged.

31.3.3 Close members of the family of an individual are family members who might be expected to influence, or be influenced by, that individual in their dealings with the entity. They may include:

- the individual's domestic partner and children;
- children of the individual's domestic partner; and
- dependants of the individual or their domestic partner.

31.3.4 Compensation includes all employee benefits (see also IAS 19 and IFRS 2) and all forms of such consideration paid, payable, or provided by the reporting entity, or on behalf of the reporting entity, in exchange for services rendered to the entity. It also includes such consideration paid on behalf of a parent of the reporting entity in respect of the entity. Compensation includes:

- short-term employee benefits and nonmonetary benefits for current employees;
- postemployment benefits;
- other long-term employee benefits;
- termination benefits; and
- share-based payments.

FIGURE 31.1 Illustration of Related Parties of a Reporting Entity

Crossed-out entities are not related to the reporting entity in the black box.

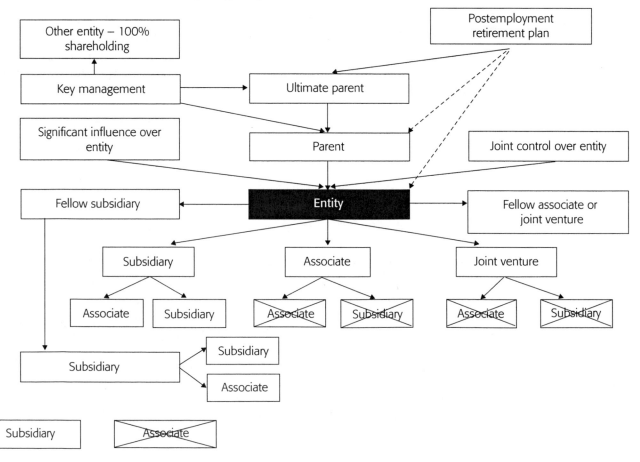

31.4   **ACCOUNTING TREATMENT**

31.4.1 When assessing a related-party relationship, the reporting entity must consider the substance of the relationship over its legal form. Examples of entities that are not related include:

- two entities that have a mutual director or manager, unless that director has a substantial interest and voting power;
- two venturers that jointly control an entity (the entity is a related party of the venturers but the venturers are not related parties of each other);
- financers, public utilities, trade unions, and government departments that are parties with the reporting entity simply due to normal business dealings; and
- customers, agents, suppliers, and similar entities with whom a significant volume of business occurs merely due to the dependence the entity may have on these parties.

31.4.2 A related-party transaction comprises a transfer of resources or obligations between related parties, regardless of whether a price is charged; this transfer of resources includes transactions concluded on an arm's-length basis. The following are examples of related-party transactions:

- purchase or sale of goods;
- purchase or sale of property or other assets;
- rendering or receipt of services;
- agency arrangements;
- lease agreements;
- transfer of research and development;
- transfers under license agreements;
- transfers under finance agreements, including loans and equity contributions;
- provision of guarantees and collaterals; and
- participation by a parent or subsidiary in a defined benefit plan that shares risks between group entities.

31.5   **PRESENTATION AND DISCLOSURE**

31.5.1 An entity's financial statements should contain the disclosures necessary to draw attention to the possibility that the financial position and profit or loss could have been affected by the existence of related parties and by transactions and outstanding balances with them.

31.5.2 Relationships between parents and subsidiaries (that is, where control exists) should be disclosed, irrespective of whether there have been transactions between the parties. The name of the parent and, if different, the name of the ultimate controlling party should be disclosed. If neither the parent nor ultimate controlling parent produces consolidated financial statements for public use, the name of the next most senior parent that does so must be disclosed.

31.5.3 Although relationships with associates and joint ventures do not require specific disclosure under this standard, these relationships are required to be disclosed under IAS 28 and IAS 31.

31.5.4 The amount of related-party transactions and balances must be disclosed whether these are at arm's length or not. Transactions can only be described as being at arm's length if this can be substantiated.

31.5.5 Compensation of key management personnel should be disclosed in total and for each of the following categories of compensation:

- short-term employee benefits;
- postemployment benefits;
- other long-term benefits;
- termination benefits; and
- share-based payments.

31.5.6 If **related-party transactions** occur, the following should be disclosed:

- the nature of related-party relationship;
- the nature of the transactions;
- transactions and outstanding balances, including:
  - the amount of transactions;
  - the amount of outstanding balances;
  - terms and conditions related to outstanding balances;
  - guarantees given or received on outstanding balances; and
  - expense recognized in respect of bad or doubtful debts originating from related parties.

31.5.7 The items in 31.5.6 should be separately disclosed for:

- the parent;
- entities with joint control or significant influence over the entity;
- subsidiaries;
- associates;
- joint ventures in which the entity is a venturer;
- key management personnel of the entity or its parent; and
- other related parties.

31.5.8 Items of a similar nature may be disclosed in aggregate except when separate disclosure is necessary to understand the effects of the transaction on the entity.

31.5.9 Related-party relationships are a normal feature in commerce. Many entities carry on separate parts of their activities through subsidiaries, associates, joint ventures, and so on. These parties sometimes enter into transactions through atypical business terms. For these reasons, knowledge of related parties may affect assessments of the entity by users of the financial statements, including assessments of risks and opportunities facing the entity.

31.5.10 Related parties have a degree of flexibility in the price-setting process that is not present in transactions between nonrelated parties. For example, they can use a comparable uncontrolled price method, resale method, or cost-plus method.

TABLE 31.1   Illustration of Related Parties of an Entity

Entity	Relationship	Related party per IAS 24	Disclosure requirement
Entity X holds controlling interest in Entity Y	Parent & subsidiary	✔	Each of these entities must list the other as a related party in their financial statements.
Entity X holds controlling interest in Entity Y and Entity Z	Parent & subsidiary (X & Y/Z) Fellow subsidiaries (Y & Z)	✔	For X: both Y & Z For Y: both X & Z For Z: both X & Y
Mr P is the CEO of X X is the parent of Y	Parent & subsidiary Member of key management	✔	For both X & Y, Mr P will be a related party in each of their financials.
Mr P is the CEO of X Mr P is 100% shareholder in Entity K	Member of key management Substantial interest held in another entity by management	✔	Entity X will include both Mr P and Entity K in its financials.
Entity X and Entity B have the same director	Mutual director	✗	Both entities need only disclose the director as a related party but not each other (i.e., the two entities are not related parties)
Entity X has the following investments: • significant influence over Z • joint control over T	Investor & associate Investor & joint venture	✗	Entity X will include both investments as related parties in its financials.
Entity Y is a subsidiary of Entity X Entity Y controls Entity Z Entity Y also has significant influence over Entity T	Parent & subsidiary (X & Y and Y and Z) Investor & associate (Y and T)	✔	For X: Z, Y, & T For Y: Z, X, & T For Z: X, Y, & T For T: X, Y, & Z
X and Y are fellow subsidiaries Y has an associate T	Fellow subsidiaries Investor & associate	✔	For X: Y & T For Y: X & T For T: X & Y
X has a associate Y Y has an associate Z	Investor: associate	✔	For X: only Y For Y: X & T For Z: only Y
Entity T is the main supplier of raw materials to Entity X	Customer/supplier	✗	None
Entity X makes most of its sales to Entity P	Customer/supplier	✗	None

31.6   FINANCIAL ANALYSIS AND INTERPRETATION

31.6.1 Transactions with related parties often raise questions of governance, especially when the impact is not clear from the amounts disclosed.

31.6.2 These types of transactions, and the related approval processes, can give rise to negative publicity. For example, amounts paid to management and directors have been the focus of significant attention in terms of governance processes in recent years.

31.6.3 For this reason, the disclosure of pricing policies and approval processes for related-party transactions should be taken into account when considering the impact of those transactions on the business.

31.6.4 The potential disempowerment of groups such as non-controlling interests should be considered, particularly where payments are made to other group companies.

31.7 COMMENTARY

31.7.1 As a practical expedient, a number of entities do not disclose information in the consolidated financial statements of transactions and balances that have been eliminated on consolidation.

31.7.2 Obtaining the related-party information for key management personnel is often difficult as the information is sensitive, voluminous, and difficult to obtain.

31.7.3 In a country where publicly owned or government-related entities are prevalent, the reporting entity will have numerous related parties. Identifying related-party transactions and obtaining the required information would be an onerous task. This could also be applicable in small economies where there are a few very large investment holding companies.

31.7.4 As part of its projects to improve a number of standards, the IASB issued a revised IAS 24 in November 2009. The revised standard will be effective for annual periods beginning on or after January 1, 2011.

31.7.5 The revisions to IAS 24 mainly include the following:

- a simplified definition of a related party and clarification on what relationships fall within this definition; and
- partial exemption from disclosure requirements for government-related entities.

31.7.6 For the purposes of the revised standard, the term "government" includes government agencies and similar bodies that are local, national, and international. A government-related entity will be any entity that is a subsidiary, associate, or joint venture of the government. A reporting entity will be exempt from the disclosure requirements for related-party transactions and outstanding balances when the related party is a government-related entity or another entity that is a related party because the government has control, significant influence, or joint control over both entities.

31.8 IMPLEMENTATION DECISIONS

The following table sets out some of the strategic and tactical decisions that should be considered when applying IAS 24:

Strategic decisions	Tactical decisions	Problems to overcome
Related-party relationships need to be identified by management per IAS 24 definitions.	Policies and procedures must be put in place to identify related parties.	An entity may not always realize it has a related-party relationship as identification can get complex. Entities within the group also may not realize that they are dealing with a related party.
Transactions and balances with the related parties must be identified.	The terms of transactions entered into must be carefully considered to ensure they are at arm's length. Policies and procedures must be put in place to identify and track such transactions.	It is not always easy to determine whether or not transactions are at arm's length.
Other statutory requirements must be considered, for example the disclosure of directors' emoluments in terms of the companies act or listing requirements.	Processes must be in place to identify any related-party disclosures required by other regulations.	Accounting and other statutory disclosure requirements may not be the same but are equally important. Care must be taken to ensure they do not contradict each other in the disclosures made.
Certain related-party information may be confidential and sensitive in nature, for example directors' emoluments.	A process should be developed regarding the appropriate person to obtain information from directors.	

EXAMPLE: RELATED-PARTY DISCLOSURES

EXAMPLE 31.1

Habitat Inc. is a subsidiary in a group structure, as indicated by the following diagram:

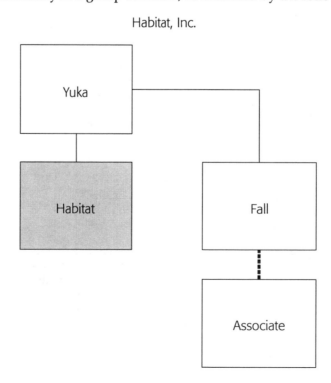

Habitat, Inc.

Solid lines indicate **control,** whereas dotted lines indicate the exercise of **significant influence.**

During the year, Habitat acquired plant and equipment from Associate at an amount of $23 million, on which Associate earned a profit of $4 million.

EXPLANATION

Habitat and Associate are deemed to be related parties in terms of IAS 24. The full details of the transaction should therefore be disclosed in the financial statement of **both** entities as required by IAS 24, namely:

- the nature of the related-party relationship;
- the nature of the transaction;
- the amount involved; and
- any amount still due from Habitat to Associate.

Examples 31.2 and 31.3 illustrate related-party disclosures made in practice for both a banking and nonbanking entity. The data in these examples are obtained from the published annual reports of the relevant entities.

EXAMPLE 31.2: BANKING ENTITY

The financial statements shown are those of Barclays PLC, a winner of the 2009 Golden Peacock Global Award for Corporate Governance, which is annually awarded by the World Council for Corporate Governance. This extract was obtained from the published annual report of Barclays PLC as available on their Web site: www.barclays.com.

Barclays provides the majority of its related-party disclosures in a single note.

Notes to the accounts
For the year ended 31st December 2008

Related party transactions and Directors' remuneration

(a) Related party transactions Parties are considered to be related if one party has the ability to control the other party or exercise significant influence over the other party in making financial or operation decisions, or one other party controls both. The definition includes subsidiaries, associates, joint ventures and the Group's pension schemes, as well as other persons.

Subsidiaries Transactions between Barclays PLC and subsidiaries also meet the definition of related party transactions. Where these are eliminated on consolidation, they are not disclosed in the Group financial statements. Transactions between Barclays PLC and its subsidiary, Barclays Bank PLC are fully disclosed directly in its balance sheet and income statement. A list of the Group's principal subsidiaries is shown in Note 41.

Associates, joint ventures and other entities The Group provides banking services to its associates, joint ventures, the Group pension funds (principally the UK Retirement Fund) and to entities under common directorships, providing loans, overdrafts, interest and non-interest bearing deposits and current accounts to these entities as well as other services. Group companies, principally within Barclays Global Investors, also provide investment management and custodian services to the Group pension schemes. The Group also provides banking services for unit trusts and investment funds managed by Group companies and are not individually material. All of these transactions are conducted on the same terms as third-party transactions.

Amounts included in the accounts, in aggregate, by category of related party entity are as follows:

For the year ended and as at 31st December 2008

Amounts of related parties transactions and balances split per main categories of related parties	Associates £m	Joint ventures £m	Entities under common directorships £m	Pension funds unit trusts and investment funds £m	Total £m
Income statement:					
Interest received	–	105	3	–	108
Interest paid	–	(73)	–	–	(73)
Fees received for services rendered (including investment management and custody and commissions)	–	15	–	5	20
Fees paid for services provided	(44)	(146)	–	–	(190)
Principal transactions	8	59	60	(25)	102
Assets:					
Loans and advances to banks and customers	110	954	34	–	1,098
Derivative transactions	–	9	311	15	335
Other assets	67	276	–	3	346
Liabilities:					
Deposits from banks	–	592	–	–	592
Customer accounts	–	167	74	10	251
Derivative transactions	–	–	111	41	152
Other liabilities	3	18	–	28	49

For the year ended and as at 31st December 2007[a]

	Associates £m	Joint ventures £m	Entities under common directorships £m	Pension funds unit trusts and investment funds £m	Total £m
Income statement:					
Interest received	5	88	1	–	94
Interest paid	(1)	(58)	(1)	–	(60)
Fees received for services rendered (including investment management and custody and commissions)	1	34	–	26	61
Fees paid for services provided	(52)	(78)	–	–	(130)
Principal transactions	(27)	45	(16)	–	2
Assets:					
Loans and advances to banks and customers	142	1,285	40	–	1,467
Derivative transactions	–	4	36	–	40
Other assets	213	106	–	14	333
Liabilities:					
Deposits from banks	11	–	–	–	11
Customer accounts	–	61	33	12	106
Derivative transactions	–	10	50	–	60
Other liabilities	4	125	–	–	129

(continued)

EXAMPLE 31.2, CONTINUED

For the year ended and as at 31st December 2006[a]

	Associates £m	Joint ventures £m	Entities under common directorships £m	Pension funds unit trusts and investment funds £m	Total £m
Income statement:					
Interest received	45	38	–	2	85
Interest paid	(31)	(57)	–	–	(88)
Fees received for services rendered (including investment management and custody and commissions)	14	7	–	28	49
Fees paid for services provided	(115)	(51)	–	(1)	(167)
Principal transactions	3	–	(2)	–	1
Assets:					
Loans and advances to banks and customers	784	146	65	–	995
Derivative transactions	–	–	–	–	–
Other assets	19	3	–	17	39
Liabilities:					
Deposits from banks	9	–	–	3	12
Customer accounts	19	18	5	34	76
Derivative transactions	–	–	2	–	2
Other liabilities	13	8	–	–	21

Note
a. The amounts reported in prior periods have been restated to reflect new related parties.

No guarantees, pledges or commitments have been given or received in respect of these transactions in 2008, 2007 or 2006. Derivatives transacted on behalf of the Pensions Funds Unit Trusts and Investment Funds amounted to £318m (2007: £22m, 2006: £1,209m).

In 2008 Barclays paid £12m (2007: £18m) of its charitable donations through the Charities Aid Foundation, a registered charitable organisation, in which a Director of the Company is a Trustee.

> It is required that the details of any guarantees over related party balances be disclosed

Key Management Personnel

The Group's Key Management Personnel, and persons connected with them, are also considered to be related parties for disclosure purposes. Key Management Personnel are defined as those persons having authority and responsibility for planning, directing and controlling the activities of Barclays PLC (directly or indirectly) and comprise the Directors of Barclays PLC and the Officers of the Group, certain direct reports of the Group Chief Executive and the heads of major business units.

In the ordinary course of business, the Bank makes loans to companies where a Director or other member of Key Management Personnel (or any connected person) is also a Director or other member of Key Management Personnel (or any connected person) of Barclays.

There were no material related party transactions with companies where a Director or other member of Key Management Personnel (or any connected person) is also a Director or other member of Key Management Personnel (or any connected person) of Barclays.

The Group provides banking services to Directors and other Key Management Personnel and persons connected to them. Transactions during the year and the balances outstanding at 31st December 2008 were as follows:

Directors, other Key Management Personnel and connected persons

		2007 £m	2006 £m
Loans outstanding at 1st January		7.8	7.4
Loans issued during the year		2.7	2.7
Loan repayments during the year		(3.2)	(2.3)
Loans outstanding at 31st December		7.3	7.8
Interest income earned	**0.4**	0.4	0.3

> The amounts of any transactions or balances with related parties including key management must be disclosed

No allowances for impairment were recognised in respect of loans to Directors or other members of Key Management Personnel (or any connected person) in 2008, 2007 or 2006.

	2007 £m	2006 £m
Deposits outstanding at 1st January	15.0	4.7
Deposits received during the year	114.4	105.2
Deposits repaid during the year	(115.0)	(94.8)
Deposits outstanding at 31st December	14.4	15.1
Interest expense on deposits	0.6	0.2

> The terms and conditions and any allowances for impairment must be disclosed for all related party balances

Of the loans outstanding above, £1.6m (2007: £nil, 2006: £nil) relates to Directors and other Key Management Personnel (and persons connected to them) that left the Group during the year. Of the deposits outstanding above, £6.1m (2007: £2.8m, 2006: £0.1m) related to Directors and other Key Management Personnel (and persons connected to them) that left the Group during the year.

All loans are provided on normal commercial terms to Directors and other Key Management Personnel (and persons connected to them), with the exception of £692 of loans which are provided on an interest free basis.

The loans of £692 provided on an interest free basis relate to the granting of loans to one non-Director member of Barclays key management to purchase commuter rail tickets. The commuter rail ticket loans are still provided to all Barclays staff members upon request on the same terms.

All loans to Directors and other key management personnel (a) were made in the ordinary course of business, (b) were made on substantially the same terms, including interest rates and collateral, as those prevailing at the same time for comparable transactions with other persons and (c) did not involve more than a normal risk of collectability or present other unfavourable features.

Directors, other Key Management Personnel and connected persons

	2008 £m	2007 £m	2006 £m
Salaries and other short-term benefits	10.7	23.7	34.2
Pension costs	0.9	1.1	0.8
Other long-term benefits	1.6	9.2	9.3
Termination benefits	–	–	1.4
Share-based payments	11.8	31.7	27.2
Employer social security charges on emoluments	2.7	7.8	10.0
	27.7	73.5	82.9

> Total key management personnel compensation must be disclosed per compensation type

(continued)

EXAMPLE 31.2, CONTINUED

(b) Disclosure required by the Companies Act 1985

The following information is presented in accordance with the Companies Act 1985:

Directors' remuneration

	2008 £m	2007 £m
Aggregate emoluments	6.0	29.2
Gains made on the exercise of share options	–	0.3
Amounts paid under long-term incentive schemes	7.4	–
Actual pension contributions to money purchase scheme (2008: one Director, £11,745 and 2007: one Director, £10,233)	–	–
Notional pension contributions to money purchase scheme (2008: no Directors and 2007: no Directors)	–	–
	13.4	29.5

As at 31st December 2008, two Directors were accruing retirement benefits under a defined benefit scheme (2007: three Directors).

One Director (Frits Seegers) agreed to waive his fees as non-executive Director of Absa Group Limited and Absa Bank Limited. The fees for 2008 were ZAR 0.4m (£0.03m). The fees for 2007 were ZAR 0.5m (£0.03m). In both 2007 and 2008 the fees were paid to Barclays.

Directors' and Officers' shareholdings and options The beneficial ownership of the ordinary share capital of Barclays PLC by all Directors and Officers of Barclays PLC (involving 20 persons) and Barclays Bank PLC (involving 21 persons) at 31st December 2008 amounted to 8,036,962 ordinary shares of 25p each (0.10% of the ordinary share capital outstanding) and 8,037,498 ordinary shares of 25p each (0.10% of the ordinary share capital outstanding), respectively.

Executive Directors and Officers of Barclays PLC as a group (involving 8 persons) held, at 31st December 2008, options to purchase 2,185,380 Barclays PLC ordinary shares of 25p each at prices ranging from 255p to 510p under Sharesave and at 397p under the Executive Share Option Scheme and ranging from 317p to 534p under the Incentive Share Option Plan, respectively.

Contracts with Directors (and their connected persons) and Managers The aggregate amounts outstanding at 31st December 2008 under transactions, arrangements and agreements made by banking companies within the Group for persons who are, or were during the year, Directors of Barclays PLC and persons connected with them, as defined in the Companies Act 2006, and for Managers, within the meaning of the Financial Services and Markets Act 2000, of Barclays Bank PLC were:

	Number of Directors or Managers	Number of connected persons	Amount £m
Directors			
Loans	1	1	6.1
Quasi-loans and credit card accounts	8	1	–
Managers			
Loans	3	n/a	14.0
Quasi-loans and credit card accounts	7	n/a	–

(c) US disclosures

For US disclosure purposes, the aggregate emoluments of all Directors and Officers of Barclays PLC who held office during the year (2008: 24 persons, 2007: 22 persons, 2006: 24 persons) for the year ended 31st December 2008 amounted to £26.8m (2007: £64.6m, 2006: £72.1m). In addition, the aggregate amount set aside for the year ended 31st December 2008, to provide pension benefits for the Directors and Officers amounted to £0.9m (2007: £1.1m, 2006: £0.8m). The aggregate emoluments of all Directors and Officers of Barclays Bank PLC who held office during the year (2008: 25 persons, 2007: 23 persons, 2006: 25 persons) for the year ended 31st December 2008 amounted to £26.9m, (2007: £64.9m and 2006: £72.2m). In addition, the aggregate amount set aside by the Bank and its subsidiaries for the year ended 31st December 2008, to provide pension benefits for the Directors and Officers amounted to £0.9m (2007: £1.1m, 2006: £0.8m).

Principal subsidiaries

> All parent and subsidiary relationships must be disclosed, including the relationship and the names of the entities

Country of registration or incorporation	Company name	Nature of business	Percentage of equity capital held %
Botswana	Barclays Bank of Botswana Limited	Banking	74.9
Egypt	Barclays Bank Egypt SAE	Banking	100
England	Barclays Bank PLC	Banking, holding company	100*
England	Barclays Mercantile Business Finance Limited	Loans and advances including leases to customers	100*
England	Barclays Global Investors UK Holdings Limited	Holding company	95.5
England	Barclays Global Investors Limited	Investment management	95.5*
England	Barclays Bank Trust Company Limited	Banking, securities industries and trust services	100*
England	Barclays Stockbrokers Limited	Stockbroking	100*
England	Barclays Capital Securities Limited	Securities dealing	100*
England	Barclays Global Investors Pensions Management Limited	Investment management	95.5*
England	FIRSTPLUS Financial Group PLC	Secured loan provider	100
England	Gerrard Investment Management Limited	Investment management	100*
Ghana	Barclays Bank of Ghana Limited	Banking	100
Ireland	Barclays Insurance (Dublin) Limited	Insurance provider	100*
Ireland	Barclays Assurance (Dublin) Limited	Insurance provider	100*
Isle of Man	Barclays Private Clients International Limited[a]	Banking	100*
Japan	Barclays Capital Japan Limited	Securities dealing	100*
Jersey	Barclays Private Bank & Trust Limited	Banking, trust company	100*
Kenya	Barclays Bank of Kenya Limited	Banking	68.5
Russia	Barclays Bank LLC	Banking	100*
South Africa	Absa Group Limited	Banking	58.6
Spain	Barclays Bank SA	Banking	99.7
Switzerland	Barclays Bank (Suisse) S.A.	Banking and trust services	100
USA	Barclays Capital Inc.	Securities dealing	100*
USA	Barclays Financial Corporation	Holding company for US credit card issuer	100*
USA	Barclays Global Investors, National Association	Investment management and securities industry	95.5*
USA	Barclays Group USA Inc.	Holding company	100
Zimbabwe	Barclays Bank of Zimbabwe Limited	Banking	67.8*

Note. In accordance with Section 231(5) of the Companies Act 1985, the above information is provided solely in relation to principal subsidiaries. The country of registration or incorporation is also the principal area of operation of each of the above subsidiaries. Investments in these subsidiaries are held directly by Barclays Bank PLC except where marked *. Full information of all subsidiaries will be included in the Annual Return to be filed at Companies House.

a. BBPLC is the beneficial owner of 38.1% of shares and Barclays Holdings (Isle of Man) Limited is the beneficial owner of 61.9% of shares.

(continued)

The financial statements shown are those of Sasol Limited Group. This extract is directly from the annual report of Sasol Limited Group as on their Web site: www.sasol.com.

Unlike Barclays, Sasol provides its related-party disclosures throughout the financial statements' notes where relevant and does not dedicate a single note to related parties. Either method is correct as long as all the required disclosures are included in the financial statements.

for the year ended 30 June	2009 Rm	2008 Rm	2007 Rm
Related party transactions			
Group companies, in the ordinary course of business, entered into various purchase and sale transactions with associates and joint ventures. The effect of these transactions is included in the financial performance and results of the group. Terms and conditions are determined on an arm's length basis.			
Disclosure in respect of joint ventures is provided on page 166 and of associates in note 8.			
Material related party transactions were as follows			
Sales and services rendered to related parties			
joint ventures			
associates	286	1 975	
third parties	1 241	742	1 759
retirement funds	3 188	944	632
	–	4	160
	4 715	3 661	2 555
Purchases from related parties			
joint ventures	306	88	135
associates	923	795	712
third parties	1 820	1 056	832
retirement funds	408	338	374
	3 457	2 277	2 053

> The amounts and nature of the relationship of any transactions with related parties must be disclosed

Amounts owing (after eliminating intercompany balances) to related parties are disclosed in the respective notes to the financial statements for those statement of financial position items. No impairment of receivables related to the amount of outstanding balances is required.

Included in the above amounts are a number of transactions with related parties which are individually insignificant.

Identity of related parties with whom material transactions have occurred

Except for the group's interests in joint ventures and associates, there are no other related parties with whom material individual transactions have taken place.

Directors and senior management

Details of the directors' and group executive committee remuneration and the shareholding in Sasol Limited are disclosed in the remuneration report on page 46 to 56.

Shareholders

An analysis of major shareholders is provided on pages 36 and 37.

	2009 Rm	2008 Rm	2007 Rm
Trade receivables	12 052	18 864	12 076
Trade receivables	705	952	484
Related party receivables third parties	549	664	238
joint ventures	156	288	246
Impairment of trade receivables	(258)	(144)	(118)
Receivables	12 499	19 672	12 442
Duties recoverable from customers	1 972	1 826	1 625
Value added tax	705	1 340	666
	15 176	22 838	14 733
Trade receivables to turnover (%)	11,0%	17,6%	15,0%
Currency analysis			
Euro	2 906	5 406	3 572
US dollar	3 635	5 506	3 074
Rand	5 423	8 069	5 414
Pound sterling	94	123	94
Other currencies	441	568	288
	12 499	19 672	12 442

The amounts of any balances with related parties must be disclosed

for the year ended 30 June	2009 Rm	2008 Rm	2007 Rm
Long-term debt continued			
Currency analysis	5 733	6 723	5 252
Euro	180	2 638	3 404
US dollar	11 878	7 346	7 534
Rand	96	96	244
Pound sterling			
Other currencies			
	17 887	16 803	16 434
Interest bearing status			
Interest bearing debt	17 244	16 166	15 834
Non-interest bearing debt	643	637	600
	17 887	16 803	16 434
Maturity profile			
Within one year	4 272	1 121	3 075
One to two years	911	4 816	1 553
Two to three years	1 181	1 392	4 398
Three to four years	1 106	1 450	1 276
Four to five years	1 172	1 429	1 256
More than five years	9 245	6 595	4 876
	17 887	16 803	16 434
Related party long-term debt included in long-term debt			
Third parties	215	134	107
Joint ventures	33	803	460
	248	937	567

The amounts of any balances with related par ties must be disclosed

(continued)

EXAMPLE 31.3, CONTINUED

Trade payables and accrued expenses

Trade payables	**5 709**	8 609	5 946
Accrued expenses	**2 440**	2 487	1 423
Related party payables	**1 080**	1 317	273
third parties	**490**	773	191
joint ventures	**590**	544	82

The amounts of any balances with related parties must be disclosed

	9 229	12 413	7 642
Duties payable to revenue authorities	**2 044**	1 692	1 381
Value added tax	**191**	589	353
	11 464	14 694	9 376

Trade payables and accrued expenses to cost of sales and services rendered (%)	**13,0%**	19,7%	15,6%

Currency analysis   2009   2008   2007

Euro	**1 782**	3 152	2 224
US dollar	**2 747**	3 528	2 343
Rand	**3 935**	4 680	2 826
Other currencies	**765**	1 053	249
	9 229	12 413	7 642

interest in significant operating subsidiaries

All parent and subsidiary relationships must be disclosed including the relationship and the names of the entities

Name	Nature of business				Investment at cost		Long-term loans to subsidiaries	
					2009 Rm	2008 Rm	2009 Rm	2008 Rm
Operating subsidiaries								
Direct								
Sasol Mining (Pty) Limited	Coal mining activities.	Rm	215	100	**456**	456	**122**	31
Sasol Synfuels (Pty) Limited	Production of liquid fuels, gases, chemical products and refining of tar acids.	Rm	100	100	**676**	676	–	518
Sasol Technology (Pty)	Limited Engineering services, research and development and technology transfer.	Rm	1	100	**1**	1	**1 384**	827
Sasol Financing (Pty) Limited	Management of cash resources, investment and procurement of loans for South African operations.	R	200	100	–	–	**5 454**	3 647
Sasol Investment Company (Pty) Limited	Holding company of the group's foreign investments and investment in movable and immovable property.	R	300	100	**12 083**	–	**266**	17 545
Sasol Chemical Industries Limited	Production and marketing of mining explosives, gases, petrochemicals and fertilisers.	R	152	100	–	–	**7 516**	5 792
Sasol Gas Holdings (Pty) Limited	Holding company of the group's gas interests.	R	100	100	–	–	–	537
Sasol Oil (Pty) Limited	Marketing of fuels and lubricants.	R	1 200	75	**378**	378	–	–

Executive directors' emoluments

Remuneration and benefits paid and incentives approved in respect of the 2009 financial year for executive directors were as follows:

Executive directors

	Salary R'000	Total key management personnel compensation must be disclosed per compensation type		nual ntives oved[1] 000	Total 2009[3] R'000	Total 2008[4] R'000
LPA Davies	6 790			572	10 280	14 744
VN Fakude	3 394	653	528	848	5 423	6 657
AMB Mokaba	3 961	764	712	553	5 990	7 806
TS Munday[2]	n/a	n/a	n/a	n/a	n/a	16 165
KC Ramon	3 506	675	399	975	5 555	6 689
Total	17 651	3 488	2 161	3 948	27 248	52 061

1. *Incentives approved on the group results for the 2009 financial year and payable in the following year. Incentives are calculated as a percentage of total guaranteed package. The difference between the total amount approved as at 11 September 2009 and the total amount accrued as at 30 June 2009 represents an over-provision of R3,4 million. The under provision (R1,4 million) for 2008 was also expensed in 2009.*
2. *Mr Munday retired as an employee with effect from 1 July 2007.*
3. *Total remuneration for the financial year excludes gains derived from share incentives, details of which are disclosed on page 54.*
4. *Includes incentives approved on the group results for the 2008 financial year and paid in 2009.*

Benefits and payments made in the 2009 financial year disclosed in the table above as "other benefits" include:

Executive directors

	Vehicle benefits R'000	Medical benefits R'000	Vehicle insurance fringe benefits R'000	Security benefits R'000	Exchange rate fluctuation[1] R'000	Total other benefits 2009 R'000	Total other benefits 2008 R'000
LPA Davies	321	45	5	44	107	522	497
VN Fakude	303	42	5	164	14	528	448
AMB Mokaba	303	50	5	351	3	712	631
TS Munday[2]	n/a	n/a	n/a	n/a	n/a	n/a	16 165
KC Ramon	303	45	5	27	19	399	352
Total	1 230	182	20	586	143	2 161	18 093

1. *Rand equivalent of exchange rate fluctuations on cash salary and incentive of offshore components.*
2. *Payments made to Mr Munday include a payment of R16 million in respect of a restraint of trade agreement which became effective after his retirement on 1 July 2007, proceeds of a retirement policy payable on retirement (R138 000) and security benefits (R27 000).*

(continued)

Group executive committee

The total remuneration of members of the GEC other than the executive directors was reviewed by the committee at its meeting held on 5 September 2008 by applying principles consistent with those for executive directors. The members of the GEC participate in the group short-term incentive and long-term incentive schemes under similar terms as detailed above. The aggregate short-term incentive in respect of the 2008 financial year calculated as a percentage of the total guaranteed package and paid during 2009 was R18,7 million.

Non-executive directors' remuneration for the year was as follows:

Non-executive directors	Board meeting fees[7] R'000	Committee fees R'000	Share incentive trustee fees R'000	Total 2009 R'000	Total 2008 R'000
E le R Bradley[1]		178	63	400	747
BP Connellan		514	127	989	931
PV Cox[2]		238	–	1 562	3 750
HG Dijkgraaf[3]		384	11	1 494	1 060
MSV Gantsho		159	–	477	490
A Jain[3]	1 038	–	–	1 038	747
IN Mkhize	348	98	–	446	410
S Montsi[4]	27	33	5	65	744
MJN Njeke[5]	148	66	–	214	n/a
TH Nyasulu (Chairman)[6]	2 138	212	11	2 361	422
JE Schrempp (Lead independent director)[3]	1 273	159	–	1 432	897
TA Wixley	348	257	–	605	513
Total	8 568	2 298	217	11 083	10 711

> Total key management personnel compensation must be disclosed per compensation type

1. Retired as director of Sasol Limited on 31 December 2008.
2. Retired as chairman of Sasol Limited on 28 November 2008.
3. Board meeting fees paid in US dollars. Rand equivalent of US$110 000 at actual exchange rates.
4. Resigned as a director of Sasol Limited on 31 July 2008.
5. Appointed as non-executive director of Sasol Limited on 4 February 2009. The fees are paid directly to Mr Njeke's employer.
6. Appointed as chairman of Sasol Limited with effect from 28 November 2008.
7. Includes fees for ad hoc meetings attended during the year.

> Total key management personnel compensation including share base payments must be disclosed

Long-term incentive plans

The interests of the directors in the form of share options are shown in the tables below. During the year to 30 June 2009 the highest and lowest closing market prices for the company's shares were R471,00 (on 1 July 2008) and R216,56 (on 24 November 2008), and the closing market price on 30 June 2009 was R269,98.

No variations have been made to the terms and conditions of the options during the relevant period.

	Balance at beginning of year (number)[1]	Share options implemented (number)	Balance at end of year[2] (number)
Executive directors			
LPA Davies	636 300	65 000	**571 300**
VN Fakude	81 900	–	**81 900**
AMB Mokaba	94 000	–	**94 000**
KC Ramon	81 700	–	**81 700**
Non-executive directors			
PV Cox[3]	116 700	–	**116 700**
Total share options	1 010 600	65 000	**945 600**

1. *The balance of options represents the accumulated number of options granted (less implemented) over the preceding years.*
2. *No share options were granted during the period under review as a result of the replacement of the Sasol Share Incentive Scheme with the SAR Scheme with effect from 1 March 2007.*
3. *The share options were granted to Mr Cox while he was an executive director.*

Share appreciation rights granted during 2009—directors

	Balance at beginning of year (number)	Granted (number)	Average offer price per share (Rand)	Grant date	Balance at end of year (number)
Executive directors					
LPA Davies	55 200	70 800	352,10	11 Sep 2008	**126 000**
VN Fakude	17 100	22 400	352,10	11 Sep 2008	**39 500**
AMB Mokaba	–	25 900	352,10	11 Sep 2008	**25 900**
KC Ramon	–	23 200	352,10	11 Sep 2008	**23 200**
Total share appreciation rights	72 300	142 300			**214 600**

Sasol Inzalo Management Scheme rights granted during 2009—directors

	Balance at beginning of year (number)	Rights granted (number)	Value of underlying share (Rand)	Grant date	Effect of resignations/ retirements (number)	Balance at end of year (number)
Executive directors						
VN Fakude	25 000	–	–	–	–	**25 000**
AMB Mokaba	25 000	–	–	–	–	**25 000**
KC Ramon Total Sasol Inzalo Management Scheme	25 000	–	–	–	–	**25 000**
Vested rights	75 000	–	–	–	–	**75 000**

At grant date on 3 June 2008, the issue price of the underlying share of R366,00 was the 60 day volume weighted average price of Sasol ordinary shares to 18 March 2008. The shares were issued to The Sasol Inzalo Management Trust at R0,01 per share.

(continued)

Share options implemented and share appreciation rights granted during 2009—group executive committee[1]

	Balance at beginning of year (number)	Effect of change in composition of group executive committee (number)	Granted (number)	Average offer price per share (Rand)	Grant date	Share options implemented (number)	Balance at end of year (number)
Share options[2]	559 600	66 500	–	–	–	20 100	**606 000**
Share appreciation rights	157 000	(27 700)	145 100	352,10	11 Sept 2008	–	**274 400**

1. *Excluding the executive directors disclosed separately in the table above.*
2. *Includes share options issued to individuals during the year before they became members of the GEC.*

Share options implemented—directors

					Gain on implementation of share options	
	Implementation dates	Share options implemented (number)	Average offer price per share (Rand)	Market price per share (Rand)	2009 R'000	2008 R'000
Executive directors						
LPA Davies	12 September 2008	13 600	42,30	360,01	**4 321**	5 395
	25 September 2008	51 400	54,00	357,99	**15 625**	–
VN Fakude		–	–	–	–	6 258
Non-executive directors						
PV Cox[1]		–	–	–	–	20 297
Total		65 000			**19 946**	31 950

1. *The share options implemented were granted to Mr Cox when he was an executive director.*

Share options implemented—group executive committee[1]

		Gain on implementation of share options	
	Share options implemented (number)	2009 R'000	2008 R'000
Group executive committee[2]	20 100	4 797	38 406

1. *Excluding the executive directors disclosed separately in the table above.*
2. *Included in the total share options implemented are the gains on the implementation of 20 100 share options on which the shares were retained by members. A gain of R4 796 908 on the implementation of these share options was determined using the closing share price on the date of implementation.*

Share options outstanding at the end of the year vest during the following periods:

	Already vested (number)	Within one year (number)	One to two years (number)	Two to five years (number)	More than five years (number)	Total (number)
Executive directors						
LPA Davies	385 400	11 100	29 000	145 800	–	**571 300**
VN Fakude	41 200	–	–	40 700	–	**81 900**
AMB Mokaba	31 300	–	31 300	31 400	–	**94 000**
KC Ramon	27 200	–	27 200	27 300	–	**81 700**
Non-executive directors						
PV Cox1	116 700	–	–	–	–	**116 700**
Total	601 800	11 100	87 500	245 200	–	**945 600**

1. *The share options were granted to Mr Cox when he was an executive director.*

Share appreciation rights outstanding at the end of the year vest during the following periods:

	Already vested (number)	Within one year (number)	One to two years (number)	Two to five years (number)	More than five years (number)	Total (number)
Executive directors						
LPA Davies	–	18 400	23 600	60 400	23 600	**126 000**
VN Fakude	–	5 700	7 500	18 900	7 400	**39 500**
AMB Mokaba	–	–	8 600	8 600	8 700	**25 900**
KC Ramon	–	–	7 700	7 700	7 800	**23 200**
Total	–	24 100	47 400	95 600	47 500	**214 600**

Share options and share appreciation rights outstanding at the end of the year vest during the following periods:

	Already vested (number)	Within one year (number)	One to two years (number)	Two to five years (number)	More than five years (number)	Total (number)
Group executive committee[1]	374 900	93 900	48 900	88 300	–	606 000
Share options						
Share appreciation rights	–	64 100	55 300	118 900	36 100	274 400

1. *Excluding the executive directors disclosed separately in the table above.*

(continued)

Beneficial shareholding

The aggregate beneficial shareholding at 30 June 2009 of the directors of the company and the group executive committee and their associates (none of which have a holding greater than 1%) in the issued ordinary share capital of the company are detailed below.

| Beneficial shareholding | 2009 | | | | 2008 | | | |
| | Number of shares | | Number of share options[2] | Total beneficial shareholding | Number of shares | | Number of share options[2] | Total beneficial shareholding |
	Direct	Indirect[1]			Direct	Indirect[3]		
Executive directors								
LPA Davies	86 700	221	385 400	472 321	21 700	212	277 800	299 712
VN Fakude	1 500	–	41 200	42 700	–	–	600	600
AMB Mokaba	–	–	31 300	31 300	–	–	–	–
KC Ramon	21 500	41 556	27 200	90 256	–	–	–	–
Non-executive directors								
E le R Bradley[4]	n/a	n/a	n/a	n/a	97 494	–	–	97 494
BP Connellan	10 500	–		10 500	10 500	–	–	10 500
PV Cox[4,5]	n/a	n/a	n/a	n/a	281 409	–	116 700	398 109
IN Mkhize	1 313	18 626	–	19 939	–	–	–	–
TH Nyasulu	–	1 450	–	1 450	–	–	–	–
TA Wixley	2 500	–	–	2 500	1 300	–	–	1 300
Total	**124 013**	**61 853**	**485 100**	**670 966**	412 403	212	395 100	807 715

1. *Includes units held in the Sasol Share Savings Trust and shares held through Sasol Inzalo Public Limited.*
2. *Including share options which have vested or which vest within sixty days of 30 June 2009.*
3. *Includes units held in the Sasol Share Savings Trust.*
4. *Retired during 2009.*
5. *The share options were granted when Mr Cox was still an executive director.*

There have been no changes in the direct or indirect beneficial interests of the directors and their associates between 30 June 2009 and 28 September 2009.

CHAPTER 32

Earnings per Share
(IAS 33)

OBJECTIVE

Earnings per share is a prime variable used for evaluating the performance of an entity. It allows investors to make an accurate comparison of the results of entities functioning in different sectors and industries.

The objective of IAS 33 is to prescribe principles for the determination and presentation of earnings per share, focusing on the denominator (number of shares) of the calculation because a consistently determined denominator results in enhanced performance reporting. This improves the performance comparisons between different entities and different reporting periods of the same entity. The standard distinguishes between the notions, calculation methods, and disclosures of basic as well as diluted earnings per share.

32.2   **SCOPE OF THE STANDARD**

This standard applies to entities whose shares are **publicly traded** (or in the process of being issued in public securities markets) and other entities that choose to disclose earnings per share. It is applicable to consolidated information only if the parent prepares consolidated financial statements. Where an entity prepares both separate and consolidated financials, this information need only be presented in the consolidated financials.

32.3   **KEY CONCEPTS**

32.3.1 Earnings per share is the interest of each ordinary share of an entity in the profit or loss of the entity for the reporting period.

32.3.2 Earnings are the amounts attributable to all the ordinary equity holders of the parent entity (controlling and non-controlling interest).

32.3.3 An **ordinary share** is an equity instrument that is subordinate to all other classes of equity instruments. An entity may issue more than one class of ordinary shares.

32.3.4 A **potential ordinary share** is a financial instrument or other contract that can entitle its holder to ordinary shares of an entity (for example, debt or equity instruments that are convertible into ordinary shares, and share warrants and options that give the holder the right to purchase ordinary shares).

32.3.5 **Dilution** is a reduction in earnings per share or an increase in loss per share resulting from the assumption that convertible instruments are converted, that options or warrants are exercised, or that ordinary shares are issued upon the satisfaction of specified conditions.

32.3.6 **Options, warrants, and their equivalents** are financial instruments that give the holder the right to purchase ordinary shares at a specified price.

32.3.7 **Put options** on ordinary shares are contracts that give the holder the right to sell ordinary shares at a specified price for a given period.

32.4 ACCOUNTING TREATMENT

Basic Earnings per Share

32.4.1 **Basic earnings per share** is the profit or loss attributable to each ordinary share in issue at reporting date. It is calculated by dividing basic earnings (numerator) by the weighted average number of ordinary shares outstanding during the period (denominator):

$$\frac{\text{Basic earnings as adjusted}}{\text{(Weighted average number of ordinary shares outstanding)}}$$

32.4.2 **Basic earnings (numerator)** is profit or loss attributable to ordinary equity holders and (if presented) profit or loss from continuing operations attributable to those equity holders adjusted for the effect of preference dividends.

32.4.3 The effect of preference shares on earnings includes the following:

- the deduction of the after-tax amount of **noncumulative preference dividends** actually declared for the period;
- the deduction of the full after-tax amount of **cumulative preference dividends** for the period, whether declared or not;
- the deduction of any after-tax interest expense on preference shares classified as liabilities;
- the discount on any preference shares issued at a discount (that is, the amount that is amortized to retained earnings as this is regarded as a deemed dividend);
- for preference shares that also participate in the profits remaining after all preference dividends have been paid out (that is, participatory preference shares), the amount of profits attributable to them, which must be deducted to calculate basic earnings;
- for preference shares that are repurchased from the holders in the period, the difference between the consideration paid for the repurchase and the carrying amount of the shares, which is deducted from earnings if a loss is made and added to earnings if a profit is made; and
- the deduction of any excess fair value of ordinary shares issued on the early conversion of preference shares to ordinary shares within the period.

32.4.4 When calculating the weighted average number of shares (denominator), the following aspects should be considered:

- The **weighted number of shares** is the average number of ordinary shares outstanding during the period (that is, the number of ordinary shares outstanding at the beginning of the period, adjusted by those bought back or issued during the period). This number is multiplied by a time-weighting factor.
- The **time-weighting factor** is the number of days that the shares are outstanding during the period in proportion to the total number of days in the period. A reasonable approximation of the weighted average is adequate.

▓ Contingently **issuable ordinary shares** are ordinary shares issuable at no consideration or for consideration which is lower than the market value, upon the satisfaction of specified conditions. These shares are included in the computation of basic earnings per share, but only from the date when all necessary conditions have been satisfied.

▓ The number of shares for **current** and all **previous periods** presented should be adjusted for changes in shares without a corresponding change in resources (for example, bonus issue and share split).

▓ The number of **ordinary shares** should be adjusted for all periods prior to a rights issue (which includes a bonus element), multiplied by the following adjusting factor:

$$\frac{\text{Fair value per share immediately prior to the exercise of rights}}{\text{Theoretical ex-rights fair value per share}}$$

Theoretical ex-rights fair value per share calculation:

$$\frac{\substack{\text{Fair value of all outstanding shares before rights issue} \\ \text{+ total amount received from rights issued}}}{\text{Number of shares before rights issue + number of shares in rights issue}}$$

TABLE 32.1   Calculation of Weighted Average Number of Shares

Shares	Effect on number of shares	Effect on current period number of shares	Effect of current period on prior period number of shares
Opening balance of ordinary shares in issue	Starting point of calculation	Adjusted closing balance of prior period	None
Normal issue of ordinary shares during current period for cash	Increase	From date consideration receivable multiplied by the number of days in issue over 365	None
Issue of shares as consideration for business combination	Increase	From date of acquisition multiplied by the number of days in issue over 365	None
Issue of mandatorily convertible preference shares or debentures	Increase	From date of issue even though not converted yet multiplied by the number of days in issue over 365	None
Contingently issuable ordinary shares	Increase	Once all conditions are met multiplied by the number of days in issue over 365	None
Ordinary shares with contingent recall	Increase	Only from date no longer subject to recall multiplied by the number of days over 365	None
Share splits and reverse share splits; that is, current shares are split into more shares of a lower value or fewer shares of a higher value	Increase if share split Decrease if reverse share split	The number of shares comprising the increase or decrease is the total number before the split less the total number after the split	The number of shares comprising the increase or decrease is the total number before the split less the total number after the split. This must be the same total at end as current year

TABLE 32.1 Calculation of Weighted Average Number of Shares *(continued)*

Shares	Effect on number of shares	Effect on current period number of shares	Effect of current period on prior period number of shares
Capitalization or bonus issue; that is, when additional ordinary shares are issued to existing shareholders for no consideration in proportion to their current holdings	Increase	Number of shares up to the date of capitalization issue divided by the number of shares issued for every share held	Total number at period end divided by number of shares for every share held
Rights issue at less than fair value; that is, when the entity issues shares at less than their fair value	Increase	Number of shares before rights issue multiplied by the adjusting factor for the number of days over 365. This is then added to the number of shares per rights issue for the number of days over 365	Total number at period end multiplied by the adjusting factor
Ordinary shares issued after reporting date before authorization of financial statements for issue	If at fair value: there is no effect If at less than fair value: change the number as above	See above dependent in type of issue	See above: dependent on type of issue

Diluted Earnings per Share

32.4.5 Diluted earnings per share is the profit or loss attributable to each ordinary and **potential ordinary share** in issue at reporting date. It is calculated by adjusting the basic earnings per share calculation for the effect of **dilutive** potential ordinary shares:

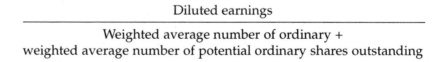

$$\frac{\text{Diluted earnings}}{\text{Weighted average number of ordinary } + \text{ weighted average number of potential ordinary shares outstanding}}$$

32.4.6 Diluted earnings (numerator) is the profit or loss attributable to ordinary equity holders of the parent entity and (if presented) profit or loss from continuing operations attributable to those equity holders, adjusted for the effects of all dilutive potential ordinary shares.

32.4.7 Diluted earnings consist of the basic earnings *adjusted for after-tax effects* of the following items associated with dilutive potential ordinary shares:

- dividends or other related items (for example, the savings in preference dividends) that would not be distributed if the convertible preference shares were already converted;
- interest recognized for the period (for example, the interest savings on convertible debentures if they were already converted); and
- other changes in income or expense that would result from a conversion of the shares (for example, the savings on interest related to these shares, which can increase expenses for a non-discretionary employee profit-sharing plan).

32.4.8 The weighted average number of shares (denominator) used for basic earnings per share is adjusted by the weighted average number of ordinary shares that would be issued on conversion of all dilutive potential ordinary shares. These shares are deemed to have been converted into ordinary shares at the beginning of the period or, if actually converted in the current year, at the date the shares were issued.

The following adjustments are made to the **weighted number of shares:**

- Include the number of all dilutive potential ordinary shares issued in prior periods that have not yet been converted. These shares are not weighted; that is, the full number is included for the entire period unless they are converted, lapse, or cancel within the current period.
- Include new issues of dilutive potential ordinary shares in the current year, weighted for days in issue in the current period.
- Include dilutive potential ordinary shares allowed to lapse or that are cancelled in the current period weighted for period before lapse.
- Include dilutive potential ordinary shares that have converted in the current period as part of diluted earnings per share for the period up to conversion. Thereafter include these shares in basic earnings per share as actual ordinary shares in issue.
- Include contingently issuable shares at the number that would have been issued if the conditions were already met. If these conditions are in fact met in the current period, include the amount in diluted earnings per share only up until the date the actual shares are issued.

32.4.9 Potential ordinary shares are treated as dilutive only when their conversion to ordinary shares would decrease earnings per share (or increase loss per share) from *continuing operations*. In determining whether potential ordinary shares are dilutive or anti-dilutive, and whether they should be included in the weighted average number of shares or not, each series of potential ordinary shares in a period must be considered separately. The separately determined dilutive shares are then put in sequence from the most to the least dilutive.

32.4.10 Basic earnings per share and diluted earnings per share for all periods presented are adjusted for the effect of

- prior period errors; or
- changes in accounting policies.

TABLE 32.2   Dilutive Potential Ordinary Shares and Their Effect on the Weighted Average Number of Shares

Potential ordinary shares	Effect on number of shares	Test for and sequence of dilution
Dilutive warrants and options	It must be assumed that they will all be converted or exercised. Increase the weighted average number of shares by the shares deemed to be issued for no consideration (that is, the difference between the number of shares to be issued in terms of the contracts and the number that would have been issued at average market period in order to raise the same proceeds as the options or warrants).	These items are dilutive when they would result in the issue of the ordinary shares for less than average market price for the shares. These are mostly dilutive as they have no effect on earnings.
Convertible preference shares or debentures	Increase the weighted average number of shares by the expected future increase in ordinary shares resulting from the conversion.	These items are dilutive when the dividends or interest after tax per ordinary share receivable is less than basic earnings per share.* This would increase earnings with the after-tax future saving in dividends or interest when these items are converted.
Contingently issuable shares (see definition)	Assume the end of the reporting period is the end of the contingency period. Increase weighted average number of shares that will be issued when the conditions are met. Include them until the conditions are met (after which they are included in basic earnings per share).	These items are dilutive when the issue will decrease basic earnings per share.* These are most dilutive as they have no effect on earnings.
Contracts that can be settled in ordinary shares (such as convertible debentures)	If the entity has the option to settle in equity: all the shares are included unless it is the entity's policy to settle in cash. If the holder has the option to settle in equity: shares are only included if the issue of shares is the most dilutive option.	These items are dilutive when the issue will decrease basic earnings per share.* Increase in earnings by any changes in profit or loss if the contract was wholly equity.
Written put options, that is, the right of holder to have the entity repurchase the shares at a fixed price in future	Increase the weighted average number of shares with all shares that must be issued at beginning of year to make the proceeds to buy back shares, that is, the number of shares that will probably be bought back (assume they will all be exercised).	These items are dilutive when the entity has to buy them back at a price that is more than market price at the time. These are mostly dilutive as they have no effect on earnings.
Purchased options	None as they will always be anti-dilutive. The entity cannot be assumed to exercise as it will act in its own benefit, and a decreased earnings per share is not beneficial.	These items will always be anti-dilutive.

The control earnings per share used to determine the dilutive effect and sequence of dilution is calculated as follows:

$$\frac{Profit\ from\ continuing\ operations\ only}{Weighted\ average\ number\ of\ shares\ for\ basic\ earnings\ per\ share}$$

32.5   **PRESENTATION AND DISCLOSURE**

32.5.1 Basic and diluted earnings per share are shown with equal prominence on the face of the Statement of Comprehensive Income for **each** class of ordinary shares with different rights. Information presented should include:

- profit or loss from continuing operations attributable to ordinary equity holders of the parent entity;
- profit or loss attributable to ordinary equity holders of the parent entity; and
- any reported discontinued operation.

32.5.2 Basic and diluted **losses** per share are disclosed when they occur.

32.5.3 Amounts used as numerators for basic and diluted earnings per share and a reconciliation of those amounts to the net profit or loss for the period should be disclosed.

32.5.4 The weighted average number of ordinary shares used as the denominator in calculating basic and diluted earnings per share, and a reconciliation of these denominators to each other, must be disclosed.

32.5.5 If an earnings per share figure in addition to that required by IAS 33 is disclosed, the following effects must be disclosed:

- The amounts shall be calculated using the weighted average number of shares determined in accordance with IAS 33.
- Related basic and diluted amounts per share should be disclosed with equal prominence.
- That figure should be disclosed in the notes
- The basis on which the numerator is determined should be indicated, including whether amounts are before or after tax.
- A reconciliation of the numerator and reported line item should be provided in the Statement of Comprehensive Income.
- The same denominator should be used as for basic earnings per share or dilutive earnings per share (as appropriate).

32.6   **FINANCIAL ANALYSIS AND INTERPRETATION**

32.6.1 When discussing companies, investors and others commonly refer to **earnings per share.** If a company has a simple capital structure, one that contains no convertible bonds or preferred shares, no warrants or options, and no contingent shares, it will present only its **basic earnings per share.**

32.6.2 For complex capital structures, **both basic earnings per share and diluted earnings per share** are generally reported. A complex capital structure is one where the company does have one or more of the following types of securities: convertible bonds, preferred shares, warrants, options, and contingent shares.

32.7   COMMENTARY

32.7.1 Earnings per share of a company is a very important indicator of performance used by investors in analyzing companies as it is a base part of the price-earnings ratio. Investors may estimate the fair value of the shares of a company by referring to the earnings per share alone. This figure could also be applied as a benchmark in due diligence assessments before mergers and other similar transactions are entered into. As companies may possibly reflect a growth in profits without a corresponding growth in earnings per share, their earnings per share figures will be more reliable to investors as a measurement of company performance. It is thus of vital importance that the amounts disclosed are accurately calculated.

32.7.2 Dividends per share is also a useful tool in analyzing company performance and potential returns. It can be used by investors as an indicator of the dividend policy of the company. There is no specific standard that deals with the calculation and disclosure of dividends per share, nor is this topic covered by IAS 33. Reference is made in IAS 1, which states that dividends per share must be disclosed on the face of the income statement or in the notes to the financial statements. There is no guidance on how to calculate this amount but generally accepted practice is as follows:

$$\frac{\text{Dividends for the current period}}{\text{Actual ordinary shares in issue at date of payment}}$$

32.7.3 The IASB embarked on a project to simplify earnings per share and converge the current requirements with those of U.S. GAAP. An exposure draft to this effect was issued in December 2008. The main proposals in this exposure draft included the following:

- provide a clear principle to determine which instruments are included in the calculation;
- clarify the calculation for particular instruments such as contracts for a company to repurchase its own shares;
- amend the calculation of diluted earnings per share for participating instruments and two-class ordinary shares; and
- simplify the calculation for instruments that are accounted for at fair value through profit or loss.

32.7.4 In an April 2009 meeting of the IASB it was discussed, based on the comments received on the exposure draft, whether this project should be continued, delayed, or discontinued. Many of the respondents to the exposure draft commented that the IASB should suspend this project until it finalizes the project on financial instruments and financial presentation as these have a direct impact on earnings per share calculations. The IASB did not favor discontinuing the project but agreed to suspend work on the project until the consolidation project was complete, after which work would continue on finalizing the exposure draft. Currently there have been no revisions or amendments of IAS 33 related to this project.

32.8   **IMPLEMENTATION DECISIONS**

The following table sets out some of the strategic and tactical decisions that should be considered when applying IAS 33.

Strategic decisions	Tactical decisions	Problems to overcome
Management must determine if the entity falls within the scope and has to apply this standard.	Processes must be in place to identify the related statutory requirements that support or override this requirement. Legal assistance must be obtained where possible.	Accounting and other statutory disclosure requirements may not always be the same but are equally important. Care must be taken to ensure they do not contradict each other in the disclosures made.
	Adjustments that may be required to earnings such as preference shares must be identified.	
	All instruments that are currently convertible into ordinary shares, or any other potential ordinary shares that may have a dilutive effect, must be identified.	

EXAMPLES: EARNINGS PER SHARE

EXAMPLE 32.1

The issued and fully paid share capital of Angli Inc., unchanged since the date of incorporation until the financial year ended March 31, 20X4, include the following:

- 1,200,000 ordinary shares with no par value
- 300,000 6% participating preference shares of $1 each

The corporation has been operating at a profit for a number of years. As a result of a very conservative dividend policy in previous years, there is a large accumulated profit balance on the Statement of Financial Position. On July 1, 20X4, the directors decided to issue to all ordinary shareholders two capitalization shares for every one previously held.

The following abstract was taken from the (noncompliant) consolidated Statement of Comprehensive Income for the year ending March 31, 20X5:

	20×5 $	20×4 $
Profit after Tax	400,000	290,000
Noncontrolling interest (not IFRS compliant)	(30,000)	(20,000)
Net Profit from Ordinary Activities	370,000	270,000
Extraordinary Item (not IFRS compliant)	–	(10,000)
Profit for the Year	370,000	260,000

The following dividends have been paid or declared at the end of the reported periods:

	20×5 $	20×4 $
Ordinary	165,000	120,000
Preference	34,500	30,000

The participating preference shareholders are entitled to share profits in the same ratio in which they share dividends, after payment of the fixed preference dividend. The shareholders will share the same benefits if the company is liquidated.

EXPLANATION

The earnings per share (required by IAS 33) and the dividends per share (required by IAS 1) to be presented in the group financial statements for the year ending March 31, 20X5, are calculated as follows:

	20×5	20×4
EARNINGS PER SHARE		
Attributable earnings (Calculation b)		
divided by weighted number of shares (Calculation c)		
Ordinary Shares	320,000	220,000
	3,600,000	3,600,000
	= $0.089	= $0.061
Participating Preference Shares		
	50,000	40,000
	300,000	300,000
	= $0.167	= $0.133

	20×5	20×4
DIVIDENDS PER SHARE		
Dividends divided by actual number of shares in issue		
Ordinary Shares	165,000	120,000
(20×4 adjusted for the capitalization issue for the purposes of comparability)	3,600,000	3,600,000
	= $0.046	= $0.033
Preference Shares	34,500	30,000
	300,000	300,000
	= $0.115	= $0.10

CALCULATIONS

a. Percentage of profits attributable to classes of equity shares

	20×5	20×4
Total preference dividend	34,500	30,000
Fixed portion (6% x $300,000)	(18,000)	(18,000)
	16,500	12,000
Dividend paid to ordinary shareholders	165,000	120,000

Therefore, the participating preference shareholders share profits in the ratio 1:10 with the ordinary shareholders after payment of the fixed preference dividend out of profits.

b. Earnings per class of share

	20×5 $	20×4 $
Net profit for the period	370,000	260,000
Fixed preference dividend	(18,000)	(18,000)
	352,000	242,000
Attributable to ordinary shareholders: 10/11	320,000	220,000
Attributable to participating preference shareholders: 1/11	2,000	22,000
Fixed dividend	18,000	18,000
	50,000	40,000

c. Weighted number of ordinary shares in issue

	20×5 Shares	20×4 Shares
Balance, April 1, 20X3	1,200,000	1,200,000
Capitalization issue	2,400,000	2,400,000
	3,600,000	3,600,000

EXAMPLE 32.2

L. J. Pathmark reported net earnings of $250,000 for the year ending 20X1. The company had 125,000 shares of $1 par value common stock and 30,000 shares of $40 par value convertible preference shares outstanding during the year. The dividend rate on the preference shares was $2 per share. Each share of the convertible preference shares can be converted into two shares of L. J. Pathmark Class A common shares. During the year no convertible preference shares were converted.

What were L. J. Pathmark's basic earnings per share?

a. $0.89 per share
b. $1.52 per share
c. $1.76 per share
d. $2.00 per share

EXPLANATION

Choice b. is correct. The answer was derived from the following calculation:

$$\text{Basic earnings per share} = \frac{(\text{Net income} - \text{preference dividends})}{(\text{Weighted average common shares})}$$

$$= \frac{\$250,000 - (\$2 \times 30,000 \text{ shares})}{125,000 \text{ shares}}$$

$$= \frac{\$190,000}{125,000}$$

$$= \$1.52 \text{ per share}$$

Choice a. is incorrect. This answer does not correctly apply the formula above.

Choice c. is incorrect. The preference dividends were improperly determined by using the shares (only), and not deriving a dollar dividend.

Choice d. is incorrect. When determining the basic earnings per share, preference dividends were not subtracted.

EXAMPLE 32.3

L. J. Pathmark reported net earnings of $250,000 for the year ending 20X1. The company had 125,000 shares of $1 par value common stock and 30,000 shares of $40 par value convertible preference shares outstanding during the year. The dividend rate on the preference shares was $2 per share. Each share of the convertible preference shares can be converted into two shares of L. J. Pathmark Class A common shares. During the year no convertible preference shares were converted.

What were L. J. Pathmark's diluted earnings per share?

a. $0.70 per share.
b. $1.35 per share.
c. $1.68 per share.
d. $2.00 per share.

EXPLANATION

Choice b. is correct. The answer was derived from the following calculation:

$$\text{Diluted earnings per share} = \frac{(\text{Net income} - \text{preference dividends} + \text{Dividends on converted securities})}{(\text{Shares outstanding} + \text{Additional shares if securities were converted})}$$

$$= \frac{\$250,000 - \$60,000 + \$60,000)}{125,000 + (30,000)}$$

$$= \frac{\$250,000}{185,000}$$

$$= \underline{\$1.35 \text{ per share}}$$

Choice a. is incorrect. Dividends on converted securities were incorrectly subtracted in the numerator.

Choice c. is incorrect. Preference dividends were ignored in the numerator of the calculation.

Choice d. is incorrect. This represents an incorrect application of both fully diluted and basic earnings per share, as net income is divided by shares outstanding.

CHAPTER 33

Financial Instruments: Presentation (IAS 32)

Note: IAS 32, IAS 39, and IFRS 7 were issued as separate standards but are applied in practice as a unit because they all deal with the accounting for and disclosure of financial instruments.

33.1   OBJECTIVE

IAS 32 establishes the principles for the classification of financial instruments as *financial assets, financial liabilities,* or *equity instruments.* This classification is an important aspect of accounting for financial instruments as it drives the recognition and measurement requirements of IAS 39 and the disclosure requirements of IFRS 7.

IAS 32 also provides guidance for the presentation of financial instruments in the financial statements, including requirements for offsetting financial assets and financial liabilities. Additionally, the standard deals with the accounting treatment of treasury shares.

The principles in IAS 32 complement the principles of recognition and measurement in IAS 39, and disclosure in IFRS 7.

33.2   SCOPE OF THE STANDARD

The standard deals with **all types of financial instruments**, both recognized and unrecognized, and should also be applied to contracts to buy or sell a nonfinancial item that **can be settled** net as follows:

- in cash;
- by another financial instrument; or
- by exchanging financial instruments, as if the contracts were financial instruments.

Presentation issues addressed by IAS 32 relate to:

- distinguishing financial liabilities from equity;
- classifying compound instruments;
- reporting interest, dividends, losses, and gains; and
- offsetting of financial assets and liabilities.

IAS 32 applies to all financial instruments, except:

- interests in subsidiaries, associates, and joint ventures (covered by, respectively, IAS 27, Consolidated and Separate Financial Statements; IAS 28, Investments in Associates; and IAS 31, Joint Ventures);
- employers' rights and obligations arising from employee benefit plans (IAS 19, Employee Benefits);
- financial instruments within the scope of IFRS 2, Share-Based Payments (if the way in which a company structures its share-based payment scheme involves the acquisition of its own shares, for example a share trust, those treasury shares will be in the scope of IAS 32; judgment will have to be applied on a case by case basis to determine whether a share-based payment scheme does result in treasury shares);
- contracts for contingent consideration in a business combination (IFRS 3, Business Combinations); and
- insurance contracts and financial instruments within the scope of IFRS 4, Insurance Contracts (except for derivatives that are embedded in insurance contracts if IAS 39 requires the entity to account for them separately).

33.3   KEY CONCEPTS

33.3.1 A **financial instrument** is any contract that gives rise to a financial asset in one entity and a financial liability or equity instrument in another entity.

33.3.2 A **financial asset** is any asset that is:

- cash (for example, cash deposited at a bank);
- an equity instrument of another entity;
- a contractual right to receive cash or a financial asset (for example, the right of a debtor);
- a contractual right to exchange financial instruments under conditions that are potentially favorable to the entity; or
- a contract that will or may be settled in an entity's own equity instruments and is:
  - a nonderivative for which the entity is or may be obliged to receive a variable number of the entity's own equity instruments; or
  - a derivative that will or may be settled other than by the exchange of a fixed amount of cash or another financial asset for a fixed number of the entity's own equity instruments.

Physical assets (for example, inventories and patents) are not financial assets because they do not give rise to a present contractual right to receive cash or other financial assets.

33.3.3 A **financial liability** is a contractual obligation to:

- deliver cash or another financial asset to another entity;
- exchange financial instruments with another entity under conditions that are potentially unfavorable to the entity; or
- a contract that will or may be settled in the entity's own equity instruments and is:
  - a nonderivative for which the entity is or may be obliged to deliver a variable number of the entity's own equity instruments; or
  - a derivative that will or may be settled other than by the exchange of a fixed amount of cash or another financial asset for a fixed number of the entity's own equity instruments.

Liabilities imposed by statutory requirements (for example, income taxes) are not financial liabilities because they are not contractual.

33.3.4 An **equity instrument** is any contract that evidences a residual interest in the assets of an entity after deducting all of its liabilities. An obligation to issue an equity instrument is not a financial liability because it results in an increase in equity and cannot result in a loss to the entity.

33.3.5 **Fair value** is the amount for which an asset could be exchanged, or a liability settled, between knowledgeable, willing parties in an arm's-length transaction.

33.4   PRESENTATION

33.4.1 The issuer of a financial instrument should classify the instrument, or its component parts, **on initial recognition** as a financial liability, a financial asset, or an equity instrument in accordance with the substance of the contractual arrangement and the definitions of a financial liability, a financial asset, and an equity instrument.

33.4.2 In order for an instrument to be classified as an equity instrument the instrument should not include any contractual obligation to pay cash or another financial asset or exchange financial assets and financial liabilities under potentially unfavorable conditions. If this instrument will or may be settled in the issuer's own equity, then the contract must result in the issue of a fixed number of shares for a fixed amount of cash. If either the number of shares or the amount of cash is variable, then the instrument is a financial liability and not an equity instrument.

33.4.3 A financial instrument that is puttable by the holder is classified as an equity instrument if it has all of the following features:

- It entitles the holder to a pro rata share of the entity's net assets in the event of liquidation of the entity, where the entity's net assets are those that remain after deducting all other claims on its assets.
- The instrument is in the class of instruments that is subordinate to all other classes of instruments.
- All financial instruments in the class of instruments that is subordinate to all other classes of instruments have identical features.
- Apart from the contractual obligation of the issuer to repurchase or redeem the instrument for cash or another financial asset, the instrument does not include any contractual obligation to deliver cash or another financial asset or exchange financial assets under conditions that potentially are unfavorable.
- The total expected cash flows attributable to the instruments over the life of the instrument are based substantially on the profit or loss, the change in recognized net assets, or the change in fair value of the recognized and unrecognized net assets of the entity over the life of the instrument.

33.4.4 The classification of instruments as financial liabilities or equities requires judgment and is based on the substance of a financial instrument and not its legal form. There is an exception for instruments described in 33.4.5 below.

33.4.5 An instrument is not necessarily equity just because it may be settled by the delivery of an entity's own equity instruments. Such instruments are only classified as equity if the result is the entity transferring a fixed number of equity instruments for a fixed amount of cash. As soon as either the number of equity instruments or the amount of cash is variable the contract does not evidence a residual interest in the entity's net assets and is accordingly classified as a financial liability.

33.4.6 A financial instrument may require an entity to deliver cash or other financial asset in the event of the occurrence or nonoccurrence of uncertain future events that are beyond the control of the issuer and the holder of the instruments. Because the entity does not have an unconditional right to avoid the delivery of cash or another financial asset, the instrument is a financial liability unless the contingent settlement provisions are not genuine or settlement would only occur on the liquidation of the entity.

33.4.7 The issuer of a **compound financial instrument** that contains **both** a liability and equity component (for example, convertible bonds) should classify the instrument's component parts separately. The equity component is the difference between the consideration received and the fair value of the liability component. The fair value of the liability component is determined as the present value of the contractual cash flows discounted at the market rate of interest for a similar instrument but without the conversion option. Once a financial instrument has been classified the classification is not changed, even if economic circumstances change. No gain or loss arises from recognizing and presenting the parts separately.

33.4.8 Interest, dividends, losses, and gains relating to a financial liability should be reported in the Statement of Comprehensive Income as expense or income. Distributions to holders of equity instruments should be debited directly to equity. The classification of the financial instrument therefore determines its accounting treatment in the Statement of Comprehensive Income:

- Dividends on shares classified as liabilities would thus be classified as an expense in the same way that interest payments on a loan are classified as an expense.
- Gains and losses (premiums and discounts) on redemption or refinancing of instruments classified as liabilities are reported in the Statement of Comprehensive Income.

33.4.9 A financial asset and a financial liability should be **offset** only when:

- a currently enforceable legal right to set off exists, and
- an intention exists to either settle on a net basis or to realize the asset and settle the related liability simultaneously.

33.4.10 Treasury shares are equity instruments that an entity or other members of the consolidated group hold in itself. Treasury shares should be deducted from equity and no gain or loss on such transactions may be recognized. The amount of treasury shares should be disclosed.

33.5   **DISCLOSURE**

33.5.1 See chapter 34 (IFRS 7) for information about disclosure requirements.

33.6   **COMMENTARY**

33.6.1 If an instrument is classified as a financial liability it is because the entity is obligated to make certain cash payments in respect of the balance. If an instrument is classified as equity, cash flows in respect of that instrument are entirely at the discretion of the entity. The debt equity classification therefore illustrates what cash flows the entity is obligated to make in the future and what cash flows the entity can exercise discretion in making in the future. This information provides some insight into the amount, timing, and uncertainty related to future cash flows.

33.6.2 The rules relating to offsetting of financial assets and liabilities ensure that the presentation of financial information is consistent with how the instrument will be settled. This provides users of financial statements with information about the expected cash flows that arise from settling a financial instrument.

33.6.3 The classification of instruments as equity or liability requires significant judgment, particularly for complex or compound instruments. Each instrument should be assessed on a case-by-case basis and the contractual terms compared to the definitions in IAS 32.

33.6.4 The offset rules also require the application of judgment, especially in considering whether the intention to settle on a net basis or to realize the asset and settle the related liability simultaneously exists. The offset should be assessed on a case-by-case basis and the terms of the agreements, as well as the entity's business practice and intention, must be considered.

33.6.5 In response to criticism in respect of IAS 32 and whether the rules provide appropriate classification of amounts as equity or liabilities, the IASB and the FASB undertook a project on the classification of financial instruments with characteristics of equity. A discussion paper was issued early in 2008 and an exposure draft is expected to be issued in the second quarter of 2010. This is a project being undertaken in terms of the memorandum of understanding between the IASB and FASB.

33.7 IMPLEMENTATION DECISIONS

The following table sets out some of the strategic and tactical decisions that should be considered when applying IAS 32.

Strategic decisions	Tactical decisions	Problems to overcome
Management should confirm the extent to which the entity may hold treasury shares. Management should also have a thorough understanding of the impact on the capital ratios and whether this impacts any of the regulatory requirements. Management may decide that there are only specific circumstances under which treasury shares may be acquired.	Processes should be put in place to identify and monitor the extent of investments in treasury shares.	Treasury shares may be difficult to identify and could have a significant impact on profit or loss, particularly when the shares are held on behalf of third parties, for example in sinking fund policies. The effect of IAS 32 is that the full sinking fund liability is reflected at fair value through profit or loss whereas the assets held to back that liability are not reflected in the statement of financial position.
Management may decide on a target debt/equity ratio that it would like to maintain. Certain instruments classified as equity pre-IFRS may be classified as debt under IFRS. This could negatively impact the debt equity ratios and could potentially result in the entity breaking certain covenants. This could also impact the regulatory capital held and the entity's compliance with the regulatory requirements.	The classification of all debt and equity items should be performed at initial recognition in line with the guidance in IAS 32.	IAS 32 requires the classification of instruments as debt or equity based on their substance rather than their legal form. This can result in instruments having the legal form of equity being classified as debt.
Management should decide to what extent they would like to make use of the offsetting requirements in IAS 32.	For contracts where the current legal right of set off exists, the entity should decide whether or not to settle net and consider how that intention can be demonstrated.	Both the current legal right to set off and the intention to settle simultaneously or net should be present before set off may be applied. The absence of one of those aspects will result in gross presentation of financial assets and liabilities.

CHAPTER 34

Financial Instruments: Disclosures
(IFRS 7)

34.1 | **OBJECTIVE**

Users of financial statements need information about an entity's exposure to risks and how those risks are managed. Such information can influence a user's assessment of the financial position and financial performance of an entity or of the amount, timing, and uncertainty of its future cash flows. Greater transparency regarding those risks allows users to make more informed judgments about risk and return.

IFRS 7 adopts a dichotomous approach to disclosures in respect of financial instruments. The first part of the standard requires entities to provide disclosures in their financial statements that enable users to evaluate the **significance of financial instruments** for the entity's financial position and performance. The second part of the standard requires entities to disclose quantitative and qualitative information about the **nature and extent of risks** arising from financial instruments to which they are exposed during the period under review and at the reporting date, and how they manage those risks.

34.2 | **SCOPE OF THE STANDARD**

IFRS 7 applies to all entities and for all financial instruments, whether recognized or unrecognized. This includes, for example, some loan commitments and other instruments falling outside the direct scope of IAS 39, as well as contracts to buy and sell nonfinancial items that are in the scope of IAS 39. The forward purchase of wheat is an example. If the contract can be settled net and the wheat will not be consumed or sold in the entity's ordinary course of business, then it is considered to be a derivative. If the wheat will be used in the ordinary course of business, by a miller for example, then the forward purchase agreement will be excluded from the scope of IAS 39. Other scope exclusions include the following:

- interests in subsidiaries, associates, and joint ventures (IAS 27, 28, and 31);
- employers' rights and obligations arising from employee benefit plans (IAS 19);
- contracts for contingent consideration in a business combination (IFRS 3);
- insurance contracts as defined in IFRS 4 (except for derivatives that are embedded in insurance contracts if IAS 39 requires the entity to account for them separately); and
- financial instruments, contracts, and obligations under share-based payment transactions (IFRS 2).

367

IFRS 7 requires disclosure of the following:

■ the significance of financial instruments, in each category of asset (assets held at fair value through profit and loss, assets available for sale, assets held to maturity, and loans and receivables) or liability (liabilities at fair value and liabilities shown at amortized cost), and by class of instrument;

■ the carrying values of financial assets and financial liabilities;

■ the nature and extent of the risk exposures arising from financial instruments used by the entity;

■ qualitative and quantitative information about exposure to credit risk, liquidity risk, and market risk arising from financial instruments; and

■ management information regarding exposures to credit and liquidity risk.

34.3   KEY CONCEPTS

34.3.1 Four categories of financial assets: The four categories of financial assets are defined in IAS 39: assets carried at fair value through profit and loss, held-to-maturity securities, available-for-sale securities, and loans and receivables.

34.3.2 Two categories of financial liabilities: IAS 39 defines two categories of financial liabilities: liabilities carried at fair value through profit and loss, and liabilities measured at amortized cost (see also chapter 17).

34.3.3 Classes of financial instruments: IFRS 7 introduces the concept of providing disclosures based on classes of financial instruments. The classes of financial instruments are distinct from the categories defined in IAS 39. When determining the classes of financial instruments for disclosure entities should consider:

■ the appropriate classification based on the nature of the information disclosed; and
■ the characteristics of those financial instruments.

34.3.4 Reconciliations: Sufficient information must be provided to enable reconciliations between the disclosures and the line items presented in the Statement of Financial Position.

34.4   ACCOUNTING TREATMENT/DISCLOSURE OVERVIEW

34.4.1 Overview of disclosure requirements (see figure 34.1 and table 34.1). IFRS 7 requires a determination of the significance of key disclosures, as well as the financial instruments affected, for the financial position and performance of an entity. In addition, the qualitative and quantitative nature and extent of risks arising from financial instruments must be disclosed.

34.4.2 Overview of Statement of Financial Position disclosure (see table 34.2). The carrying values of all financial assets and liabilities must be disclosed. The broad categories of Statement of Financial Position disclosures relate to credit risk and related collateral issues, recognition and reclassification issues, liabilities with embedded options, and loans payable but in default.

34.4.3 Overview of Statement of Comprehensive Income disclosure (see table 34.3). Statement of Comprehensive Income disclosures focus on net gains and losses on financial assets and liabilities. The disclosures require a split between the different classes of assets and liabilities—specifically to enable the reader to distinguish between those instruments that have been designated fair value through profit or loss, those that are traded, and those that are measured at amortized cost.

FIGURE 34.1   Overview of the IFRS 7 Reporting Requirements

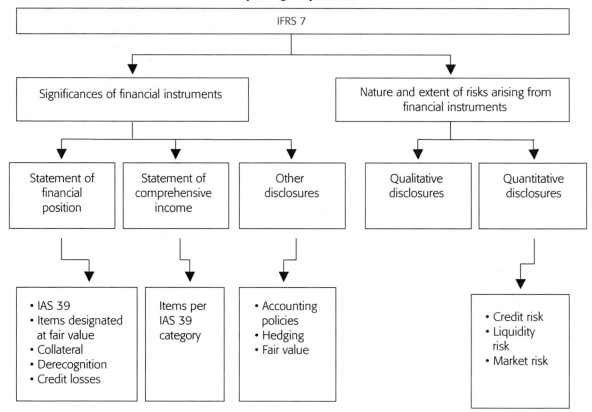

TABLE 34.1   Information to Be Disclosed and Financial Instruments Affected

Information to be Disclosed and Financial Instruments Affected

A. Determination of Significance (for example, evidenced by carrying value) for Financial Position and Performance

A1. Statement of Financial Position

A2. Statement of Comprehensive Income and Equity

A3. Other Disclosures—accounting policies, hedge accounting, and fair value

B. Nature and Extent of Risks Arising from Financial Instruments

B1. Qualitative disclosures (nature and how arising)—not necessarily by instrument

B2. Quantitative disclosures

34.4.4 Overview of other disclosure types (see table 34.4). IFRS 7 also requires that the annual financial statements provide information regarding the accounting policies and measurement bases adopted in respect of financial instruments. In addition, detailed disclosure relating to all hedges for which hedge accounting is applied is required. For all instruments not measured at fair value disclosure is required of what their fair value is. For financial instruments that are measured at fair value, an entity is required to disclose the methods and assumptions used in determining fair value and the level of the fair value hierarchy into which the valuation falls.

TABLE 34.2   Overview of Statement of Financial Position Disclosures

IAS 39 categories	Instruments	Statement of Financial Position disclosures applicable to all instruments	Specific disclosures required for the Statement of Financial Position
Financial Assets			
Fair value through profit or loss	Derivatives	Carrying value	Derecognition
	Instruments held for trading	Carrying value	Reclassification Derecognition
	Instruments designated at fair value	Carrying value	Fair value movements attributable to credit risk Derecognition
Fair value through other comprehensive income	Available for sale debt instruments	Carrying value	Reclassification Derecognition Collateral held
	Available for sale equity instruments	Carrying value	Derecognition
Amortized cost instruments	Held to maturity	Carrying value	Reclassification Derecognition Collateral held Allowance account for credit losses
	Loans and receivables	Carrying value	Derecognition Collateral held Allowance account for credit losses
Financial Liabilities			
Fair value through profit or loss	Derivatives	Carrying value	Collateral pledged
	Instruments held for trading	Carrying value	Collateral pledged
	Instruments designated at fair value	Carrying value	Fair value movements attributable to credit risk Collateral pledged Details of multiple embedded derivatives Defaults and breaches
Amortized cost	Liabilities at amortised cost	Carrying value	Collateral pledged Defaults and breaches

34.4.5 Overview of disclosure of nature and extent of risks arising from financial instruments. Once the entity has complied with Statement of Financial Position and Statement of Comprehensive Income disclosures, the user needs qualitative and quantitative information regarding the different types of risks arising from all financial instruments, as well as specific quantitative information with regard to credit, liquidity, and market risks. Table 34.5 summarizes the required disclosures of risk.

TABLE 34.3   Overview of Statement of Comprehensive Income Disclosure

IAS 39 categories	Instruments	Statement of Comprehensive Income disclosures Profit or loss	Statement of Comprehensive Income disclosures Other comprehensive income
Financial Assets			
Fair value through profit or loss	Derivatives	Net gains or losses included in the net gains or losses on instruments held for trading, unless specifically designated as a hedging instrument	
	Instruments held for trading	Net gains or losses presented separately from instruments designated at fair value	
	Instruments designated at fair value	Net gains or losses presented separately from instruments classified as held for trading	
Fair value through other comprehensive income	Available for sale debt instruments	Amounts reclassified from other comprehensive income into profit or loss Total interest income Fee income and expense Impairment losses Interest income on impaired assets	Amount of gains or losses recognized in other comprehensive income
	Available for sale equity instruments	Amounts reclassified from other comprehensive income into profit or loss Fee income and expense Impairment losses Interest income on impaired assets	Amount of gains or losses recognized in other comprehensive income
Amortized cost instruments	Held to maturity	Net gains or losses Total interest income Fee income and expense Impairment losses Interest income on impaired assets	
	Loans and receivables	Net gains or losses Total interest income Fee income and expense Impairment losses Interest income on impaired assets	
Financial Liabilities			
Fair value through profit or loss	Derivatives	Net gains or losses included in the net gains or losses on instruments held for trading, unless specifically designated as a hedging instrument	
	Instruments held for trading	Net gains or losses presented separately from instruments designated at fair value	
	Instruments designated at fair value	Net gains or losses presented separately from instruments classified as held for trading	
Amortized cost	Liabilities at amortized cost	Net gains or losses Total interest expense Fee income and expense	

TABLE 34.4 Overview of Other Disclosure

IAS 39 categories	Instruments	Other disclosures		
		Accounting policies	Hedge accounting	Fair value
Financial Assets				
Fair value through profit or loss	Derivatives	How net gains or losses are determined Accounting policies for regular way transactions	Description of each type of hedge Description of hedging instruments and fair values at reporting date Nature of the risks being hedged	Description of how fair value is determined Levels of the fair value hierarchy into which the values are classified If the instruments fall into level 3 of the fair value hierarchy disclosures are required for the sensitivity of the valuation Reconciliation of day-one gains or losses not recognized if applicable
	Instruments held for trading	How net gains or losses are determined Accounting policies for regular way transactions		Description of how fair value is determined Levels of the fair value hierarchy into which the values are classified If the instruments fall into level 3 of the fair value hierarchy, disclosures are required for the sensitivity of the valuation Reconciliation of day-one gains or losses not recognized if applicable
	Instruments designated at fair value	Nature of instruments designated and how the criteria for designation in IAS 39 have been complied with How net gains or losses are determined Accounting policies for regular-way transactions		Description of how fair value is determined Levels of the fair value hierarchy into which the values are classified If the instruments fall into level 3 of the fair value hierarchy, disclosures are required for the sensitivity of the valuation Reconciliation of day-one gains or losses not recognized if applicable
Fair value through other comprehensive income	Available for sale debt instruments	The criteria used for designating instruments as available for sale Impairment policies Accounting policies for regular-way transactions How net gains or losses are determined		Levels of the fair value hierarchy into which the values are classified If the instruments fall into level 3 of the fair value hierarchy, disclosures are required for the sensitivity of the valuation Reconciliation of day-one gains or losses not recognized if applicable
	Available for sale equity instruments	The criteria used for designating instruments as available for sale Impairment policies Accounting policies for regular way transactions How net gains or losses are determined		Description of how fair value is determined Levels of the fair value hierarchy into which the values are classified If the instruments fall into level 3 of the fair value hierarchy, disclosures are required for the sensitivity of the valuation Reconciliation of day-one gains or losses not recognized if applicable

IAS 39 categories	Instruments	Other disclosures		
		Accounting policies	Hedge accounting	Fair value
Amortized cost instruments	Held to maturity	Impairment policies Accounting policies for regular way transactions How net gains or losses are determined Policy for renegotiated assets		Fair value of the instruments
	Loans and receivables	Impairment policies How net gains or losses are determined Policy for renegotiated assets		Fair value of the instruments
Financial Liabilities				
Fair value through profit or loss	Derivatives	Accounting policies for regular way transactions How net gains or losses are determined	Description of each type of hedge Description of hedging instruments and fair values at reporting date Nature of the risks being hedged	Description of how fair value is determined Levels of the fair value hierarchy into which the values are classified If the instruments fall into level 3 of the fair value hierarchy, disclosures are required for the sensitivity of the valuation Reconciliation of day-one gains or losses not recognized if applicable
	Instruments held for trading	Accounting policies for regular way transactions How net gains or losses are determined.		Description of how fair value is determined Levels of the fair value hierarchy into which the values are classified If the instruments fall into level 3 of the fair value hierarchy, disclosures are required for the sensitivity of the valuation Reconciliation of day-one gains or losses not recognized if applicable
	Instruments designated at fair value	Nature of instruments designated and how the criteria for designation in IAS 39 has been complied with How net gains or losses are determined	Description of each type of hedge Description of hedging instruments and fair values at reporting date Nature of the risks being hedged	Description of how fair value is determined Levels of the fair value hierarchy into which the values are classified If the instruments fall into level 3 of the fair value hierarchy, disclosures are required for the sensitivity of the valuation Reconciliation of day-one gains or losses not recognized if applicable
Amortized cost	Liabilities at amortized cost	How net gains or losses are determined	Description of each type of hedge Description of hedging instruments and fair values at reporting date Nature of the risks being hedged	Fair value of the instruments

TABLE 34.5 Nature and Extent of Risks Arising from Financial Instruments

IAS 39 categories	Instruments	Credit risk	Market risk	Liquidity risk
Financial Assets				
Fair value through profit or loss	Derivatives	Maximum exposure to credit risk	Sensitivity analysis for each type of market risk	
	Instruments held for trading		Sensitivity analysis for each type of market risk	
	Instruments designated at fair value	Maximum exposure to credit risk Collateral Information about credit quality Age analysis for amounts that are past due but not impaired	Sensitivity analysis for each type of market risk	
Fair value through other comprehensive income	Available-for-sale debt instruments	Maximum exposure to credit risk Collateral Information about credit quality Age analysis for amounts that are past due but not impaired	Sensitivity analysis for each type of market risk	
	Available-for-sale equity instruments		Sensitivity analysis for each type of market risk	
Amortized cost instruments	Held to maturity	Maximum exposure to credit risk Collateral Information about credit quality Age analysis for amounts that are past due but not impaired	Sensitivity analysis for each type of market risk	
	Loans and receivables	Maximum exposure to credit risk Collateral Information about credit quality Age analysis for amounts that are past due but not impaired	Sensitivity analysis for each type of market risk	
Liquid assets				
Fair value through profit or loss	Derivatives		Sensitivity analysis for each type of market risk	Maturity analysis showing the remaining contractual maturities, which are essential for the understanding of the timing of the cash flows
	Instruments held for trading		Sensitivity analysis for each type of market risk	Maturity analysis based on undiscounted contractual cash flows
	Instruments designated at fair value		Sensitivity analysis for each type of market risk	Maturity analysis based on undiscounted contractual cash flows
Amortized cost	Liabilities at amortized cost		Sensitivity analysis for each type of market risk	Maturity analysis based on undiscounted contractual cash flows

34.5 **DISCLOSURE—DETAILED/MICRO VIEW**

34.5.1 Credit risk on the Statement of Financial Position. The fair value movement attributable to changes in credit risk related to loans and receivables, as well as movement attributable to liabilities designated at fair value, must be disclosed.

For instruments that would be classified as loans and receivables in terms of IAS 39 if it were not for the option to designate them at fair value through profit or loss (for example corporate debt instruments for which there is no quoted price), the following information is required:

- maximum exposure to credit risk;
- mitigation by using credit derivatives;
- the change in fair value attributable to credit risk (not market risk events) as well as the methods used to achieve this specific credit risk disclosure; and
- the change in the fair value of credit derivatives for the current period and cumulatively after the loan was designated at fair value.

For liabilities designated at fair value, entities are required to disclose the following:

- the change in fair value attributable to credit risk (not market risk events) as well as the methods used to achieve this specific credit risk disclosure; and
- the difference between the current carrying amount and the required contractual payment when the liability matures.

34.5.2 Reclassification of financial instruments. IAS 39 describes very specific circumstances under which a financial instrument may be reclassified. IFRS 7 provides guidance on how such reclassifications are to be disclosed. IAS 39 describes mandatory and optional reclassifications. The disclosure required by IFRS 7 depends on the type of reclassification.

The following information is required for mandatory reclassifications (for example when a held-to-maturity portfolio is reclassified as a result of a breach of the tainting rules):

- the amount reclassified between cost, amortized cost, or fair value; and
- the reason for the reclassification.

For optional reclassifications (for example, instruments classified as held for trading for which managements intention has changed and that are unlikely to be disposed of in the foreseeable future), a two-fold disclosure approach is followed. First, the following disclosure is required in the period in which the reclassification is made:

- the amount reclassified into and out of each category;
- the carrying amount and fair value;
- if the reclassification was due to a rare circumstance, then disclosure is required of the rare circumstance that give rise to the reclassification;
- gain or loss recognized in profit or loss and other comprehensive income in the current and prior period; and
- the effective interest rate and the amount the entity expects to recover at the date of reclassification.

Second, the following disclosure is required for all periods until the instrument is derecognized:

- the carrying amount and fair value of all instruments reclassified; and
- the fair value gain or loss that would have been recognized in profit or loss or other comprehensive income had the instrument not been reclassified.

34.5.3 **Derecognition of Statement of Financial Position items.** All transfers of assets not qualifying for derecognition must be identified as follows:

- the nature of assets transferred that do not qualify for derecognition (for example, certain special-purpose vehicles for asset-backed securities);
- the nature of the risks/rewards still exposed; and
- the carrying amount of assets still recognized—disclose the original total and associated liabilities.

34.5.4 **Collateral related to items on the Statement of Financial Position.** The following must be disclosed:

- the carrying amount of financial assets pledged as collateral for liabilities or contingent liabilities and the terms and conditions relating to the pledge; and
- for financial assets received as a collateral that are available to be resold or repledged in the absence of default:
  - the fair value of collateral held if available to be sold or repledged (even if the owner does not default);
  - the fair value of collateral sold or repledged (whether there is any obligation to return the collateral at the contract maturity); and
  - terms and conditions for the use of collateral.

34.5.5 **Allowance for credit losses on the Statement of Financial Position.** Reconciliation of changes during the current period should be provided for all impaired financial assets, by class of asset.

34.5.6 **Embedded options in the Statement of Financial Position** (structured liabilities with equity components using interdependent, multiple embedded derivatives). Disclose the existence of features and interdependencies for all financial liabilities with multiple embedded derivatives.

34.5.7 **Loans payable in default.** For loans payable, where loans are in default or conditions have been breached, disclose the following:

- the carrying amount of such liabilities;
- details related to the principal, interest, sinking fund, or redemption terms; and
- any remedy of default or renegotiation of loan terms that had taken place prior to the issue of the financial statements.

34.5.8 **Hedge accounting in the financial statements.** The types of hedges and risks related to hedging activities must be disclosed as follows (table 34.6).

34.5.9 **Fair value disclosure in the financial statements** (see table 34.7). The fair value information required depends on how the financial instrument is measured in the Statement of Financial Position.

34.5.10 **Nature and extent of risks arising from financial instruments: qualitative disclosures.** Qualitative disclosures (the nature of risks and how they arose) do not necessarily have to be broken down by individual financial instruments. However, each type of risk arising from all financial assets and financial liabilities must be discussed, as follows:

- the exposure to risk and how risks arise;
- the objectives, policies, and processes to manage risk, as well as any changes in risk management processes from the previous period; and

TABLE 34.6 **Disclosure of Hedging Activities**

Information to be disclosed	Hedge type
Description of the type of hedge	Required for all types of hedges
Type of instruments designated as hedging instruments and their fair value at the reporting date	
The nature of the risks being hedged	
The periods when the cash flows are expected to occur and when they are expected to affect profit or loss	Cash flow hedges
A description of a forecast transaction for which hedge accounting had been applied but which is no longer expected to occur	
The amount that was recognized in other comprehensive income during the period	
The amount that was reclassified from other comprehensive income to profit or loss for the period	
The amount that was removed from other comprehensive income in the current period and included in the initial cost or carrying amount of a nonfinancial asset or liability	
Ineffectiveness recognized in profit or loss	
Fair value gains or losses on the hedging instruments	Fair value hedges
Fair value gains or losses on the hedged item attributable to the hedged risk	
Ineffectiveness recognized in profit or loss	Hedges of a net investment in a foreign operation

TABLE 34.7 **Disclosure of Fair Value Information**

Instruments measured at amortized cost	Instruments measured at fair value		
	Level 1	Level 2	Level 3
Description of the methods and assumptions used to determine fair value			
	Instruments for which the fair value is determined based on a price quoted in an active market	Instruments for which the fair value is based on a valuation technique for which the significant inputs are observable in the market	Instruments for which the fair value is based on a valuation technique for which the significant inputs are not observable in the market
The fair value measured in a way that permits comparison with the carrying amount	Carrying value	Carrying value	Carrying value
	Description of transfers into and out of level 1	Description of transfers into and out of level 2	Detailed reconciliation showing: • opening and closing balance • purchases, sales, and settlements • gains or losses • transfers into and out of level 3
			Gains or losses recognized in profit or loss in respect of instruments recognized in the Statement of Financial Position at reporting date
			If changing one or more inputs would have a significant impact on the fair value the fact and a sensitivity analysis must be disclosed

- the methods used to measure risk as well as any changes in risk measurement processes from the previous period

34.5.11 Quantitative disclosures. For each type of risk arising from all financial assets and financial liabilities, provide the following:

- summary quantitative data as supplied internally to key management personnel;
- detail of all risk concentrations;
- further information if data provided are not representative of the risk during the period; and
- credit, liquidity, and market risk information (specified below), where material.

34.5.12 Credit risk: quantitative disclosures. The maximum exposure (ignoring collateral or netting) to credit risk must be provided for each class of financial asset and financial liability. In addition, the following information must be provided for each class of financial asset:

- a description of any collateral held;
- information regarding the credit quality of financial assets that are neither past due nor impaired;
- the carrying value of assets that have been renegotiated and would be impaired if it were not for the renegotiation;
- an age analysis of past due (but not impaired) items, including the fair value of any collateral held;
- analysis of impaired items, including any factors considered in determining the impairment as well as the fair value of collateral; and
- a discussion of the nature and carrying value of collateral acquired and recognized, including the policies for disposal or usage of collateral.

34.5.13 Liquidity risk: quantitative disclosures. For all financial liabilities, the following must be provided:

- an analysis of remaining contractual maturities; and
- a description of the management of inherent liquidity risk.

34.5.14 Market risk: quantitative disclosures. For each type of market risk arising from all financial assets and financial liabilities, the following must be disclosed:

- sensitivity analysis, including the impact on income and equity—value at risk (VAR) may be used, as long as objectives and key parameters are disclosed;
- methods and assumptions used for sensitivity analysis, as well as changes from the previous period; and
- further information if data provided are not representative of risk during the period.

34.6   FINANCIAL ANALYSIS AND INTERPRETATION

34.6.1 Historically, generally accepted accounting practices did not place heavy burdens of disclosure of financial risk management practices. This situation changed in the 1990s with the introduction of IAS 30 (subsequently scrapped with introduction of IFRS 7) and IAS 32 (disclosure requirements transferred to IFRS 7). IAS 30 and IAS 32, which are now largely superseded by IFRS 7, required many financial regulators to adopt a "full disclosure" approach. IAS 30 encouraged management to add comments on financial statements describing the way liquidity, solvency, and other risks associated with the operations of a bank were managed and controlled.

34.6.2 Users need information to assist them with their evaluation of an entity's financial position, financial performance, and risk management so that they are in a position to make economic decisions (based on their evaluation). Of key importance are a realistic valuation of assets, including sensitivities to future events and adverse developments, and the proper recognition of income and expenses. Equally important is the evaluation of the entire risk profile, including on- and off-balance-sheet items, capital adequacy, the capacity to withstand short-term problems, and the ability to generate additional capital.

34.6.3 Market participants also need information that enhances their understanding of the significance of on- and off-balance-sheet financial instruments to an entity's financial position, performance, and cash flows. This information is necessary to assess the amounts, timing, and certainty of future cash flows associated with such instruments. For several years, but especially in the wake of the East Asia financial crises of the late 1990s, there has been criticism regarding deficiencies in accounting practices that have resulted in the incomplete and inadequate presentation of risk-based financial information in annual financial reports. Market participants perceived the opacity of financial information as not only an official oversight, but also as the Achilles heel of effective corporate governance and market discipline.

34.6.4 Disclosure is an effective mechanism to expose financial risk management practices to market discipline. Disclosure should be sufficiently comprehensive to meet the needs of users within the constraints of what can reasonably be required. Improved transparency through better disclosure may reduce the chances of a systemic financial crisis or the effects of contagion because creditors and other market participants will be better able to distinguish between the financial circumstances that face different institutions or countries.

34.6.5 Lastly, disclosure requirements should be accompanied by active regulatory enforcement—and perhaps even fraud laws—to ensure that the information disclosed is complete, timely, and not deliberately misleading. Regulatory institutions should also have adequate enforcement capacities. IFRS 7 aims to rectify some of the remaining gaps in financial risk disclosure by adding the following requirements to the existing accounting standards:

- new disclosure requirements for loans and receivables designated as fair value through profit or loss;
- disclosure of the amount of change in a financial liability's fair value that is not attributable to changes in market conditions;
- the method used to determine the effects of changes from a benchmark interest rate;
- where an impairment of a financial asset is recorded through an allowance account (for example, a provision for doubtful debts as opposed to a direct reduction to the carrying amount of the receivable), a reconciliation of changes in carrying amounts in that account during the period, for each class of financial asset;
- the amount of ineffectiveness recognized in profit or loss on cash flow hedges and hedges of net investments;
- gains or losses in fair value hedges arising from remeasuring the hedging instrument and on the hedged item attributable to the hedged risk; and
- the net gain or loss on held-to-maturity investments, loans and receivables, and financial liabilities measured at amortized cost.

34.6.6 Table 34.7 presents a summary of the information to be disclosed and the financial instruments affected by such disclosure.

34.7 **COMMENTARY**

34.7.1 The standard is only a disclosure standard and does not require any changes to the recognition or measurement of financial instruments. However, the complexities and effort involved in meeting the requirements of the standard should not be underestimated.

34.7.2 Some of the required disclosure cannot be sourced from information used by management, but rather comes from information that is used almost exclusively by analysts and other investors. Entities are therefore required to develop systems to generate additional information. Investors may then make decisions based on information that management does not evaluate or use to make their decisions, for example, the undiscounted contractual cash flow maturity analysis for financial liabilities.

34.7.3 Some of the requirements result in onerous and subjective calculations, for example calculating the fair value of financial instruments not recognized at fair value such as retail advances and deposits. Retail advances and deposits are managed and the cash flows realized on an amortized cost basis. Forcing entities to calculate the fair value results in management applying a significant amount of judgment to a very onerous calculation to provide information that is irrelevant to themselves and should be irrelevant to investors.

34.7.4 As part of the second annual improvements project of the IASB, certain improvements to IFRS 7 have been proposed. These are as follows:

- The standard will explicitly state that the qualitative disclosures should enhance the quantitative disclosures.
- Reference to materiality in the section dealing with qualitative risk disclosures has been removed.
- The fair value of collateral is no longer required but the financial effect thereof is required.
- The standard will clarify that collateral recognized on balance sheets is foreclosed collateral.
- Entities will no longer be required to disclose renegotiated assets.
- Disclosure of the maximum exposure to credit risk is only required when the carrying amount is not representative of the maximum exposure.

34.8   IMPLEMENTATION DECISIONS

The following table sets out some of the strategic and tactical decisions that should be considered when applying IFRS 7.

Strategic decisions	Tactical decisions	Problems to overcome
IFRS 7 is driven by the IAS 39 classifications and elections, for example whether instruments are designated at fair value or whether hedge accounting is applied. The most significant strategic decisions relating to financial instruments are therefore made when considering IAS 39.	When management is deciding on the IAS 39 classifications and elections, the decisions should incorporate the impact of IFRS 7 and whether the information required is available. If information is not available or impossible or costly to develop, management should potentially consider alternative options.	Management decisions being driven by accounting and disclosure considerations. Some information may be sensitive. If that is the case, management should discuss the matter with external auditors to find a suitable solution, potentially through aggregation.
Decisions need to be taken in respect of how much emphasis is placed on different aspects of information reported.	Decisions need to be made about how and where the information will be presented in the annual report. If an entity is also required to disclose information for regulatory purposes, for example Basel II Pillar 3 disclosures, the entity should consider how the IFRS 7 information and the Basel II information are presented together to provide the users of financial statements with insight into the risks associated with financial instruments.	Some of the information required by the standard may not be readily available in the entity's systems. A detailed gap analysis should be performed to determine what information is available and a plan implemented to obtain any information that is not readily available. Despite the standard only dealing with disclosure, there are still interpretation and judgment involved, for example renegotiated advances, how the movement in credit risk is determined, the treatment of net settled derivatives in the liquidity analysis, and so forth.
The extent to which information is to be aggregated should be considered. There needs to be a balance between overburdening the users of financial statements and obscuring important differences between individual transactions or associated risks.	Determine the classes of financial instruments based on their characteristics and their significance to the overall financial position of the entity.	The entity's systems may provide detailed information at a different level to what is required for the disclosures. This may require further aggregation or additional disaggregation.
A decision needs to be taken as to whether the entity will disclose the results of any internal sensitivity analysis used to manage the business, for example VaR, or whether the market risk sensitivity analysis required by IFRS 7 will be disclosed.	The reasonable possible alternatives of the various market risk variables should be determined for purposes of preparing the sensitivity analysis.	Detailed sensitivity information may not be available across the organization.

34.9   EXAMPLES: FINANCIAL INSTRUMENTS: DISCLOSURE AND PRESENTATION

EXAMPLE 34.1: MARKET RISK DISCLOSURE BY A NONFINANCIAL ENTITY

Commodity price risk

The group makes use of derivative instruments, including commodity swaps, options and futures contracts of short duration as a means of mitigating price and timing risks on crude oil purchases and sales. In effecting these transactions, the business units concerned operate within procedures and

(continued)

EXAMPLE 34.1, CONTINUED

policies designed to ensure that risks, including those relating to the default of counterparties, are minimised. For the year under review, the strategy was to hedge the equivalent of approximately 30% of Sasol Synfuels' production (16,4 million barrels) and 30% of Sasol Petroleum International's West Africa output (550 000 barrels). These zero cost collar hedges have been used to mitigate the risk of substantial volatility in the oil prices in the past and their suitability for the future oil hedge strategy is monitored on a regular basis.

Dated Brent crude prices applied during the year:

	2009 US$	2008 US$
High	143,95	139,98
Average	68,14	95,51
Low	39,41	33,73

The following commodity derivative contracts were in place at 30 June:

	Contract foreign currency amount 2009 million	Contract amount – Rand equivalent 2009 Rm	Average price 2009 US$	Estimated fair value losses 2009 Rm	Contract foreign currency amount 2008 million	Contract amount – Rand equivalent 2008 Rm	Average price 2008 US$	Estimated fair value gains 2008 Rm
Commodity derivatives								
Derivative instruments— cash flow hedges								
Futures								
Crude oil (US dollar)	10	76	70,01	(1)	19	147	140,53	–
Derivative instruments— held for trading								
Futures								
Crude oil (US dollar)	38	295	70,29	(2)	88	685	133,76	31

The high crude oil prices seen over the recent years are expected to decline over the next ten years. For every US$1/b increase in the average crude oil price, group operating profit increased by approximately R572 million during 2009 (2008: R402 million).

The average crude oil price achieved during 2009 was cushioned by the effect of the oil hedges during the year which resulted in a net gain of R4 605 million. The recognition of the fair value of the oil hedges resulted in an unrealised fair value loss of R2 million at the end of the year owing to the significant decrease in crude oil prices from 2008.

The maturity profile of contract amounts of commodity derivatives at 30 June were as follows:

	Contract amount 2009 Rm	Within one year 2009 Rm	Contract amount 2008 Rm	Within one year 2008 Rm
Commodity derivatives				
Futures				
Crude oil	371	371	832	832

Source: Sasol Annual Financial Statements 2008.

EXAMPLE 34.2: FAIR VALUE DISCLOSURE BY A FINANCIAL ENTITY

Sensitivity of fair values to reasonably possible alternative assumptions

	Favourable changes US$m	Unfavourable changes US$m	Favourable changes US$m	Unfavourable changes US$m
At 31 December 2009				
Derivatives, trading assets and trading liabilities[23]	984	(577)	–	–
Financial assets and liabilities designated at fair value	102	(98)	–	–
Financial investments: available for sale	–	–	1,161	(1,157)
At 31 December 2008				
Derivatives, trading assets and trading liabilities[23]	1,266	(703)	–	–
Financial assets and liabilities designated at fair value	30	(30)	–	–
Financial investments: available for sale	–	–	984	(1,005)

For footnote, see page 195.

The decrease in the effect of changes in significant unobservable inputs in relation to derivatives, trading assets and trading liabilities during the year primarily reflected the decreased sensitivity to the assumptions for the derivative portfolios. The increase in the effect of changes in significant unobservable inputs for available-for-sale assets arose from the increase in private equity holdings in Level 3 and from increased sensitivity to the assumptions for ABSs.

Sensitivity of fair values to reasonably possible alternative assumptions by Level 3 instrument type

	Reflected in profit or loss		Reflected in equity	
	Favourable changes US$m	Unfavourable changes US$m	Favourable changes US$m	Unfavourable changes US$m
At 31 December 2009				
Private equity investments	54	(54)	302	(299)
Asset-backed securities	41	(41)	734	(735)
Leveraged finance	1	(1)	–	–
Loans held for securitisation	16	(16)	–	–
Structured notes	3	(3)	–	–
Derivatives with monolines	333	(25)	–	–
Other derivatives	309	(332)	–	–
Other portfolios	329	(203)	125	(123)

Source: HSBC Holdings Plc Annual Report and Accounts 2009.

EXAMPLE 34.3: CREDIT RISK DISCLOSURE BY A FINANCIAL ENTITY

Credit risk loans comprise loans and advances to banks and customers 90 days overdue or more and those subject to individual impairment. The coverage ratio is calculated by reference to the total impairment allowance and the carrying value (before impairment) of credit risk loans.

As at 31st December 2009	Neither past due nor individually impaired[a] £m	Past due but not individually impaired[b] £m	Individually impaired £m	Total £m	Impairment allowance £m	Total carrying value £m	Credit Risk Loans £m	Coverage ratio %
The Group								
Trading portfolio:								
Traded loans	2,962	–	–	2,962	–	2,962	–	–
Financial assets designated at fair value held on own account:								
Loans and advances	22,210	180	–	22,390	–	22,390	–	–
Other financial assets	557	–	–	557	–	557	–	–
Loans and advances to banks	38,859	2,280	57	41,196	(61)	41,135	57	100.0
Loans and advances to customers:								
Residential mortgage loans	139,199	8,846	1,693	149,738	(639)	149,009	3,604	17.7
Credit card receivables	20,195	1,544	2,459	24,198	(2,309)	21,889	3,068	75.3
Other personal lending	23,796	2,175	2,372	28,343	(2,908)	25,435	3,466	83.9
Wholesale and corporate loans and advances	199,800	7,598	10,088	217,486	(4,558)	212,928	11,497	39.6
Finance lease receivables	10,128	664	402	11,194	(321)	10,873	696	46.1
Total	457,706	23,287	17,071	498,064	(10,796)	487,268	22,388	48.2
The Bank								
Trading portfolio:								
Traded loans	2,945	–	–	2,945	–	2,945	–	–
Financial assets designated at fair value held on own account:								
Loans and advances	21,467	169	–	21,636	–	21,636	–	–
Other financial assets	423	–	–	423	–	423	–	–
Loans and advances to banks	40,784	2,183	57	43,024	(61)	42,963	57	100.0
Loans and advances to customers:								
Residential mortgage loans	104,037	5,900	816	110,753	(148)	110,605	1,532	9.7
Credit card receivables	10,920	582	1,363	12,865	(1,342)	11,523	1,578	85.0
Other personal lending	13,043	1,030	1,959	16,032	(1,907)	14,125	2,485	76.7
Wholesale and corporate loans and advances	365,778	3,854	9,825	379,457	(3,944)	375,513	10,584	37.3
Finance lease receivables	362	–	–	362	–	362	–	–
Total	559,759	13,718	14,020	587,497	(7,402)	580,095	16,236	45.6

Notes

a. Financial assets subject to collective impairment allowance are included in this column if they are not past due.
b. Financial assets subject to collective impairment allowance are included in this column if they are past due.

Credit quality of loans and advances neither past due nor individually impaired

	2009				2008			
	Strong £m	Satisfactory £m	Higher risk £m	Total £m	Strong £m	Satisfactory £m	Higher risk £m	Total £m
The Group								
Trading portfolio:								
Traded loans	1,366	1,290	306	2,962	759	220	91	1,070
Financial assets designated at fair value held on own account:								
Loans and advances	15,909	3,809	2,492	22,210	25,665	2,792	725	29,182
Other financial assets	261	–	296	557	–	1,469	–	1,469
Loans and advances to banks	35,825	2,492	542	38,859	40,181	6,384	100	46,665
Loans and advances to customers:								
Residential mortgage loans	66,956	69,919	2,324	139,199	86,937	42,770	1,310	131,017
Credit card receivables	–	20,038	157	20,195	–	20,426	666	21,092
Other personal lending	3,417	18,108	2,271	23,796	2,975	21,750	1,160	25,885
Wholesale and corporate loans and advances	119,764	70,132	9,904	199,800	141,868	94,453	10,184	246,505
Finance lease receivables	2,664	7,082	382	10,128	4,214	7,504	649	12,367
Total loans and advances	246,162	192,870	18,674	457,706	302,599	197,768	14,885	515,252
The Bank								
Trading portfolio:								
Traded loans	1,366	1,273	306	2,945	759	220	68	1,047
Financial assets designated at fair value held on own account:								
Loans and advances	17,657	2,892	918	21,467	21,211	1,518	1,054	23,783
Other financial assets	423	–	–	423	–	1,472	–	1,472
Loans and advances to banks	37,160	1,851	1,773	40,784	34,708	1,981	89	36,778
Loans and advances to customers:								
Residential mortgage loans	60,025	42,964	1,048	104,037	83,139	17,182	105	100,426
Credit card receivables	–	10,920	–	10,920	–	10,783	–	10,783
Other personal lending	2,911	8,178	1,954	13,043	4,838	11,656	957	17,451
Wholesale and corporate loans and advances	303,545	54,510	7,723	365,778	329,384	68,385	9,560	407,329
Finance lease receivables	–	362	–	362	2	342	–	344
Total loans and advances	423,087	122,950	13,722	559,759	474,041	113,539	11,833	599,413

(continued)

EXAMPLE 34.3, CONTINUED

For the purposes of the analysis of credit quality, the following internal measures of credit quality have been used:

Financial statements description	Retail lending Probability of default	Wholesale lending Probability of default	Default grade
Strong	0.0–0.60%	0.0–0.05%	1–3
		0.05–0.15%	4–5
		0.15–0.30%	6–8
		0.30–0.60%	9–11
Satisfactory	0.60–10.00%	0.60–2.15%	12–14
		2.15–11.35%	15–19
Higher risk	10.00% +	11.35% +	20–21

Financial statement descriptions can be summarised as follows:

Strong—there is a very high likelihood that the asset being recovered in full.

Satisfactory—whilst there is a high likelihood that the asset will be recovered and therefore, of no cause for concern to the Group, the asset may not be collateralised, or may relate to retail facilities, such as credit card balances and unsecured loans, which have been classified as satisfactory, regardless of the fact that the output of internal grading models may have indicated a higher classification. At the lower end of this grade there are customers that are being more carefully monitored, for example corporate customers, which are indicating some evidence of some deterioration, mortgages with a high loan to value ratio, and unsecured retail loans operating outside normal product guidelines.

Higher risk—there is concern over the obligor's ability to make payments when due. However, these have not yet converted to actual delinquency. There may also be doubts over value of collateral or security provided. However, the borrower or counterparty is continuing to make payments when due and is expected to settle all outstanding amounts of principal and interest.

Loans and advances that are past due but not individually impaired

An age analysis of loans and advances that are past due but not individually impaired is set out below.

For the purposes of this analysis an asset is considered past due and included below when any payment due under strict contractual terms is received late or missed. The amount included is the entire financial asset, not just the payment, of principal or interest or both, overdue.

The table below provides a breakdown of total financial assets past due but not individually impaired. In general, retail and wholesale loans fall into this category for two separate reasons. Retail loans and advances to customers may come under this category because the impairment allowance on such loans is calculated on a collective—not individual—basis. This reflects the homogenous nature of the assets, which allows statistical techniques to be used, rather than individual assessment.

In contrast, some loans to wholesale and corporate customers and banks may come under this category because of instances where a payment on a loan is past due without requiring an individual impairment allowance. For example, an individual impairment allowance will not be required when a loss is not expected due to a corporate loan being fully secured or collateralised. As a result, it is past due but not individually impaired.

As at 31st December 2009	Past due up to 1 month £m	Past due 1–2 months £m	Past due 2–3 months £m	Past due 3–6 months £m	Past due 6 months and over £m	Total £m	Of which Credit Risk Loans £m
The Group Financial assets designated at fair value held on own account: Loans and advances	170	–	1	–	9	180	–
Loans and advances to banks	2,280	–	–	–	–	2,280	–
Loans and advances to customers: Residential mortgage loans Credit card receivables Other personal lending Wholesale and corporate loans and advances Finance lease receivables	4,849 501 369 5,403 186	1,453 214 295 292 86	633 220 417 494 98	1,410 459 413 866 282	501 150 681 543 12	8,846 1,544 2,175 7,598 664	1,911 609 1,094 1,409 294
Total loans and advances to customers	11,308	2,340	1,862	3,430	1,887	20,827	5,317
Total financial assets past due but not individually impaired	13,758	2,340	1,863	3,430	1,896	23,287	5,317
The Bank Financial assets designated at fair value held on own account: Loans and advances	169	–	–	–	–	169	–
Loans and advances to banks	2,183	–	–	–	–	2,183	–
Loans and advances to customers: Residential mortgage loans Credit card receivables Other personal lending Wholesale and corporate loans and advances Finance lease receivables	3,648 209 87 2,629 –	1,183 67 185 161 –	353 91 232 305 –	546 207 290 377 –	170 8 236 382 –	5,900 582 1,030 3,854 –	716 215 526 759 –
Total loans and advances to customers	6,573	1,596	981	1,420	796	11,366	2,216
Total financial assets past due but not individually impaired	8,925	1,596	981	1,420	796	13,718	2,216

Source: Barclays Bank PLC Annual Report 2009.

EXAMPLE 34.4: DISCLOSURE OF INSTRUMENTS DESIGNATED AT FAIR VALUE BY A FINANCIAL ENTITY

22. Financial assets and financial liabilities designated at fair value through profit or loss

22.1 loans and advances

The maximum exposure to credit risk for loans and advances designated at fair value through profit or loss for the group and company is R2 309 million (2008: R3 673 million). No credit derivatives were used to mitigate credit risk on these instruments.

There are no cumulative gains or losses due to credit risk. The change in fair value of the designated loans and advances that is attributable to changes in credit risk is determined as the amount of change in fair value that is not attributable to changes in market conditions.

22.2 Financial liabilities

The fair value movement of financial l liabilities attributable to changes in credit risk cumulative to date is negligible (2008: negligible) for the group and company.

The change in fair value of the designated financial liabilities attributable to changes in credit risk has been calculated by reference to the change in credit risk implicit in the market value of the bank's senior notes.

The amount that would contractually be paid at maturity for financial liabilities designated at fair value through profit or loss for the group is R49 039 million (2008: R45 514 million) and for the company is R46 805 million (2008: R44 838 million), R1 953 million (2008: R7 506 million) for the group and R1 993 million (2008: R7 487 million) for the company higher than the carrying amount.

Source: Standard Bank of South Africa Annual Report 2009.

EXAMPLE 34.5: MARKET RISK DISCLOSURE BY A FINANCIAL ENTITY

The VaR risk measure estimates the potential loss over a 10-day holding period at a 99% confidence level. The scenario set used in the calculation of these figures comprises the most recent 250 days, as required for regulatory capital measurement purposes under the internal model based approach. The following table provides the aggregate risk exposure per asset class across different trading activities:

VaR analysis by instrument (audited)

			2009		2008
R million	Min	Max	Ave	Year end	Year end
Risk type					
Equities	142.7	411.9	247.2	287.4	233.8
Interest rates	65.3	229.1	123.5	158.0	100.7
Foreign exchange	26.8	170.9	82.5	117.7	69.0
Commodities	16.4	122.7	69.0	71.2	119.8
Traded credit	1.2	59.2	22.4	8.4	46.5
Diversification				(263.7)	(243.7)
Total				379.0	326.1

VaR calculations are validated on a daily basis through a comparison of 1-day VaR figures (at the 99% confidence level) to actual trading profits or losses for the particular day.

Market risk stress analysis (distressed ETL)

The portfolio is also re-valued over a set of 500 scenarios of which 250 represent a distressed market period. The scenario set is supplemented with additional relevant data points over time, including, for example, the period of the current financial crisis, as and when appropriate. The following table provides a summary of distressed ETL figures by asset class, based on a 10-day liquidity horizon over a 99% confidence level:

Distressed ETL analysis by instrument (audited)

			2009		2008
R million	Min	Max	Ave	Year end	Year end
Risk type					
Equities	229.2	639.4	387.8	431.8	346.4
Interest rates	181.2	561.1	346.6	525.2	270.1
Foreign exchange	45.8	267.6	131.9	169.7	124.6
Commodities	24.8	193.3	107.7	108.9	180.5
Traded credit	4.1	93.3	27.6	15.0	67.6
Diversification				(457.3)	(390.8)
Total				793.3	598.4

Source: FirstRand Bank Limited Annual Report 2009.

CHAPTER 35

Operating Segments
(IFRS 8)

<table>
<tr><td>35.1</td><td>

OBJECTIVE

IFRS 8 establishes principles for reporting information by operating segments, that is, information about the different business activities of an entity and the different economic environments in which it operates.

IFRS 8 requires the identification of operating segments on the basis of internal reports that senior management (also referred to as the chief operating decision maker) use when determining the allocation of resources to a segment and assessing its performance. The presentation of segment information based on the management approach will enable the users of financial statements to review the entity's performance through the eyes of management and allow users to make their decisions based on the information presented to management.

</td></tr>
</table>

35.1

OBJECTIVE

IFRS 8 establishes principles for reporting information by operating segments, that is, information about the different business activities of an entity and the different economic environments in which it operates.

IFRS 8 requires the identification of operating segments on the basis of internal reports that senior management (also referred to as the chief operating decision maker) use when determining the allocation of resources to a segment and assessing its performance. The presentation of segment information based on the management approach will enable the users of financial statements to review the entity's performance through the eyes of management and allow users to make their decisions based on the information presented to management.

35.2

SCOPE OF THE STANDARD

This standard applies to the stand-alone financial statements of individual entities and the consolidated financial statements of a group with a parent, whose equity or debt securities are traded in a public securities market or that are in the process of issuing such instruments. Other entities that voluntarily choose disclosure under this standard should comply fully with the requirements of IFRS 8.

A parent entity is required to present segment information only on the basis of its consolidated financial statements. If a subsidiary's own securities are publicly traded, it will present segment information in its own separate financial report. (Financial statement disclosure of equity information for associated investments would mirror this requirement.)

35.3

KEY CONCEPTS

35.3.1 **An operating segment** is a component of an entity:

- that engages in business activities from which it may earn revenues and incur expenses;
- whose operating results are regularly reviewed by the entity's chief operating decision maker for allocating resources to the segment and assessing its performance; and
- for which discrete financial information is available.

Business activities include revenues and expenses from transactions with other operating segments of the same entity.

35.3.2 **A reportable segment** is an operating segment or results from the aggregation of two or more operating segments that meets any of the following quantitative thresholds:

- Its reported **revenue**, including both sales to external customers and intersegment sales or transfers, is 10 percent or more of the combined revenue (internal and external) of all operating segments.
- Its absolute reported **profit** is 10 percent or more of the combined reported profit of all operating segments that did not report a loss, or its absolute reported **loss** is 10 percent or more of the combined reported loss of all operating segments that reported a loss.
- Its **assets** are 10 percent or more of the combined assets of all operating segments.

35.3.3 **The chief operating decision maker** identifies a function and not necessarily a person; for example, it could be the board of directors or the executive management team. The function of the chief operating decision maker is to allocate resources to operating segments and assess the performance of the operating segments of an entity.

35.4   **ACCOUNTING TREATMENT**

35.4.1 The amount of each segment item reported is the measure reported to the chief operating decision maker for the purposes of allocating resources to the segment and assessing its performance, irrespective of whether this measure is IFRS compliant. Adjustments, eliminations, and allocations made in preparing an entity's financial statements should be included in determining the segment profit or loss only if they are included in the measure of the segment's profit or loss that is used by the chief operating decision maker.

35.4.2 IFRS 8 does not define segment revenue, segment expense, segment profit or loss, segment assets, or segment liabilities. The standard does however require that an entity should explain the measurements of segment profit or loss, segment assets, and segment liabilities for each reportable segment. At a minimum, an entity must disclose the nature of any differences between the following:

- the basis of accounting for any transactions between reportable segments;
- measurements of the reportable segments' profits or losses and the entity's profit or loss;
- measurements of the reportable segments' assets and the entity's assets;
- measurements of the reportable segments' liabilities and the entity's liabilities;
- accounting periods and the measurement methods used to determine reported segment profit or loss and the effect of those differences on the measure of segment profit or loss; and
- allocations to reportable segments—for example, if the entity allocates depreciation expense to a segment without allocating the related depreciable assets to that segment.

35.4.3 An entity should report information for each operating segment that:

- meets the definition of an operating segment or results from the aggregation of two or more segments in line with the requirements set out in paragraphs 35.3.1 and 35.3.2; and
- exceeds the quantitative thresholds.

35.4.4 Operating segments often exhibit similar long-term financial performance if they have similar economic characteristics. For example, similar long-term average gross margins would be expected for two operating segments with similar economic characteristics. Two or more operating segments may be aggregated into a single operating segment for disclosure purposes if aggregation is consistent with the core principle of IFRS 8, the segments have similar economic characteristics, and the segments are similar in each of the following respects:

- products and services;
- production processes;
- the type or class of customer for their products and services;
- the methods used to distribute their products or provide their services; and
- the nature of the regulatory environment (for example, banking, insurance, or public utilities).

35.4.5 If the total revenue from external customers for all *reportable* segments combined is less than 75 percent of the total entity revenue, additional reportable segments should be identified until the 75 percent level is reached.

35.4.6 Operating segments that do not meet any of the quantitative thresholds may be considered reportable, and separately disclosed, if management believes that information about the segment would be useful to users of the financial statements.

35.4.7 Small segments might be combined as one if they share a substantial number of factors that define a business or geographical segment, or they might be combined with a similar significant reportable segment. If they are not separately reported or combined, they are included as an unallocated reconciling item.

35.4.8 A segment that is not judged to be a reportable segment in the current period should none the less be reported if it is significant for decision-making purposes (for example, future market strategy).

35.5   **PRESENTATION AND DISCLOSURE**

35.5.1 An entity must disclose the factors used to identify its reportable segments, including:

- the basis of organization (products and services, geographic areas, regulatory environments, or a combination thereof);
- whether operating segments have been aggregated; and
- types of products and services from which each reportable segment derives its revenues.

35.5.2 An entity should report:

- a measure of profit or loss and total assets for each reportable segment; and
- a measure of liabilities for each reportable segment if such an amount is regularly provided to the chief operating decision maker.

35.5.3 An entity should also disclose the following about each reportable segment if the specified amounts are included in the measure of segment profit or loss reviewed by the chief operating decision maker, or are otherwise regularly provided to the chief operating decision maker:

- revenues from external customers;
- revenues from transactions with other operating segments of the same entity;
- interest revenue;

- interest expense;
- depreciation and amortization;
- material items of income and expenses disclosed in accordance with paragraph 97 of IAS 1 (refer to chapter 3);
- the entity's interest in the profit or loss of associates and joint ventures accounted for using the equity method;
- income tax expense or income; and
- material noncash items other than depreciation and amortization.

35.5.4 The interest revenue should be reported separately from the interest expense for each reportable segment, unless the majority of the segment's revenues are from interest and the chief operating decision maker relies primarily on the net interest revenue for making decisions and assessing performance.

35.5.5 The following amounts should be disclosed for each reportable segment, if the amounts are included in the measure of segment assets reviewed by the chief operating decision maker or are otherwise regularly provided to the chief operating decision maker, even if the amounts are not included in the measure of segment assets:

- the amount of investments in associates and joint ventures accounted for using the equity method; and
- the amounts of additions to noncurrent assets (other than financial instruments, deferred tax assets, postemployment benefit assets, and rights arising under insurance contracts).

35.5.6 An entity should provide reconciliations of the following and all material reconciling items should be separately identified and described:

- The total of the reportable segments' revenues to the entity's revenue.
- The total of the reportable segments' measures of profit or loss to the entity's profit or loss before tax expense (tax income) and discontinued operations. However, if an entity allocates to reportable segments items such as tax expense (tax income), then the entity may reconcile the total of the segments' measures of profit or loss to the entity's profit or loss after those items.
- The total of the reportable segments' assets to the entity's assets.
- The total of the reportable segments' liabilities to the entity's liabilities.
- The total of the reportable segments' amounts for every other material item of information disclosed to the corresponding amount for the entity.

35.5.7 IFRS 8 also requires entities to make certain entity-wide disclosures. These entity-wide disclosures are however not required if the information is not available and the cost to develop the information would be excessive. The following disclosures are required:

- The revenue from external customers for each group of similar products and services.
- Per geographical segment:
  - Revenues from external customers attributed to the entity's country of domicile and attributed to all foreign countries in total.
  - Noncurrent assets (other than financial instruments, deferred tax assets, postemployment benefit assets, and rights arising under insurance contracts) located in the entity's country of domicile and located in all other foreign countries in total.
  - If the revenues from external customers or assets attributable to an individual foreign country are material, those revenues or assets should be reported separately.

■ An entity should provide information about the extent of its reliance on its major customers. If the revenues from transactions with a single customer exceed 10 percent of an entity's revenue, the entity should disclose the fact and the amount of revenues from each such a customer, and the identity of the segment(s) reporting the revenues.

35.5.8 As a result of issuing IFRS 8, certain consequential amendments were also made to IAS 34 (refer to chapter 36). Additional information relating to segment reporting should also be presented in an entity's interim financial reporting.

35.6   **COMMENTARY**

35.6.1 The core principle of IFRS 8 is that an entity should disclose information to enable users of its financial statements to evaluate:

■ the nature and financial effects of the business activities in which it is engaged; and

■ the economic environments in which it engages, viewed in the same way that management views it (that is, the management approach).

35.6.2 This approach to reporting segment information will benefit both the preparers and users of financial statements. It should reduce the cost of providing disaggregated information for many entities because it uses segment information generated for management's use. The majority of disclosures required by IFRS 8 are only required if they are included in the information that is regularly reviewed by the chief operating decision maker.

35.6.3 IFRS 8 requires that a measure of segment profit or loss and segment assets be disclosed regardless of whether those measures are reviewed by the chief operating decision maker. This requirement was subsequently amended through the IASB's Annual Improvements Project to clarify that the measure of segment assets will be nil when such information is not provided to the chief operating decision maker. In other words, if the chief operating decision maker does not review information, for example segment assets, that number is not required to be disclosed in the segment report.

35.6.4 In the instance that an entity only has one reportable segment, the entity-wide disclosures will still be required.

35.6.5 IFRS 8 was released by the IASB in November 2006 and replaced IAS 14, Operating Segments. The IASB issued IFRS 8 as part of their project to converge IFRSs with U.S. GAAP. The IASB's current project agenda does not include any future amendments to segment reporting.

35.6.6 The effective date of IFRS 8 was on or after January 1, 2009. At this early stage of application of the standard, complications and inconsistency are difficult to identify.

35.7   **IMPLEMENTATION ISSUES**

The following table sets out some of the strategic and tactical decisions that should be considered when applying IFRS 8.

Strategic decisions	Tactical decisions	Problems to overcome
Defining the chief operating decision maker and identifying the operating segments.	In a group structure there are different reporting levels with more aggregation as the information is reported up the line. Defining the chief operating decision maker as the reporting entity level should be separated from reporting at the lower reporting levels.	Management should apply their judgment to determine whether a part of a business is an operating segment, specifically in the following instances: • start-up operations; • corporate headquarters and other functional departments; and • components with outputs transferred exclusively to other segments. The term "regularly" is not defined in IFRS 8 and management will need to apply judgment to determine whether information about the operating segment is regularly reviewed.
Identify the entity's reportable segments.	Determine whether any of the operating segments identified meet the aggregation criteria and whether these operating segments should be aggregated and reported together.	The users of financial statements may take a different view as to whether the operating segments identified have similar economic characteristics. If an entity aggregates operating segments then they should disclose their justification for doing so. It may be difficult to establish what similar economic characteristics exist if the gross margins of the operating segments differ significantly. However, other performance factors such as trends in sales growth, returns on assets employed, and operating cash flow may also be considered in making this decision.
	Ensure that the all operating segments that meet the quantitative thresholds as set out are reported separately. Ensure that the requirements for the minimum number of reportable segments are met (that is, at least 75 percent of the entity's revenue is included in the reportable segments).	The reportable segments may vary from one year to the next based on fluctuations in the reported revenue, profit or loss, or assets. If an operating segment becomes a reportable segment during the current year, the entity will have to obtain the information for the previous period and the comparative information will need to be restated. In addition, the segment report for the prior year is restated.

EXAMPLE: SEGMENT REPORTING

EXAMPLE 35.1

Hollier Inc. is a diversified entity that operates in nine operating segments organized around differences in products and geographical areas. The following financial information relates to the year ending June 30, 20X5.

	Total sales	External sales	Total profit	Total assets
Nature of Business				
Beer	2,249	809	631	4,977
Beverages	1,244	543	−131	3,475
Hotels	4,894	4,029	714	5,253
Retail	3,815	3,021	−401	1,072
Packaging	7,552	5,211	1,510	8,258
Totals	19,754	13,613	2,323	23,035
Geographical Areas				
Finland	7,111	6,841	1,536	9,231
France	1,371	1,000	−478	5,001
United Kingdom	3,451	2,164	494	3,667
Australia	7,821	3,608	771	5,136
Totals	19,754	13,613	2,323	23,035

EXPLANATION

The **first** step in identifying the reportable segments of the entity is to identify those which represent at least 10 percent of any of the entity's sales, profit, or assets.

	Exceeds 10% of			Qualify
	Total sales = $1,975	Total profit/ absolute loss = $232	Total assets = $2,303	
Nature of Business				
Beer	Yes	Yes	Yes	Yes
Beverages	No	No	Yes	Yes
Hotels	Yes	Yes	Yes	Yes
Retail	Yes	No	No	Yes
Packaging	Yes	Yes	Yes	Yes
Geographical Areas				
Finland	Yes	Yes	Yes	Yes
France	No	No	Yes	Yes
United Kingdom	Yes	Yes	Yes	Yes
Australia	Yes	Yes	Yes	Yes

The **second** step would be to check if total external revenue attributable to reportable segments constitutes at least 75 percent of the total consolidated or entity revenue of $13,613,000.

As all operating segments qualify as reportable segments, the external revenue requirement of 75 percent is met.

If that had not been the case, IFRS 8 would have required that additional operating segments be identified as reportable even if they do not meet the 10 percent thresholds in step one.

CHAPTER 36

Interim Financial Reporting
(IAS 34)

36.1   OBJECTIVE

In order to make economic decisions, users require the latest financial information of an entity and cannot wait a full year for the annual report. Interim financial information enhances the accuracy of forecasting earnings and share prices and improves users' ability to understand the financial conditions and liquidity of the entity by providing information on a more regular basis. Interim reporting also helps users understand seasonal fluctuations, trends, and liquidity of the entity.

The objective of IAS 34 is to prescribe the following for interim financial reports:

- minimum content; and
- the principles for recognition and measurement in complete or condensed financial statements.

36.2   SCOPE OF THE STANDARD

This standard applies to all entities that publish interim financial reports covering a period shorter than a full financial year (for example, a half year or a quarter). This standard applies whether such reporting is **required** by law or regulations or if the entity **voluntarily** publishes such reports. Publicly traded entities are encouraged to publish interim financial reports that comply with this standard at least at the end of the first half of the financial year and to make these reports available within 60 days of the interim period.

IAS 34 defines and prescribes the minimum content of an interim financial report, including disclosures, and identifies the accounting recognition and measurement principles that should be applied in an interim financial report.

36.3   KEY CONCEPTS

36.3.1 An **interim period** is a financial reporting period which is shorter than a full financial year (12 months).

36.3.2 An **interim financial report** is a financial report that contains either a complete or condensed set of financial statements for an interim period.

36.3.3 A **condensed set of financial statements** includes condensed primary statements (financial position, comprehensive income, equity, and cash flow) and selected explanatory notes.

36.3.4 A **complete set of financial statements** includes detailed primary statements and all required notes, including accounting policies, as required by IAS 1.

36.3.5 A **condensed statement of financial position** is produced at the end of an interim period with comparative balances provided for the end of the prior full financial year.

36.3.6 A **condensed statement of comprehensive income** is produced for the current interim period and cumulative for the current financial year to date, with comparatives for the comparable interim periods of the prior financial year. An entity that publishes interim financial reports quarterly would, for example, prepare four statements of comprehensive income in its third quarter: one for the nine months cumulatively since the beginning of the year, one for the third quarter only, and comparative statements of comprehensive income for the exact comparable periods of the prior financial year.

36.3.7 A **condensed statement of cash flows** is a cumulative statement for the current financial year to date, and a comparative statement for the comparable interim period of the prior financial year.

36.3.8 A **condensed statement of changes in equity** is cumulative for the current financial year to date and comparative for the comparable interim period of the prior financial year.

36.4   ACCOUNTING TREATMENT

36.4.1 An interim financial report includes the following minimum components:

- a condensed statement of financial position;
- a condensed statement of comprehensive income;
- a condensed statement of cash flows;
- a condensed statement of changes in equity; and
- selected explanatory notes.

TABLE 36.1   Minimum Components of Interim Financial Reports

Component	Periods for which component is required to be presented	Comparatives to be presented
Statement of Financial Position	Balances at the end of the current interim period	Balances at the end of the immediately preceding financial year
Statement of Comprehensive Income	• Current interim period • Cumulative year-to-date	• Corresponding interim period of the preceding financial year • Corresponding year-to-date of the preceding financial year
Statement of cash flows	Cumulative for the current financial year-to-date	Corresponding year-to-date of the preceding financial year
Statement of changes in equity	Cumulative for the current financial year-to-date	Corresponding year-to-date of the preceding financial year

36.4.2 The purpose of interim reporting is to provide an **update** of the latest annual report. For this reason, it is not necessary for an entity to repeat all the information and detail of the annual report in the interim report. Information should be limited to what is useful—in other words, what has changed since the annual reporting date, in line with the minimum components required by this standard. The standard does not prohibit the entity from including more information as long as the minimum requirements are disclosed.

The minimum required **form and content** of an interim financial report includes the following:

- each of the headings and subtotals that were included in the most recent annual financial statements;
- selected explanatory notes required by this standard that present significant events and transactions in order to explain changes in financial position and performance of the entity since the last annual report;
- additional items or notes only if their omission would cause the interim report to be misleading;
- basic and diluted earnings per share, which must be presented on the face of the statement of comprehensive income; and
- the interim report on a consolidated basis, prepared by a parent entity, if the most recent annual report was consolidated.

36.4.3 An entity should apply the same **accounting policies** in its interim financial statements as in its latest annual financial statements, except for accounting policy changes made subsequent to the last annual financial statements and that are to be reflected in the next annual financial statements.

36.4.4 A change in accounting policy should be reflected by **restating** the financial statements of prior interim periods of the current financial year **and** the comparable interim periods of prior years in terms of IAS 8 (if practicable).

36.4.5 The frequency of interim reporting (for example, semiannually or quarterly) does not affect the **measurement** of an entity's annual results. Measurements for interim reporting purposes are therefore made on a year-to-date basis, the so-called **discrete method.**

36.4.6 Measurements in both annual and interim financial reports are often based on reasonable estimates, but the preparation of interim financial reports generally will require a **greater use of estimation methods** than annual financial reports. For example, full stock-taking and valuation procedures cannot be realistically carried out for inventories at interim dates. For interim reporting purposes use need not be made of professional qualified valuers. Estimates can be obtained by extrapolating previous annual report figures, where these are reliable and where extrapolation is feasible.

36.4.7 In deciding how to recognize, measure, classify, and disclose items in the interim report, **materiality** must be taken into consideration. In assessing the materiality to be applied, reliance must be placed on estimates used for interim reporting and not annual results.

36.4.8 **Revenues received** seasonally, cyclically, or occasionally should not be recognized or deferred at interim date if recognition or deferral would not be appropriate at the end of the entity's financial year. For example, an entity that earns all its revenue in the first half of a year does not defer any of that revenue until the second half of the year.

36.4.9 **Costs** incurred unevenly during the financial year should not be recognized or deferred at interim date if recognition or deferral would not be appropriate at the end of the financial year. To illustrate, the cost of a planned major periodic maintenance that is expected to occur late in the year is not anticipated for interim reporting purposes unless the entity has a legal or constructive obligation. Similarly, development costs incurred are not deferred in an earlier period in the hope that they will meet the asset recognition criteria in a later period.

36.5   PRESENTATION AND DISCLOSURE

36.5.1 Selected **explanatory notes** in interim financial reports are intended to provide an update on the changes in the financial position and performance of the entity since the last annual financial statements. The minimum explanatory notes required include the following:

- a statement that accounting policies have been applied consistently and a description of any changes in policies since the last annual financial statements and the effect of such changes;
- explanatory comments about any seasonal or cyclical operations of the entity;
- the nature and amount of items affecting assets, liabilities, other comprehensive income, net income, or cash flows that are unusual because of their nature, size, or incidence;
- material changes in estimates of amounts reported in prior interim periods of the current year or prior annual reports;
- issuances, purchases, and repayments of debt and equity securities;
- dividends paid, separately for ordinary shares and other shares;
- segment revenue and results if IFRS 8 is applicable to the entity, including:
  - external revenue (if included in segment profit and loss);
  - intersegment revenues (if included in segment profit or loss);
  - a measure of segment profit and loss;
  - total assets that have materially changed in amount from the last annual report;
  - a description of differences in the basis of segmentation or measurement of segment profit since the last annual report; and
  - a reconciliation of total reportable segments' measures of profit and loss to entity profit and loss before tax and discontinued operations;
- material events occurring after the interim reporting date;
- the effect of acquisitions (business combinations) or disposals of subsidiaries and long-term investments, restructurings, and discontinued operations; and
- changes in contingent liabilities or assets since the last annual reporting date.

36.5.2 If the interim financial report is in compliance with this standard, the fact should be disclosed.

36.5.3 If an estimate of an amount reported in an interim period is changed significantly during the **final interim period** of the financial year but a separate financial report is not published for that final interim period, the nature and amount of that change should be disclosed in a note to the annual financial statements.

36.6   COMMENTARY

36.6.1 When adopting a new standard or amendment, the new requirements are applicable to the first interim period after the effective date. The condensed annual financial statements for the interim period and the comparative information therefore have to meet the new requirements. Entities that issue interim results are therefore effectively required to have restated numbers 6 and 18 months earlier than if the new requirements were just applied in the annual financial statements.

36.6.2 The preparation of interim reports is affected by other legal and regulatory requirements specific to the country in which the entity operates. These regulations for the scope and disclosure requirements of interim reporting as per the various companies, bank, taxation, and listing requirements may differ per country and need to be addressed by management in preparing the interim report.

36.6.3 As part of the second annual improvements project of the IASB, amendments to IAS 34 have been proposed. The proposed amendments suggest disclosure about:

- significant changes in the business and economic circumstances that affect the fair value of financial instruments;
- significant transfers between levels of the fair value;
- changes in the classification of assets as a result of a changes in the purpose or use of those assets; and
- changes in contingent assets and liabilities.

36.7   IMPLEMENTATION DECISIONS

The following table sets out some of the strategic and tactical decisions that should be considered when applying IAS 34.

Strategic decisions	Tactical decisions	Problems to overcome
Management must determine if the entity falls within the scope of this standard.	Processes must be in place to identify the related statutory requirements that support or override this requirement. Legal assistance must be obtained where possible.	Accounting and other statutory disclosure requirements may not always be the same but are equally important. Care must be taken to ensure they do not contradict each other in the disclosures made.
Management must determine the interim periods for which the entity will report.	There must be processes in place to ensure that the relevant information will be available for these periods and that the information at these dates will be useful.	Availability of information at these selected dates must meet all the relevant disclosure requirements.

EXAMPLE: INTERIM FINANCIAL REPORTING

EXAMPLE 36.1

The following three basic recognition and measurement principles are stated in IAS 34:

A. An entity should apply the same accounting policies in its interim financial statements as it applies in its annual financial statements, except for accounting policy changes made after the date of the most recent annual financial statements that are to be reflected in the next annual financial statements. However, the frequency of an entity's reporting (annually, semiannually, or quarterly) should not affect the measurement of its annual results. To achieve that objective, measurements for interim reporting purposes should be made on a year-to-date basis.

B.   Revenues that are received seasonally, cyclically, or occasionally within a financial year should not be anticipated or deferred because of an interim report. This would not be appropriate at the end of the entity's financial year.

C.   Costs that are incurred unevenly during an entity's financial year should be anticipated or deferred for interim reporting purposes only if it is also appropriate at the end of the financial year.

EXPLANATION

Table 36.2 illustrates the practical application of the above-mentioned recognition and measurement principles.

TABLE 36.2   Principles and Application of IAS 34

Principles and issues	Practical application
A. Same accounting policies as for annual financial statements	
A devaluation in the functional currency against other currencies occurred just before the end of the first quarter of the year. This necessitated the recognition of foreign exchange losses on the restatement of unhedged liabilities, which are repayable in foreign currencies. Indications are that the functional currency will regain its position against the other currencies by the end of the second quarter of the year. Management is reluctant to recognize these losses as expenses in the interim financial report and wants to defer recognition, based on the expectation of the functional currency. Management hopes that the losses will be neutralized by the end of the next quarter and wants to smooth the earnings rather than recognize losses in one quarter and profits in the next.	In the interim financial statements, these losses are recognized as expenses in the first quarter in accordance with IAS 21. The losses are recognized as expenses on a year-to-date basis to achieve the objective of applying the same accounting policies for both the interim and annual financial statements.

Principles and issues	Practical application
B. Deferral of revenues	
An ice cream manufacturing corporation recently had its shares listed on the local stock exchange. Management is worried about publishing the first quarter's interim results because the entity normally earns most of its profits in the third and fourth quarters (during the summer months). Statistics show that the revenue pattern is more or less as follows: First quarter = 10 percent of total annual revenue Second quarter = 15 percent of total annual revenue Third quarter = 40 percent of total annual revenue Fourth quarter = 35 percent of total annual revenue During the first quarter of the current year, total revenue amounted to $254,000. However, management plans to report one-fourth of the projected annual revenue in its interim financial report, calculated as follows: $254,000 ÷ 0.10 × 1/4 = $635,000	It is a phenomenon in the business world that some entities consistently earn more revenues in certain interim periods of a financial year than in other interim periods, for example, seasonal revenues of retailers. IAS 34 requires that such revenues are recognized when they occur, because anticipation or deferral would not be appropriate at the Statement of Financial Position date. Revenue of $254,000 is therefore reported in the first quarter.

Principles and issues	Practical application
C. Deferral of expenses	

Principles and issues	Practical application
An entity that reports quarterly has an operating loss carry forward of $10,000 for income tax purposes at the start of the current financial year, for which a deferred tax asset has not been recognized. The entity earns $10,000 in the first quarter of the current year and expects to earn $10,000 in each of the three remaining quarters. Excluding the carry forward, the estimated average annual income tax rate is expected to be 40 percent. Tax expense for the year would be calculated as follows: 40 percent × (40,000 − 10,000 tax loss) = $12,000 The effective tax rate based on the annual earnings would then be 30 percent (12,000 ÷ 40,000). The question is whether the tax charge for interim financial reporting should be based on actual or effective annual rates, which are illustrated below:	According to IAS 34, §30(c), the interim period income tax expense is accrued using the tax rate that would be applicable to expected total annual earnings, that is, the weighted average annual effective income tax rate applied to the pretax income of the interim period. This is consistent with the basic concept set out in IAS 34, §28 that the same accounting recognition and measurement principles should be applied in an interim financial report as are applied in annual financial statements. Income taxes are assessed on an annual basis. Interim period income tax expense is calculated by applying to an interim period's pretax income the tax rate that would be applicable to expected total annual earnings, that is, the weighted average annual effective income tax rate. This rate would reflect a blend of the progressive tax rate structure expected to be applicable to the full year's earnings. This particular issue is dealt with in IAS 34, Appendix B §22.

Income Tax Payable

Quarter	Actual Rate	Effective Rate
First	0*	3,000
Second	4,000	3,000
Third	4,000	3,000
Fourth	4,000	3,000
	$12,000	$12,000

* The full benefit of the tax loss carried forward is used in the first quarter.

CHAPTER 37

Accounting and Reporting by Retirement Benefit Plans
(IAS 26)

37.1 OBJECTIVE

Retirement benefit plans hold assets in a fiduciary capacity on behalf of a number of employees. The retirement benefit plans are usually referred to as pension schemes, or retirement benefit schemes. The employees that have invested in the retirement benefit plans require specific information in the financial statements of the retirement benefit plans in order to assess the value of their investments

IAS 26 prescribes the information that a retirement benefit plan should include in its financial statements for all participants. The standard specifically distinguishes between the information requirements for defined benefit and defined contribution plans.

37.2 SCOPE OF THE STANDARD

This standard should be applied in retirement benefit plans' financial statements that are directed to all participants. The standard's requirements apply to both defined contribution and defined benefit plans that are:

- funded by a separate trust or from general revenues;
- managed by an insurance company;
- sponsored by parties other than employers; and
- documented by formal or informal agreements.

37.3 KEY CONCEPTS

37.3.1 Retirement benefit plans are arrangements whereby an entity provides benefits for employees on or after termination of service (either in the form of an annual income or as a lump sum) when such benefits, or the contributions towards them, can be determined or estimated in advance of retirement from the provisions of a document or from the entity's practices.

37.3.2 Retirement benefit plans include both defined contribution plans and defined benefit plans.

37.3.3 **Defined contribution plans** are retirement benefit plans under which amounts to be paid upon retirement are determined by contributions to a fund together with investment earnings thereon. An employer's obligation is usually discharged by its contributions. An actuary's advice is therefore not normally required.

37.3.4 **Defined benefit plans** are retirement benefit plans under which amounts to be paid upon retirement are determined by a formula that is usually based on employees' earnings, years of service, or both. Periodic advice of an actuary is required to assess the financial condition of the plan, review the assumptions, and recommended future contribution levels. An employer is responsible for restoring the level of the plan's funds when deficits occur in order to provide the agreed benefits to current and former employees. Some plans contain characteristics of both defined contribution plans and defined benefit plans. Such hybrid plans are considered to be defined benefit plans for the purposes of IAS 26.

37.3.5 **Participants** are the members of a retirement benefit plan and others who are entitled to benefits under the plan's distinctive characteristics. The participants are interested in the activities of the plan because those activities directly affect the level of their future benefits. Participants are interested in knowing whether contributions have been received by the plan and whether proper control has been exercised to protect the rights of beneficiaries.

37.3.6 **Net assets available** for benefits are the assets of a plan less liabilities other than the actuarial present value of promised retirement benefits.

37.3.7 **Actuarial present value** of promised retirement benefits is the present value of the expected payments by a retirement benefit plan to existing and past employees, attributable to the service already rendered.

37.3.8 **Vested benefits** are benefits the rights to which, under the conditions of a retirement benefit plan, are not conditional on continued employment.

37.4   **ACCOUNTING TREATMENT**

Defined Contribution Plans

37.4.1 **The financial statements of a defined contribution plan** should contain a statement of net assets available for benefits and a description of the funding policy.

37.4.2 The following principles apply to the valuation of assets owned by the plan:

- Investments should be carried at fair value.
- If carried at other than fair value (for example, where assets have been acquired to match specific plan obligations), the investments' fair value should be disclosed.

Defined Benefit Plans

37.4.3 The financial statements of a defined benefit plan should contain either:

- a statement that shows the net assets available for benefits, the actuarial present value of retirement benefits (distinguishing between vested and nonvested benefits), and the resulting excess or deficit; or
- a statement of net assets available for benefits including either a **note** disclosing the actuarial present value of retirement benefits (distinguishing between vested and non vested benefits) or a **reference** to this information in an accompanying report.

37.4.4 Actuarial valuations are normally obtained every three years. The present value of the expected payments by a defined benefit plan can be calculated and reported using either current salary levels or projected salary levels up to the time of the participants' retirement.

37.4.5 Retirement benefit plan investments should be carried at fair value. In the case of marketable securities, fair value is market value. If the plan holds investments for which an estimate of fair value is not possible, the financial statements should disclose why fair value is not used.

37.4.6 The **financial statements** should explain the relationship between the actuarial present value of the promised retirement benefits and the net assets available for benefits, as well as the policy for the funding of the promised benefits.

37.5   PRESENTATION AND DISCLOSURE

37.5.1 A **description of the plan** is required, including information such as the names of the employers and the employee groups covered, number of participants receiving benefits, type of plan, and other details.

37.5.2 **Policies** to be disclosed include:

- significant accounting policies;
- investment policies; and
- the funding policy.

37.5.3 The **statement of net assets** should be made available for benefits showing the amount of assets available to pay retirement benefits that are expected to become payable in future. The statement should include:

- assets at year-end, suitably classified;
- the basis of valuation of assets;
- a note stating that an estimate of the fair value of plan investments is not possible, if any plan investments being held cannot be valued at fair market price;
- details of any single investment exceeding either 5 percent of net assets available for benefits or 5 percent of any class or type of security;
- details of any investment in the employer's securities (in the case of an employer-sponsored plan); and
- liabilities other than the actuarial present value of promised retirement benefits.

37.5.4 A **statement of changes in net assets** should be made available for benefits, including:

- investment income;
- employer contributions;
- employee contributions;
- other income;
- benefits paid or payable (analyzed per category of benefit);
- administrative expenses;
- other expenses;
- taxes on plan income;
- profits and losses on disposal of investments and changes in value of investments; and
- transfers from and to other plans.

37.5.5 Actuarial information (for defined benefit plans only) should be made available, including:

- the actuarial present value of promised retirement benefits, based on the amount of benefits promised under the terms of the plan, on service rendered to date, and on either current salary levels or projected salary levels;
- description of main actuarial assumptions;
- the method used to calculate the actuarial present value of promised retirement benefits; and
- the date of the most recent actuarial valuation.

37.6   FINANCIAL ANALYSIS AND INTERPRETATION

See chapter 25 for a discussion of analytical issues related to retirement benefit funds.

37.7   COMMENTARY

37.7.1 This standard does not introduce new recognition and measurement principles for retirement benefit plans, which are addressed in IAS 19 (see chapter 25). It merely prescribes the information that a retirement benefit plan should include in its financial statements.

37.8   IMPLEMENTATION DECISIONS

See chapter 25 for a discussion of implementation decisions.

EXAMPLE: ACCOUNTING AND REPORTING BY RETIREMENT BENEFIT PLANS

EXAMPLE 37.1

The financial statements of a retirement benefit plan should contain a statement of changes in net assets available for benefits.

EXPLANATION

The following extract was taken from the *World Bank Group: Staff Retirement Plan–2004 Annual Report*. It contains statements that comply with the IAS 26 requirements in all material respects.

Statements of Changes in Net Assets Available for Benefits (in thousands)

	Year ended December 31	
	2004	**2003**
Investment Income (Loss)		
Net appreciation in fair value of investments	881,325	1,348,382
Interest and dividends	262,406	265,212
Less: investment management fees	(45,193)	(43,618)
Net investment income	1,098,538	1,569,976
Contributions (Note C)		
Contributions by participants	77,224	76,280
Contributions by employer	184,228	85,027
Total contributions	261,452	161,307
Total additions	1,359,990	1,731,283
Benefit Payments		
Pensions	(293,908)	(271,399)
Commutation payments	(41,218)	(32,099)
Contributions, withdrawal benefits, and interest paid to former participants on withdrawal	(28,312)	(23,586)
Lump-sum death benefits	(622)	(1,671)
Termination grants	(2,375)	(3,048)
Total benefit payments	(366,435)	(331,803)
Administrative Expenses		
Custody and consulting fees	(4,516)	(4,985)
Others	(8,083)	(5,902)
Total administrative expenses	(12,599)	(10,887)
Net increase	980,956	1,388,593
Net Assets Available for Benefits		
Beginning of year	10,276,705	8,888,112
End of year	11,257,661	10,276,705

CHAPTER 38

Insurance Contracts
(IFRS 4)

| 38.1 | **OBJECTIVE** |

This standard is the first phase of the IASB's two-phase approach to insurance contracts. It is a stepping stone that provides for limited improvements to accounting and requires significant disclosure in respect of insurance contracts. The additional disclosures help users of financial statements understand the amount, timing, and uncertainty of future cash flows from insurance contracts. IFRS 4 requires entities to provide users with information about amounts recognized in financial statements in the absence of a global accounting standard.

Accounting practices for insurance contracts are diverse and differ from the accounting practices applied by other sectors. Furthermore, the industry is highly regulated and treatment is not consistent between different jurisdictions and different kinds of insurance contracts. When the IASB embarked on the insurance accounting project it was clear that all the aspects relating to insurance contracts could not be dealt with in the short or medium term. As a consequence, the project was split into two phases. The second phase will address recognition and measurement of insurance contracts.

| 38.2 | **SCOPE OF THE STANDARD** |

Entities should apply this IFRS to:

- insurance contracts (including reinsurance contracts) that it issues;
- reinsurance contracts that it holds; and
- financial instruments that it issues which contain a discretionary participation feature.

This standard does *not* apply to financial assets and financial liabilities within the scope of IAS 39.

This IFRS does *not* address:

- accounting aspects related to other assets and liabilities of an insurer;
- product warranties (IAS 37);
- employers' assets and liabilities (IFRS 2 and IAS 19);
- contingent consideration payable or receivable in a business combination (IFRS 3);
- direct insurance contacts that an entity holds (currently there is no accounting guidance for policyholders under direct insurance policies);

▪ residual value guarantee embedded in a finance lease (IAS 17); or

▪ financial guarantees (IAS 39), unless the entity has asserted explicitly that it treats such contracts as insurance contracts and has used accounting applicable to insurance contracts.

38.3

KEY CONCEPTS

38.3.1 An **insurance contract** is a contract under which one party (the **insurer**) accepts significant insurance risk from another party (the **policyholder**) by agreeing to compensate the policyholder if a specified uncertain future event (the **insured event**) adversely affects the policyholder.

38.3.2 Insurance liability is an insurer's net contractual obligations under an insurance contract.

38.3.3 Insurance risk is risk, other than financial risk, transferred from the insured to the insurer.

38.3.4 Financial risk is the risk of a possible future change in one or more of a specified interest rate, financial instrument price, commodity price, foreign exchange rate, index of prices or rates, credit rating, credit index, or other variable.

38.3.5 An **insured event** is an uncertain future event that is covered by an insurance contract and that creates insurance risk.

38.3.6 An **insurer** is the party that has the obligation under an insurance contract to compensate a policyholder if an **insured event** occurs.

38.3.7 A **policyholder** is a party that has a right to compensation under an insurance contract if an **insured event** occurs. A **cedant** is a policyholder under a reinsurance contract.

38.3.8 A **discretionary participation feature** is a contractual right to receive, as a supplement to **guaranteed benefits**, additional benefits:

▪ that are likely to be a significant portion of the total contractual benefits;

▪ whose amount or timing is contractually at the discretion of the insurer; and

▪ that are contractually based on:
   – the performance of a specified pool of contracts or a specified type of contract;
   – realized and/or unrealized investment returns on a specified pool of assets held by the insurer; or
   – the profit or loss of a company, fund, or other entity that issues the contract.

38.3.9 Guaranteed benefits are payments or other benefits to which a particular policyholder or investor has an unconditional right that is not subject to the contractual discretion of the issuer. A **guaranteed element** is an obligation to pay guaranteed benefits, including guaranteed benefits covered by a contract with a discretionary participation feature.

38.3.10 Fair value is the amount for which an asset could be exchanged or a liability settled between knowledgeable, willing parties in an arm's-length transaction.

38.4

ACCOUNTING TREATMENT

38.4.1 As described above there is currently no specific standard in IFRS that provides guidance on how insurance contracts should be recognized or measured. In terms of general IFRS principles, when no guidance exists for a particular transaction, entities are required to refer to the hierarchy in IAS 8 to identify an appropriate accounting policy. IFRS 4, however, provides a temporary exemption from the hierarchy contained in IAS 8 and thus exempts an insurer from applying those criteria when selecting accounting policies for:

- insurance contracts that it issues (including related acquisition costs and related intangible assets); and
- reinsurance contracts that it holds.

The effect of the above exemption has been that when IFRS 4 was adopted insurers could continue to apply their existing accounting policies, subject to certain limits described below.

38.4.2 Insurers may not offset reinsurance assets against insurance liabilities. They also cannot offset income and expenses from reinsurance contracts against the related insurance expenses or income.

38.4.3 Insurers must not recognize as a liability any provisions for possible future claims that arise from insurance contracts that are not in existence at the reporting date (for example, catastrophe and equalization provisions). Furthermore, an insurer can only remove an insurance liability from its Statement of Financial Position when the obligation is discharged.

38.4.4 An insurer should assess at each reporting date whether or not its recognized **insurance liabilities** are adequate, using current estimates of future cash flows under its insurance contracts.

38.4.5 A **liability adequacy test** should consider current estimates of all contractual and related cash flows and recognize the entire deficiency in profit or loss. Where a liability adequacy test is not required by its accounting policies, the insurer should:

- determine the carrying amount of the relevant insurance liabilities less the carrying amount of related deferred acquisition costs, as well as intangible assets; and
- determine whether the amount is less than the carrying amount that would be required if the relevant insurance liabilities were within the scope of IAS 37, and, if so, account for the difference in profit or loss.

38.4.6 If a cedant's **reinsurance asset is impaired,** the cedant should reduce its carrying amount accordingly and recognize that impairment loss in profit or loss. A reinsurance asset is impaired if:

- there is objective evidence that the cedant might not receive all amounts due to it under the terms of the contract, or
- an event has a measurable impact on the amounts that the cedant will receive from the reinsurer.

38.4.7 An insurer might **change its accounting policies** for insurance contracts after adopting IFRS 4, if the change makes the financial statements more relevant (but not less reliable) to users' economic decision-making needs. Greater reliability should not be obtained at the expense of relevance. Relevance and reliability should be assessed based on the criteria in IAS 8.

38.4.8 The following principles apply when considering a change in accounting policies:

- **Current market interest rates.** An insurer is permitted, but not required, to change its accounting policies so that it remeasures designated insurance liabilities to reflect current market interest rates. Changes in those liabilities must be recognized in profit or loss. This allows an insurer to change its accounting policies for designated liabilities without applying those policies consistently to all similar liabilities, which IAS 8 would otherwise require. If an insurer designates liabilities for this election, it should continue to apply current market interest rates consistently in all periods to all these liabilities until they are extinguished.

- **Continuation of existing practices.** An insurer may **continue** the following practices, but the **introduction** of any of them is not allowed:
  - measuring insurance liabilities on an undiscounted basis;
  - measuring contractual rights to future investment management fees at an amount that exceeds their fair value as implied by a comparison with current fees charged by market participants for similar services; and
  - using nonuniform accounting policies for insurance contracts issued by subsidiaries, except to the extent that current market rates are used to value designated liabilities.

- **Prudence.** An insurer need not change its accounting policies for insurance contracts to eliminate excessive prudence. However, if an insurer already measures its insurance contracts with sufficient prudence, it should not introduce additional prudence.

- **Future investment margins.** An insurer need not change its accounting policies to eliminate future investment margins. However, there is a presumption that an insurer's financial statements will become less relevant and reliable if it introduces an accounting policy that reflects future investment margins in the measurement of insurance contracts, unless those margins affect the contractual payments. Two examples of accounting policies that reflect those margins are:
  - using a discount rate that reflects the estimated return on the insurer's assets; and
  - projecting the returns on those assets at an estimated rate of return, discounting those projected returns at a different rate, and including the result in the measurement of the liability.

- The insurer might make its financial statements more relevant by switching to a comprehensive investor-oriented basis of accounting that involves:
  - current estimates and assumptions;
  - a reasonable adjustment to reflect risk and uncertainty;
  - measurements that reflect both the intrinsic value and time value of embedded options and guarantees; or
  - a current market discount rate.

- **Shadow accounting.** In some accounting models an insurer's assets have a direct effect on the measurement of some or all of its insurance liabilities. An insurer is permitted to change its accounting policies so that a recognized but unrealized gain or loss on an asset affects those measurements in the same way that a realized gain or loss does. The related adjustment to the insurance liability or other Statement of Financial Position items should be recognized in other comprehensive income if the unrealized gains or losses are recognized directly in other comprehensive income. This practice is sometimes called shadow accounting. If it were not for these provisions the full change in the liability would be recognized in profit or loss. In that case an income statement mismatch would arise as the full change in the liability would be in profit or loss while a portion of the change in the value of the assets backing the liability would be recognized in other comprehensive income.

38.4.9 IFRS 4 requires derivatives embedded in insurance contacts to be treated in terms of the IAS 39 rules applicable to embedded derivatives, unless the embedded derivative is itself an insurance contract. An option to surrender an insurance contract for a fixed amount or an amount based on a fixed interest rate is excluded from this principle and is not treated in terms of IAS 39. An option to surrender an insurance contract for an amount based on or triggered by a financial variable, for example equity prices, or if an equity index reaches a certain level, is to be treated in terms of IAS 39.

38.4.10 Some insurance contracts contain both an insurance component and a deposit component. An insurer is **required** to unbundle the deposit component, if it can be separately measured and its accounting policies do not otherwise require it to recognize all rights and obligations arising from such a deposit component. An insurer is **permitted** to unbundle the deposit component if it can be separately measured. Unbundling is prohibited if an insurer cannot measure the deposit component separately.

38.4.11 An insurer should, at the acquisition date of a business combination or portfolio transfer, measure the insurance contracts at fair value. The subsequent measurement of such assets should be consistent with the measurement of the related insurance liabilities. Insurers may elect to apply an expanded presentation to the fair value of the insurance contracts acquired. The expanded presentation splits the fair value into two components, a liability measured in accordance with the insurer's accounting policies and an intangible asset measured at the difference between the fair value of the insurance contracts and the liability measured in accordance with the insurer's accounting policies.

38.4.12 The issuer of an insurance contract that contains a **discretionary participation feature** may, but is not required to, recognize the guaranteed element separately from the discretionary participation feature. The guaranteed element is classified as a liability and the discretionary participation feature as either equity or a liability. If the guaranteed element is not recognized separately the full amount is classified as a liability. All premiums earned on these contracts are recognized as revenue without separating any portion that relates to the equity component, irrespective of whether or not the contract is classified as an insurance contract or an investment contract. For all components that are recognized as a liability the change in value of the liability is recognized in profit or loss. For those components that are recognized in equity any change in value is shown as an attribution of profit or loss rather than as an expense.

38.5 PRESENTATION AND DISCLOSURE

38.5.1 An insurer should **disclose** the following information that **identifies and explains the amounts** in its financial statements arising from insurance contracts. These disclosures include information in respect of:

- the insurer's accounting policies for insurance contracts and the related assets, liabilities, income, and expenses;
- recognized assets, liabilities, income, and expenses and cash flows (if the cash flows are presented using the direct method), including amounts in respect of reinsurance contracts;
- the process used to determine the assumptions that have the greatest effect on measurement of the amounts recognized;
- the effect of changes in assumptions used to measure insurance assets and insurance liabilities, showing separately the effect of each change that has a material effect on the financial statements; and
- reconciliations of changes in insurance liabilities and reinsurance assets.

38.5.2 If the insurer is a **cedant**, it should **disclose:**

- gains and losses recognized in profit or loss on buying reinsurance;
- amortization of deferred gains and losses for the period;
- unamortized amounts at the beginning and end of the period;
- the process used to determine assumptions underlying measurement of recognized profits and losses;
- the effect of changes in assumptions; and
- reconciliations of changes in insurance liabilities, reinsurance assets, and related deferred acquisition costs.

38.5.3 An insurer should disclose information that helps users to evaluate the nature and extent of risks arising from insurance contracts. This includes information about:

- the objectives, policies, and processes for managing risks arising from insurance contracts and the methods used to manage those risks;
- insurance risk, including:
  - the sensitivity of profit or loss and other comprehensive income to changes in applicable variables;
  - concentrations of insurance risk; and
  - actual claims compared with previous estimates, up to a maximum period of 10 years (claims development);
- credit risk, liquidity risk, and market risk that IFRS 7 would require if insurance contracts were in the scope of IFRS 7. However, an insurer need not disclose a maturity analysis required by IFRS 7 if it discloses information about the estimated timing of the net cash outflows resulting from recognized insurance liabilities. If the insurer uses an alternative method to manage sensitivities, for example embedded value, it may use that information to provide the market risk sensitivity analysis required by IFRS 7; and
- exposures to interest rate risk or market risk under embedded derivatives that are contained in a host insurance contract, where the embedded derivatives are not measured at fair value.

38.6   FINANCIAL ANALYSIS AND INTERPRETATION

38.6.1 Traditionally, insurance accounting has varied between different jurisdictions because insurance is a highly regulated industry and often recognition and measurement is based on the regulatory framework or developed by local actuarial committees. There is often a strong focus on prudence because stakeholders have demanded certainty about insurance companies' abilities to pay out cash on contracts as required.

38.6.2 Many insurance firms currently manage their financial assets and financial liabilities using fair value techniques to determine which products to underwrite, which investment strategies to adopt, and how best to manage overall risks. Moreover, those firms actively acquiring insurance firms or blocks of insurance business analyze and determine the fair value of those targets as part of their decision-making process. In addition, current and prospective investors of those insurance firms pursue similar information for making their investment decisions.

38.6.3 Currently insurance contracts are not measured at fair value. Therefore, at present, there is a distortion in reported financial performance of insurers because of an accounting model where some financial assets are measured at fair value and others are not, and not all liabilities are measured at fair value. The additional disclosures required by IFRS 4 provide users with some insight as to how insurance contracts have been recognized and measured. This enables users to better understand the amounts recognized in the financial statements.

38.7	**COMMENTARY**

38.7.1 IFRS 4 does not currently require significant changes to the recognition or measurement of insurance contracts. Therefore, implementation is focused on providing the additional disclosures that the standard requires, which is information that most insurance companies have available. The adoption of IFRS 4 is therefore not overly complex. The second phase of the insurance project will have major implications for insurers and the adoption process is likely to be more complex.

38.7.2 Some complications do arise in the classification of products between IFRS 4 and IAS 39 based on the definition of insurance contracts in IFRS 4. These complications can become particularly evident if insurers' systems do not differentiate between products based on their accounting definitions.

38.7.3 Other complications arise on the compulsory measurement and recognition changes required by IFRS 4. These include the release of catastrophe provisions that may have been allowed under local GAAP, and the gross up of reinsurance balances that may be offset under local GAAP but are not offset under IFRS.

38.7.4 The additional disclosures provide the users of insurer's financial statements with significantly more information than was available prior to the adoption of IFRS 4. This additional information provides users with insights into how balances arising from insurance contracts are recognized and measured as well as the amount, timing, and uncertainty of cash flows that arise from issuing insurance contracts.

38.7.5 The IASB is continuing to work on the second phase of the project, which will focus on recognition and measurement. In 2007 a discussion paper was issued by the IASB in which they proposed a measurement based on a current exit value. The proposals included a building-block approach to measure insurance contract liabilities based on the best estimate of the future cash flows, discounted to present value and including a risk and service margin.

38.7.6 Commentators on the discussion paper indicated that the current exit value may be difficult to apply in practice, particularly when market information was not available for certain assumptions. Many commentators raised concerns with the inclusion of own credit risk in the value of liabilities and indicated that in practice insurance contracts are likely to be settled or fulfilled rather than transferred.

38.7.7 The IASB is continuing its deliberations on phase two. The IASB has tentatively decided that the building-block approach remains the preferred measurement technique. However, the measurement attribute to be proposed in the exposure draft is unlikely to be an exit value but rather a fulfillment value calibrated to the premium on initial recognition.

38.7.8 It is worth noting that Solvency II, which focuses on risk management, is likely to be effective in many jurisdictions as the regulatory framework before phase two of IFRS 4 is completed. The measurement attribute prescribed by Solvency II is an exit value, and it will be interesting to see how the two frameworks will develop and ultimately work side by side in the same entities.

38.7.9 Policyholder accounting will be in the scope of the final standard on insurance contracts.

38.8   IMPLEMENTATION DECISIONS

The following table sets out some of the strategic and tactical decisions that should be considered when applying IFRS 4.

Strategic decisions	Tactical decisions	Problems to overcome
All contracts should be classified as either insurance contracts or financial instrument contracts. All contracts classified as insurance contracts need to be compared to the definition of an insurance contract to confirm that they are within the scope of the standard.	Where contracts have elements of both an insurance contract and a financial instrument, it should be determined whether unbundling is required or permitted. Unbundling is required if the financial instrument component can be reliably measured and the current accounting policies do not result in the recognition of all the obligations and rights of the financial instrument component. Unbundling is permitted if all of the obligations and rights relating to the financial instrument component are recognized and the entity can measure the financial instrument component separately.	In managing the insurance business, management and the actuarial valuation specialists often do not distinguish between contracts issued by the company. Therefore there may be significant additional work required to separate all contracts between insurance contracts and financial instruments and then to further unbundle insurance contracts into their component parts. Premium income is often an important indicator of performance in an insurance business, because financial instrument contracts are accounted for as balance sheet items and not income statement items in terms of IAS 39. There can often be a large decrease in premium income on adoption of IFRS 4.
A decision needs to be taken as to whether any existing accounting policies should be changed. Changes are only permitted when they result in information that is more relevant and no less reliable being included in the financial statements.	Before deciding on any change in accounting policy the entity should ensure that the change complies with the requirements of IFRS 4.	As accounting policy changes are not compulsory there should be a limited impact on the systems in place. However, although the accounting policies need not be changed, significant disclosure of the policies in place should be provided. Often this information is housed in detailed actuarial handbooks that are not considered by the accounting team of the insurer.
The methodology used to conduct the liability adequacy test should be decided on.	Decisions need to be taken on the kind of models and systems to be used to perform the liability adequacy test.	Short-term insurers in particular often do not have the models and systems available to perform a liability adequacy test.
A decision needs to be taken as to whether the guaranteed element of a discretionary participation feature is going to be recognized separately from other elements of the contract or if the whole contract is going to be recognized as a single liability.	If the guaranteed element is to be shown separately decisions need to be taken as to how the remaining part of the contract is classified, as equity or liability based on the nature of the instrument.	As the decision to show the guaranteed element separately is a choice, where information is not available in this format the entity may elect not to split the contract into its different elements.

38.9

EXAMPLES

38.9.1 The following are extracts of the disclosures explaining the amounts recognized in the financial statements arising from insurance contracts

EXAMPLE 38.1: ACCOUNTING POLICIES

DEFINITION OF INSURANCE CONTRACTS | Insurance contracts are contracts under which one party accepts significant insurance risk from another party (the policyholder) by agreeing to compensate the policyholder if a specified uncertain future event adversely affects the policyholder. Significant insurance risk exists if an insured event could cause an insurer to pay significant additional benefits in any scenario, excluding scenarios that lack commercial substance (i.e. have no discernible effect on the economics of the transaction). The classification of contracts identifies both the insurance contracts that the Group issues and reinsurance contracts that the Group holds. As a Group policy, Swiss Life considers those contracts to be insurance contracts that require the payment of additional benefits in excess of 10% of the benefits that would be payable if the insured event had not occurred, excluding some that lack commercial substance.

The Group has assessed the significance of insurance risk on a contract-by-contract basis. Contracts that do not transfer insurance risk at inception but that transfer insurance risk at a later date are classified as insurance from inception unless the Group remains free to price the insurance premium at a later date. In this case, the contract is classified as insurance when the insurance premiums are specified. A contract that qualifies as an insurance contract remains an insurance contract until all rights and obligations are extinguished or expire.

Contracts under which the transfer of insurance risk to the Group from the policyholder is not significant are classified as investment contracts.

INSURANCE LIABILITIES AND LIABILITIES FROM INVESTMENT CONTRACTS WITH DISCRETIONARY PARTICIPATION FEATURES

FUTURE LIFE POLICYHOLDER BENEFIT LIABILITIES | These liabilities are determined by using the net-level-premium method. Depending on the type of profit participation, the calculations are based on various actuarial assumptions as to mortality, interest rates, investment returns, expenses and persistency including a margin for adverse deviation. The assumptions are initially set at contract issue and are locked in except for deficiency. If the actual results show that the carrying amount of the insurance liabilities together with anticipated future revenues (less related deferred acquisition costs [DAC] and related intangible assets) are not adequate to meet the future obligations and to recover the unamortised DAC or intangible assets, the entire deficiency is recognised in profit or loss, initially by reducing the unamortised DAC or intangible assets and subsequently by increasing the insurance liabilities. The liability adequacy test is performed at each reporting date in accordance with a loss recognition test considering current estimates of future cash flows including those resulting from embedded options and guarantees.

POLICYHOLDER DEPOSITS | For investment contracts with discretionary participation, savings premiums collected are reported as deposits (deposit accounting). The liabilities relating to these contracts are not calculated actuarially; they move in line with premiums paid by the policyholders plus interest credited less expenses and mortality charges and withdrawals.

LIABILITIES FOR CLAIMS AND CLAIM SETTLEMENT COSTS | Liabilities for unpaid claims and claim settlement costs are for future payment obligations under insurance claims for which normally either the amount of benefits to be paid or the date when payments must be made is not yet fixed. They include claims reported at the balance sheet date, claims incurred but not yet reported and claim settlement expenses. Liabilities for unpaid claims and claim settlement costs are calculated at the estimated amount considered necessary to settle future claims in full, using actuarial methods. These methods are continually reviewed and updated. Claim reserves are not discounted except for claims with determinable and fixed payment terms.

(continued)

EMBEDDED OPTIONS AND GUARANTEES IN INSURANCE CONTRACTS | Insurance contracts often contain embedded derivatives. Embedded derivatives which are not closely related to their host insurance contracts are separated and measured separately at fair value. Exposure to embedded options and guarantees in insurance contracts which are closely related or which are insurance contracts themselves, such as guaranteed annuity options or guaranteed interest rates, are reflected in the measurement of the insurance liabilities.

Source: Swiss Life Group Annual Report 2008.

Liability adequacy tests

Liability adequacy testing is performed by portfolio of contracts at each reporting date, in accordance with the Group's manner of acquiring, servicing and measuring the profitability of its insurance contracts. Net unearned premiums are tested to determine whether they are sufficient to cover related expected claims, loss adjustment expenses, policyholder dividends, commission, amortization and maintenance expenses using current assumptions. If a premium deficiency is identified, the DAC asset is written down by the amount of the deficiency. If, after writing down the DAC asset to nil (for the respective portfolio of contracts), a premium deficiency still exists, then a premium deficiency reserve is recorded to provide for the deficiency in excess of the DAC asset written down.

For life contracts, the net premium reserve, calculated on a locked-in basis and reduced by the unamortized balance of DAC or present value of future profits of acquired insurance contracts (PVFP) is compared with the gross premium reserve, calculated on a best-estimate basis as of the valuation date. If there is a deficiency, the DAC or PVFP is written down to the extent of the deficiency. If, after writing down the DAC or PVFP to nil (for the respective portfolio of contracts), a deficiency still exists, the net liability is increased by the amount of the remaining deficiency.

Present value of future profits from acquired insurance contracts (PVFP)

On the acquisition of life insurance businesses a customer contract intangible asset representing the present value of future profits from the acquired insurance contracts is determined. This asset is amortized over the expected life of the policies acquired, based on a constant percentage of the present value of estimated gross profits (margins) expected to be realized, or over the premium recognition period, as appropriate. PVFP is reviewed for impairment whenever events or changes in circumstances indicate that the carrying amount may not be recovered.

Source: Zurich Financial Services Group Annual Report 2008.

b) Future life policyholders' benefits and policyholders' contract deposits
  – The future life policyholders' benefits and policyholders' contract deposits liabilities contain a number of assumptions regarding mortality (or longevity), lapses, surrenders, expenses and investment returns. These assumptions are determined with reference to past experience adjusted for new trends, current market conditions and future expectations. As such the liabilities for future life policyholders' benefits and policyholders' contract deposits may not represent the ultimate amounts paid out to policyholders. For example:
  – The estimated number of deaths determines the value of the benefit payments. The main source of uncertainty arises because of the potential for pandemics and wide-ranging lifestyle changes, such as changes in eating, smoking and exercise habits, which could result in earlier deaths for age groups in which the Group has significant exposure to mortality risk.

- For contracts that insure the risk of longevity, such as annuity contracts, an appropriate allowance is made for people living longer. Continuing improvements in medical care and social conditions could result in further improvements in longevity in excess of those allowed for in the estimates used to determine the liability for contracts where the Group is exposed to longevity risk.

- Under certain contracts, the Group has offered product guarantees (or options to take up product guarantees), including fixed minimum interest rate or mortality rate returns. In determining the value of these options and/or benefits, estimates have been made as to the percentage of contract holders that may exercise them. Changes in investment conditions could result in significantly more contract holders exercising their options and/or benefits than has been assumed.

- Estimates are also made as to future investment income arising from the assets backing long-term insurance contracts. These estimates are based on current market returns as well as expectations about future economic and financial developments.

- Assumptions are determined with reference to current and historical client data, as well as industry data. Interest rate assumptions reflect expected earnings on the assets supporting the future policyholder benefits. The information used by the Group's qualified actuaries in setting such assumptions includes, but is not limited to, pricing assumptions, available experience studies and profitability analysis.

Source: Zurich Financial Services Group Annual Report 2008.

EXAMPLE 38.3: POLICYHOLDER LIABILITY NOTE

Development of reserves for losses and loss adjustment expenses (in USD millions)

	Gross		Ceded		Net	
	2008	2007	2008	2007	2008	2007
As of January 1	67,890	64,535	(13,179)	(13,722)	54,712	50,814
Losses and loss adjustment expenses incurred:						
Current year	28,296	25,798	(2,879)	(2,424)	25,416	23,374
Prior years	(1,354)	(847)	83	(372)	(1,271)	(1,219)
Total	26,942	24,951	(2,796)	(2,796)	24,145	22,155
Losses and loss adjustment expenses paid:						
Current year	(10,190)	(9,007)	591	388	(9,599)	(8,619)
Prior years	(15,080)	(14,613)	2,528	3,375	(12,551)	(11,237)
Total	(25,269)	(23,619)	3,119	3,763	(22,150)	(19,856)
Acquisitions/(divestments) of companies and businesses	105	57	(28)	(6)	77	51
Foreign currency translation effects	(4,450)	1,967	653	(419)	(3,798)	1,548
As of December 31	**65,218**	**67,890**	**(12,232)**	**(13,179)**	**52,986**	**54,712**

Source: Zurich Financial Services Group Annual Report 2008.

(continued)

(iv) Sensitivity analysis—life assurance

Changes in key assumptions used to value insurance contracts would result in increases or decreases to the insurance contract provisions recorded, with impact on profit/(loss) and/or shareholders' equity. The effect of a change in assumption is mitigated by the following factors:

- offset (partial or full) to the bonus stabilisation reserve in the case of smoothed bonus products in South Africa;
- offset (partial or full) through DAC amortisation in the case of US business; and
- the effect of locked-in assumptions under USGAAP accounting, where assumptions underlying the insurance contract provisions are not changed until liabilities are not adequate after reflecting current best estimates.

The net increase or decrease to insurance contract provisions recorded as of 31 December 2009 has been estimated as follows:

Assumption	% Change	£m South Africa	£m US	£m Bermuda
Mortality and morbidity rates–assurance	10	209	16	—
Mortality rates–annuities	(10)	45	(4)	—
Discontinuance rates	10	(1)	15	26
Expenses (maintenance)	10	61	4	(1)

The insurance contract liabilities recorded for the South African business are also impacted by the valuation discount rate assumed. Lowering this rate by 1% would result in a net increase to the insurance contract liabilities, and decrease to profit, of £58 million (2008: £66 million).

There is no impact for the US businesses as the valuation rate is locked-in.

Source: Old Mutual Plc Annual Report 2009.

38.9.2 The following is an extract of disclosures explaining the nature and extent of risks arising from insurance contracts for a life insurer.

EXAMPLE 38.4

(iii) Management of insurance risks—life assurance

The table below summarises the variety of risks to which the Group's life assurance operations are exposed, and the methods by which the Group seeks to mitigate these risks.

Risk	Definition	Risk management
Underwriting	Misalignment of policyholders to the appropriate pricing basis or impact of anti-selection, resulting in a loss	Experience is closely monitored. For universal life business, mortality rates can be reset. Underwriting limits, health requirements, spread of risks and training of underwriters all mitigate the risk
HIV/AIDS	Impact of HIV/AIDS on mortality rates and critical illness cover	Impact of HIV/AIDS is mitigated wherever possible by writing products that allow for repricing on a regular basis or are priced to allow for the expected effects of HIV/AIDS. Tests for HIV/AIDS and other tests for lives insured above certain values are conducted. A negative test result is a prerequisite for acceptance at standard rates
Medical developments	Possible increase in annuity costs due to policyholders living longer	For non-profit annuities, improvements to mortality are allowed for in pricing and valuation. Experience is closely monitored. For with-profit annuity business, the mortality risk is carried by policyholders and any mortality profit or loss is reflected in the bonuses declared
Changing financial market conditions	Lower swap curves and higher volatilities cause investment guarantee reserves to increase	A discretionary margin is added to the value of guarantees, determined on a market-consistent stochastic basis and included in current reserves. A partial hedge is in place (South Africa). Fewer and lower guarantees are typically provided on new business (South Africa). Certain guarantees are reinsured (United States)
Policyholder behaviour	Selection of more expensive options, or lapse and re-entry when premium rates are falling, or termination of policy, which may cause the sale of assets at inopportune times	Experience is closely monitored, and policyholder behaviour is allowed for in pricing and valuation
Catastrophe	Natural and non-natural disasters, including war/terrorism, could result in increased mortality risk and payouts on policies	Catastrophe stop loss/excess of loss reinsurance treaty in place which covers claims from one incident occurring within a specified period between a range of specified limits
Policy lapse	A policyholder option to terminate the policy, which may cause the sale of assets at inopportune times. This creates the risk of capital losses and/or reinvestment risk if market yields have decreased	Experience is closely monitored, and policyholder behaviour is allowed for in pricing and valuation

(continued)

(ii) Terms and conditions of long-term insurance business—South Africa, United States and Bermuda

The terms and conditions attaching to insurance contracts determine the level of insurance risk accepted by the Group. The following tables outline the general form of terms and conditions that apply to contracts sold in each category of business, and the nature of the risk incurred by the Group:

South Africa

Category	Essential terms	Main risks	Policyholder guarantees	Policyholder participation in investment return
Individual Life Flexi business with cover	Mortality/morbidity rates may be repriced (regular premium contracts)	Mortality, morbidity	Some investment performance, cover and annuity guarantees	Varies*
Conventional with cover	Charges fixed at inception and cannot be changed	Mortality, morbidity	Some investment performance and annuity guarantees	Varies*
Greenlight	Charges fixed at inception and cannot be changed for a specified term	Mortality, morbidity, expense	Rates fixed for a specified number of years	None
Group Schemes—funeral cover	Charges fixed at inception and cannot be changed for a specified number of years	Mortality including HIV/AIDS, expense	Rates fixed for a specified number of years	None
Employee Benefits—Group Assurance	Rates are annually renewable	Mortality, morbidity	No significant guarantees, except for PHI claims in payment for which benefit payment schedule is guaranteed	None
Non-profit annuity	Regular benefit payments guaranteed in return for consideration	Mortality, investment	Benefit payment schedule is guaranteed	None
With-profit annuity	Regular benefit payments participating in profits in return for consideration	Investment	Underlying pricing interest rate is guaranteed. Declared bonuses cannot be reduced	Yes

Source: Old Mutual Plc Annual Report 2009.

CHAPTER 39

Financial Reporting in Hyperinflationary Economies
(IAS 29)

39.1	**OBJECTIVE**

In a hyperinflationary economy, reporting of operating results and financial position without restatement is not useful. Money loses purchasing power at such a rapid rate that comparison of amounts from transactions and other events that have occurred, even within the same accounting period, is misleading. This standard prescribes the accounting in the financial statements of an entity whose functional currency is in a hyperinflationary economy.

39.2	**SCOPE OF THE STANDARD**

IAS 29 should be applied by entities that report in the currency of a hyperinflationary economy. This standard does not prescribe an absolute rate at which hyperinflation is deemed to arise. It is a matter of judgment when restatement of financial statements in accordance with this standard becomes necessary. Characteristics of a hyperinflationary economy include the following:

- The general population prefers to keep its wealth in nonmonetary assets or in a relatively stable foreign currency.
- Prices are normally quoted in a stable foreign currency.
- Credit transactions take place at prices that compensate for the expected loss of purchasing power.
- Interest, wages, and prices are linked to price indexes.
- The cumulative inflation rate over three years is approaching or exceeds 100 percent (that is, an average of more than 26 percent per year).

IAS 29 requires that the financial statements of an entity operating in a hyperinflationary economy be restated in the measuring unit current at the reporting date.

IAS 21 requires that if the functional currency of a subsidiary is the currency of a hyperinflationary economy, transactions and events of the subsidiary should first be measured in the subsidiary's functional currency; the subsidiary's financial statements are then restated for price changes in accordance with IAS 29. Thereafter, the subsidiary's financial statements are translated, if necessary, into the presentation currency using closing rates. IAS 21 does not permit such an entity to use another currency, for example a stable currency, as its functional currency.

39.3

KEY CONCEPTS

39.3.1 A general **price index** that reflects changes in general purchasing power should be used.

39.3.2 **Restatement** starts from the beginning of the period in which hyperinflation is identified.

39.3.3 When **hyperinflation ceases,** restatement is discontinued.

39.4

ACCOUNTING TREATMENT

39.4.1 The financial statements of an entity that reports in the currency of a hyperinflationary economy should be **restated** in the measuring unit current at the reporting date; that is, the entity should restate the amounts in the financial statements from the currency units in which they occurred into the currency units *on the reporting date.*

39.4.2 The restated financial statements **replace** the financial statements and do not serve as a supplement to the financial statements. Separate presentation of the nonadjusted financial statements is not permitted.

Restatement of Historical Cost Financial Statements

39.4.3 Amounts not already expressed in terms of the measuring unit current at the end of the reporting period should be restated by applying a general price index. The rules applicable to the restatement of items included in the **Statement of Financial Position** are as follows:

- Monetary items are not restated as they are already expressed in the current monetary unit.
- Index-linked assets and liabilities are restated in accordance with the agreement that specifies the index to be used.
- Nonmonetary items are restated in terms of the current measuring unit by applying the changes in the index or currency unit to the carrying values since the date of acquisition (or the date on which a revaluation was performed) or fair values on dates of valuation.
- Nonmonetary assets are not restated if they are carried at net realizable value, fair value, or recoverable amount at reporting date.
- For assets under an arrangement where payment is deferred without incurring an explicit interest charge, the restatement should be done from the payment date and not the acquisition date.
- At the beginning of the first period in which the principles of IAS 29 are applied, components of owners' equity, except accumulated profits and any revaluation surplus, are restated from the dates the components were contributed.
- At the end of the first period and subsequently, all components of owners' equity are restated from the date of contribution.
- The movements in owners' equity are included in equity.

39.4.4 All items in the **Statement of Comprehensive Income** are restated by applying the change in the general price index from the dates when the income or expenses were initially recorded.

39.4.5 A **gain or loss on the net monetary position** is included in net income. This amount can be estimated by applying the change in the general price index to the weighted average of net monetary assets or liabilities.

Restatement of Current Cost Financial Statements

39.4.6 Rules applicable to the restatement of items included in the **Statement of Financial Position** are as follows:

- Items carried at current cost are not restated as they are already expressed in terms of the measuring unit current at the reporting date.
- Other items included in the Statement of Financial Position are restated in terms of the rules above.

39.4.7 All amounts included in the **Statement of Comprehensive Income** are restated into the measuring unit at reporting date by applying the general price index.

39.4.8 If a **gain or loss on the net monetary position** is calculated, such an adjustment forms part of the gain or loss on the net monetary position calculated in terms of IAS 29.

39.4.9 Temporary differences that arise as a result of the restatement in this standard should be treated in terms of IAS 12.

39.4.10 All **cash flows** are expressed in terms of the measuring unit at reporting date.

39.4.11 Corresponding figures for the previous reporting period, whether they were based on a historical cost approach or a current cost approach, are restated by applying a general price index so that the comparative financial statements are presented in terms of the measuring unit current at the end of the reporting period.

39.4.12 When a foreign subsidiary, associate, or joint venture of a parent company reports in a hyperinflationary economy, the financial statements of such entities should first be **restated** in accordance with IAS 29 and then translated at the **closing rate** as if the entities were foreign entities, per IAS 21.

39.5 PRESENTATION AND DISCLOSURE

The following should be disclosed:

- the fact that the financial statements have been restated;
- the fact that the comparative information has been restated;
- whether the financial statements are based on the historical cost approach or the current cost approach;
- the identity and the level of the price index or stable currency at the reporting date; and
- the movement in price index or stable currency during the current and previous financial years

39.6 FINANCIAL ANALYSIS AND INTERPRETATION

39.6.1 The interpretation of hyperinflated results is difficult if one is not familiar with the mathematical processes that give rise to the hyperinflated numbers.

39.6.2 Where the financial statements of an entity in a hyperinflationary economy are translated and consolidated into a group that does not report in the currency of a hyperinflationary economy, analysis becomes extremely difficult.

39.6.3 When making economic decisions, users of an entity's financial statements should consider the disclosures of the level of price indexes used to compile the financial statements and, where provided, should consider the levels of foreign exchange rates applied to the translation of financial statements.

39.6.4 When inflation rates and exchange rates do not correlate well, the carrying amounts of nonmonetary assets in the financial statements will have to be analyzed to consider how much of the change is attributable to structural issues such as hyperinflation and how much is attributable to, for example, temporary exchange rate fluctuations.

39.6.5 As accounting standards increasingly require use of fair value measurement, users of the financial statements of entities that operate in hyperinflationary economies must consider the reliability of fair value measurements in those financial statements.

39.6.6 Hyperinflationary economies often do not have active financial markets and could be subject to high degrees of regulation, such as price control. In such circumstances, the determination of fair values, as well as discount rates for defined benefit obligations and impairment tests, is very difficult.

39.7   COMMENTARY

39.7.1 Difficulties in practical application of IAS 29 arise when the general price index relating to the entity's functional currency becomes unavailable because of chronic hyperinflation and the currency lacks exchangeability. In such cases the entity no longer prepares and presents financial statements in accordance with IFRS because of its inability to comply with IAS 29.

39.7.2 The IFRIC has clarified how an entity should present its opening Statement of Financial Position and the comparatives in cases where the following conditions exist: (1) an entity ceased applying IFRSs in the previous period as a result of chronic hyperinflation and the fact that the general price index was not available, and (2) and in the subsequent period the entity changed its currency to a non-hyperinflationary currency in accordance with IAS 21. The IFRIC decided that the entity should present its opening Statement of Financial Position in accordance with IFRS 1 and should apply its judgment in presenting the comparative amounts that were not presented in terms of IFRSs.

39.7.4 The IASB has not indicated any future project regarding IAS 29.

39.8   IMPLEMENTATION DECISIONS

The following table sets out some of the strategic and tactical decisions that should be considered when applying IAS 29.

Strategic decisions	Tactical decisions	Problems to overcome
Whether the entity report in a hyperinflationary environment.	Management should make a decision as to the general price index that will be used.	

EXAMPLE: FINANCIAL REPORTING IN HYPERINFLATIONARY ECONOMIES

EXAMPLE 39.1

Darbrow Inc. was incorporated on January 1, 20X2, with an equity capital of $40 million. The statement of financial positions of the entity at the beginning and end of the first financial year were as follows:

	Beginning $'000	End $'000
Assets		
Property, plant, and equipment	60,000	50,000
Inventory	30,000	40,000
Receivables	50,000	60,000
	140,000	150,000
Equity and Liabilities		
Share capital	40,000	40,000
Accumulated profit	–	10,000
Borrowings	100,000	100,000
	140,000	150,000

The statement of comprehensive income for the first year reflected the following amounts:

	$'000
Revenue	800,000
Operating expenses	(750,000)
Depreciation of plant and equipment	(10,000)
Operating profit	40,000
Interest paid	(20,000)
Profit before tax	20,000
Income tax expense	(10,000)
Profit after tax	10,000

Additional Information

The rate of inflation was 120 percent for the year. The inventory represents two months' purchases, and all Statement of Comprehensive Income items accrued evenly during the year.

The financial statements can be restated to the measuring unit at Statement of Financial Position date using a **reliable price index,** as follows:

Statement of Financial Position

	Recorded $'000	Restated $'000	Calculations
Assets			
Property, plant, and equipment	50,000	110,000	2.20/1.00
Inventory **(Calculation a)**	40,000	41,905	2.20/2.10
Receivables	60,000	60,000	
	150,000	211,905	
Equity and Liabilities			
Share capital	40,000	88,000	2.20/1.00
Accumulated profits	10,000	23,905	Balancing
Borrowings	100,000	100,000	
	150,000	211,905	

Statement of Comprehensive Income	$'000	$'000	
Revenue **(Calculation b)**	800,000	1,100,000	2.20/1.60
Operating expenses	(750,000)	(1,031,250)	2.20/1.60
Depreciation **(Calculation c)**	(10,000)	(22,000)	2.20/1.00
Interest paid	(20,000)	(27,500)	2.20/1.60
Income tax expense	(10,000)	(13,750)	2.20/1.60
Net profit before restatement gain	10,000	5,500	
Gain arising from inflationary adjustment		18,405	Balancing Figure
Net profit after restatement gain		23,905	

Calculations
a. Index for inventory
Inventory purchased on average at November 30

Index at that date = 1.00 + (1.20 × 11/12) = 2.10

b. Index for income and expenses
Average for the year = 1.00 + (1.20 ÷ 2) = 1.60

c. Index for depreciation
Linked to the index of property, plant, and equipment = 1.00

About the Contributors

Hennie van Greuning is currently a consultant to the World Bank Treasury and the Bank's East Asia and Pacific Region. He is also an independent non-executive director of FirstRand Bank, where he chairs the audit committee.

His former roles include those of senior adviser in the World Bank's Treasury and sector manager for financial sector operations in the Bank's Europe and Central Asia Region. He has been a partner with the firm of Deloitte and a controller in a central bank, in addition to heading bank supervision in his home country of South Africa.

He is a CFA Charterholder and qualified as a Chartered Accountant in Canada and South Africa. He holds doctoral degrees in both accounting and economics. He is the coauthor of *Analyzing and Managing Banking Risk, Risk Analysis for Islamic Banks,* and *International Financial Statement Analysis.*

Darrel Scott served as chief financial officer of the FirstRand Banking Group until 30 September 2010. He was a member of the International Accounting Standards Board (IASB) Interpretations Committee (IFRIC) from July 2007 until June 2010, and joined the IASB as a full time board member in October 2010.

Simonet Terblanche heads up the Technical Accounting Division within the FirstRand Banking Group. Before joining FirstRand, she spent two years in an IFRS consulting role at Deloitte & Touche in Johannesburg after completing her training at the same firm. She is a qualified Chartered Accountant.

Other contributors:

Nicky Els is a technical accountant with the FirstRand Banking Group. She completed her training at KPMG Johannesburg in the financial services division where she qualified as a Chartered Accountant. She subsequently worked as an assistant manager and manager at KPMG before joining FirstRand.

Nicole Leith has been with the FirstRand Banking Group as a technical accountant since November 2007. Before that she was a manager at PricewaterhouseCoopers in Johannesburg after training at the same firm. She is a qualified Chartered Accountant and has a master's degree in financial management.

Nhlanhla Mungwe is a technical accountant at FirstRand Banking Group. He trained at PricewaterhouseCoopers in Johannesburg. He is a qualified Chartered Accountant.

Lufuno Israel Siphugu is a technical accountant with the FirstRand Banking Group. He trained at Deloitte & Touche in Johannesburg. He is a qualified Chartered Accountant.

Eileen van der Merwe is a technical accountant with the FirstRand Banking Group. Prior to joining FirstRand, she completed her training at a medium-sized audit firm in South Africa where she served as an audit manager for 12 months post-qualification. She is a qualified Chartered Accountant.

Jaco van Wyk heads up the Accounting Division within the Group Finance area of the FirstRand Banking Group. He spent six years in corporate finance advisory services within the financial sector in South Africa. He is a qualified Chartered Accountant and holds a Diploma in Banking.